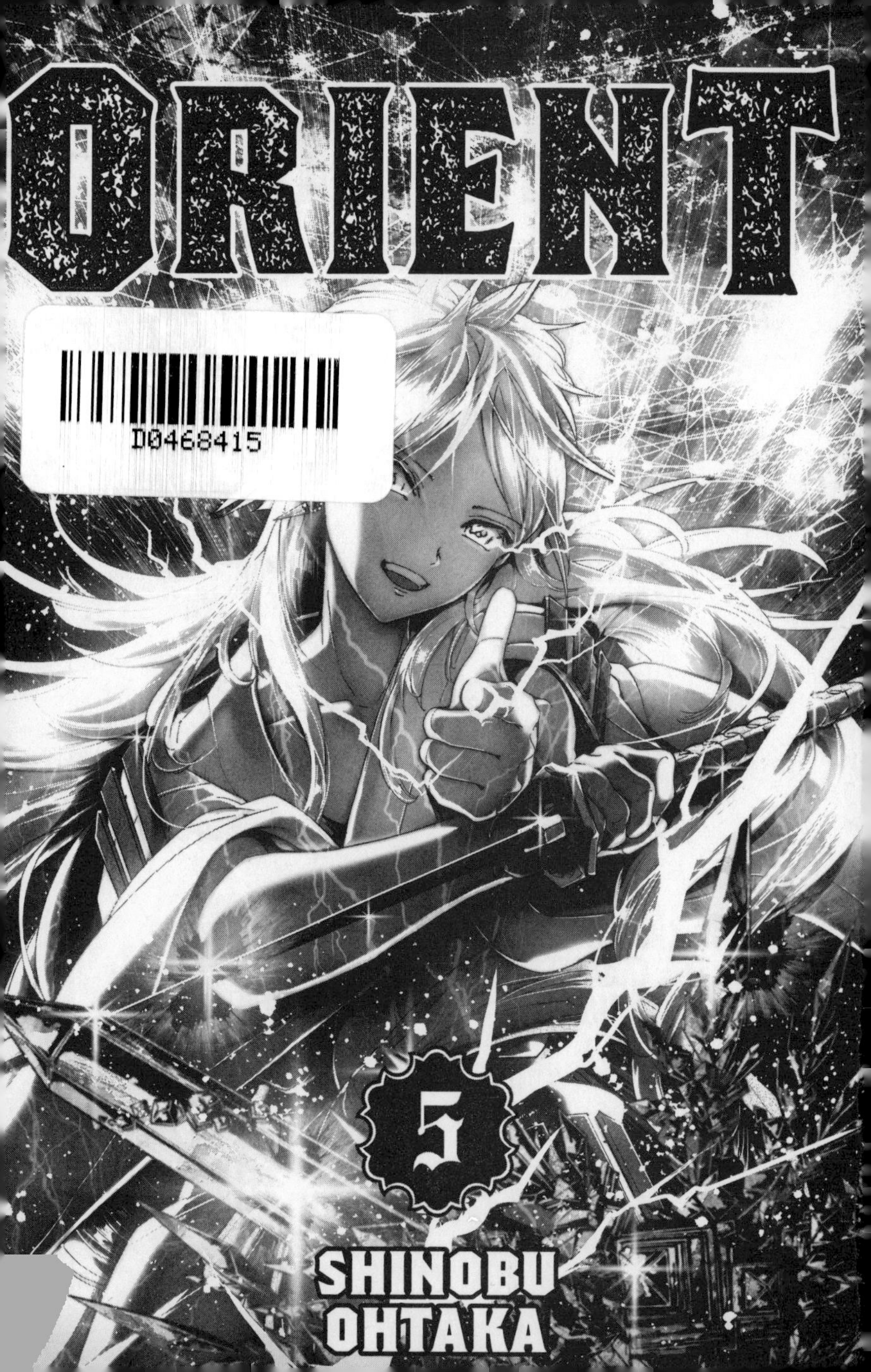
ORIENT
5
SHINOBU
OHTAKA

SHINOBU OHTAKA

CONTENTS

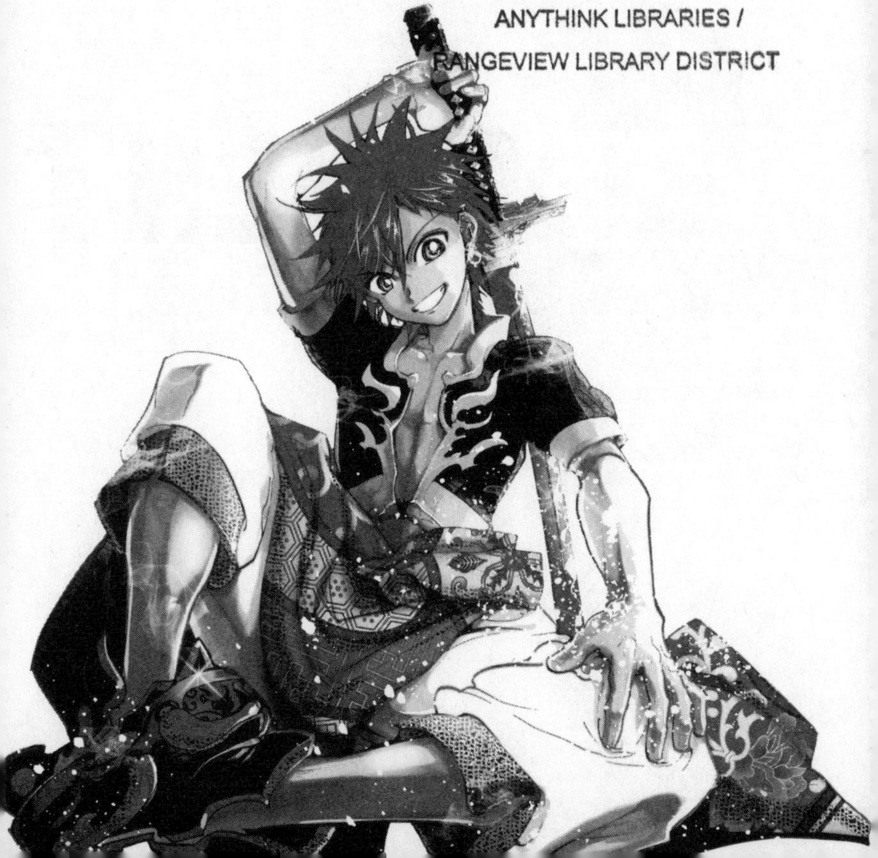

ORIENT

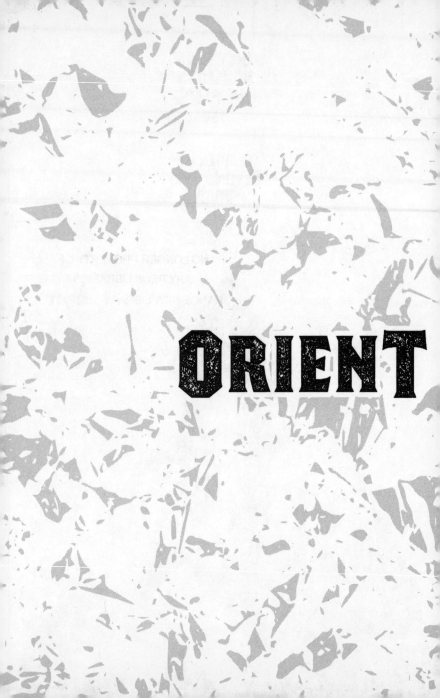

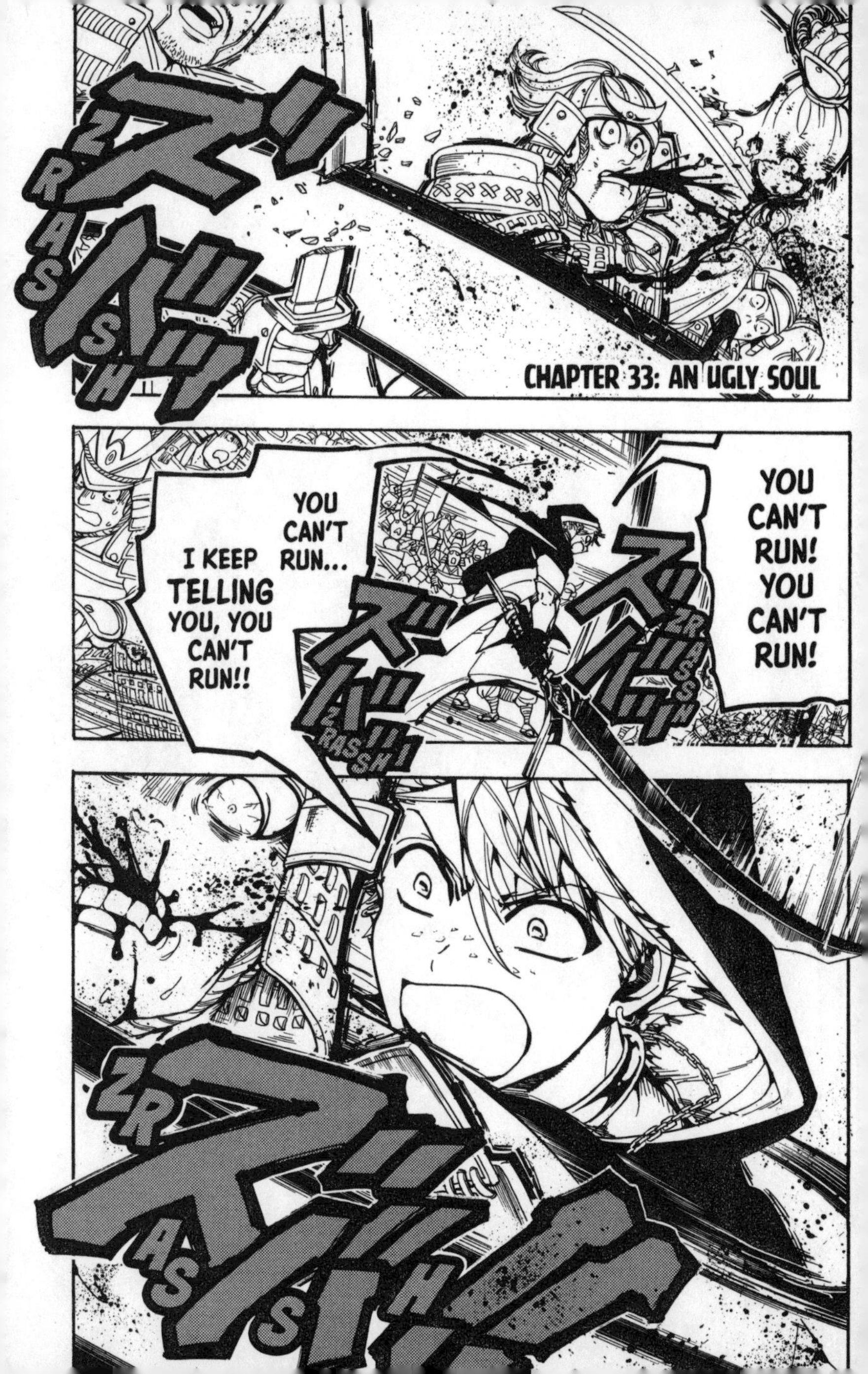
ZRASSH
CHAPTER 33: AN UGLY SOUL
YOU CAN'T RUN! YOU CAN'T RUN!
ZRASSH
YOU CAN'T RUN...
ZRASSH
I KEEP TELLING YOU, YOU CAN'T RUN!!
ZRASSH

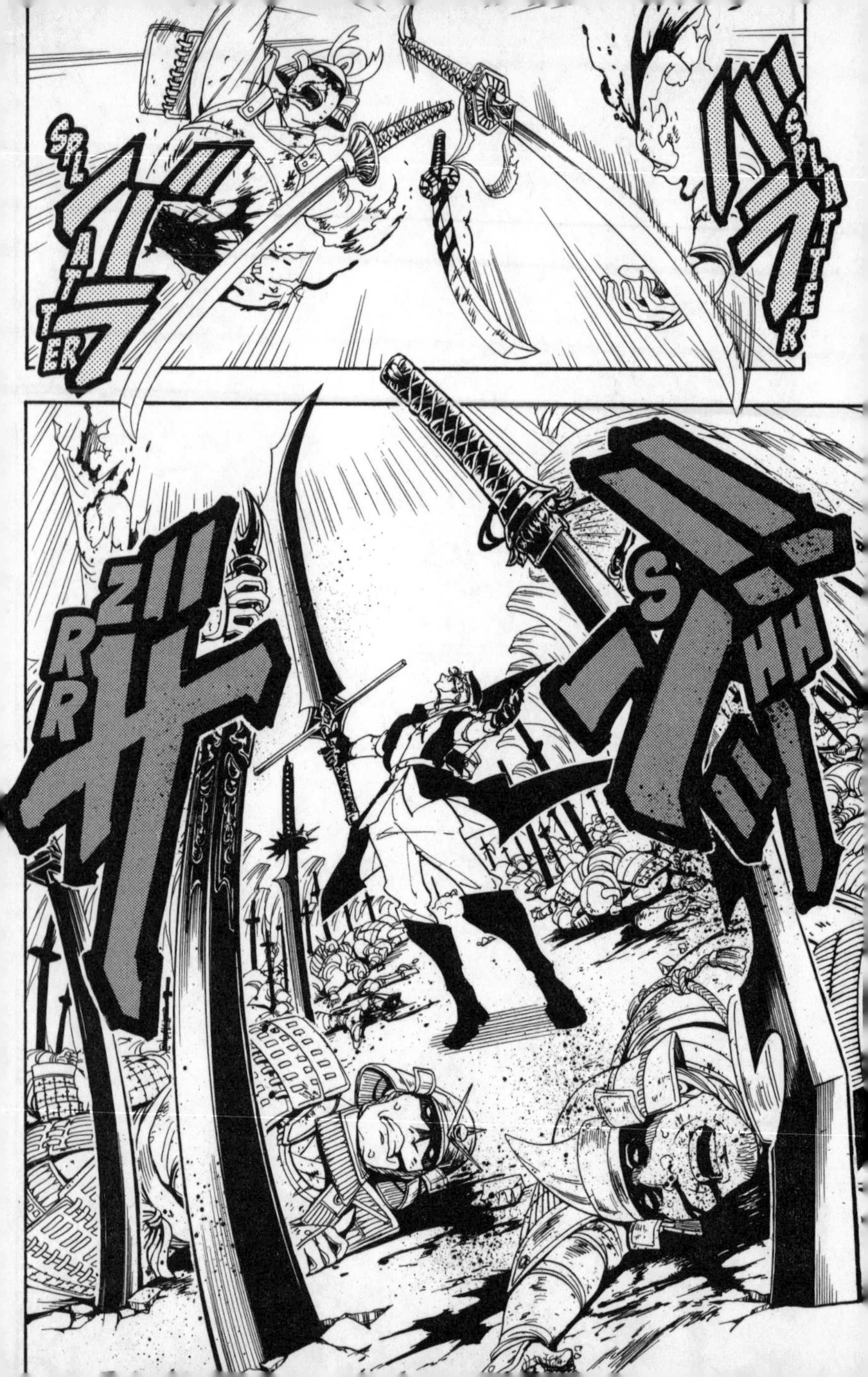
SPLATTER
SPLATTER
SHHH
ZRR

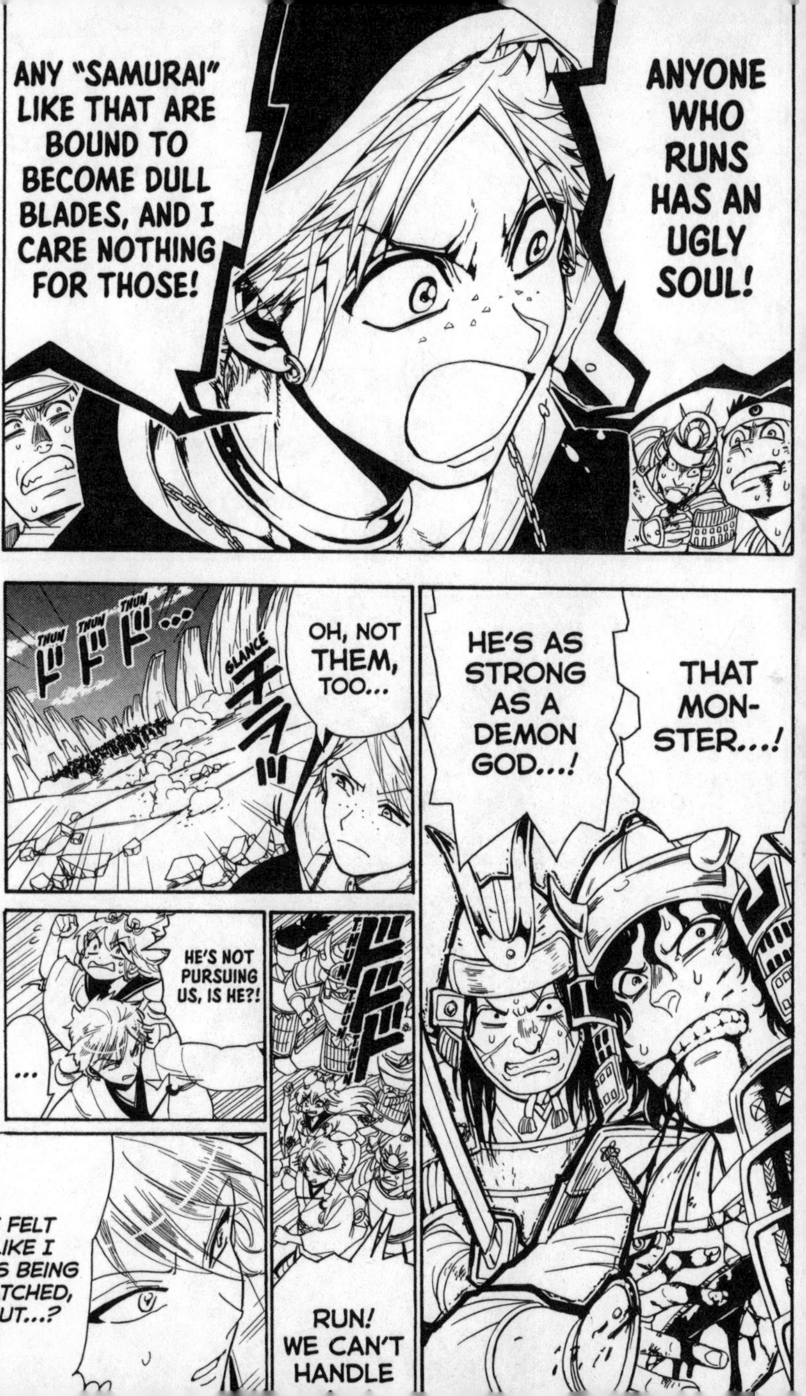
ANYONE WHO RUNS HAS AN UGLY SOUL!
ANY "SAMURAI" LIKE THAT ARE BOUND TO BECOME DULL BLADES, AND I CARE NOTHING FOR THOSE!
THAT MON-STER...!
HE'S AS STRONG AS A DEMON GOD...!
OH, NOT THEM, TOO...
GLANCE
THUN THUN THUN
THUN THUN THUN
RUN! WE CAN'T HANDLE
HE'S NOT PURSUING US, IS HE?!
...
I FELT LIKE I WAS BEING WATCHED, BUT...?

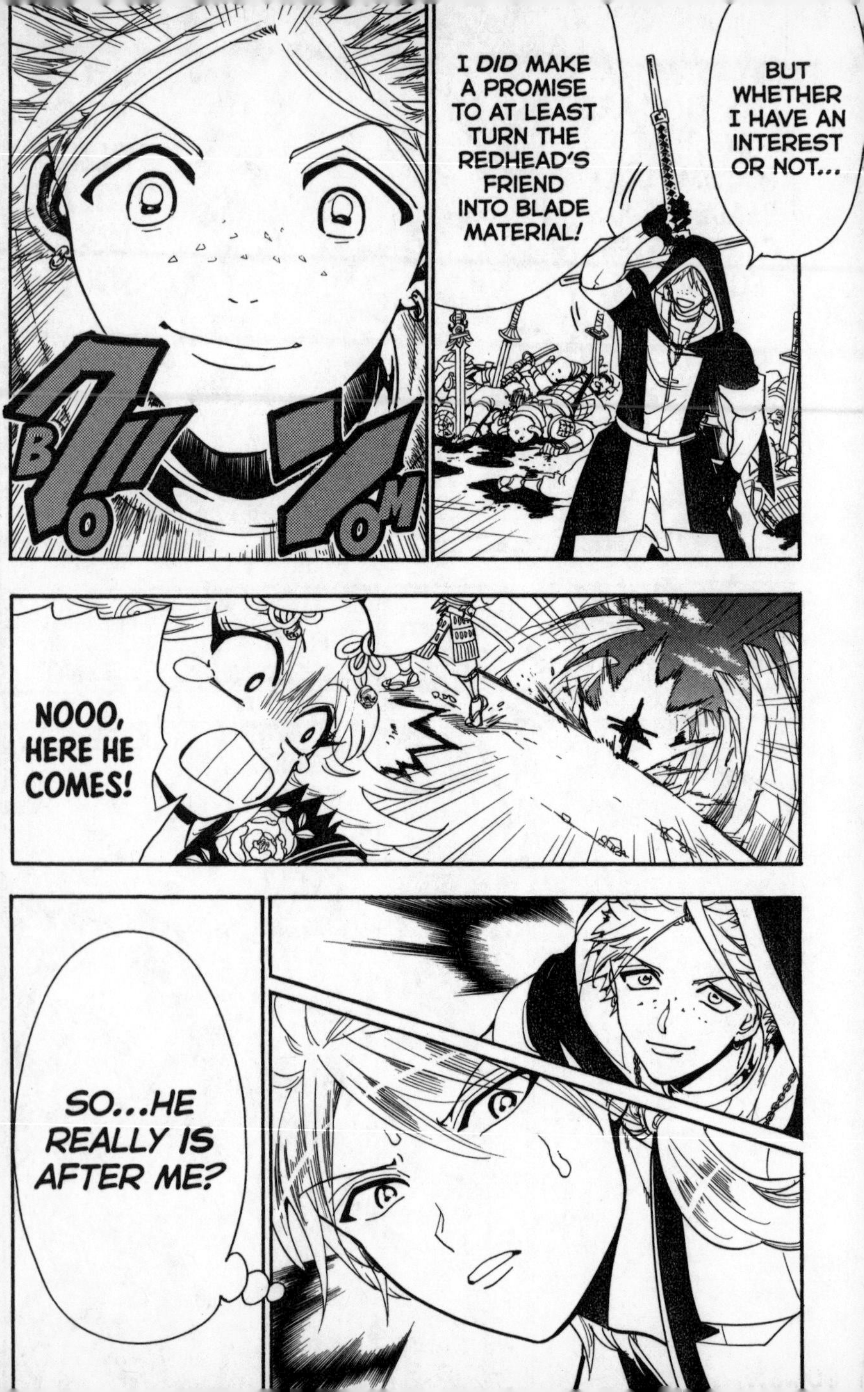
BUT WHETHER I HAVE AN INTEREST OR NOT...
I *DID* MAKE A PROMISE TO AT LEAST TURN THE REDHEAD'S FRIEND INTO BLADE MATERIAL!
BOOM
NOOO, HERE HE COMES!
SO...HE REALLY IS AFTER ME?

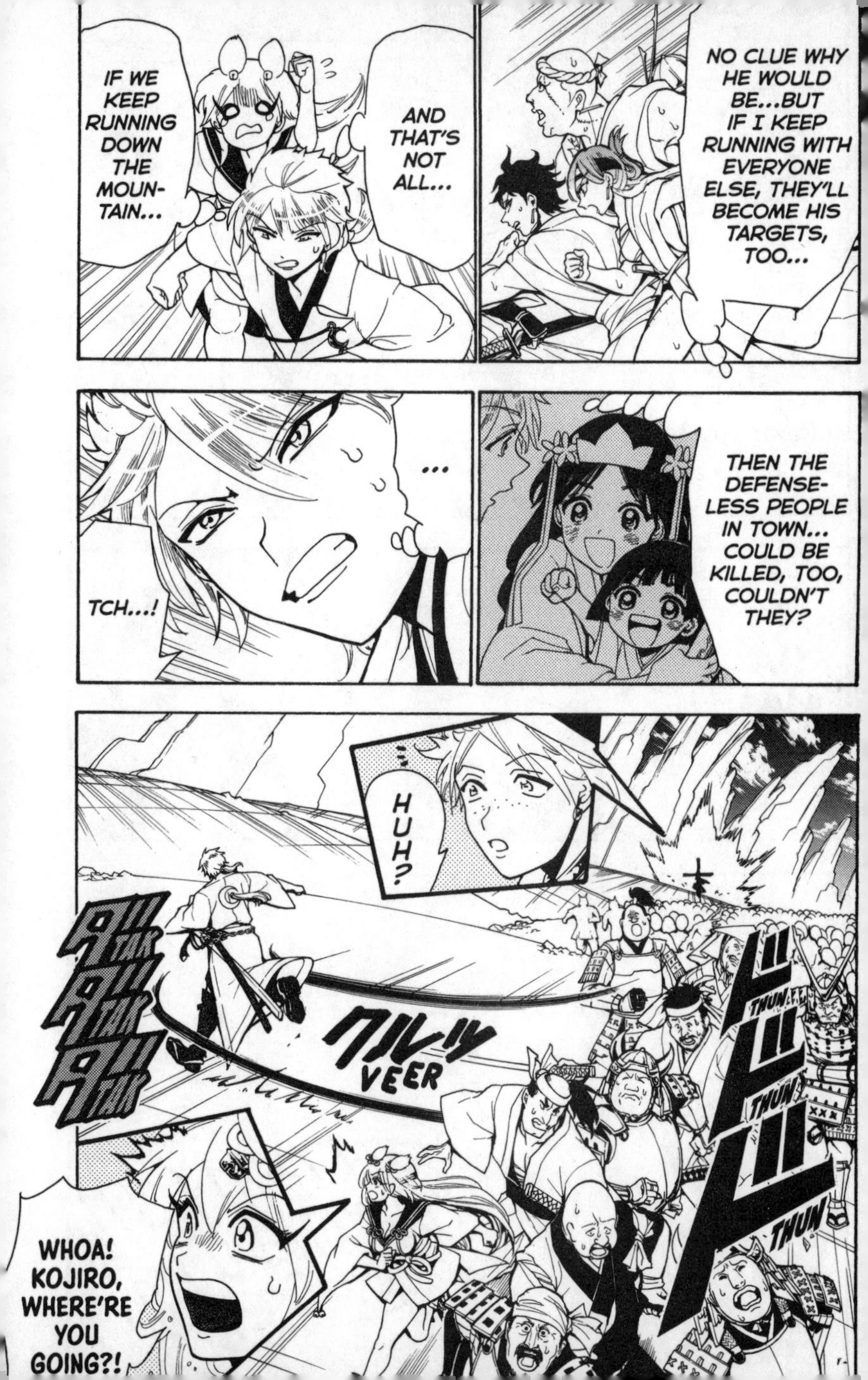
NO CLUE WHY HE WOULD BE...BUT IF I KEEP RUNNING WITH EVERYONE ELSE, THEY'LL BECOME HIS TARGETS, TOO...
IF WE KEEP RUNNING DOWN THE MOUN-TAIN...
AND THAT'S NOT ALL...
THEN THE DEFENSE-LESS PEOPLE IN TOWN... COULD BE KILLED, TOO, COULDN'T THEY?
...
TCH...!
HUH?
THUN
THUN
THUN
VEER
WHOA! KOJIRO, WHERE'RE YOU GOING?!

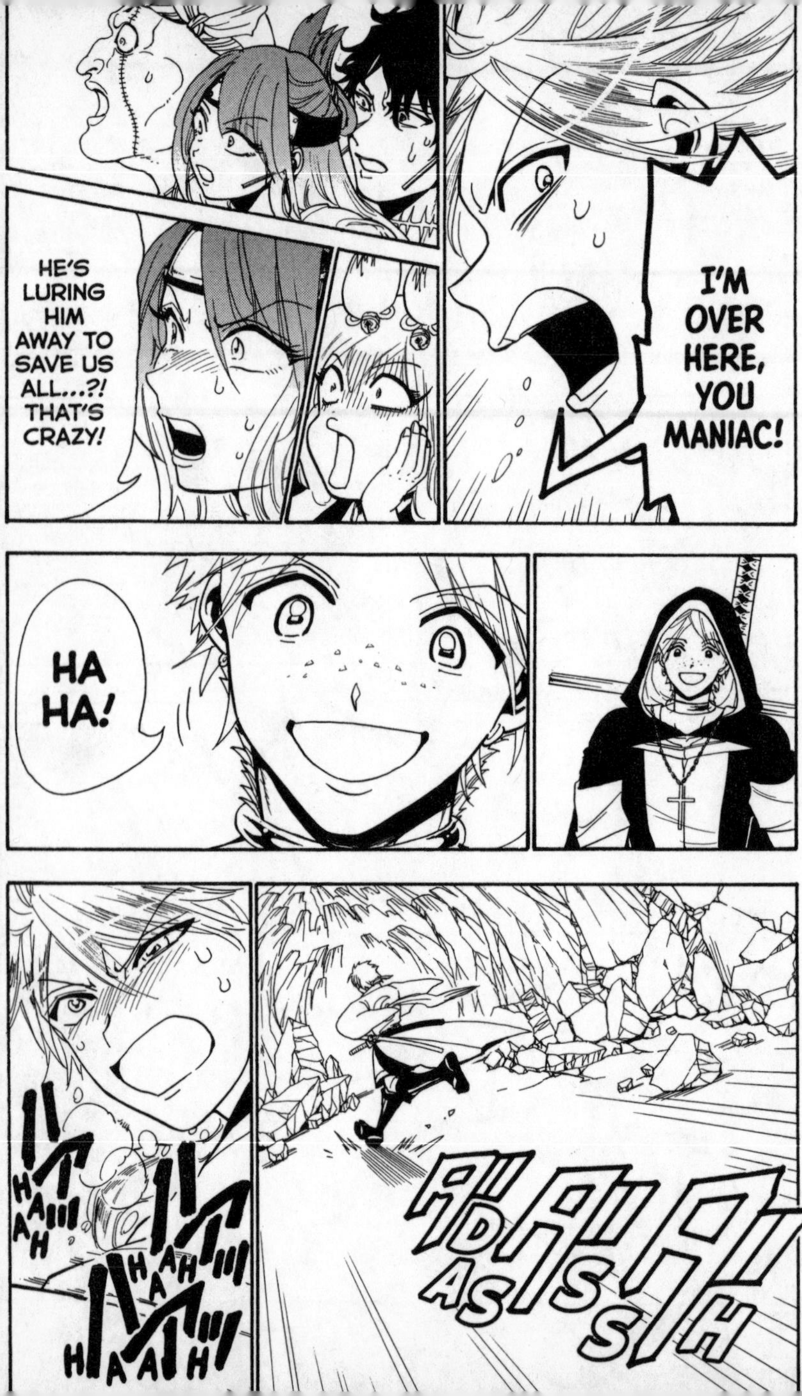
I'M OVER HERE, YOU MANIAC!
HE'S LURING HIM AWAY TO SAVE US ALL...?! THAT'S CRAZY!
HA HA!
DASSSH
HAAH
HAAH
HAAAH

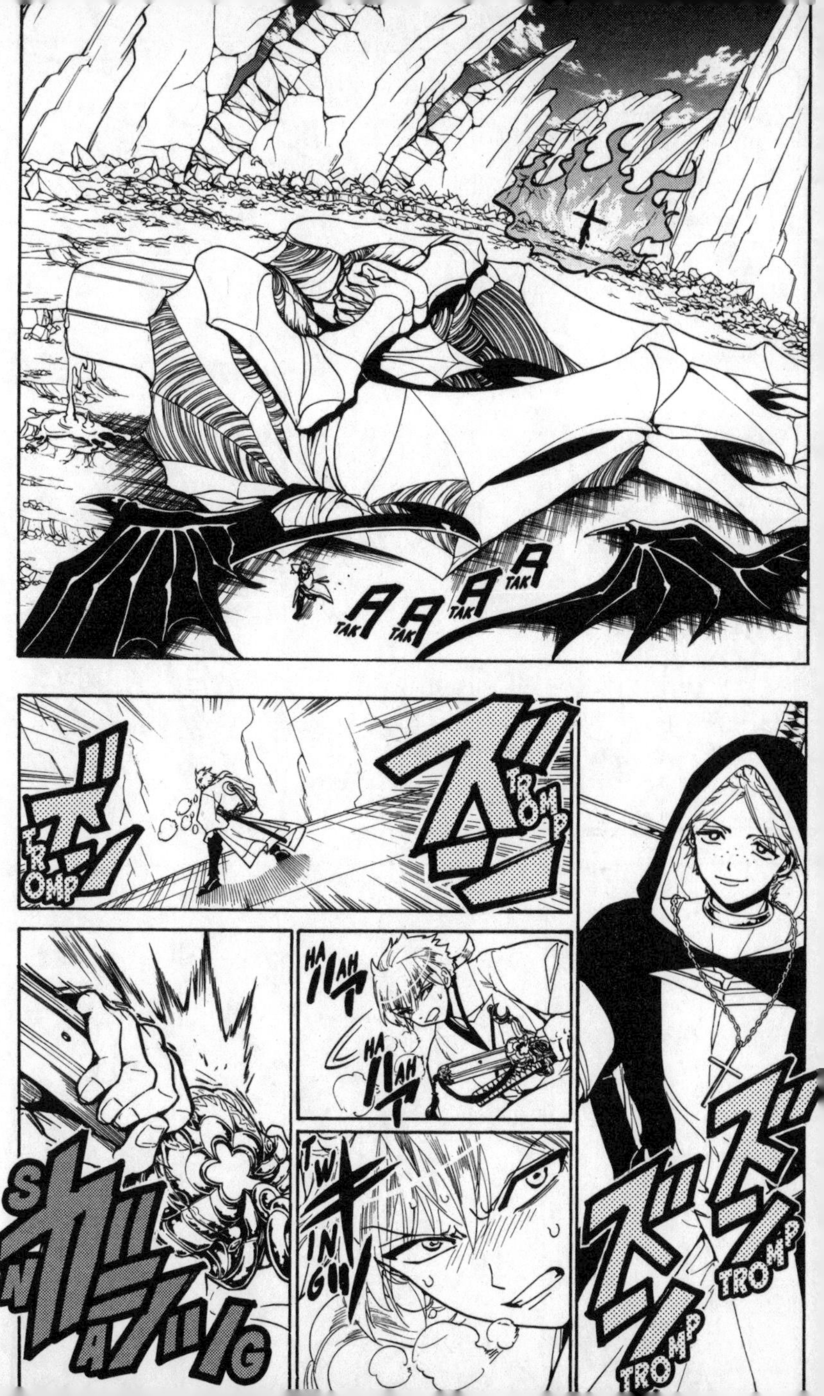
TAK TAK TAK TAK
TROMP TROMP
TROMP
TROMP
HAAH HAAH
TWING
SNAG

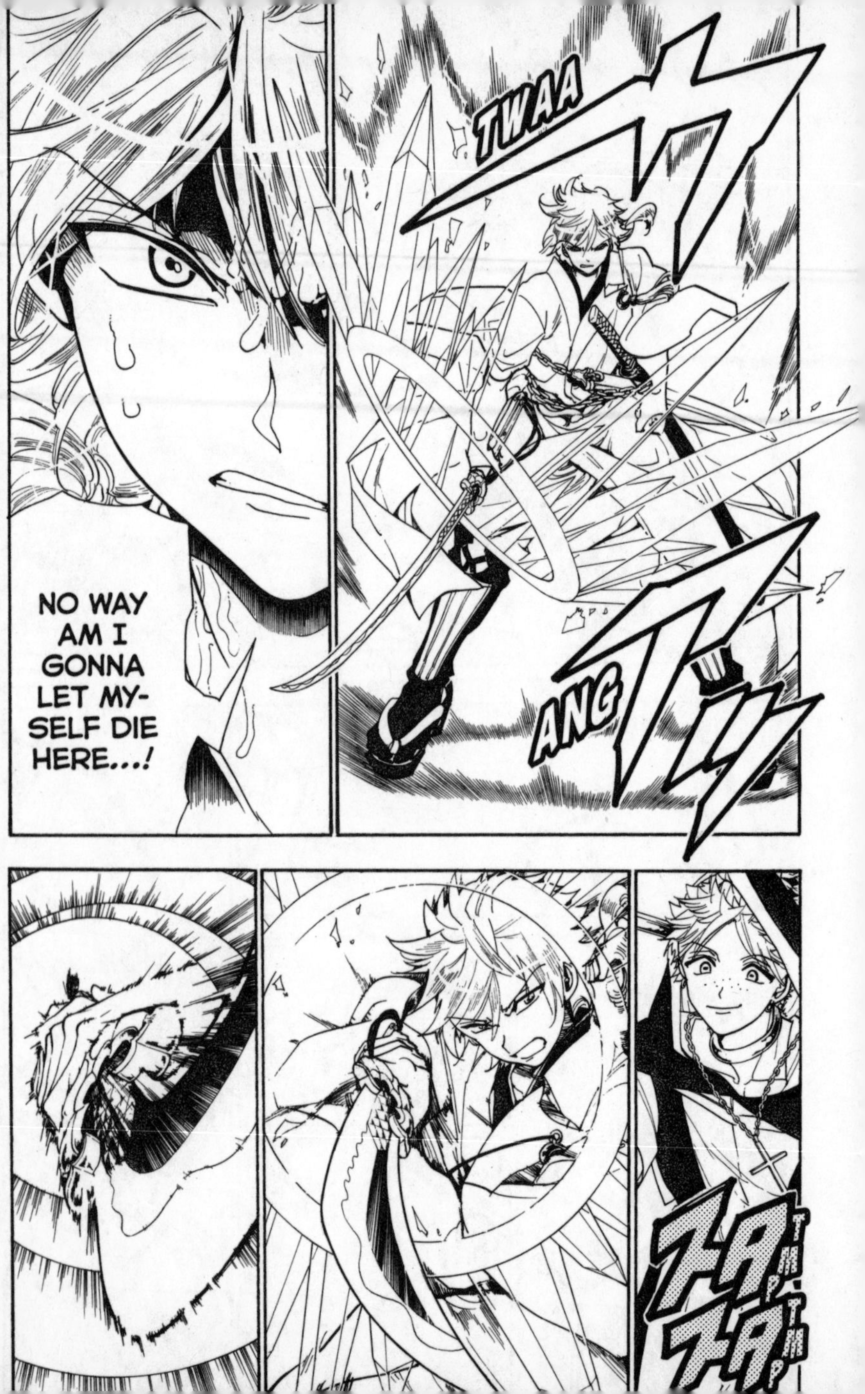
TWAA
ANG
NO WAY AM I GONNA LET MY-SELF DIE HERE...!
TMP
TMP

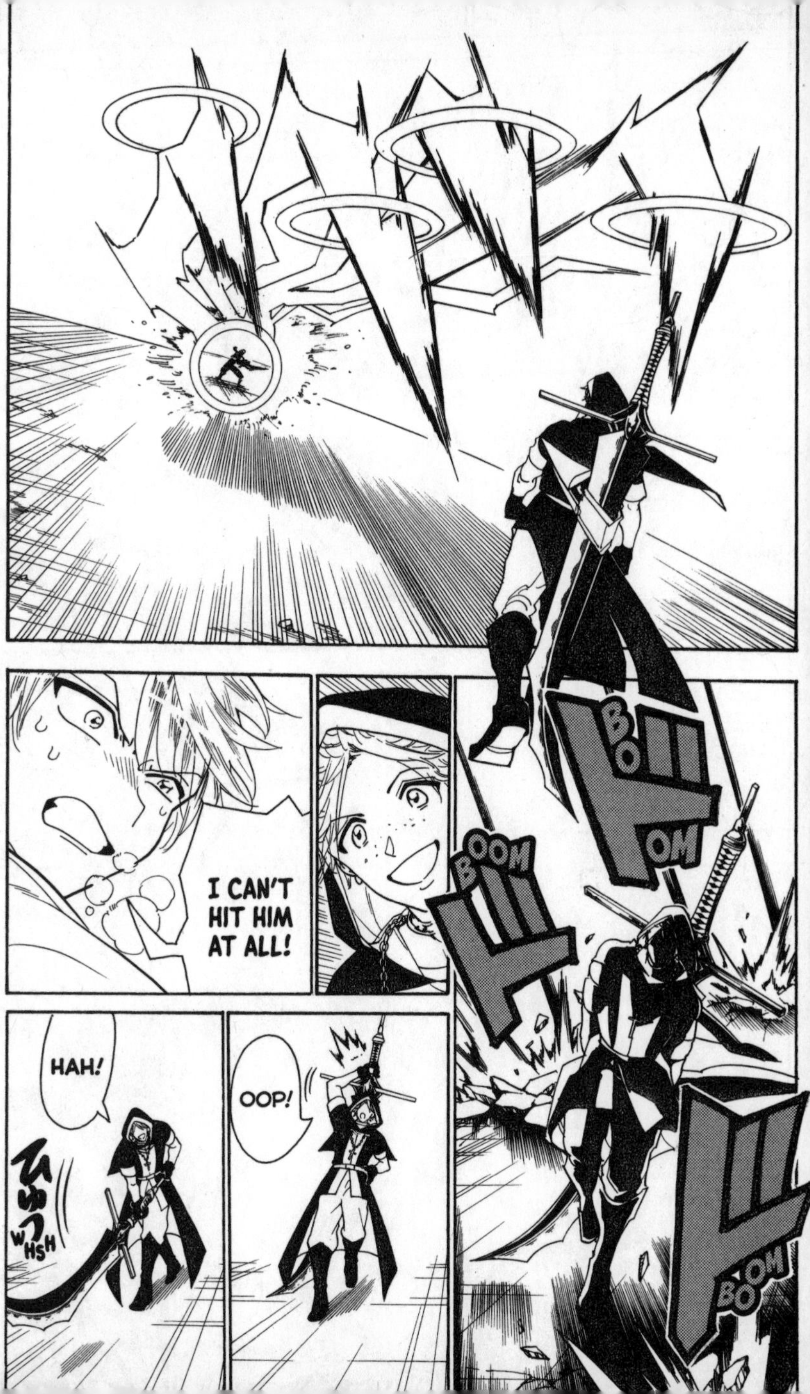

BOOM
BOOM
BOOM
I CAN'T HIT HIM AT ALL!
OOP!
HAH!
ひゅっ
WHSH

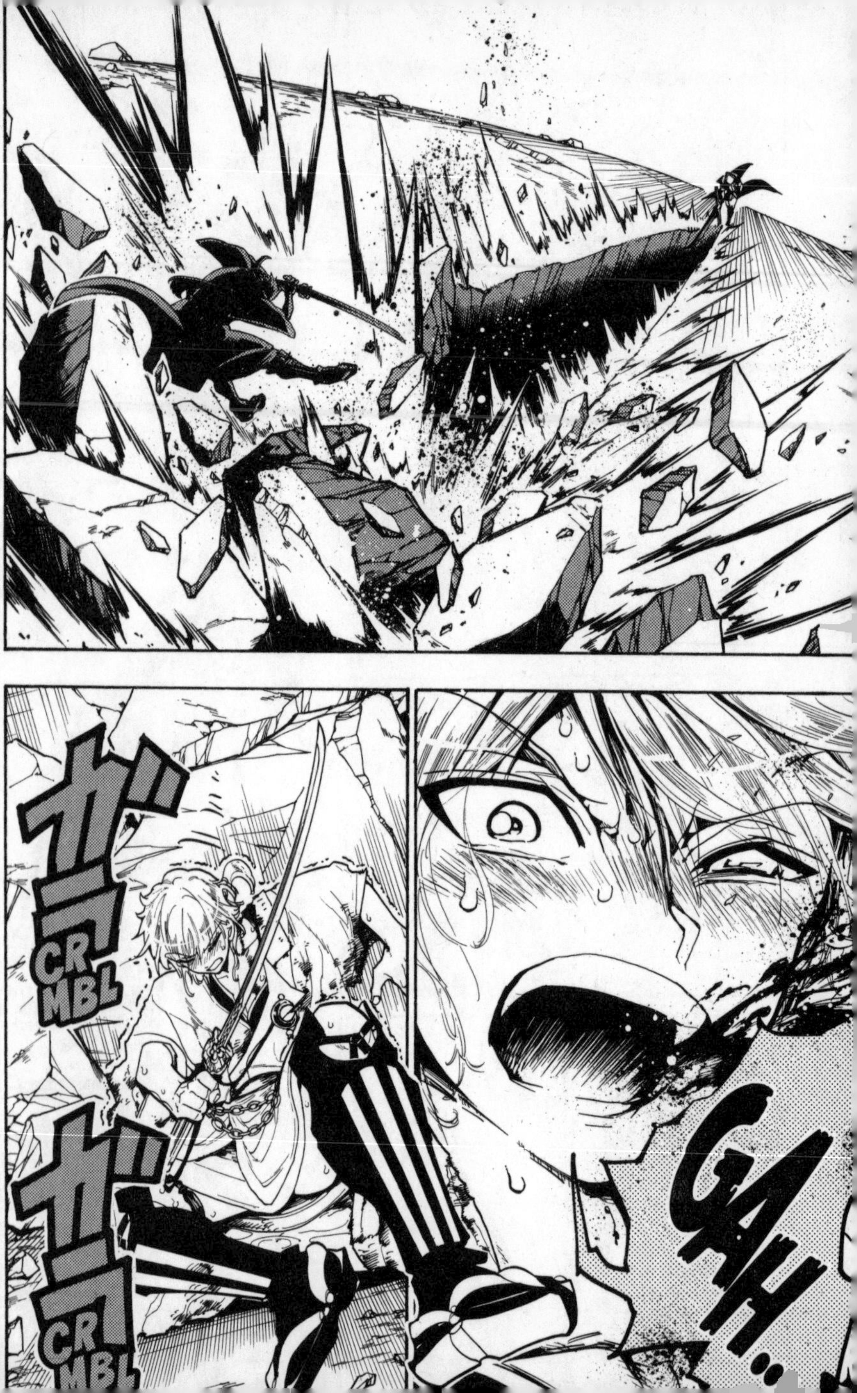
GAH...
CRMBL
CRMBL

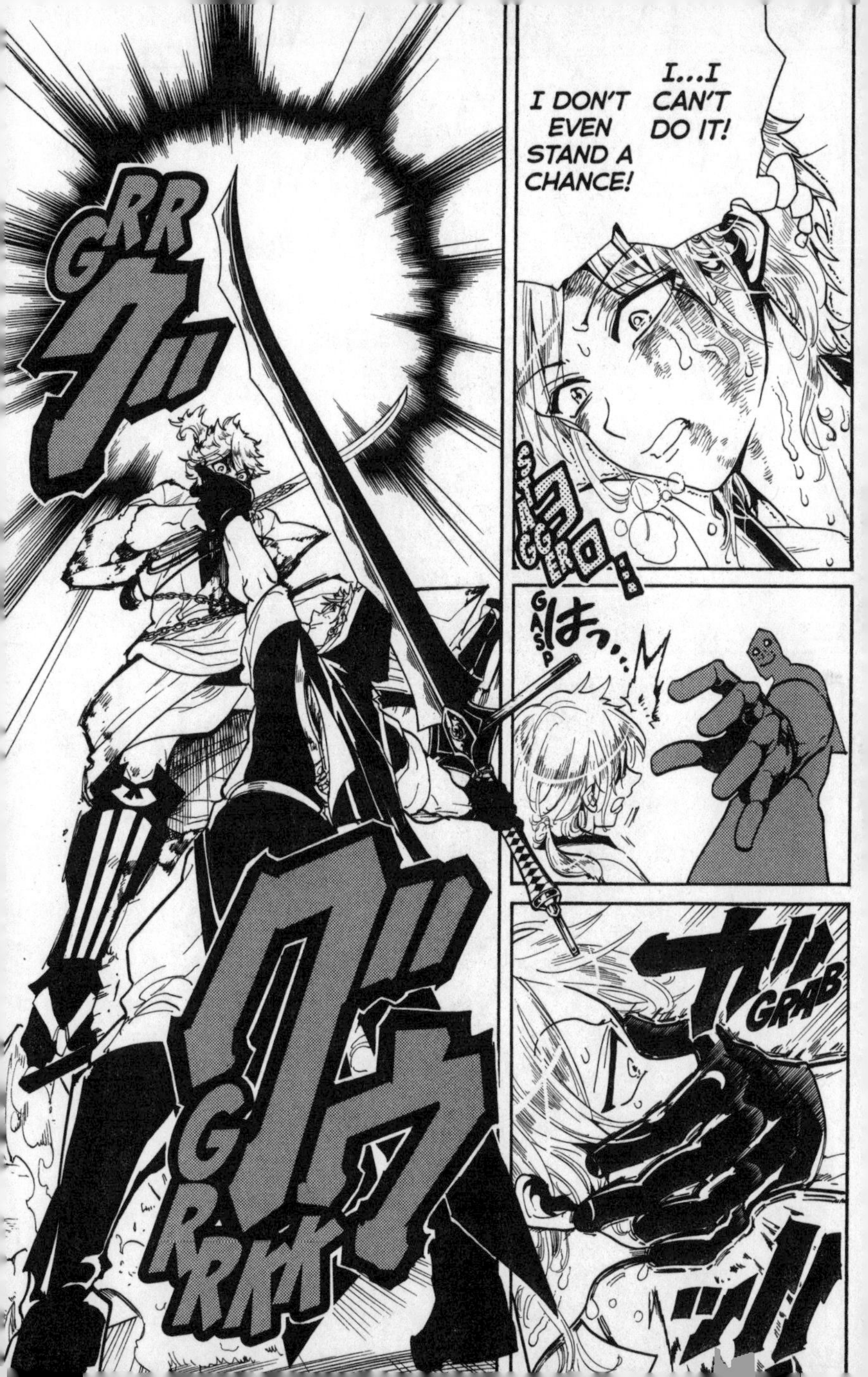
I...I CAN'T DO IT!
I DON'T EVEN STAND A CHANCE!
STAGGER
ヨロ…
GASP
はっ…
ガッ
GRAB
GRR
グ
GRRKK
グ

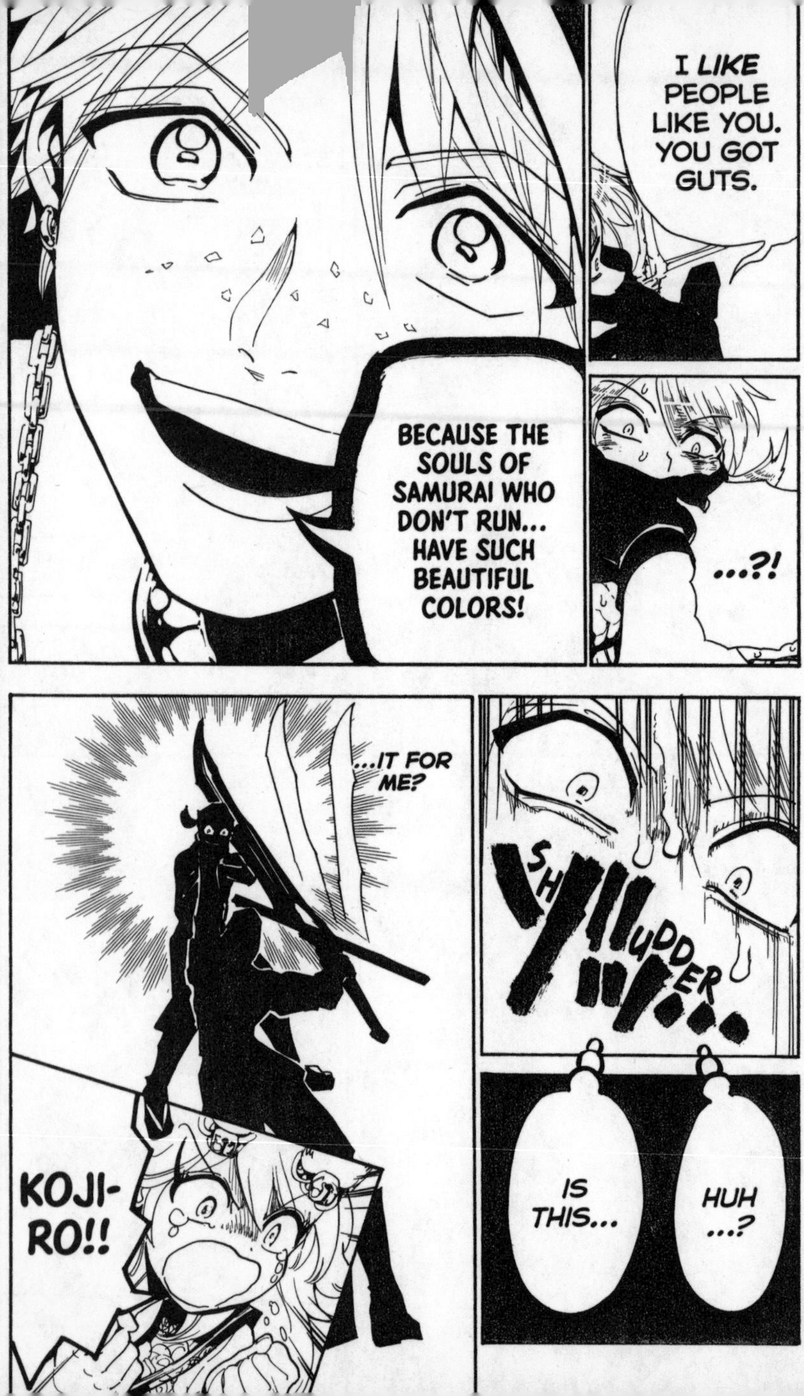
I LIKE PEOPLE LIKE YOU. YOU GOT GUTS.
...?!
BECAUSE THE SOULS OF SAMURAI WHO DON'T RUN... HAVE SUCH BEAUTIFUL COLORS!
SHUDDER...
HUH ...?
IS THIS...
...IT FOR ME?
KOJI-RO!!

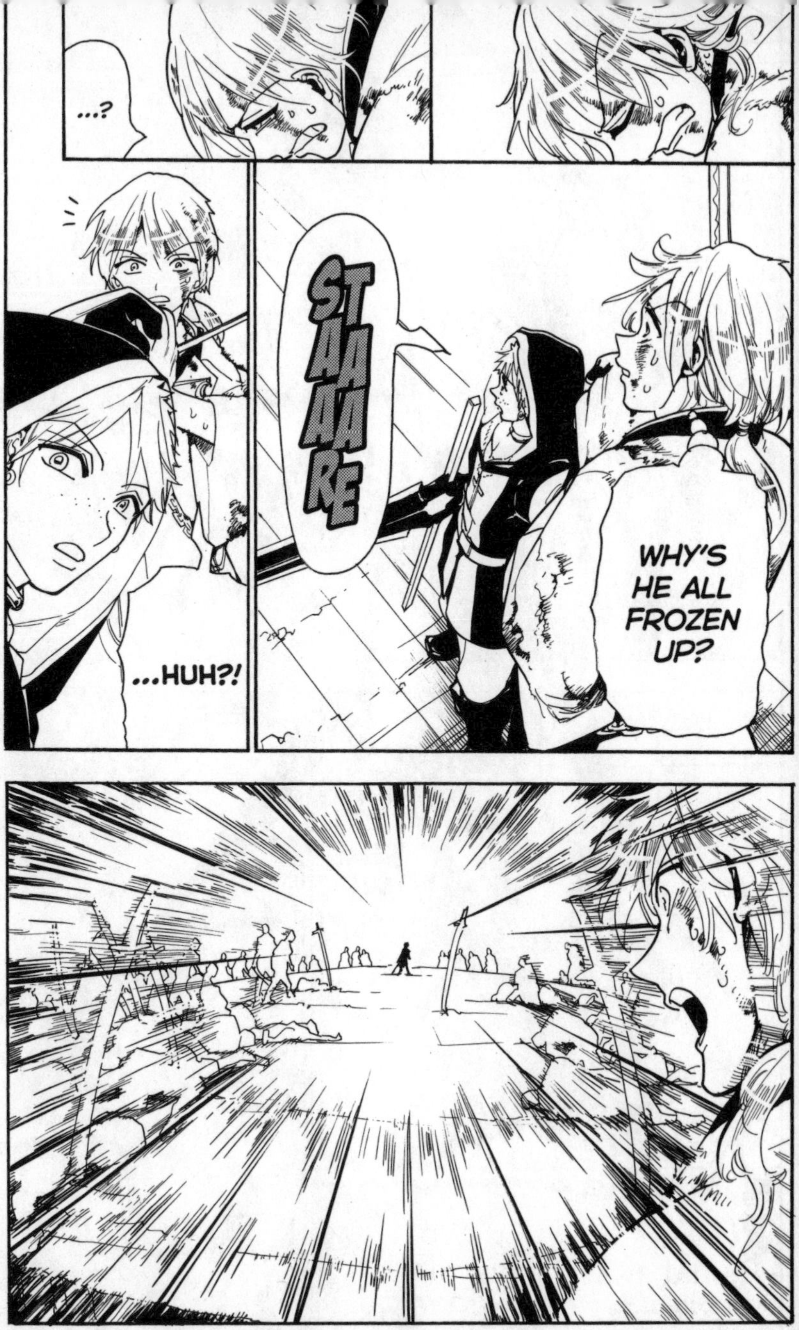
...?
STAAARE
WHY'S HE ALL FROZEN UP?
...HUH?!

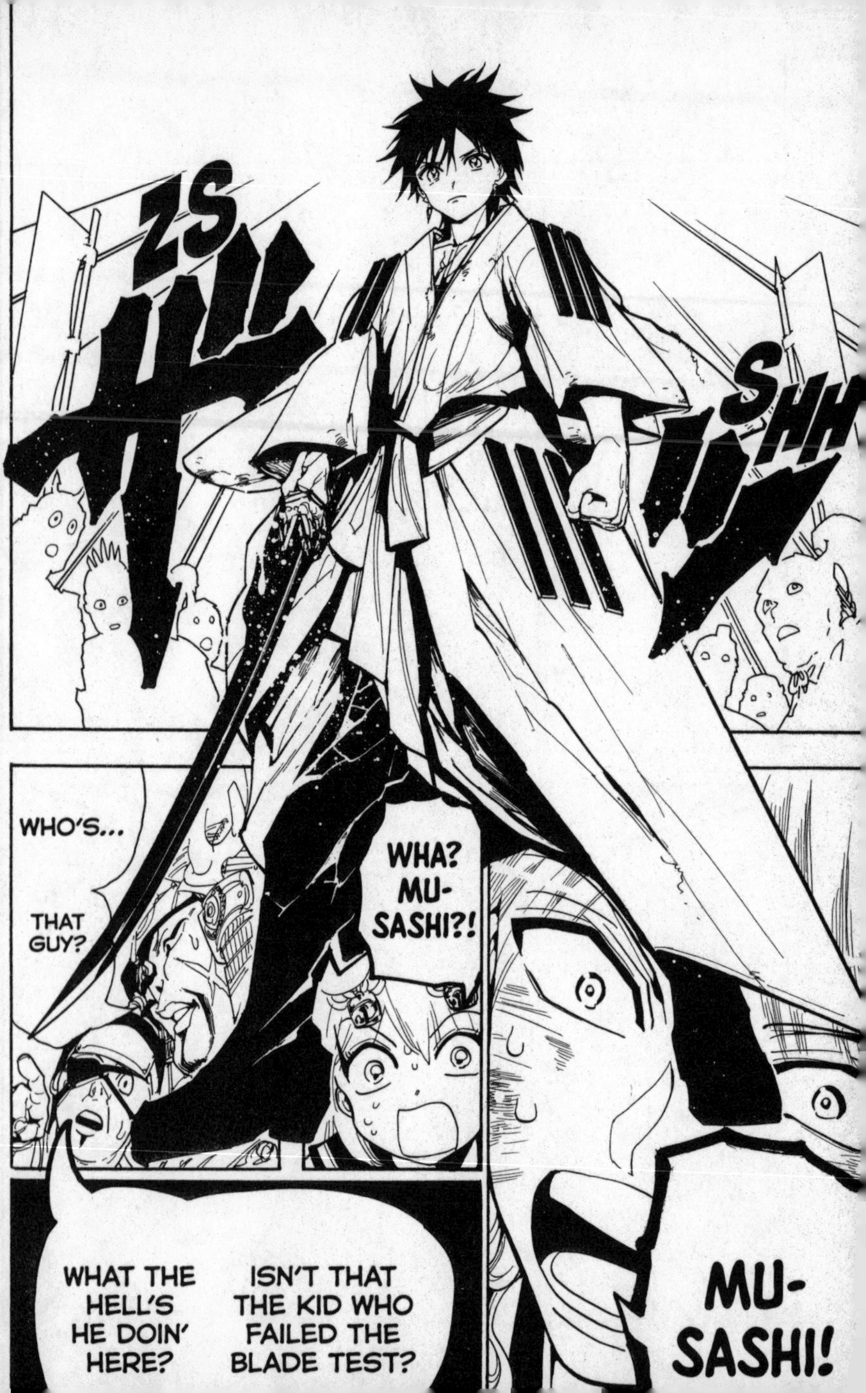
SHH
ZS
WHA? MU-SASHI?!
WHO'S...
THAT GUY?
MU-SASHI!
ISN'T THAT THE KID WHO FAILED THE BLADE TEST?
WHAT THE HELL'S HE DOIN' HERE?

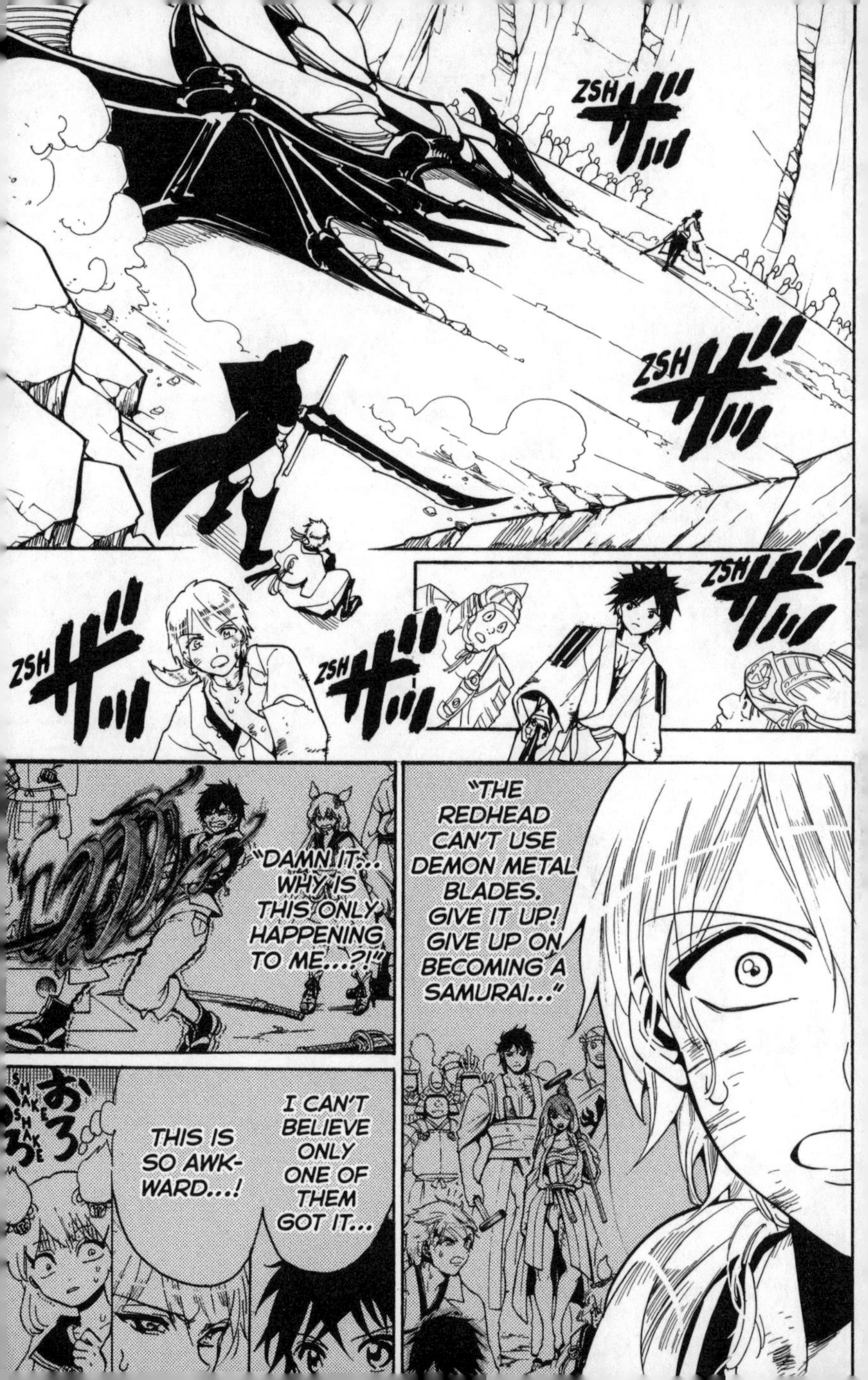
ZSH
ZSH
ZSH
ZSH
ZSH
"THE REDHEAD CAN'T USE DEMON METAL BLADES. GIVE IT UP! GIVE UP ON BECOMING A SAMURAI..."
"DAMN IT... WHY IS THIS ONLY HAPPENING TO ME...?!"
I CAN'T BELIEVE ONLY ONE OF THEM GOT IT...
THIS IS SO AWK-WARD...!
おろおろ
SHAKE SHAKE

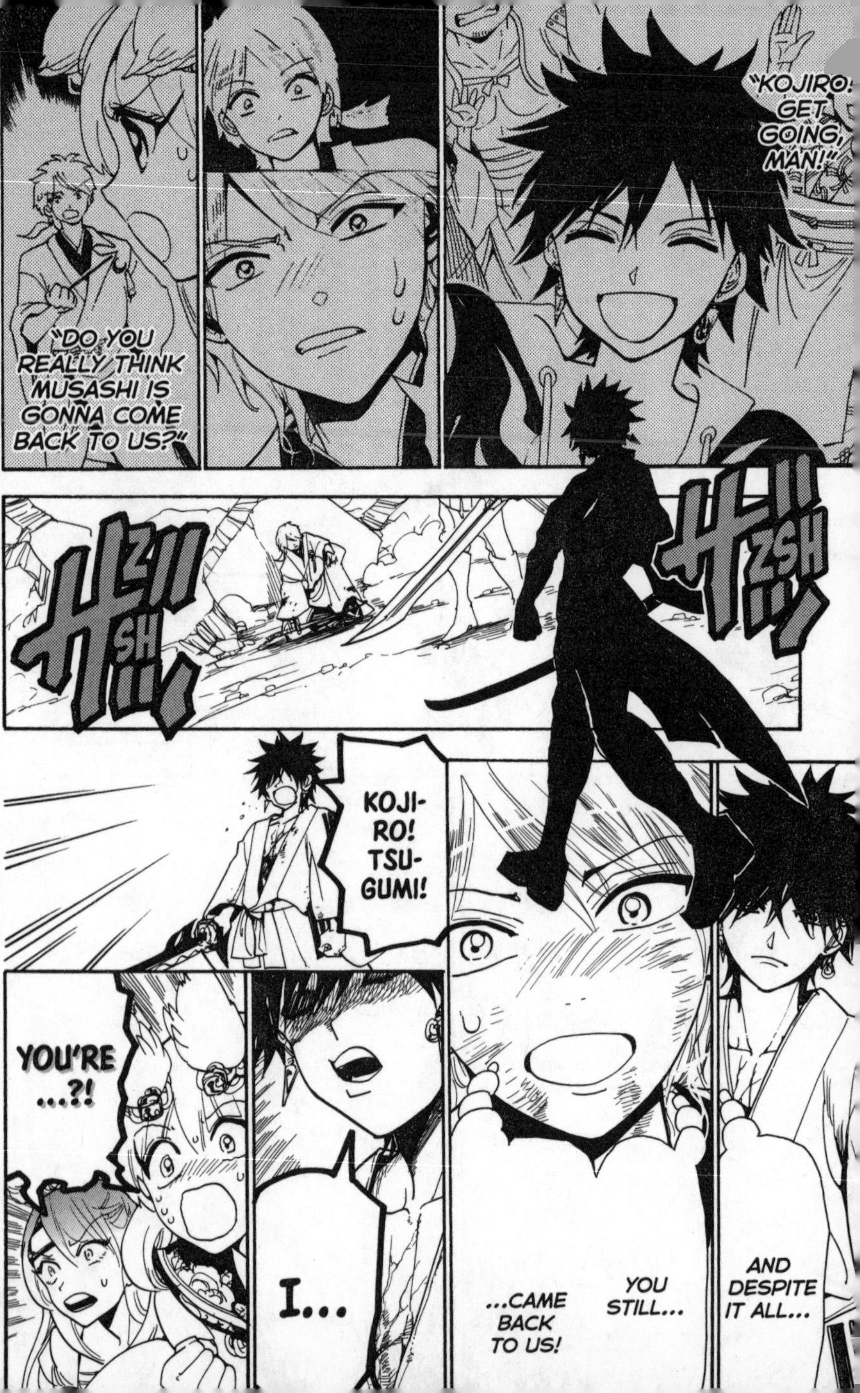
"KOJIRO! GET GOING, MAN!"
"DO YOU REALLY THINK MUSASHI IS GONNA COME BACK TO US?"
HZSH...!
HZSH...!
AND DESPITE IT ALL...
YOU STILL...
...CAME BACK TO US!
KOJI-RO! TSU-GUMI!
I...
YOU'RE ...?!

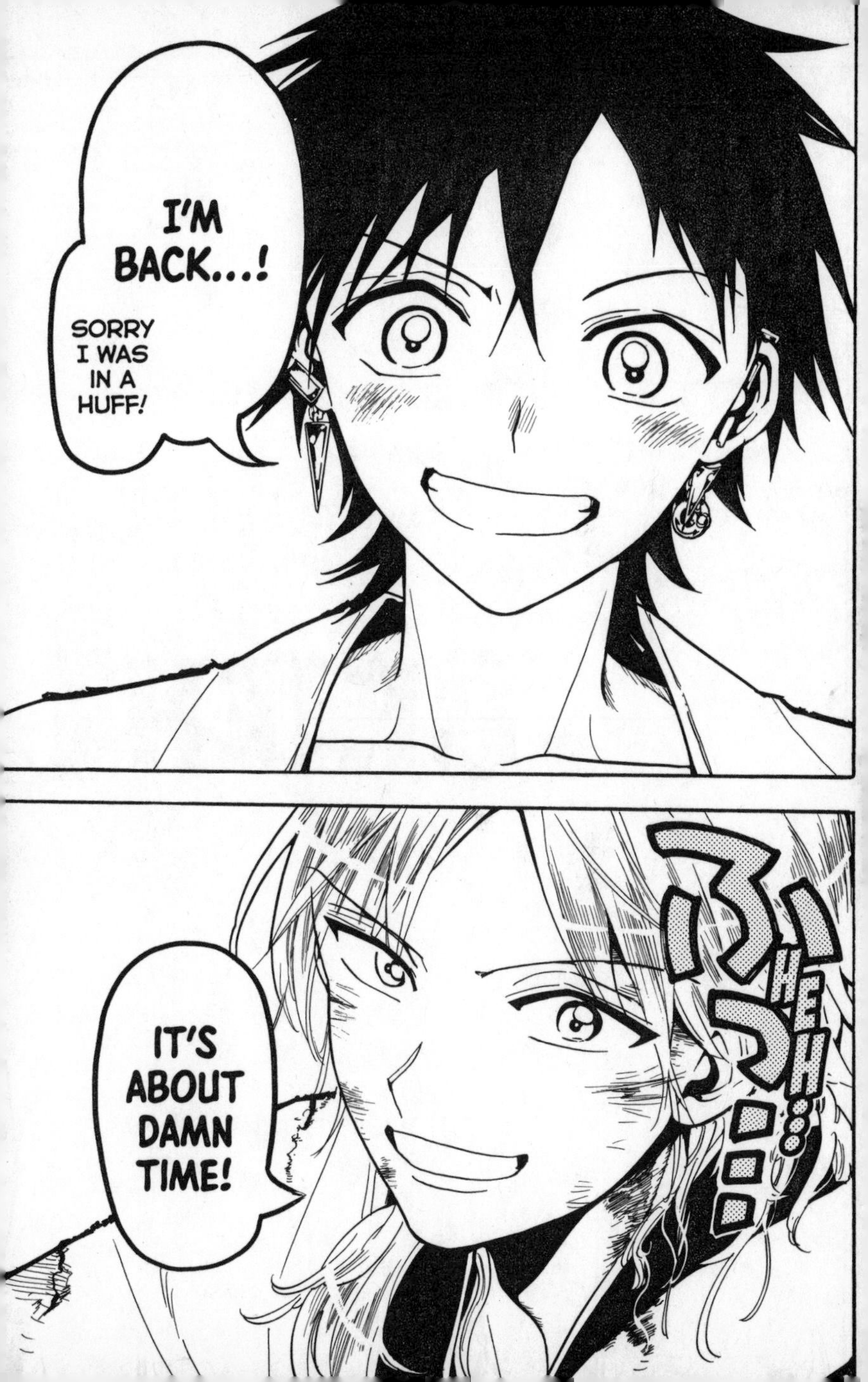
I'M BACK...!
SORRY I WAS IN A HUFF!
ふっ
HEH...!!
IT'S ABOUT DAMN TIME!

ORIENT

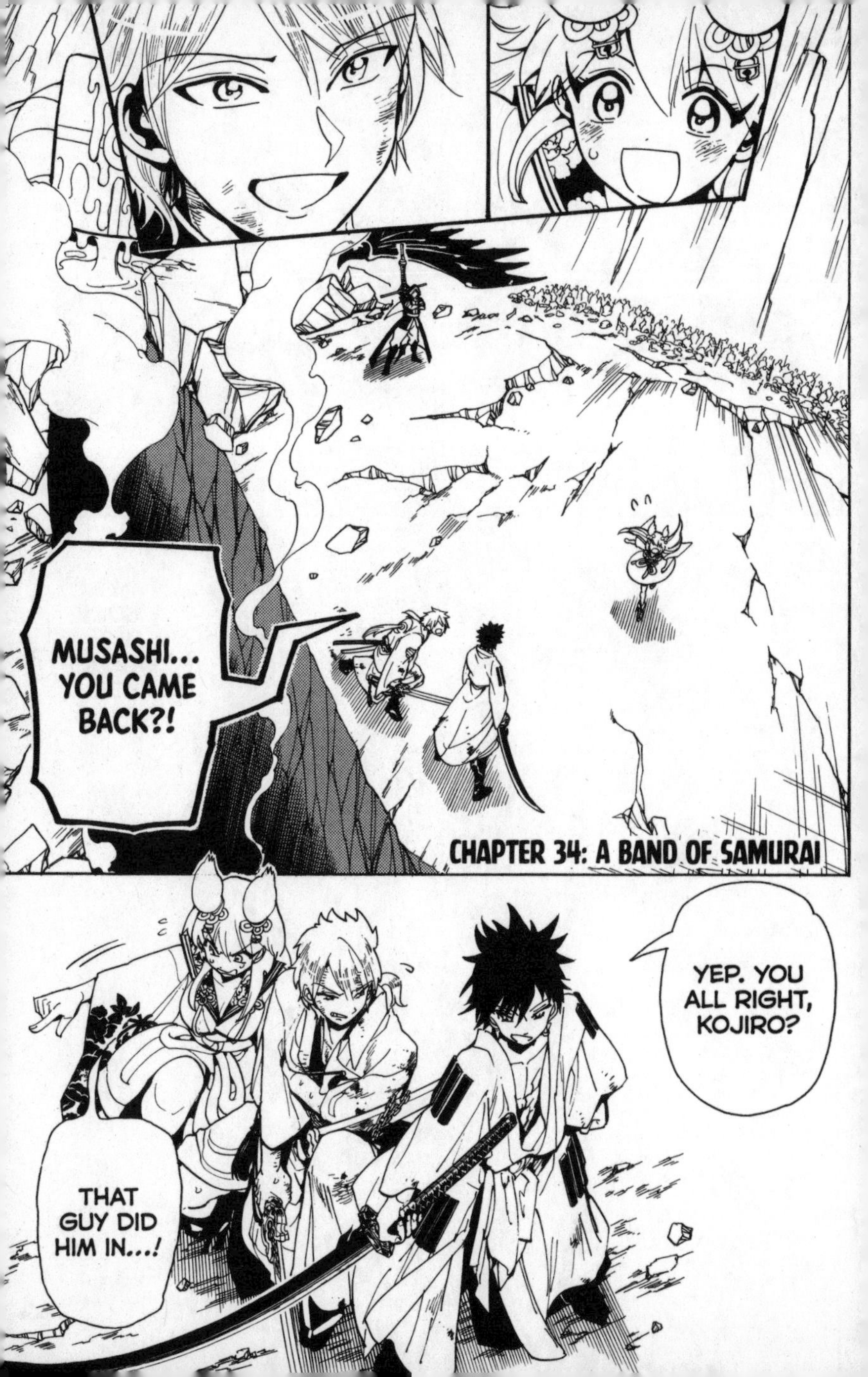
MUSASHI... YOU CAME BACK?!
CHAPTER 34: A BAND OF SAMURAI
YEP. YOU ALL RIGHT, KOJIRO?
THAT GUY DID HIM IN...!

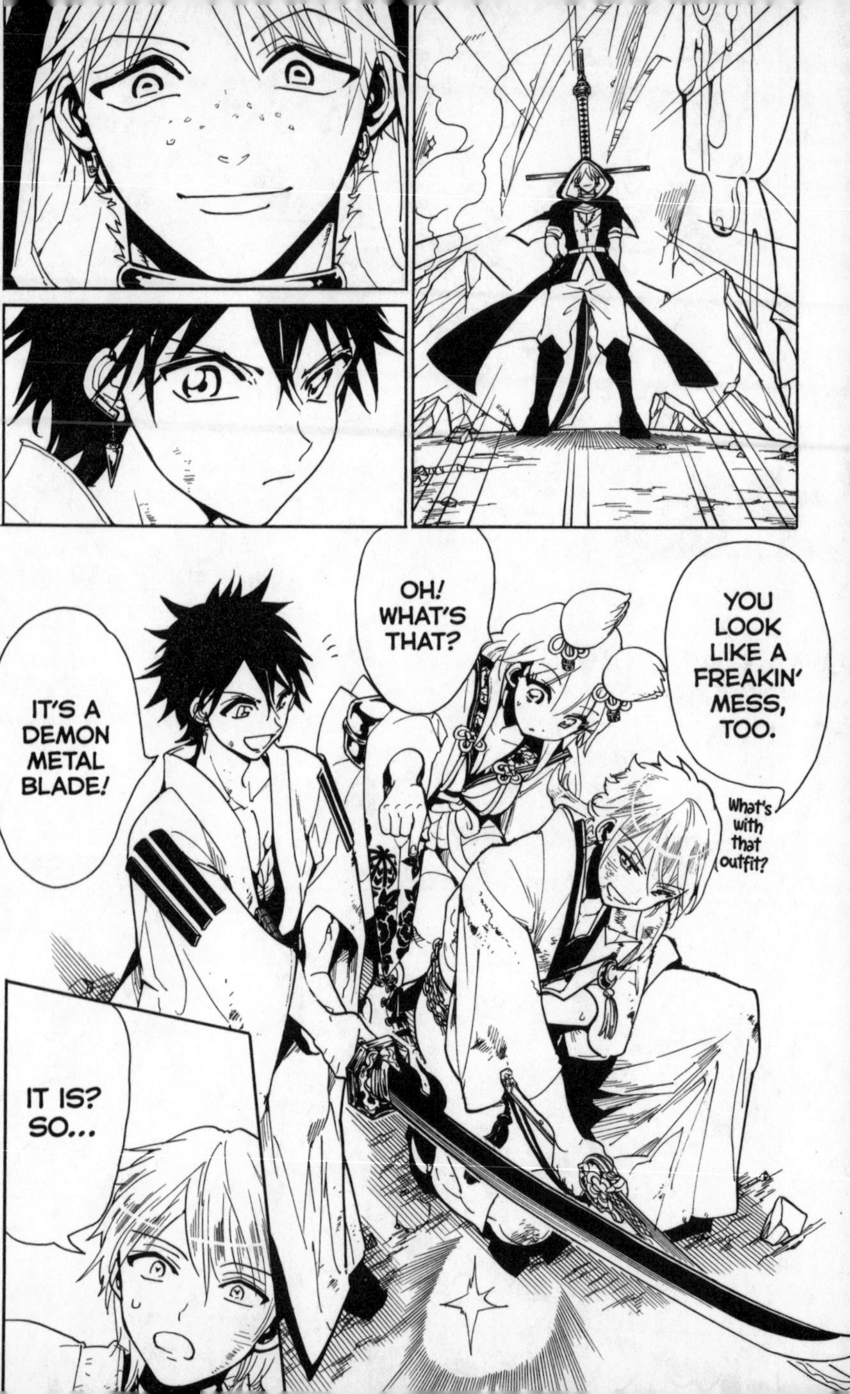
YOU LOOK LIKE A FREAKIN' MESS, TOO.
What's with that outfit?
OH! WHAT'S THAT?
IT'S A DEMON METAL BLADE!
IT IS? SO...

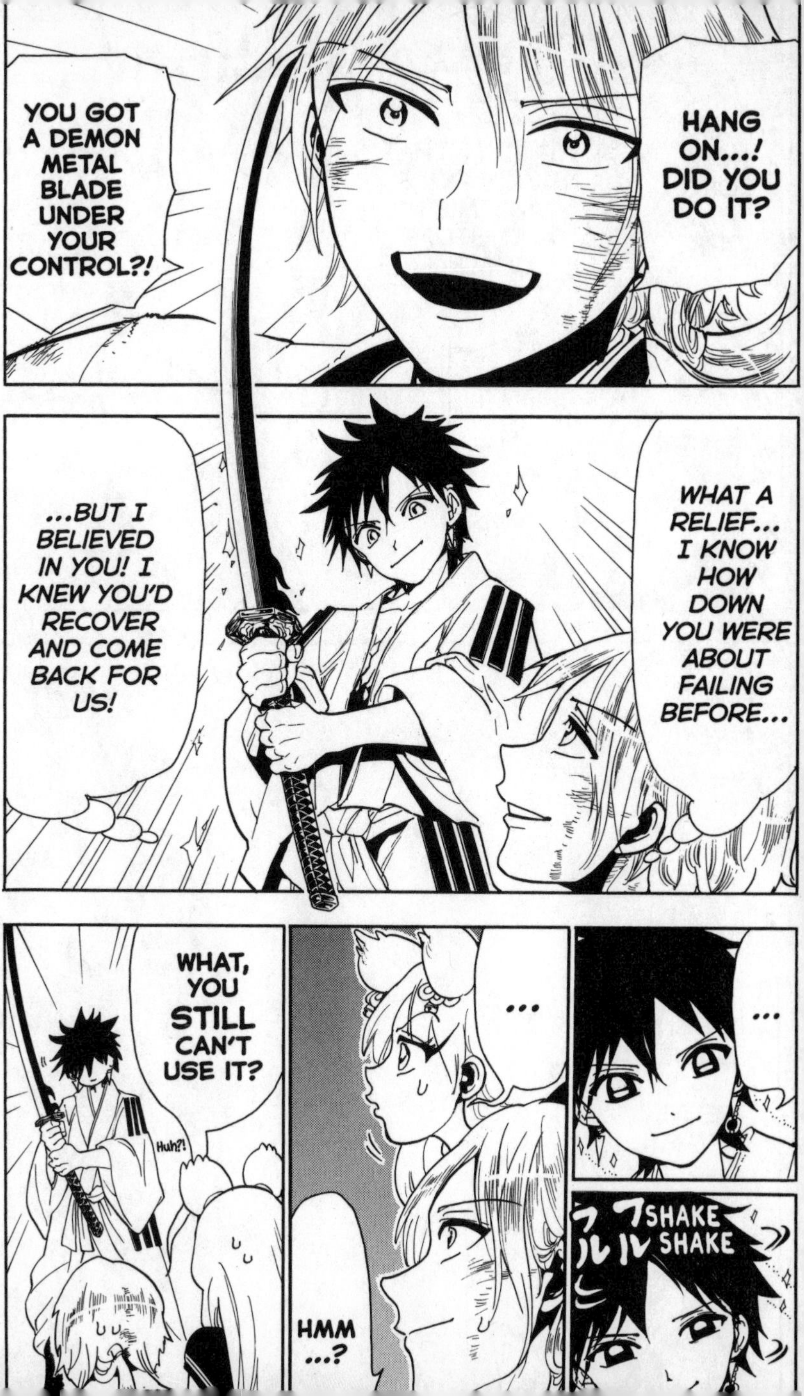
HANG ON...! DID YOU DO IT?
YOU GOT A DEMON METAL BLADE UNDER YOUR CONTROL?!
WHAT A RELIEF... I KNOW HOW DOWN YOU WERE ABOUT FAILING BEFORE...
...BUT I BELIEVED IN YOU! I KNEW YOU'D RECOVER AND COME BACK FOR US!
...
フルフル
SHAKE SHAKE
...
HMM ...?
WHAT, YOU STILL CAN'T USE IT?
Huh?!

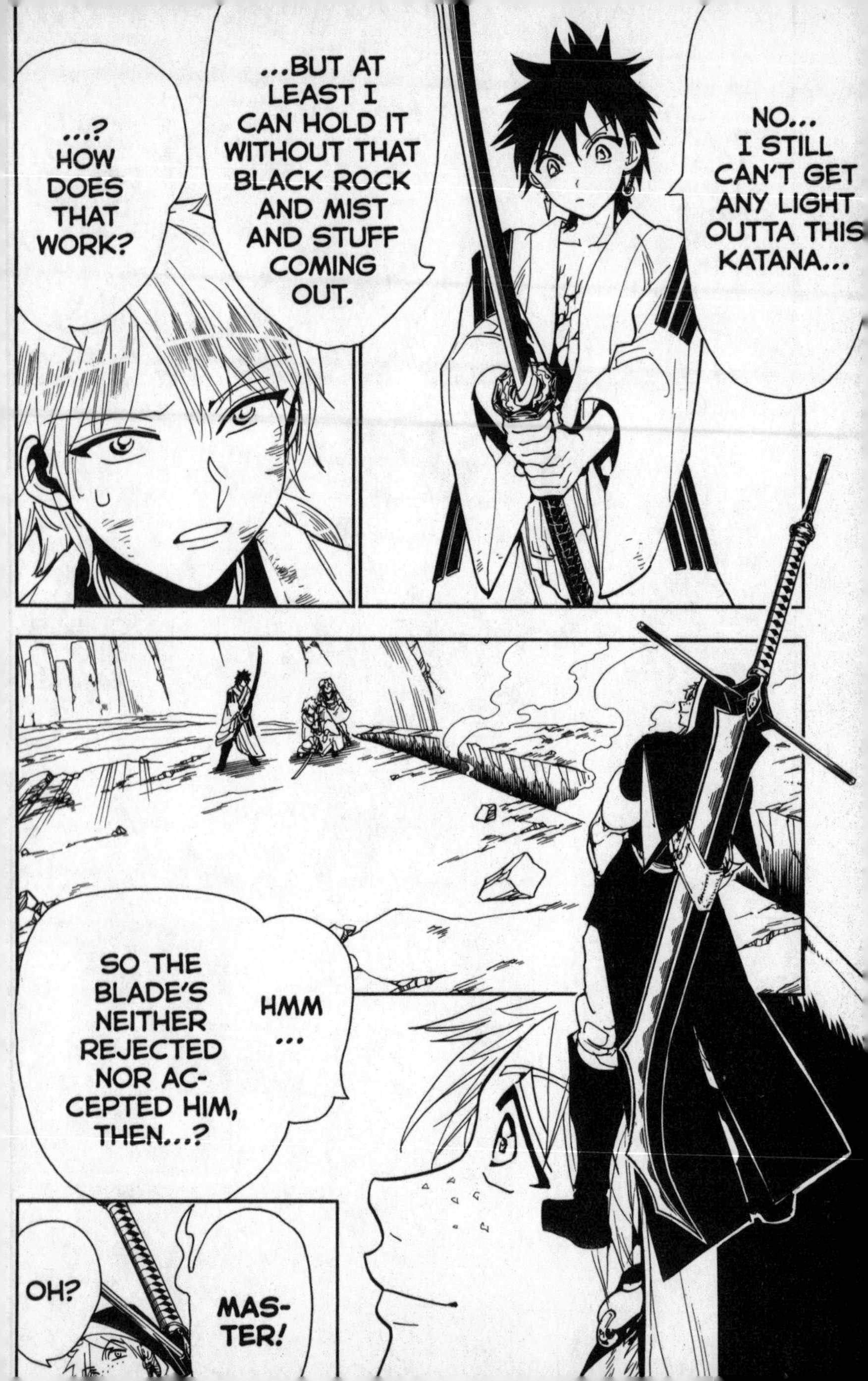
NO... I STILL CAN'T GET ANY LIGHT OUTTA THIS KATANA...
...BUT AT LEAST I CAN HOLD IT WITHOUT THAT BLACK ROCK AND MIST AND STUFF COMING OUT.
...? HOW DOES THAT WORK?
HMM ...
SO THE BLADE'S NEITHER REJECTED NOR ACCEPTED HIM, THEN...?
MASTER!
OH?

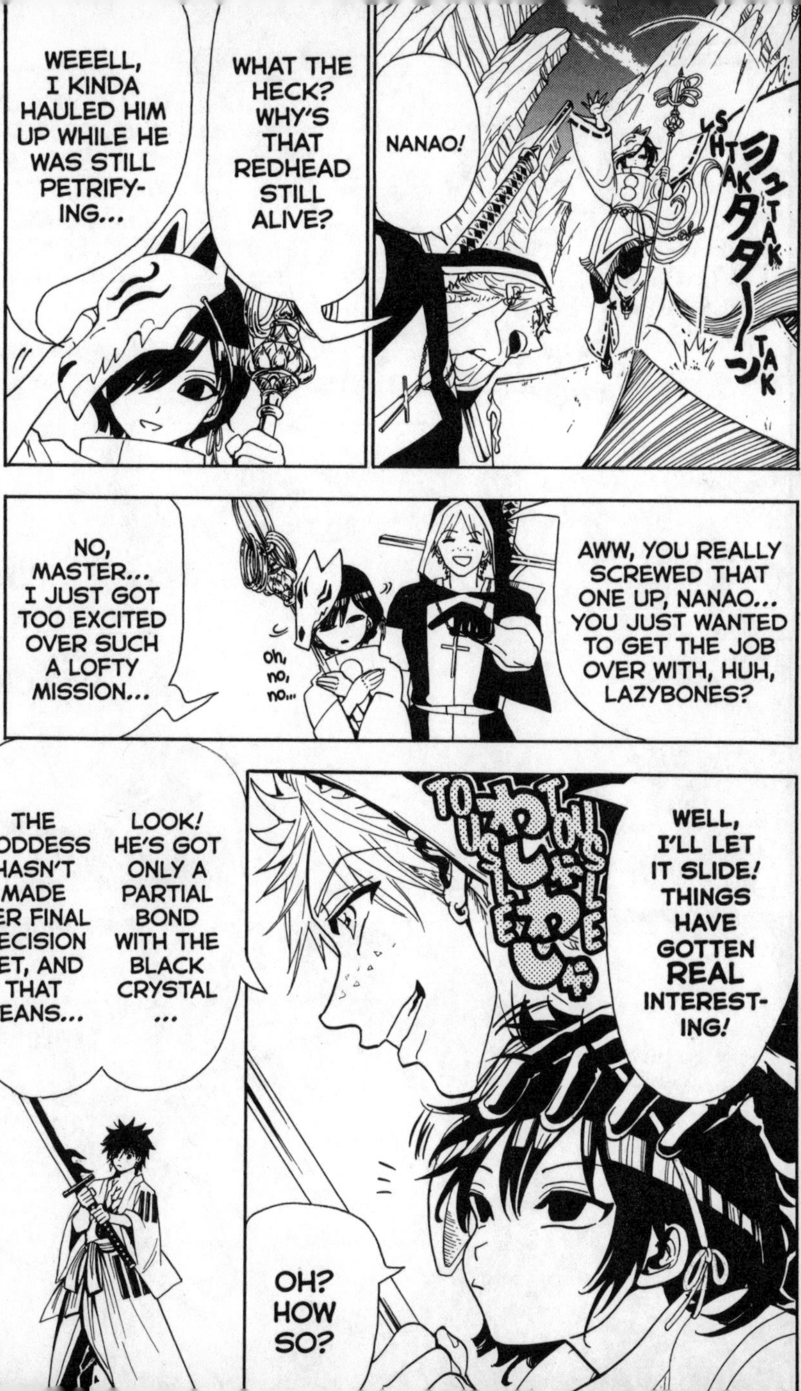
SHTAK TAK TAK
NANAO!
WHAT THE HECK? WHY'S THAT REDHEAD STILL ALIVE?
WEEELL, I KINDA HAULED HIM UP WHILE HE WAS STILL PETRIFY-ING...
AWW, YOU REALLY SCREWED THAT ONE UP, NANAO... YOU JUST WANTED TO GET THE JOB OVER WITH, HUH, LAZYBONES?
oh, no, no...
NO, MASTER... I JUST GOT TOO EXCITED OVER SUCH A LOFTY MISSION...
TOUSLE TOUSLE
WELL, I'LL LET IT SLIDE! THINGS HAVE GOTTEN REAL INTEREST-ING!
OH? HOW SO?
LOOK! HE'S GOT ONLY A PARTIAL BOND WITH THE BLACK CRYSTAL...
THE GODDESS HASN'T MADE HER FINAL DECISION YET, AND THAT MEANS...

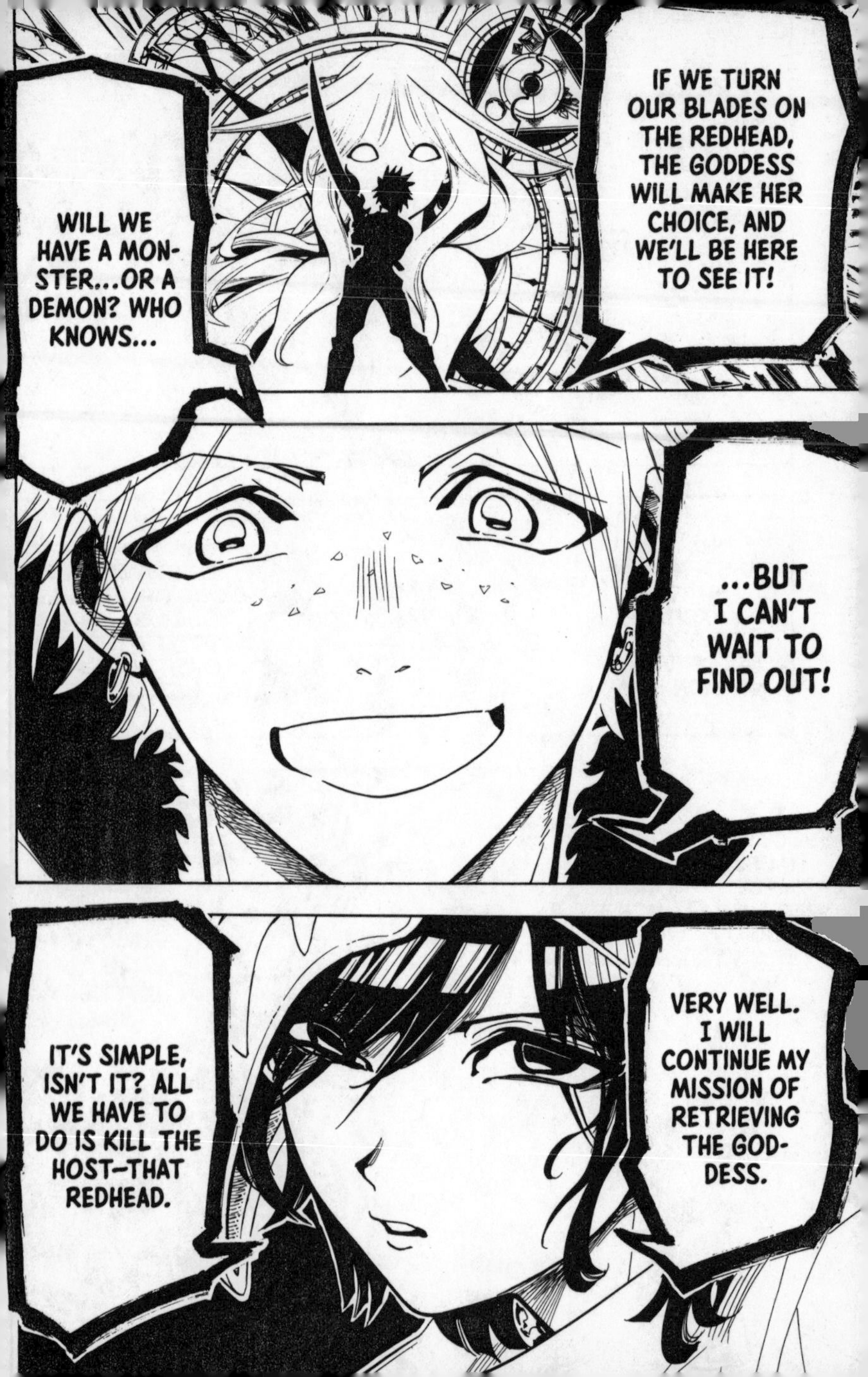
IF WE TURN OUR BLADES ON THE REDHEAD, THE GODDESS WILL MAKE HER CHOICE, AND WE'LL BE HERE TO SEE IT!
WILL WE HAVE A MON-STER...OR A DEMON? WHO KNOWS...
...BUT I CAN'T WAIT TO FIND OUT!
VERY WELL. I WILL CONTINUE MY MISSION OF RETRIEVING THE GOD-DESS.
IT'S SIMPLE, ISN'T IT? ALL WE HAVE TO DO IS KILL THE HOST—THAT REDHEAD.

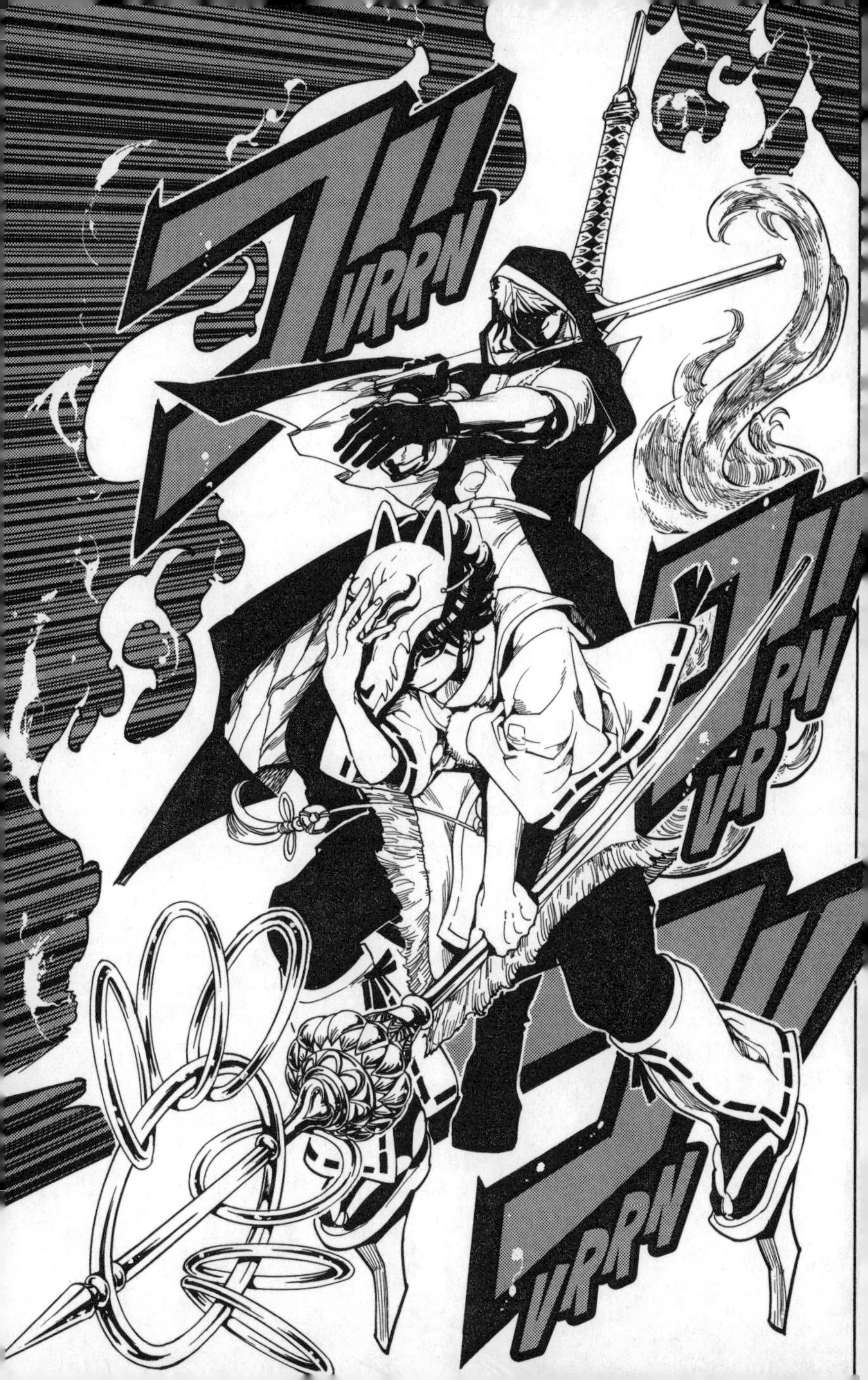
VRRN
VRRN
VRRN

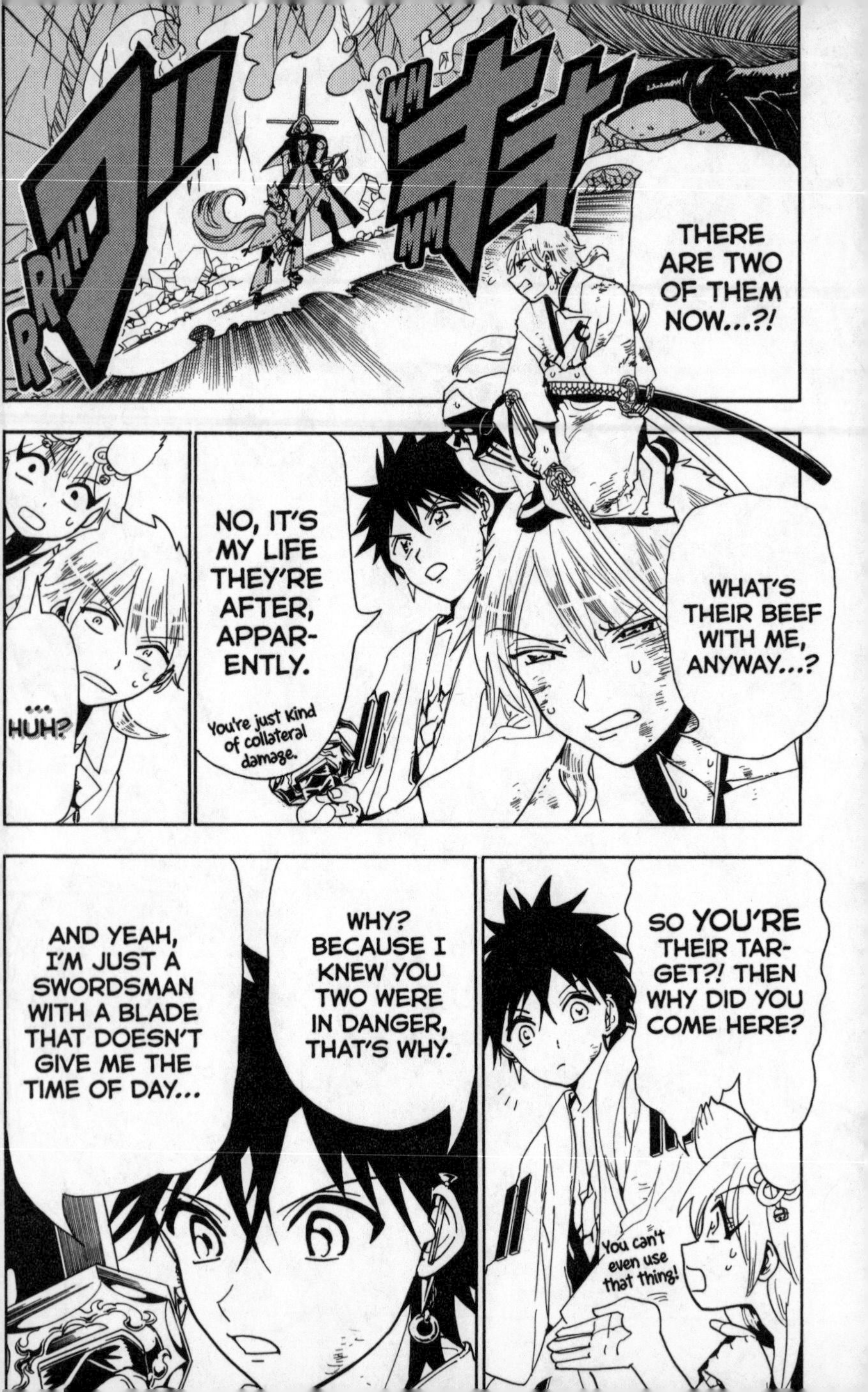
THERE ARE TWO OF THEM NOW...?!
RRHHH
WHAT'S THEIR BEEF WITH ME, ANYWAY...?
NO, IT'S MY LIFE THEY'RE AFTER, APPAR-ENTLY.
You're just kind of collateral damage.
...HUH?
SO YOU'RE THEIR TAR-GET?! THEN WHY DID YOU COME HERE?
You can't even use that thing!
WHY? BECAUSE I KNEW YOU TWO WERE IN DANGER, THAT'S WHY.
AND YEAH, I'M JUST A SWORDSMAN WITH A BLADE THAT DOESN'T GIVE ME THE TIME OF DAY...

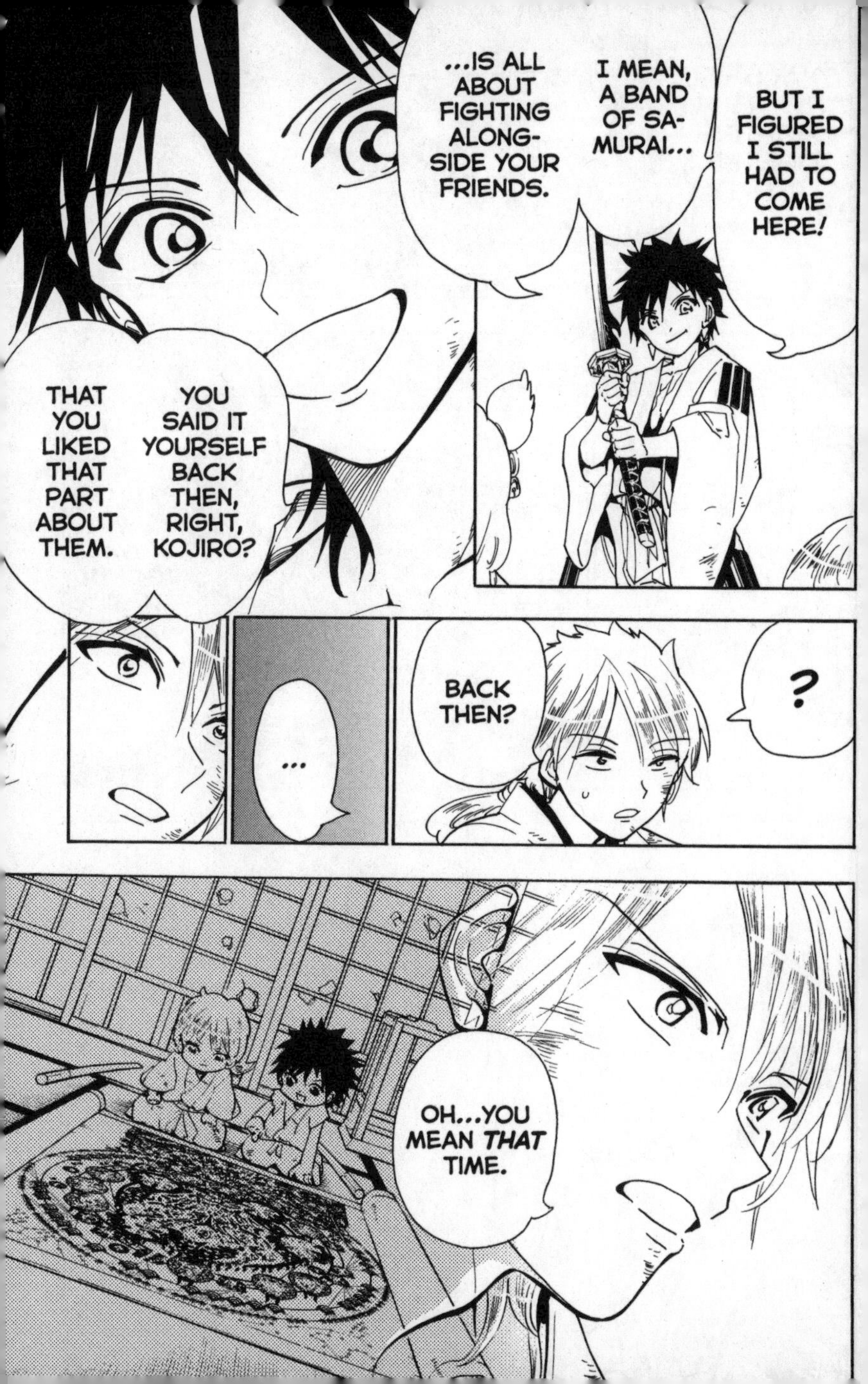
BUT I FIGURED I STILL HAD TO COME HERE!
I MEAN, A BAND OF SA-MURAI...
...IS ALL ABOUT FIGHTING ALONG-SIDE YOUR FRIENDS.
YOU SAID IT YOURSELF BACK THEN, RIGHT, KOJIRO?
THAT YOU LIKED THAT PART ABOUT THEM.
?
BACK THEN?
...
OH...YOU MEAN *THAT* TIME.

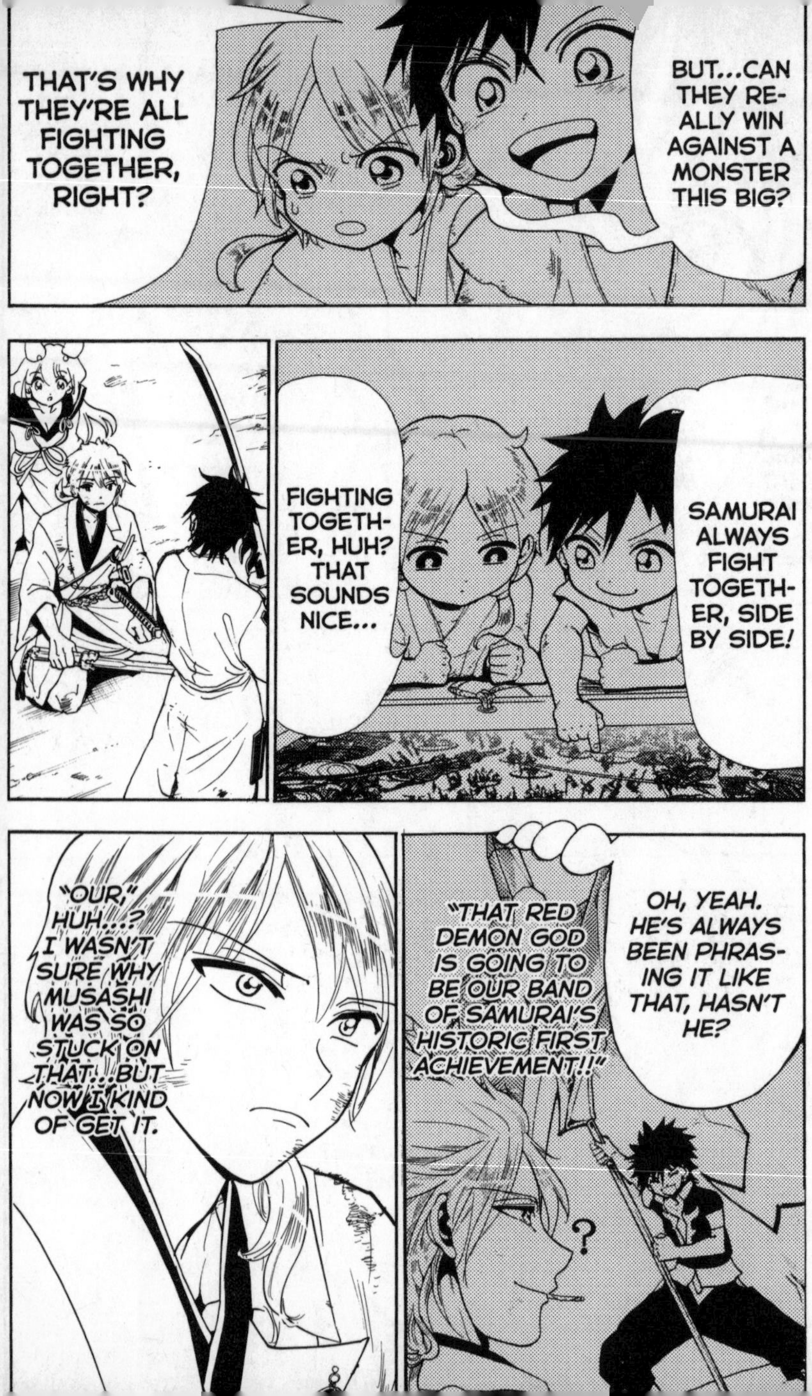
BUT...CAN THEY RE-ALLY WIN AGAINST A MONSTER THIS BIG?
THAT'S WHY THEY'RE ALL FIGHTING TOGETHER, RIGHT?
SAMURAI ALWAYS FIGHT TOGETH-ER, SIDE BY SIDE!
FIGHTING TOGETH-ER, HUH? THAT SOUNDS NICE...
OH, YEAH. HE'S ALWAYS BEEN PHRAS-ING IT LIKE THAT, HASN'T HE?
"THAT RED DEMON GOD IS GOING TO BE OUR BAND OF SAMURAI'S HISTORIC FIRST ACHIEVEMENT!!"
"OUR," HUH...? I WASN'T SURE WHY MUSASHI WAS SO STUCK ON THAT...BUT NOW I KIND OF GET IT.

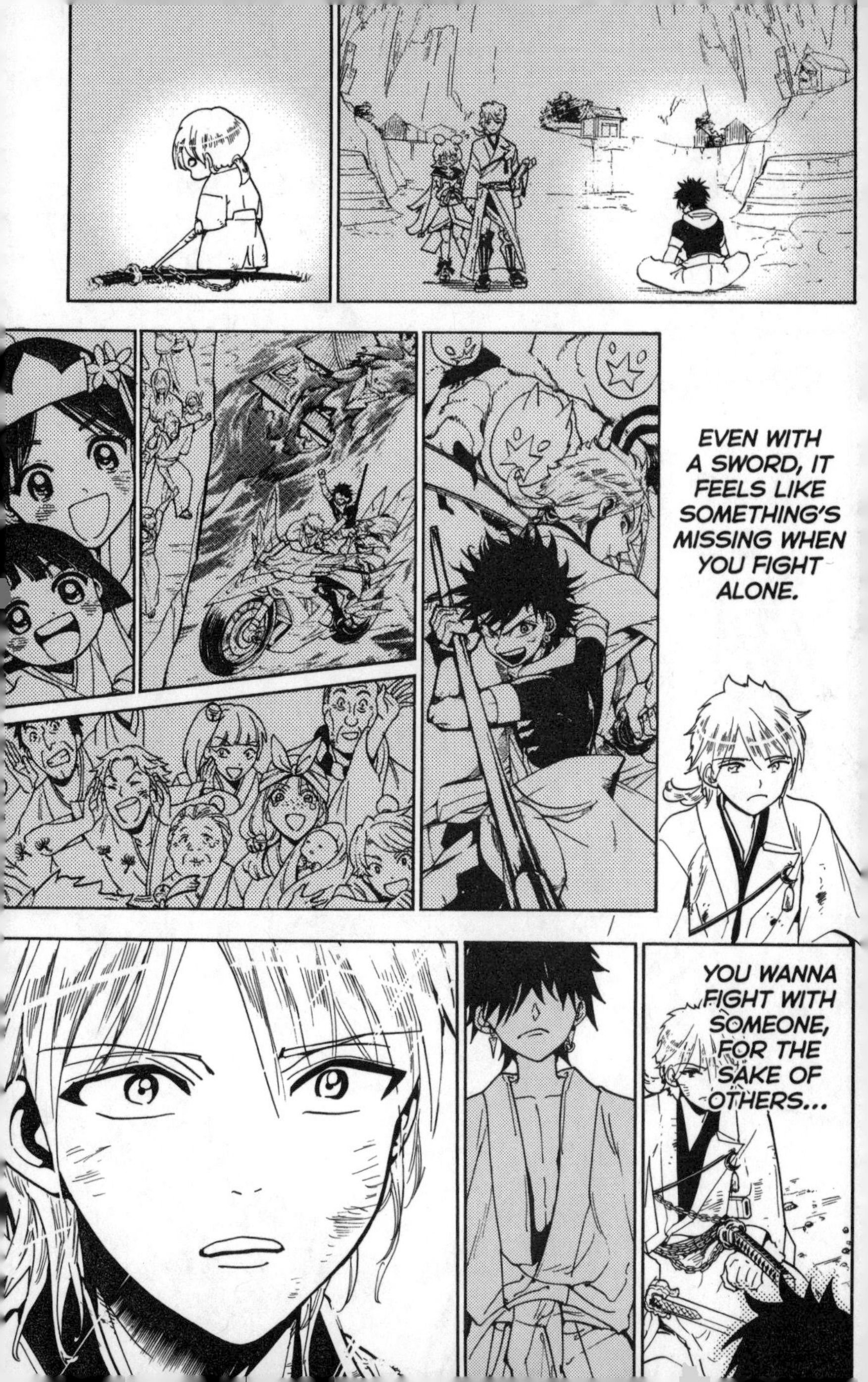
EVEN WITH A SWORD, IT FEELS LIKE SOMETHING'S MISSING WHEN YOU FIGHT ALONE.
YOU WANNA FIGHT WITH SOMEONE, FOR THE SAKE OF OTHERS...

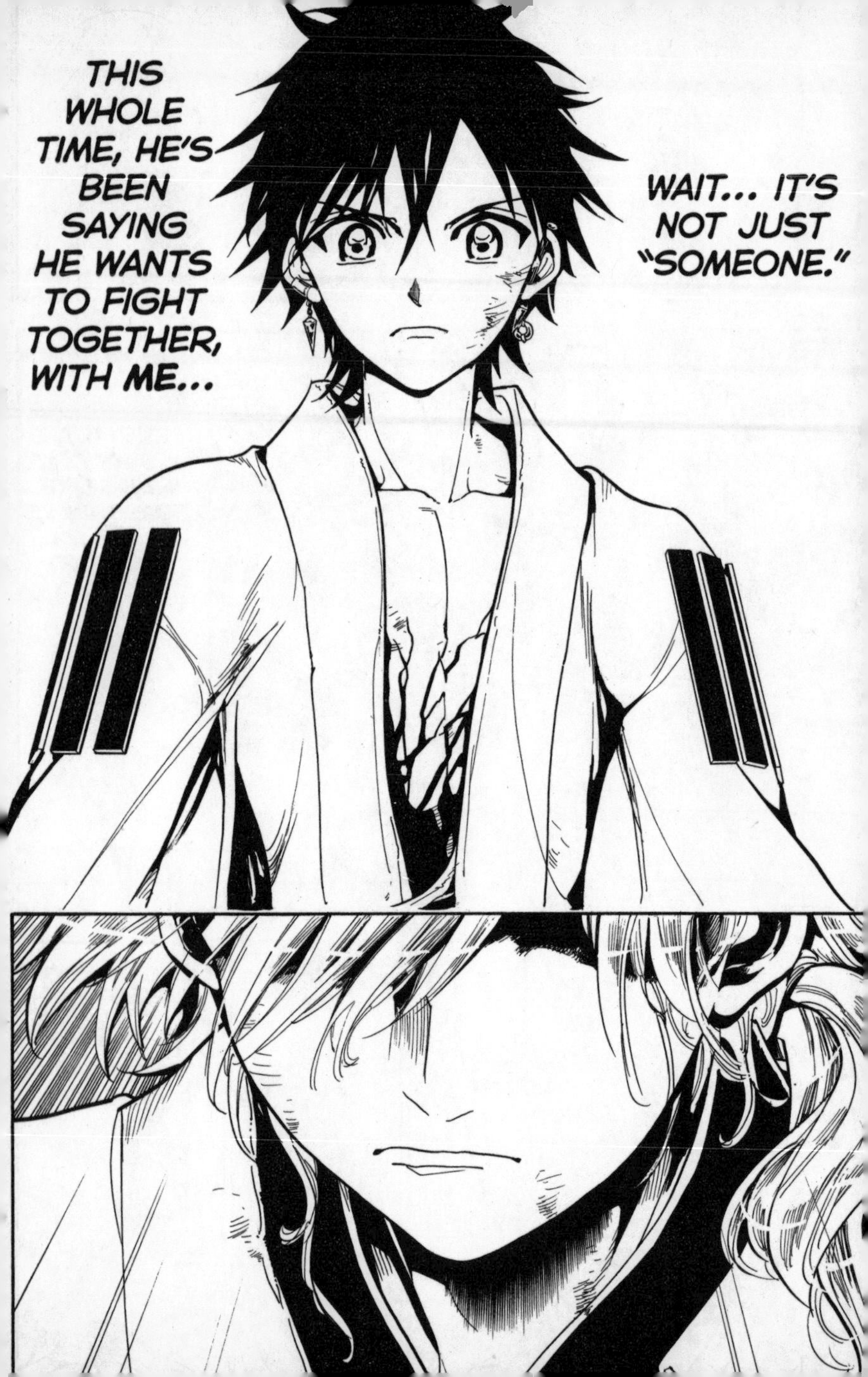
THIS WHOLE TIME, HE'S BEEN SAYING HE WANTS TO FIGHT TOGETHER, WITH ME...
WAIT... IT'S NOT JUST "SOMEONE."

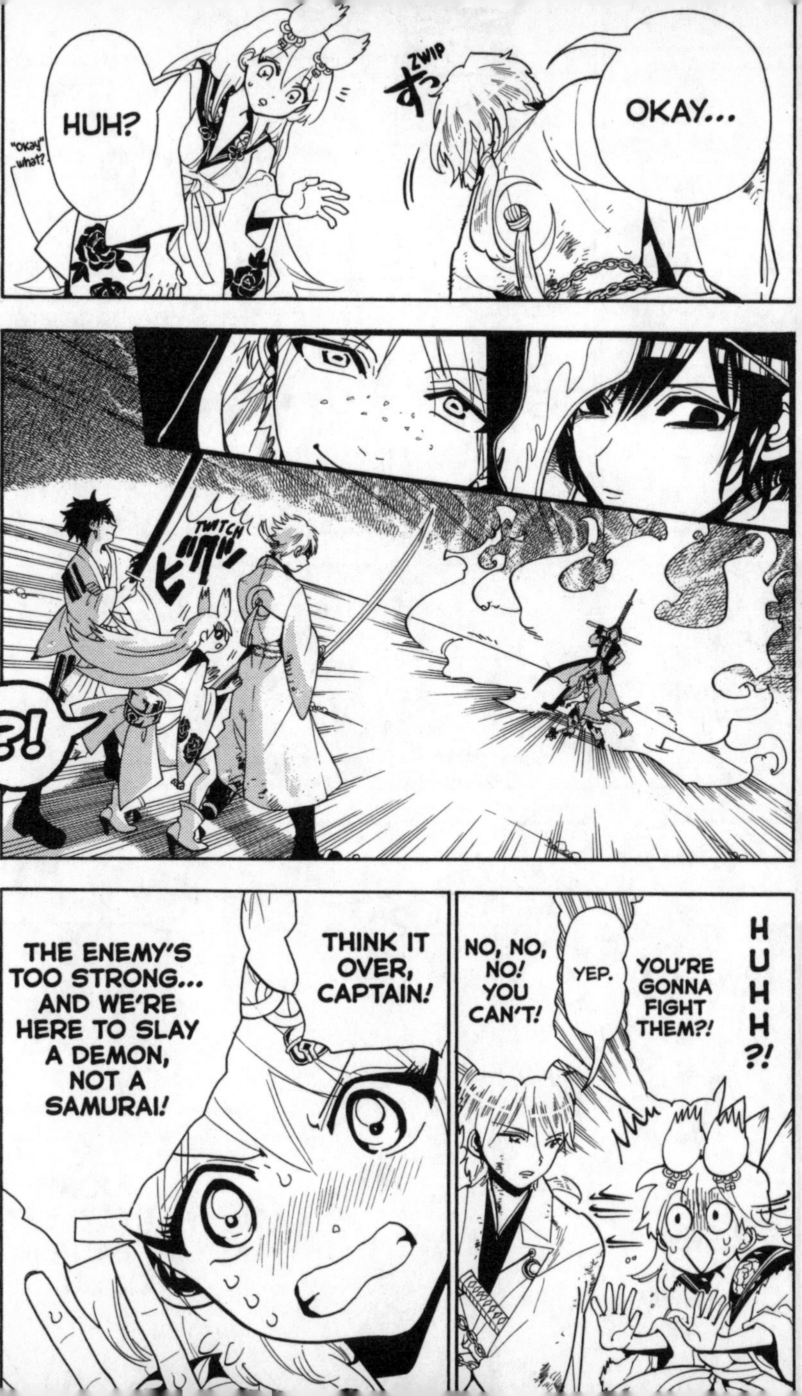
ZWIP
OKAY...
HUH?
"Okay" what?
TWITCH
?!
HUHH?!
YOU'RE GONNA FIGHT THEM?!
YEP.
NO, NO, NO! YOU CAN'T!
THINK IT OVER, CAPTAIN!
THE ENEMY'S TOO STRONG... AND WE'RE HERE TO SLAY A DEMON, NOT A SAMURAI!

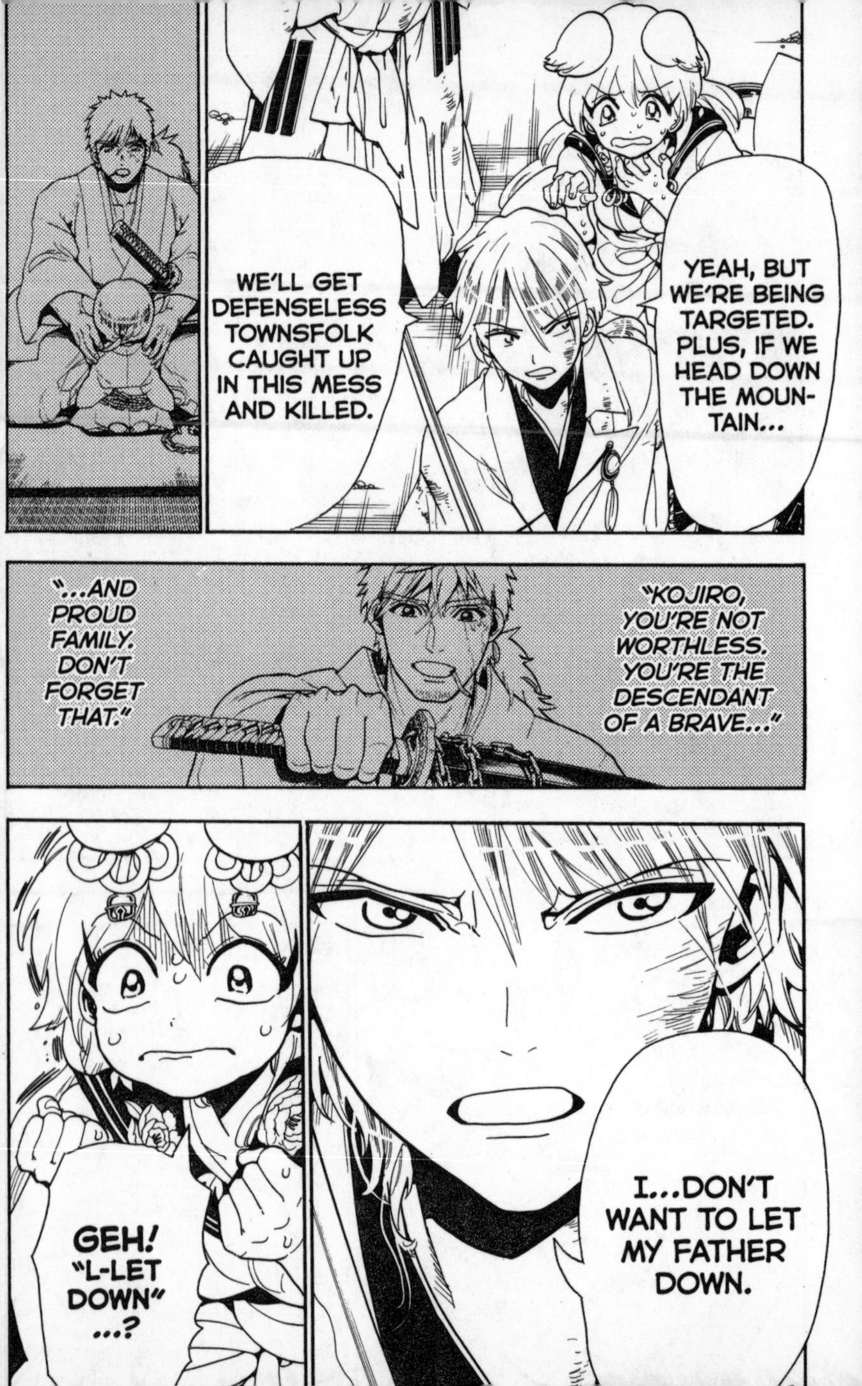
YEAH, BUT WE'RE BEING TARGETED. PLUS, IF WE HEAD DOWN THE MOUN-TAIN...
WE'LL GET DEFENSELESS TOWNSFOLK CAUGHT UP IN THIS MESS AND KILLED.
"KOJIRO, YOU'RE NOT WORTHLESS. YOU'RE THE DESCENDANT OF A BRAVE..."
"...AND PROUD FAMILY. DON'T FORGET THAT."
I...DON'T WANT TO LET MY FATHER DOWN.
GEH! "L-LET DOWN" ...?

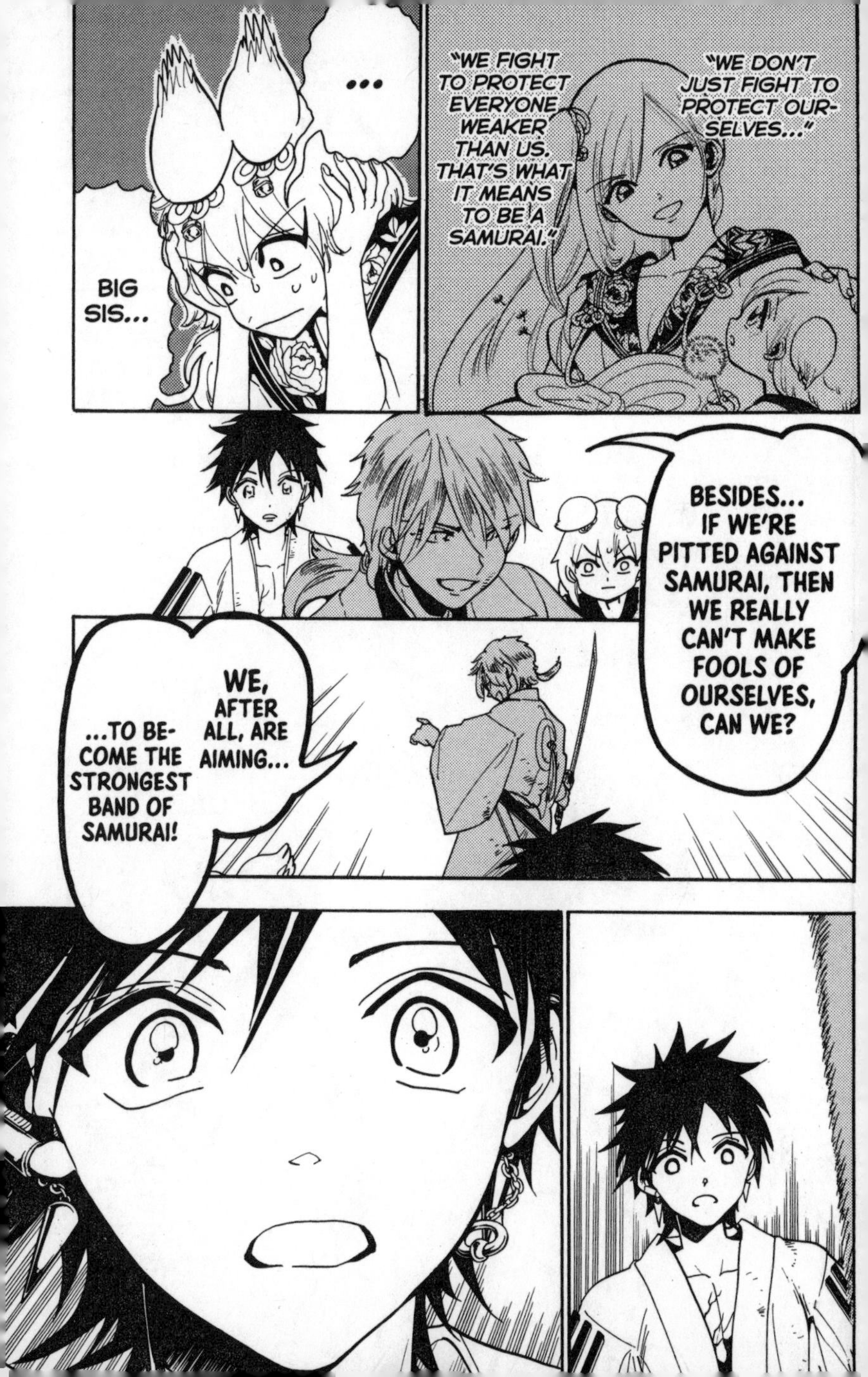
"WE DON'T JUST FIGHT TO PROTECT OURSELVES..."
"WE FIGHT TO PROTECT EVERYONE WEAKER THAN US. THAT'S WHAT IT MEANS TO BE A SAMURAI."
...
BIG SIS...
BESIDES... IF WE'RE PITTED AGAINST SAMURAI, THEN WE REALLY CAN'T MAKE FOOLS OF OURSELVES, CAN WE?
WE, AFTER ALL, ARE AIMING...
...TO BECOME THE STRONGEST BAND OF SAMURAI!

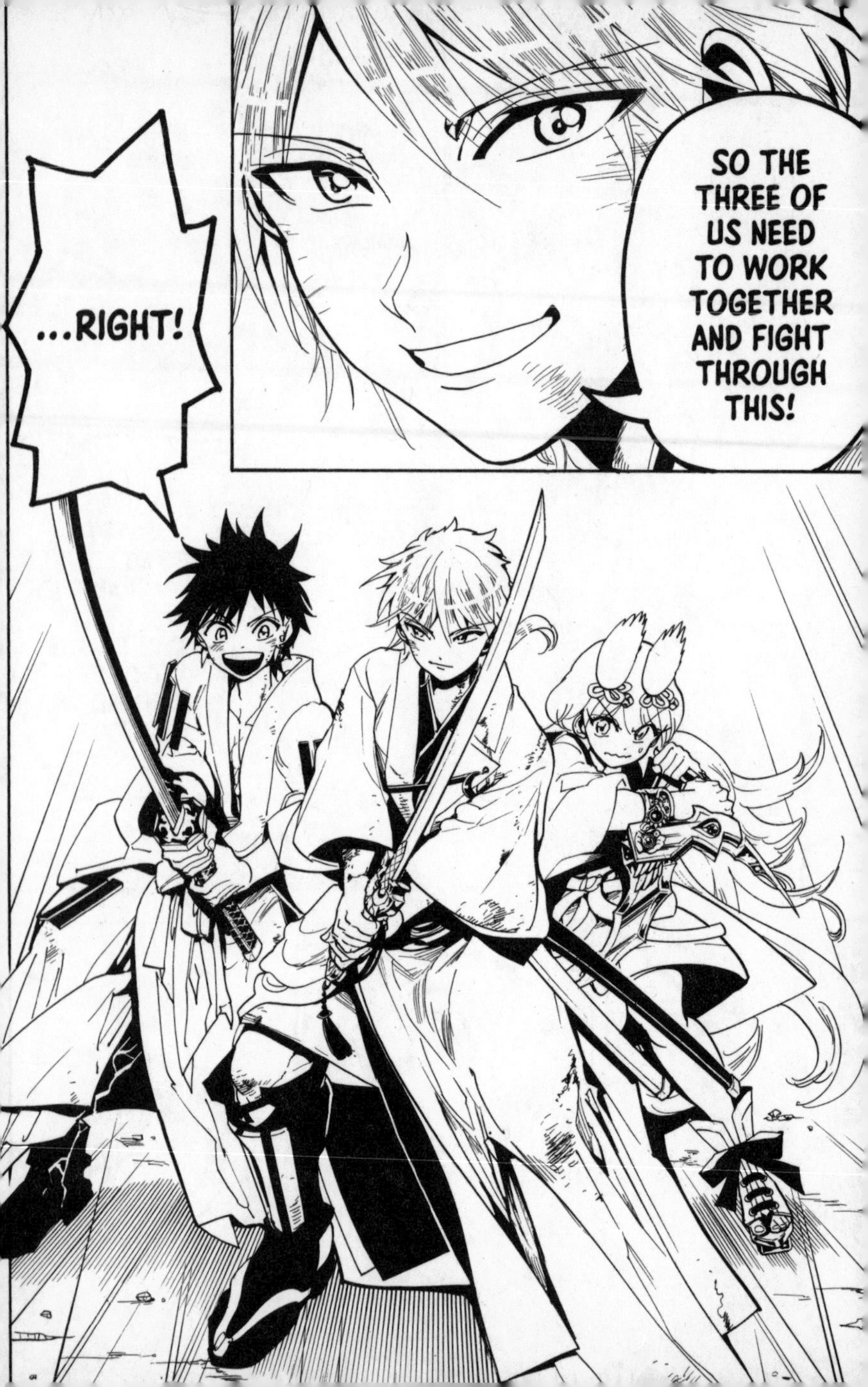
SO THE THREE OF US NEED TO WORK TOGETHER AND FIGHT THROUGH THIS!
...RIGHT!

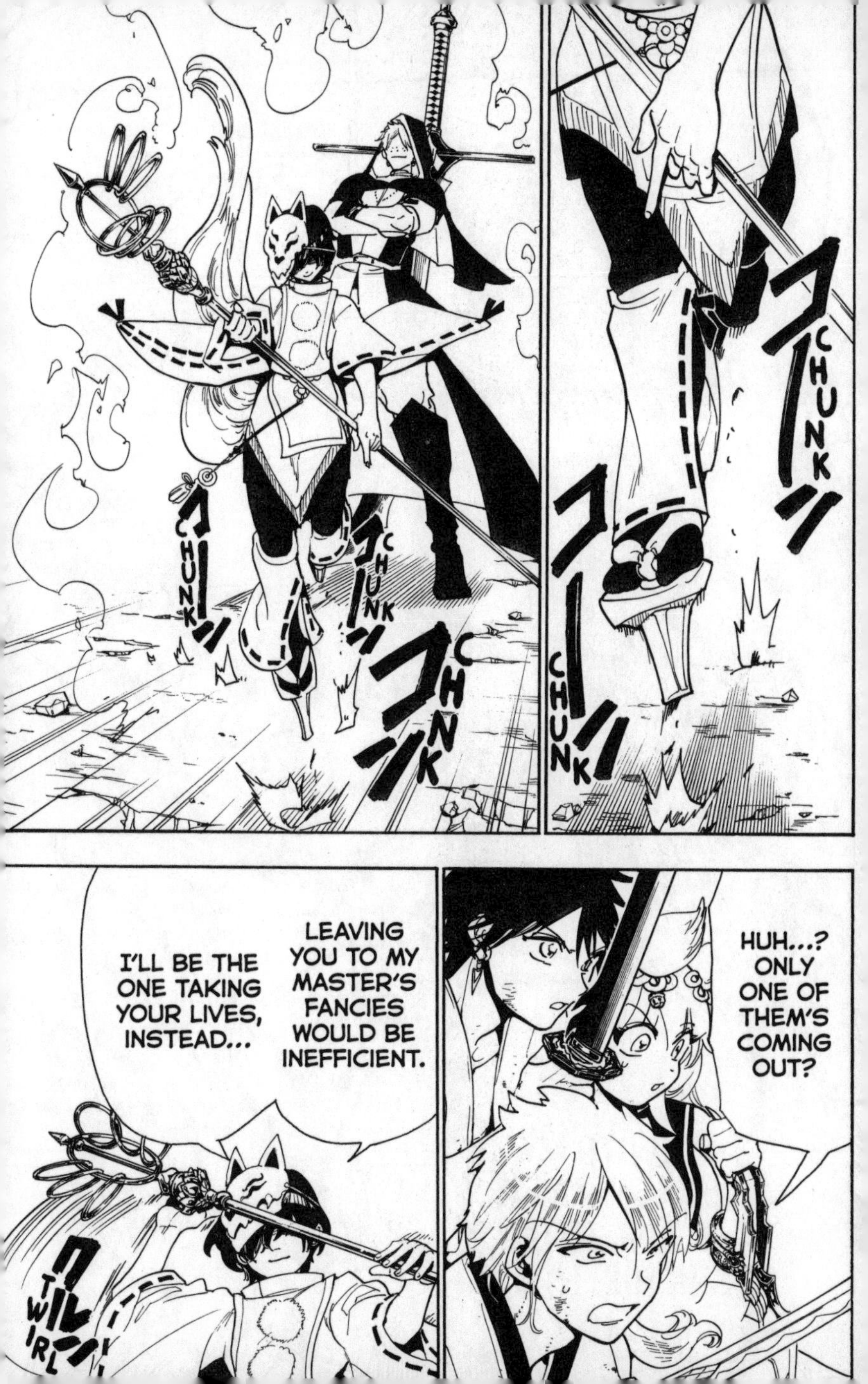
CHUNK
CHUNK
CHUNK
CHUNK
CHUNK
HUH...? ONLY ONE OF THEM'S COMING OUT?
LEAVING YOU TO MY MASTER'S FANCIES WOULD BE INEFFICIENT.
I'LL BE THE ONE TAKING YOUR LIVES, INSTEAD...
TWIRL

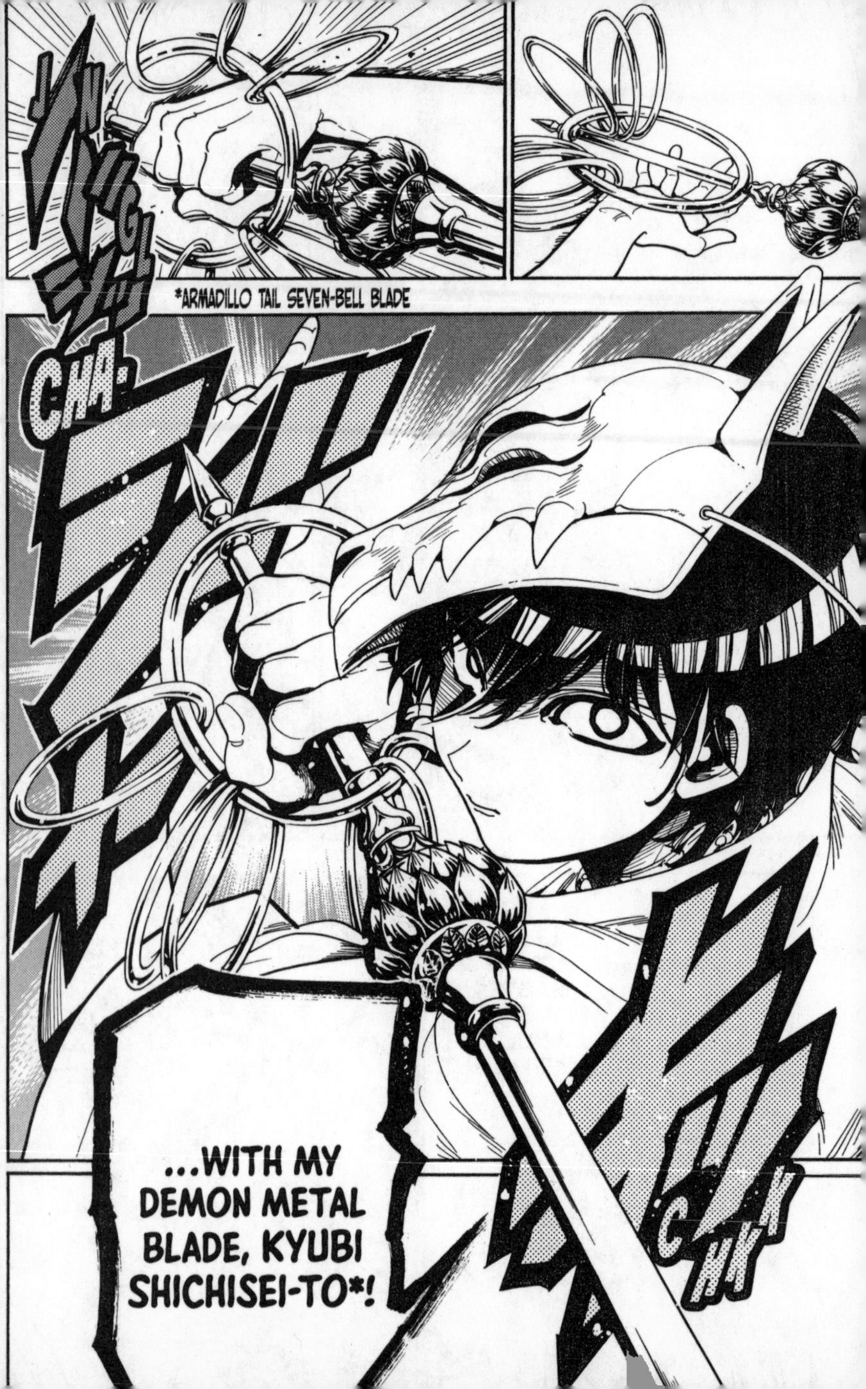
*ARMADILLO TAIL SEVEN-BELL BLADE
CHA-
...WITH MY DEMON METAL BLADE, KYUBI SHICHISEI-TO*!
CHK

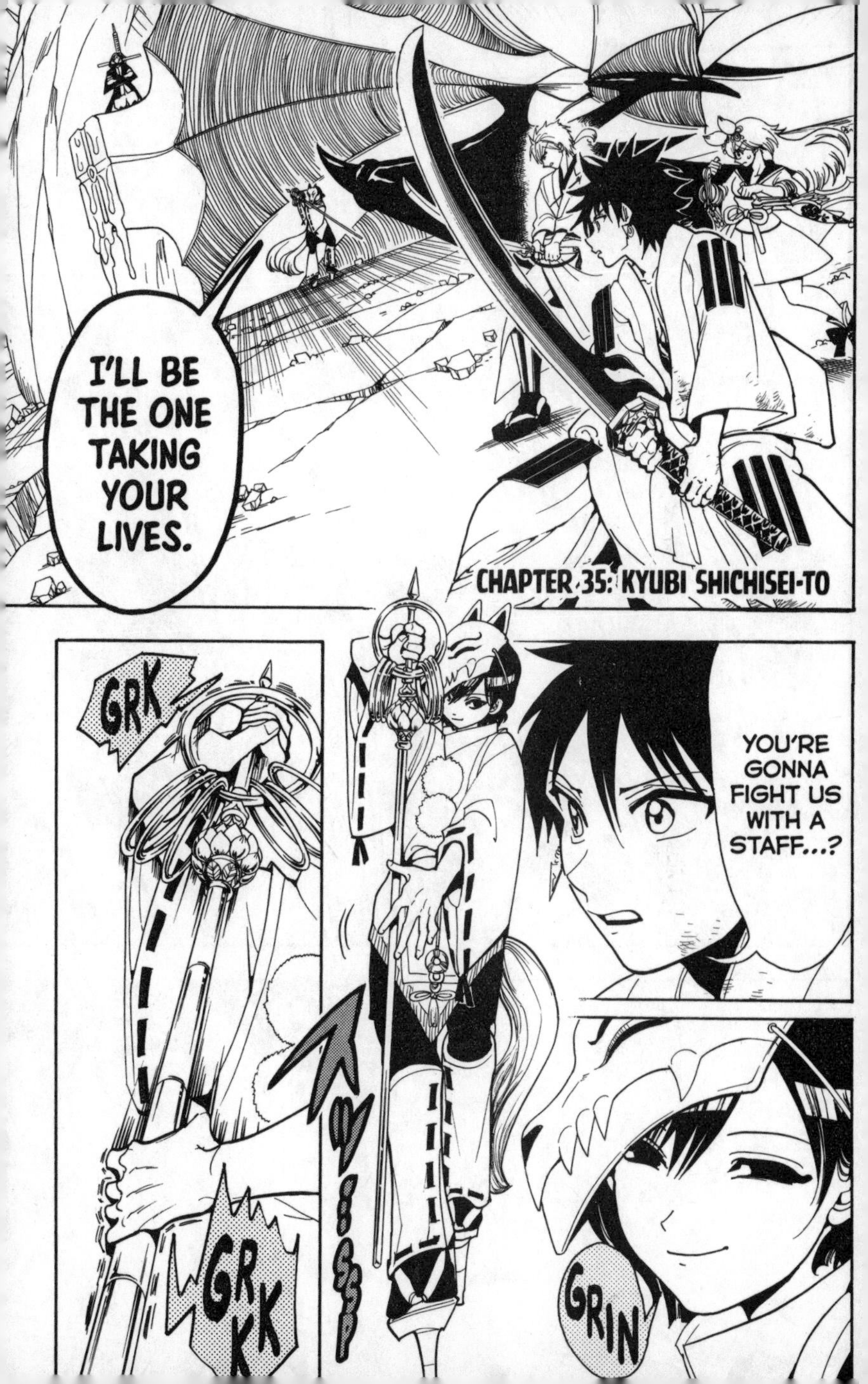
I'LL BE THE ONE TAKING YOUR LIVES.
CHAPTER 35: KYUBI SHICHISEI-TO
YOU'RE GONNA FIGHT US WITH A STAFF...?
GRIN
GRK
GRKK

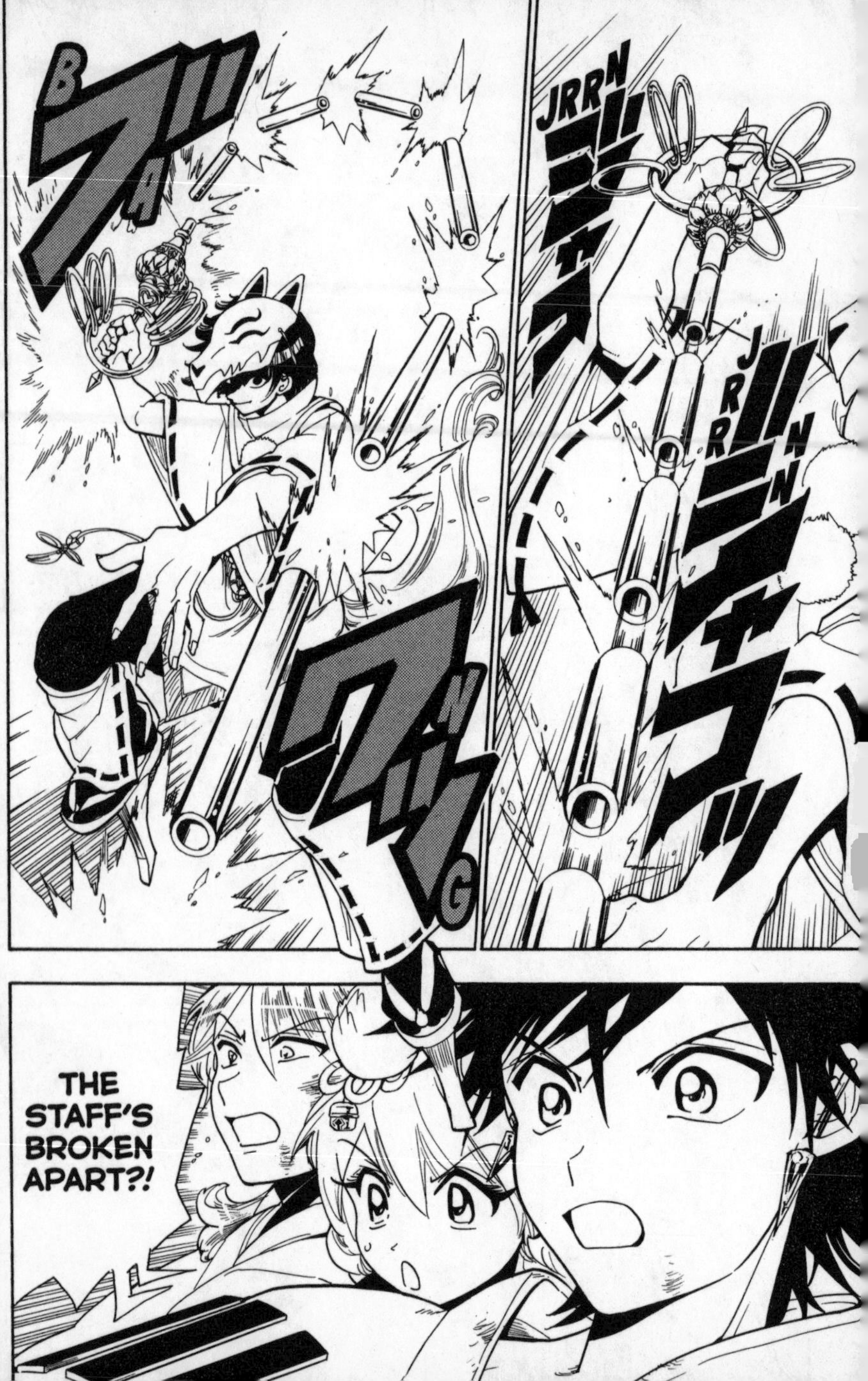

JRRN
JRRN
BA
NG
THE STAFF'S BROKEN APART?!

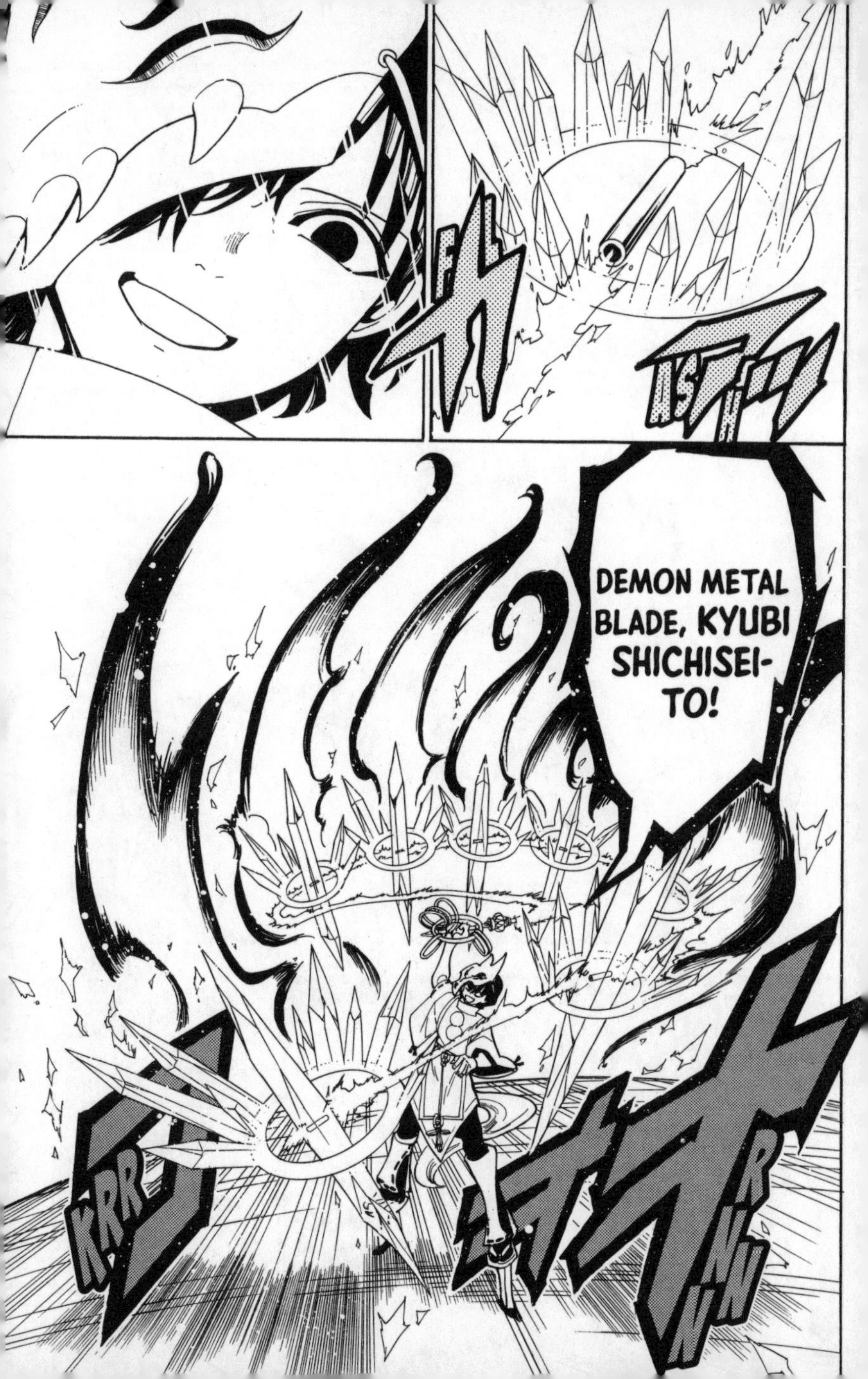
FL
ASH
DEMON METAL BLADE, KYUBI SHICHISEI-TO!
KRR
RNNN

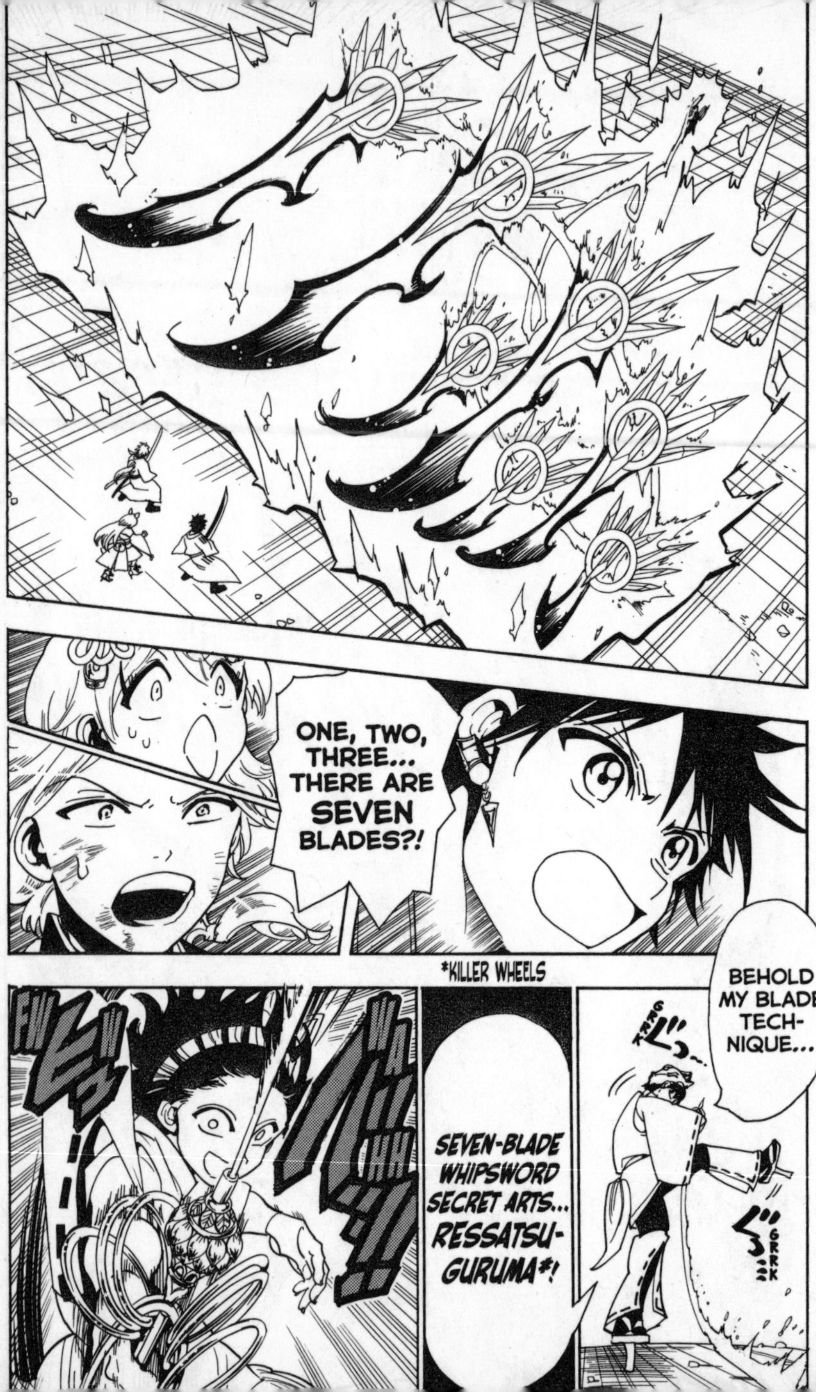
ONE, TWO, THREE... THERE ARE SEVEN BLADES?!
BEHOLD MY BLADE TECH-NIQUE...
GRRRK
GRRK
SEVEN-BLADE WHIPSWORD SECRET ARTS... RESSATSU-GURUMA*!
*KILLER WHEELS

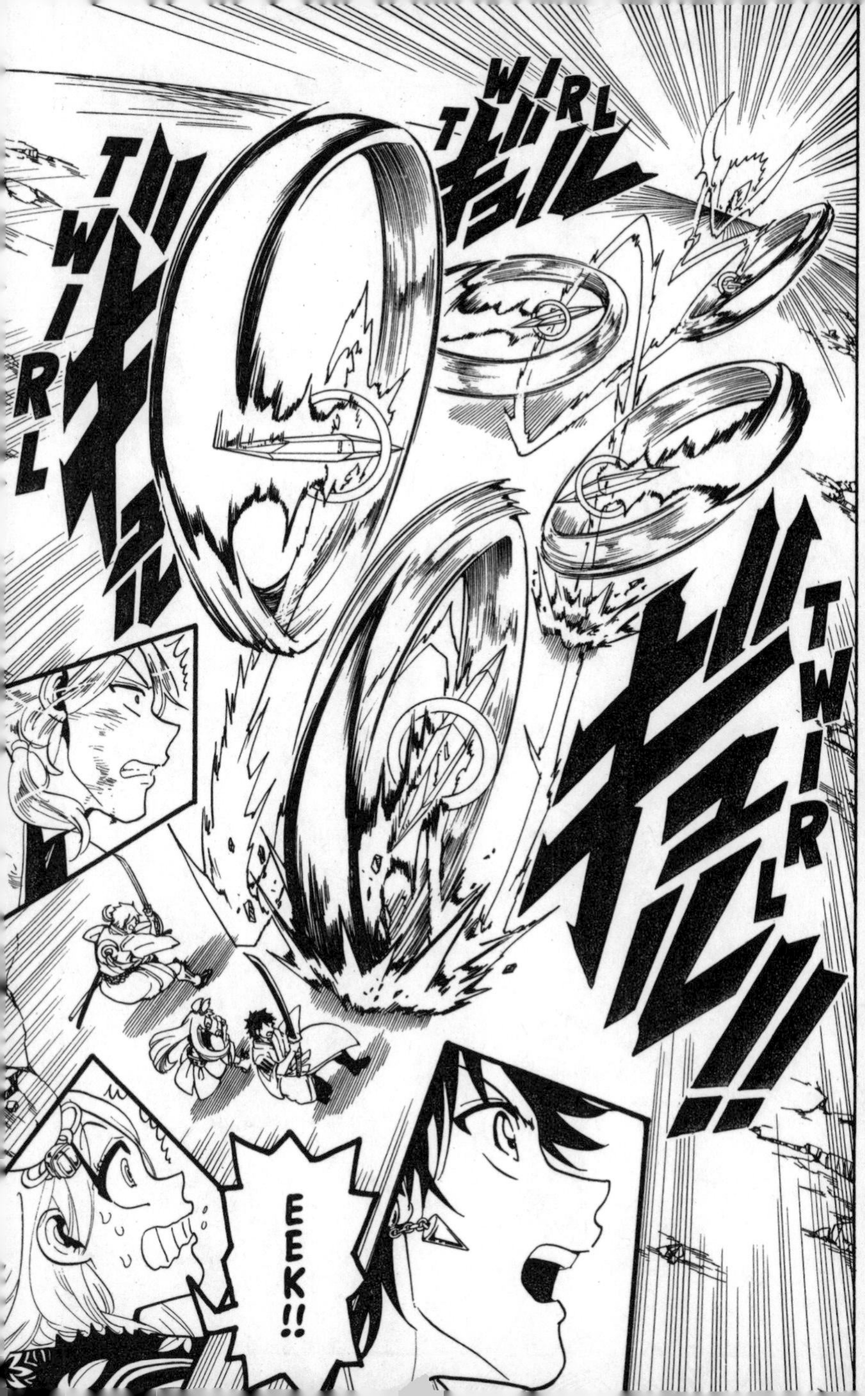
TWIRL
TWIRL
TWIRL
EEK!!

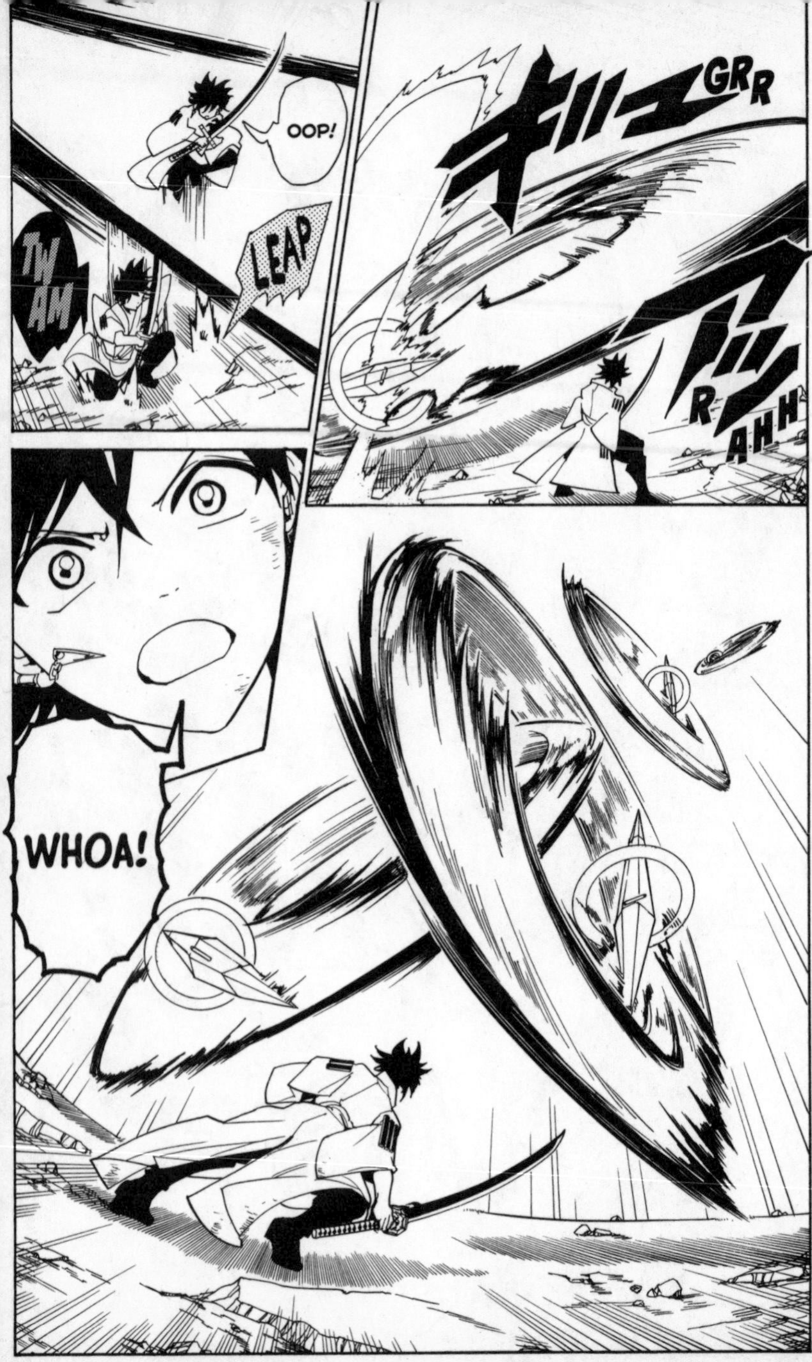
GRR
R AHH
OOP!
LEAP
TWAM
WHOA!

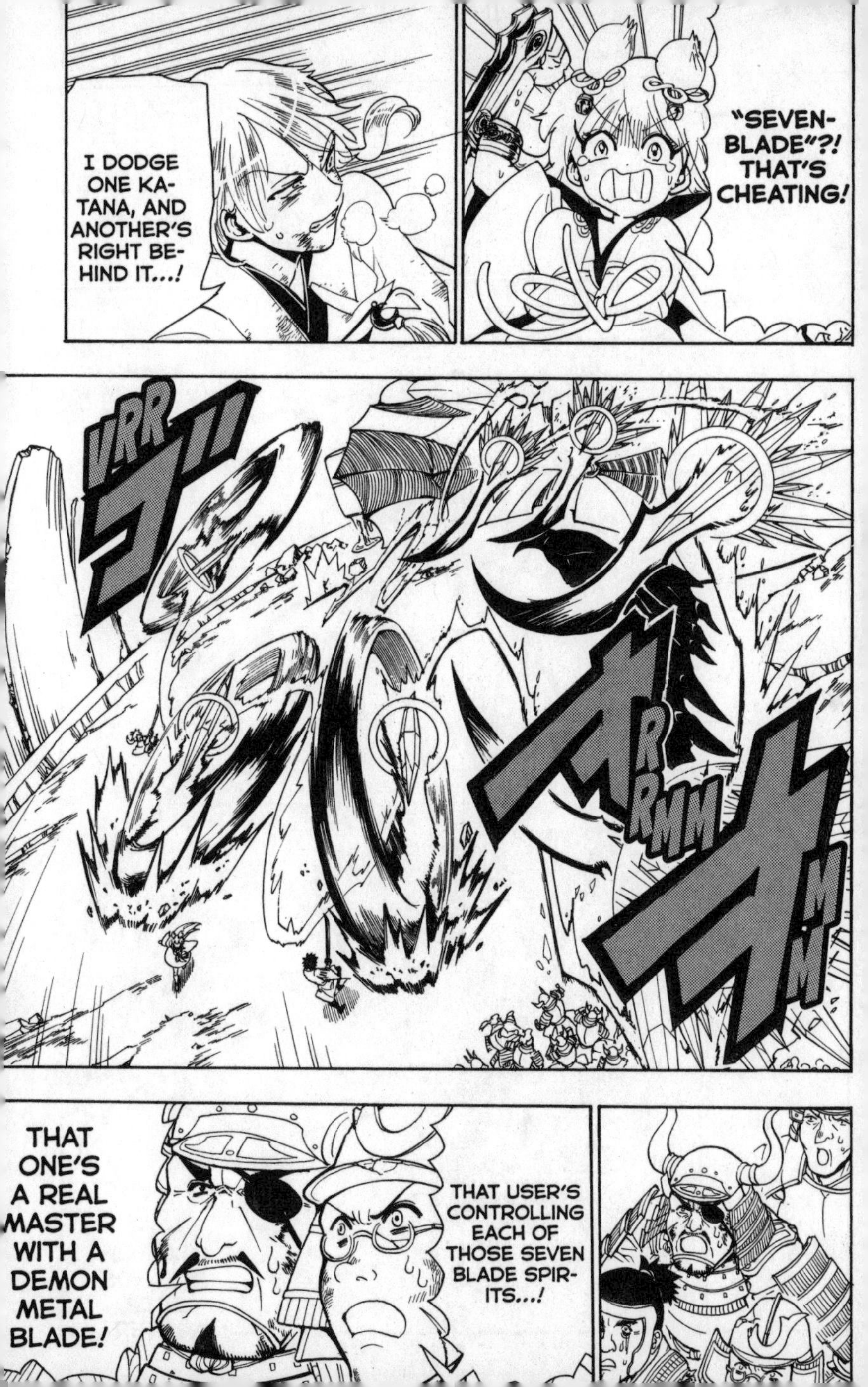
"SEVEN-BLADE"?! THAT'S CHEATING!
I DODGE ONE KATANA, AND ANOTHER'S RIGHT BEHIND IT...!
VRR
RRMM
MM
THAT USER'S CONTROLLING EACH OF THOSE SEVEN BLADE SPIRITS...!
THAT ONE'S A REAL MASTER WITH A DEMON METAL BLADE!

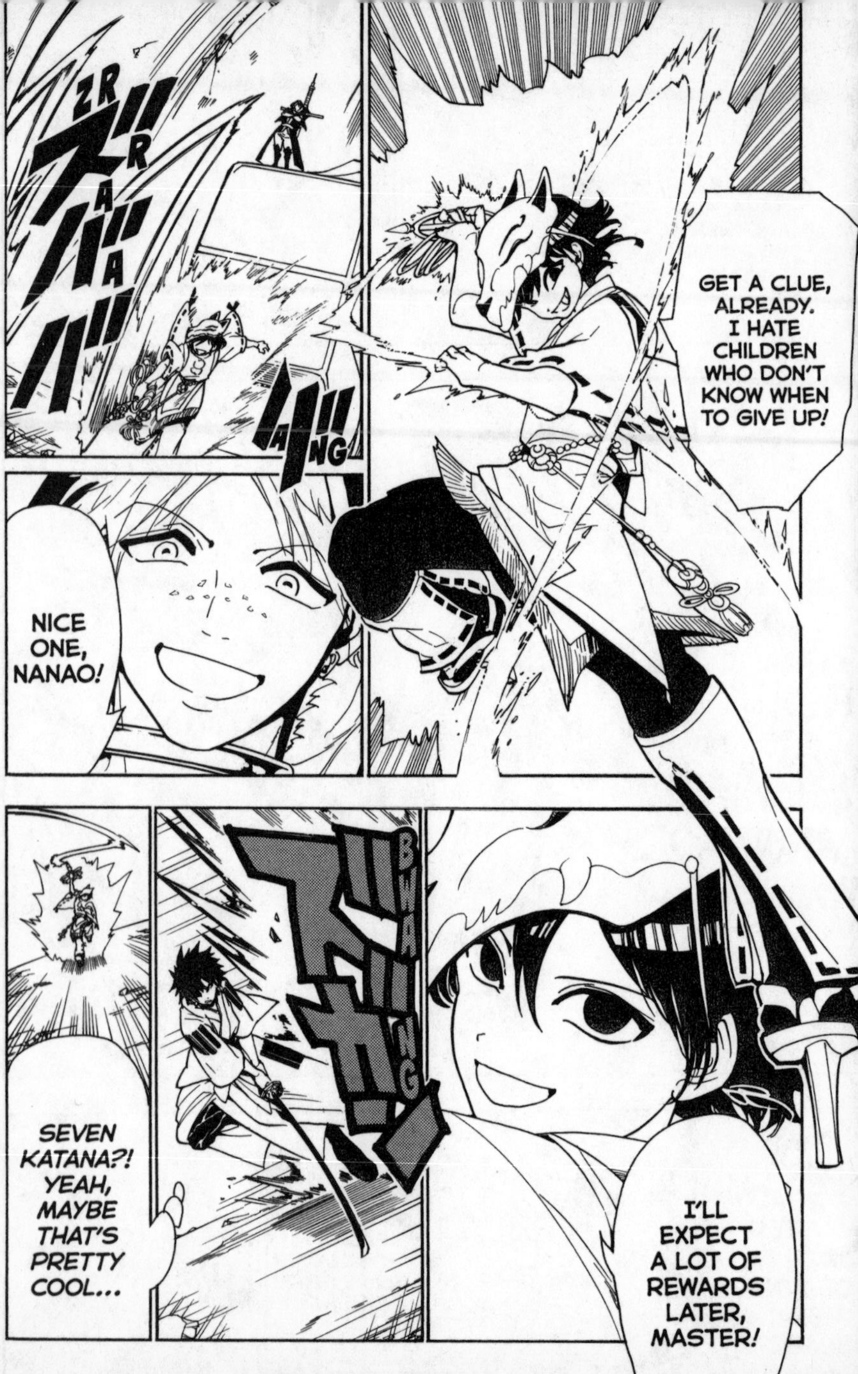
GET A CLUE, ALREADY. I HATE CHILDREN WHO DON'T KNOW WHEN TO GIVE UP!
ZRRAA
ANG
NICE ONE, NANAO!
I'LL EXPECT A LOT OF REWARDS LATER, MASTER!
BWANG
SEVEN KATANA?! YEAH, MAYBE THAT'S PRETTY COOL...

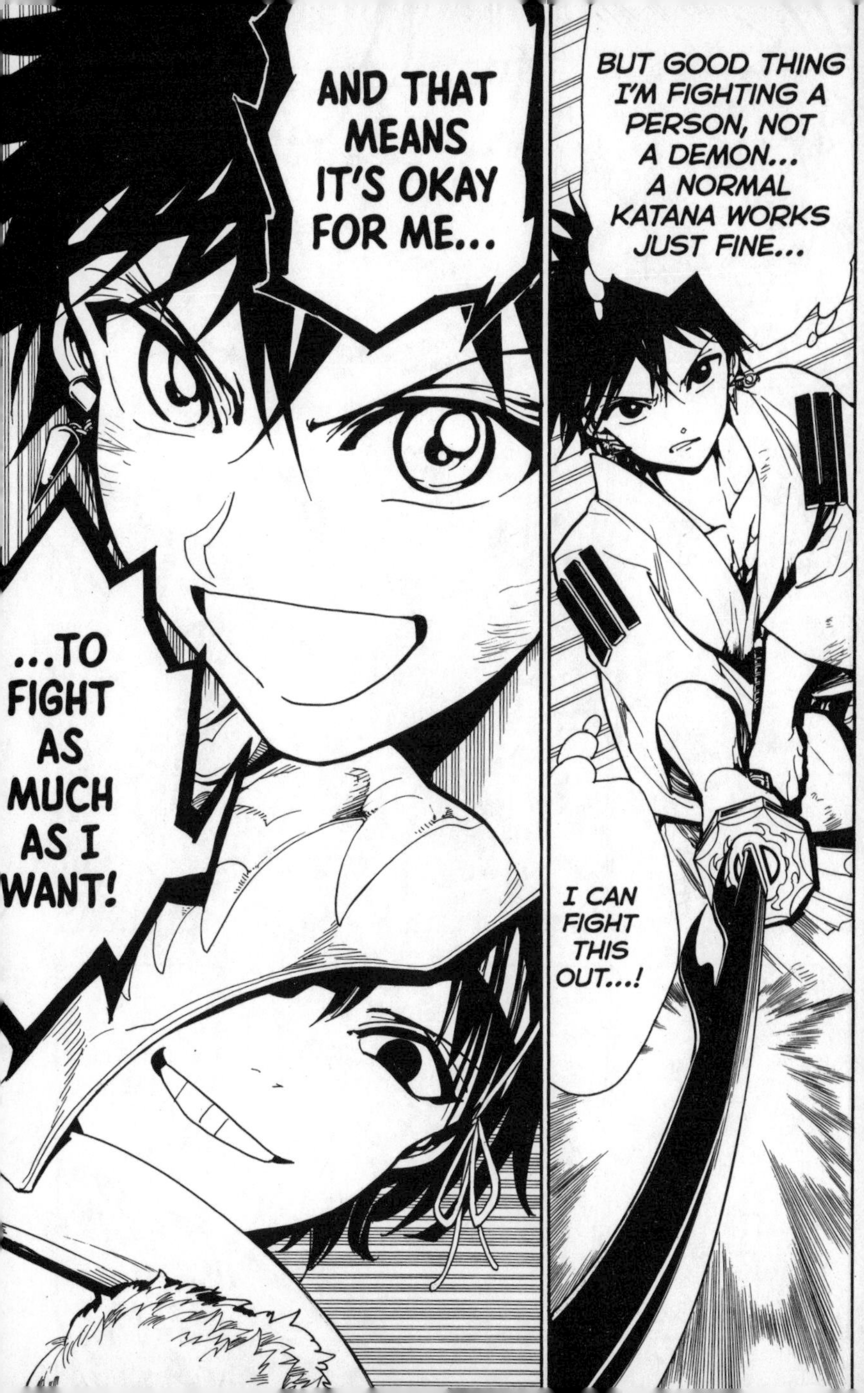
BUT GOOD THING I'M FIGHTING A PERSON, NOT A DEMON... A NORMAL KATANA WORKS JUST FINE...
I CAN FIGHT THIS OUT...!
AND THAT MEANS IT'S OKAY FOR ME...
...TO FIGHT AS MUCH AS I WANT!

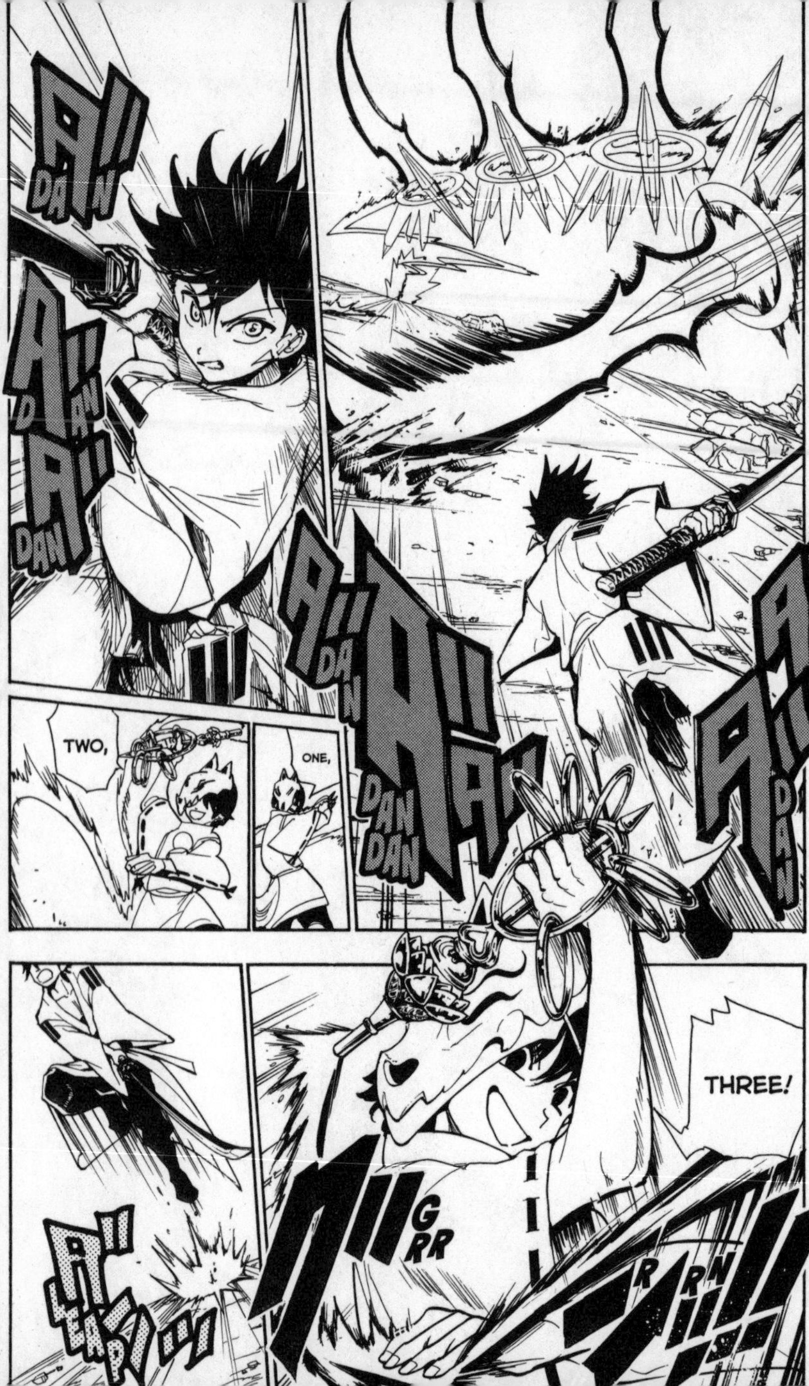
DAN
DAN DAN
ONE,
TWO,
THREE!
GRR
LEAP!!

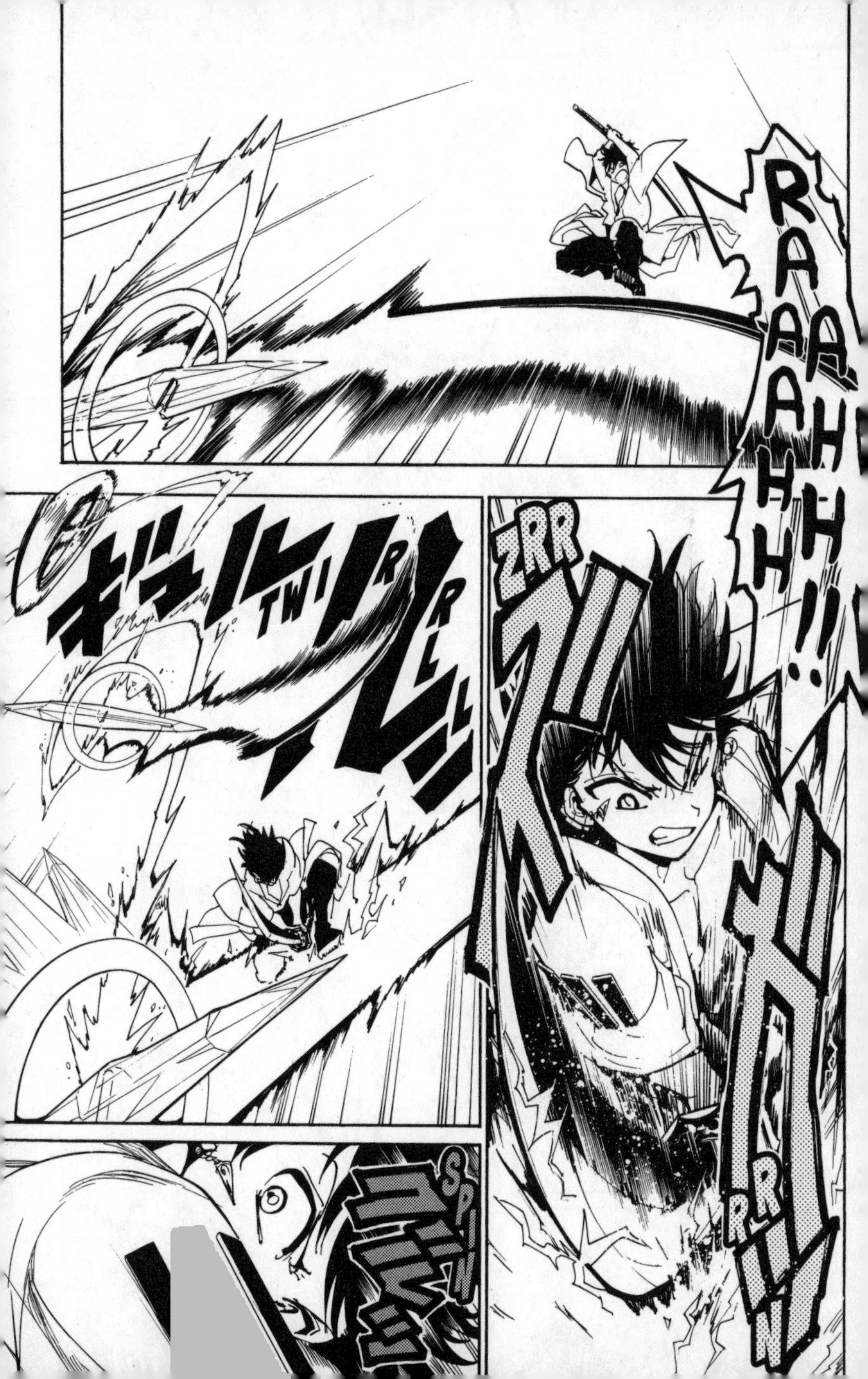
RAAAAHHHH!!
ZRR
TWIRRLL
SPIN

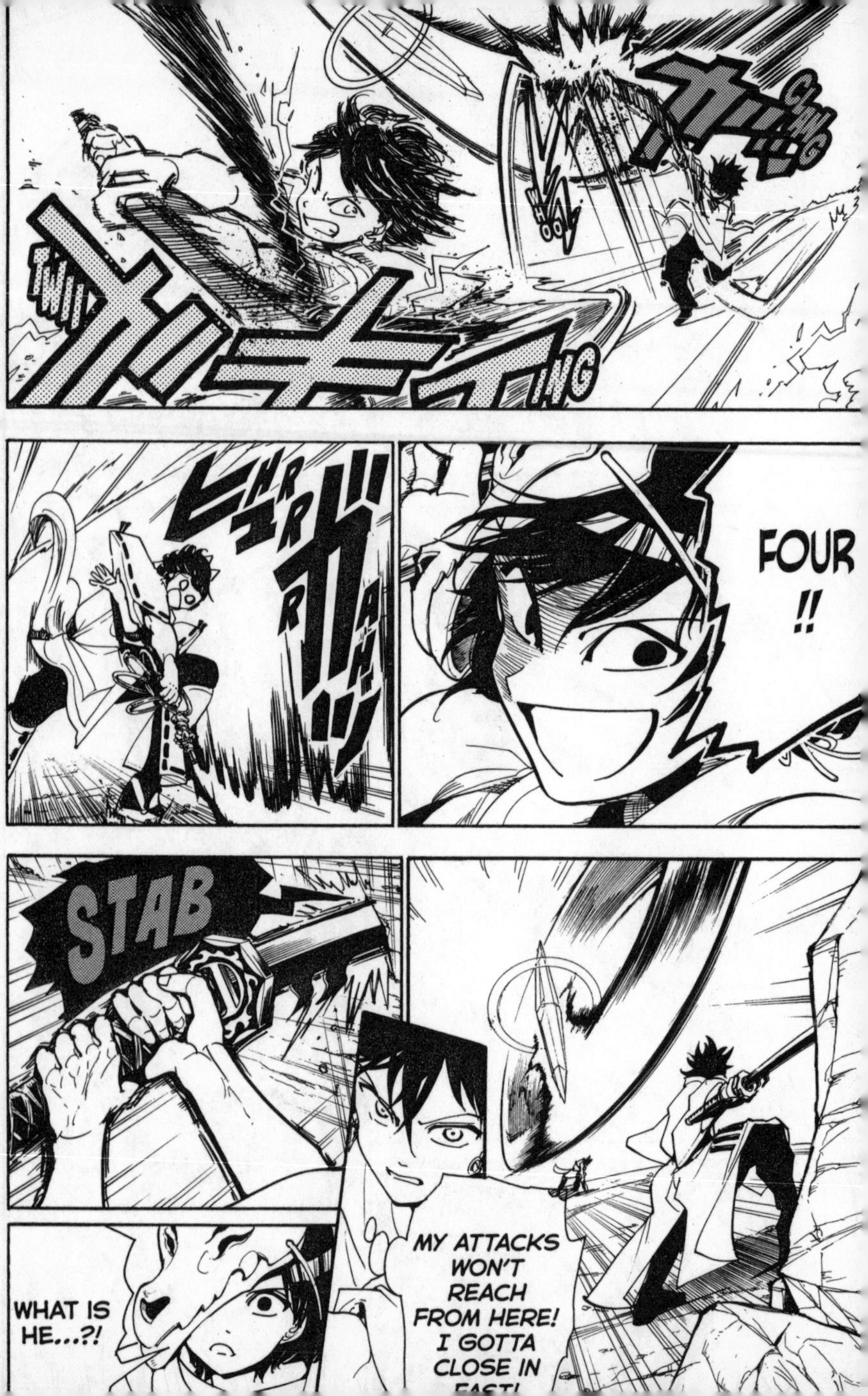
CHING
WHOO
TWING
FOUR!!
HRRR
MY ATTACKS WON'T REACH FROM HERE! I GOTTA CLOSE IN
STAB
WHAT IS HE...?!

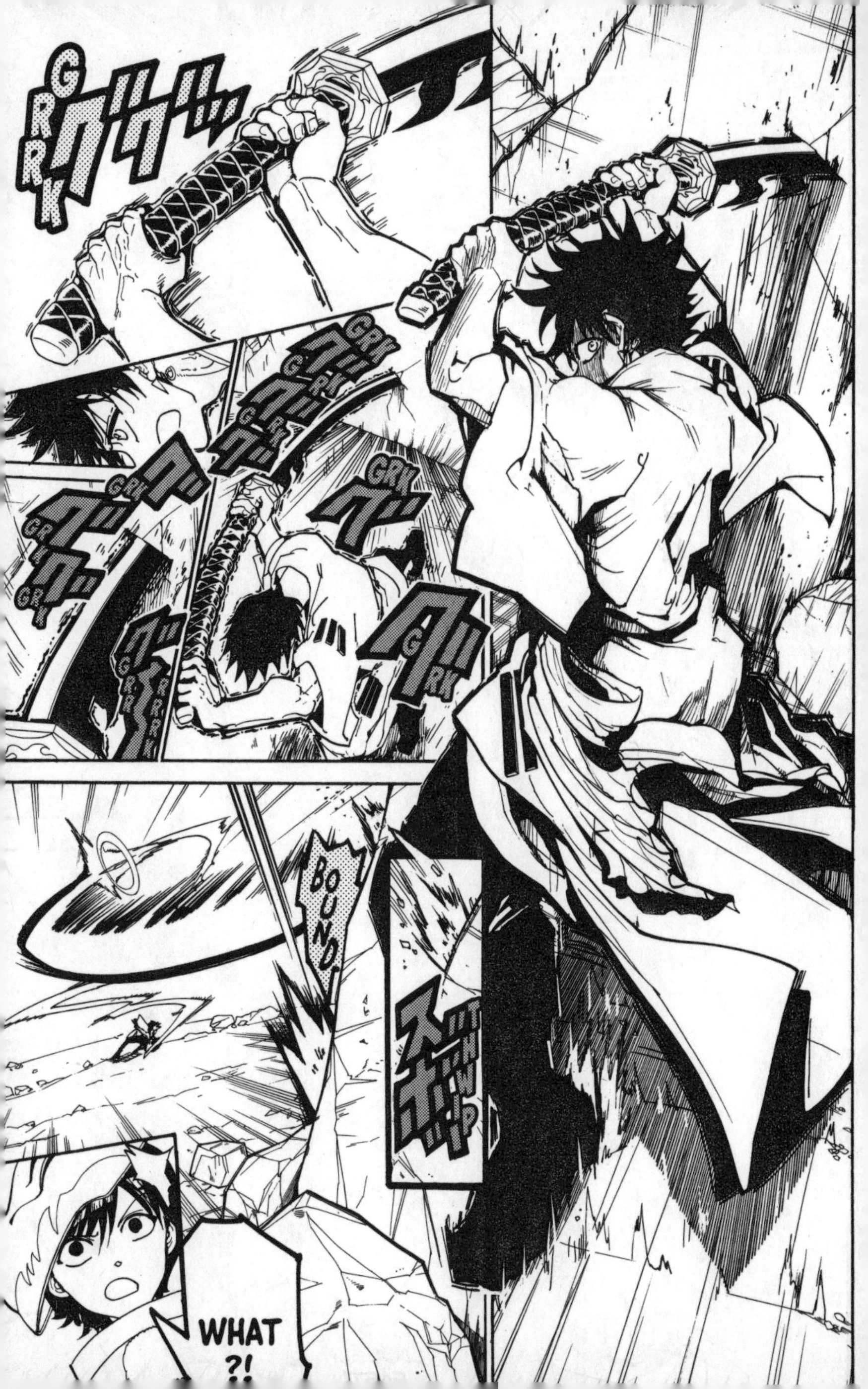
GRRK
GRK
GRK
GRK
GRK
GRK
GRK
GRK
GRRRK
THWIP
BOUND
WHAT ?!

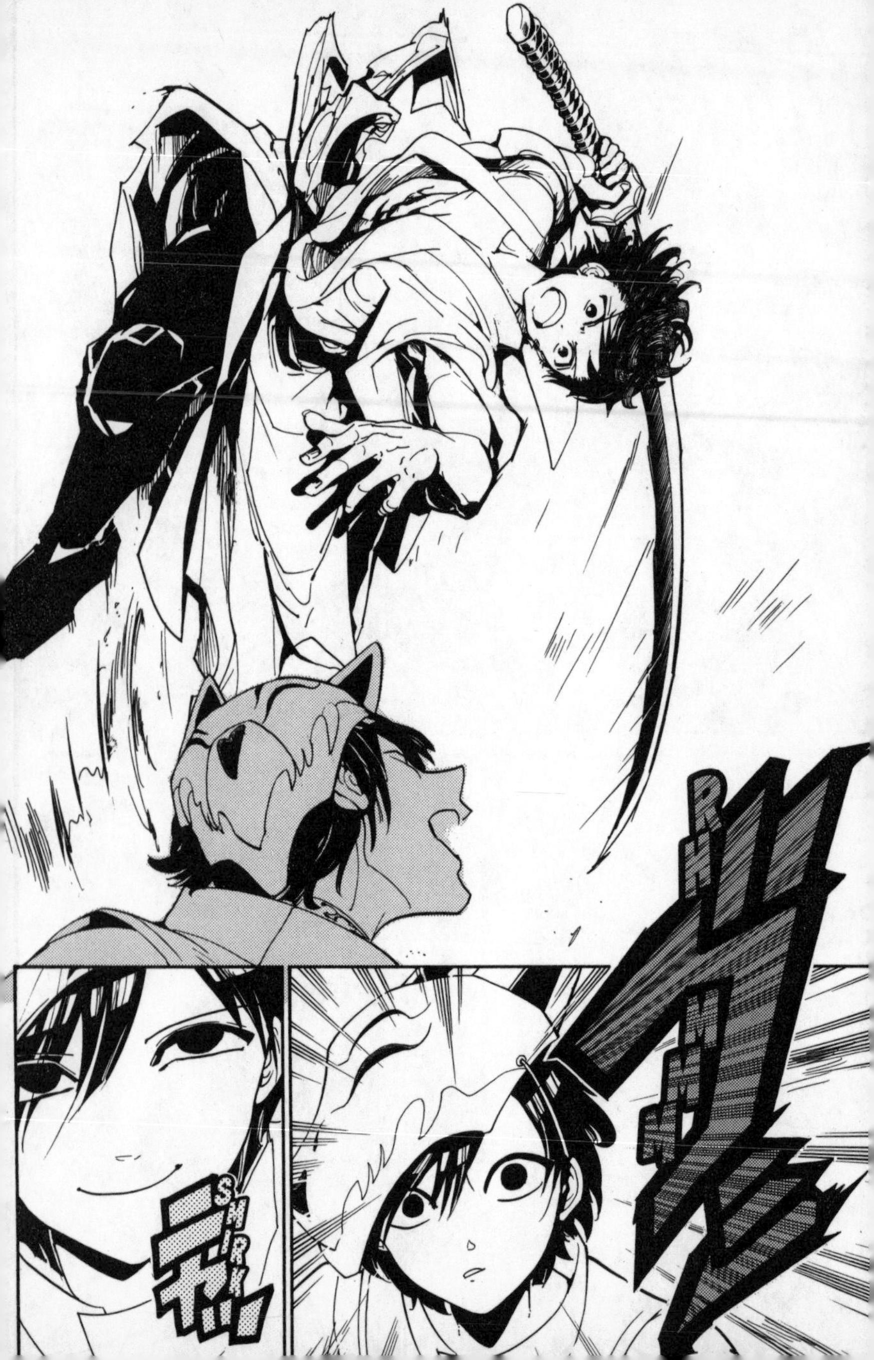
RHMMM
SMIRK
ニヤッ

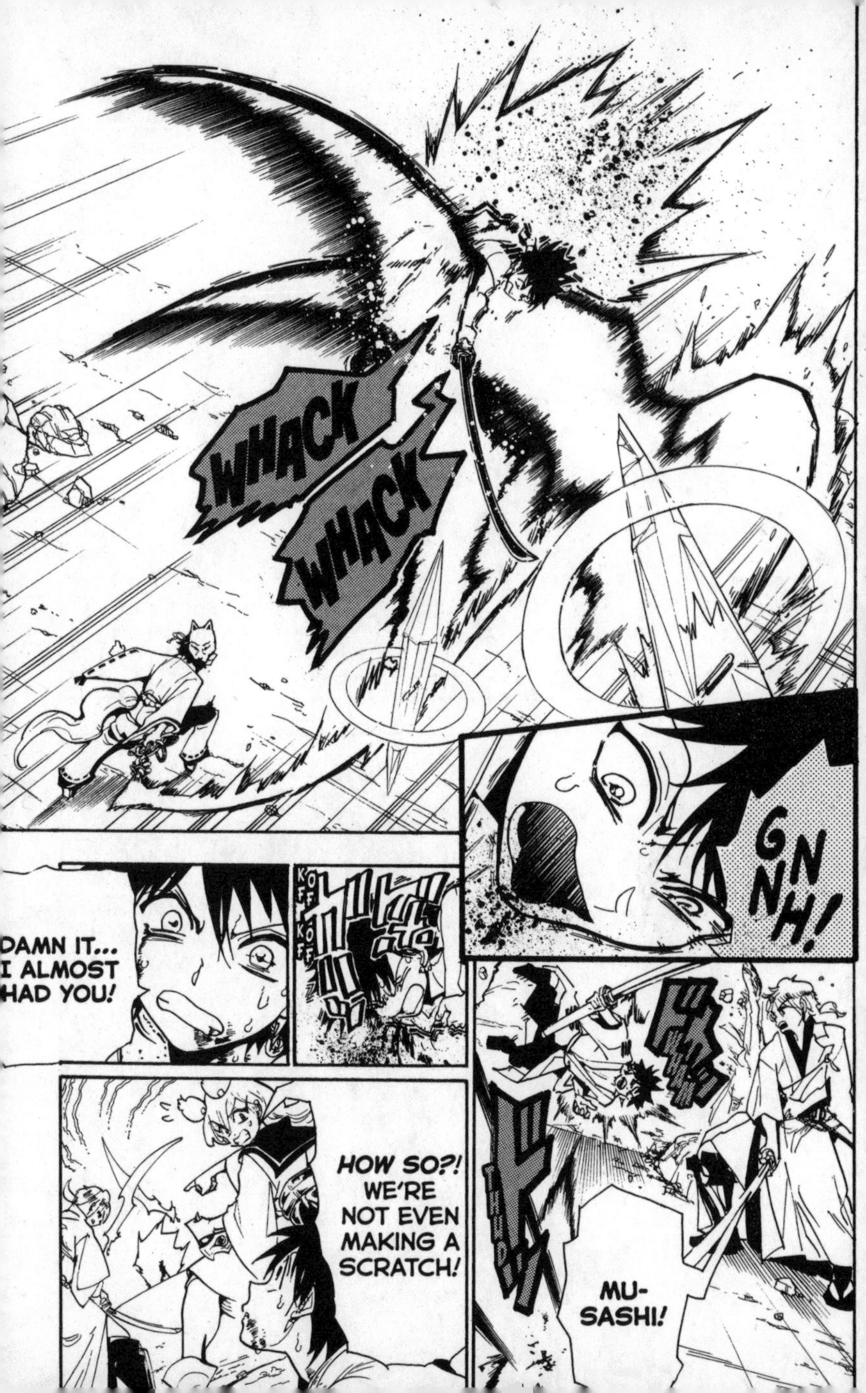
WHACK
WHACK
GNNH!
KOFF KOFF
DAMN IT... I ALMOST HAD YOU!
MU-SASHI!
HOW SO?! WE'RE NOT EVEN MAKING A SCRATCH!

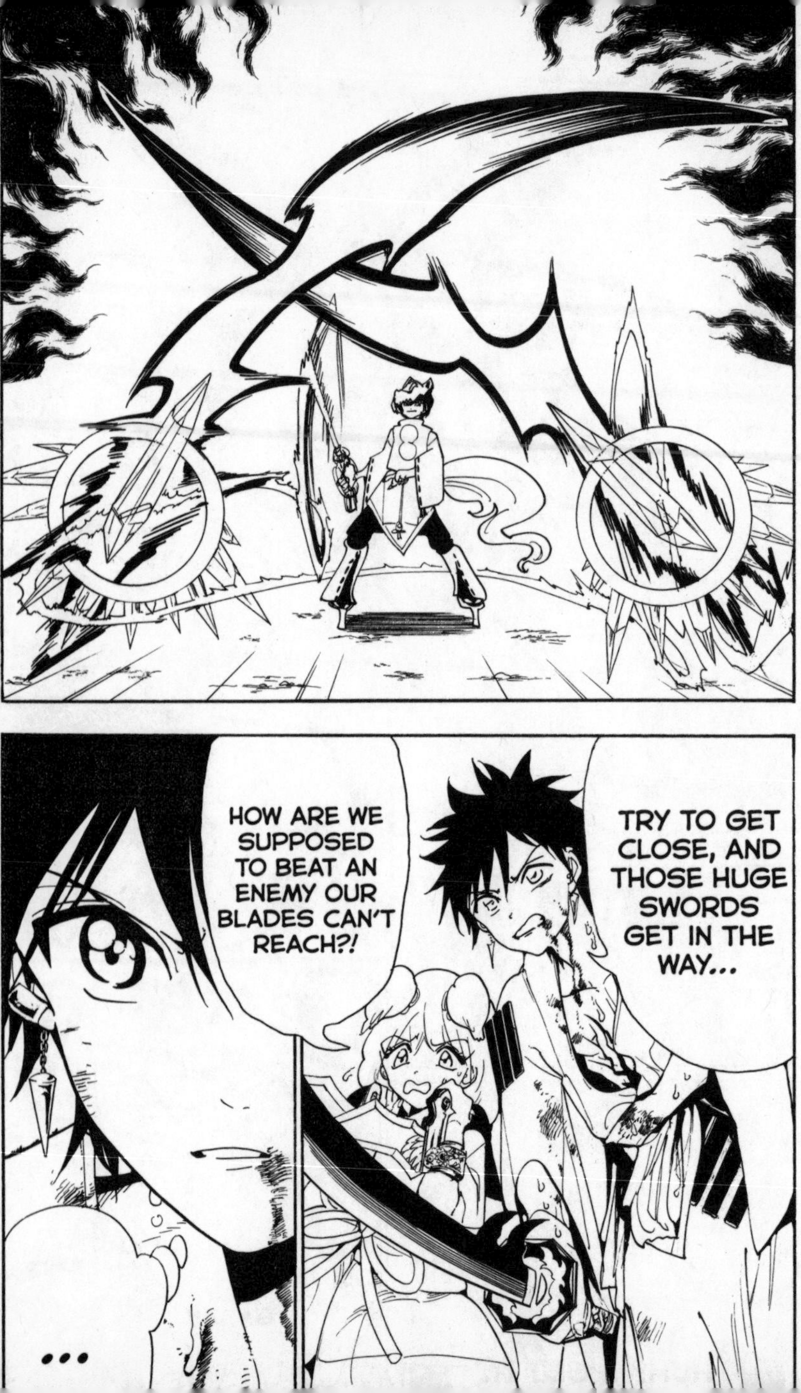
TRY TO GET CLOSE, AND THOSE HUGE SWORDS GET IN THE WAY...
HOW ARE WE SUPPOSED TO BEAT AN ENEMY OUR BLADES CAN'T REACH?!
...

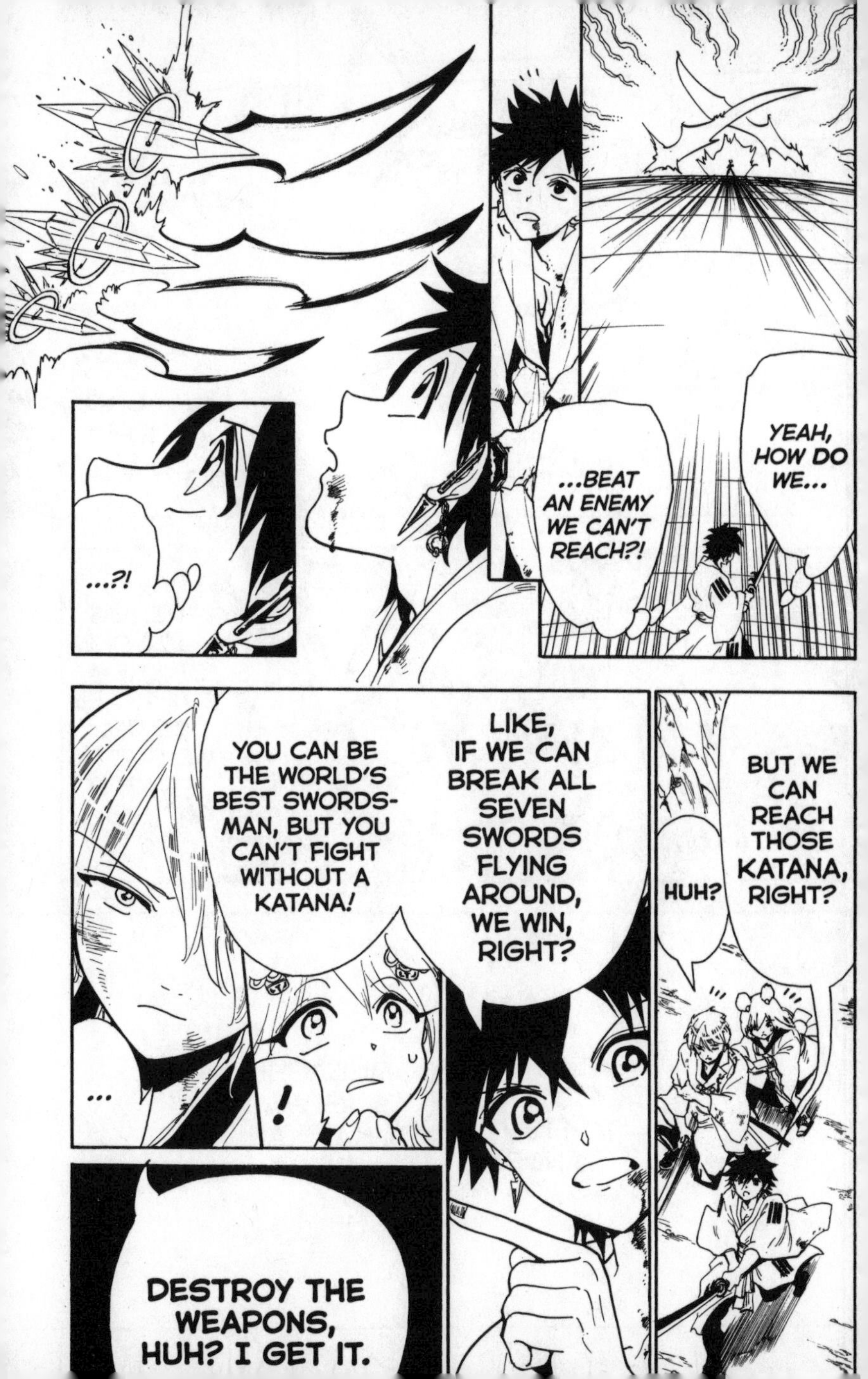
YEAH, HOW DO WE...
...BEAT AN ENEMY WE CAN'T REACH?!
...?!
BUT WE CAN REACH THOSE KATANA, RIGHT?
HUH?
LIKE, IF WE CAN BREAK ALL SEVEN SWORDS FLYING AROUND, WE WIN, RIGHT?
YOU CAN BE THE WORLD'S BEST SWORDS-MAN, BUT YOU CAN'T FIGHT WITHOUT A KATANA!
!
...
DESTROY THE WEAPONS, HUH? I GET IT.

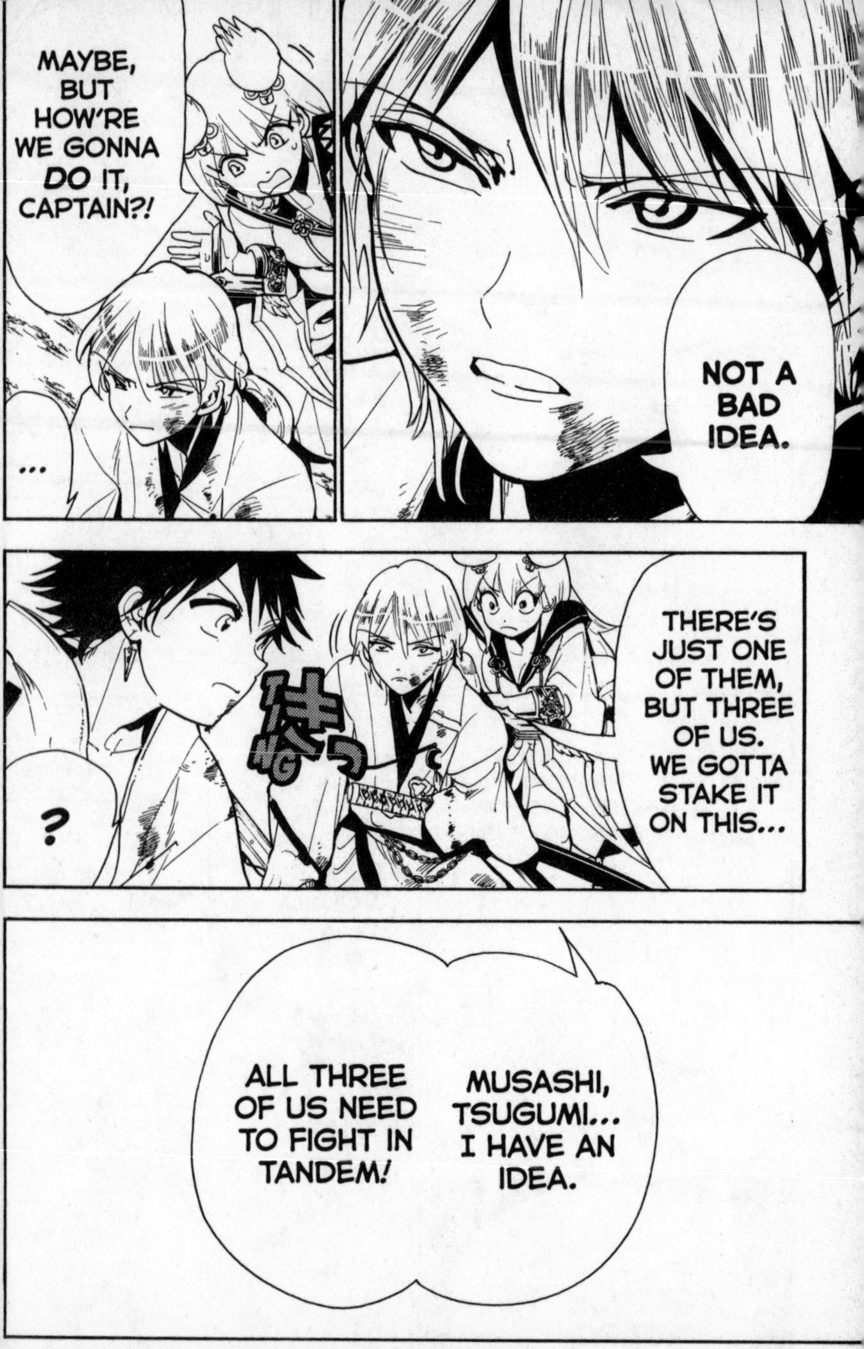
NOT A BAD IDEA.
MAYBE, BUT HOW'RE WE GONNA *DO* IT, CAPTAIN?!
...
THERE'S JUST ONE OF THEM, BUT THREE OF US. WE GOTTA STAKE IT ON THIS...
?
MUSASHI, TSUGUMI... I HAVE AN IDEA.
ALL THREE OF US NEED TO FIGHT IN TANDEM!

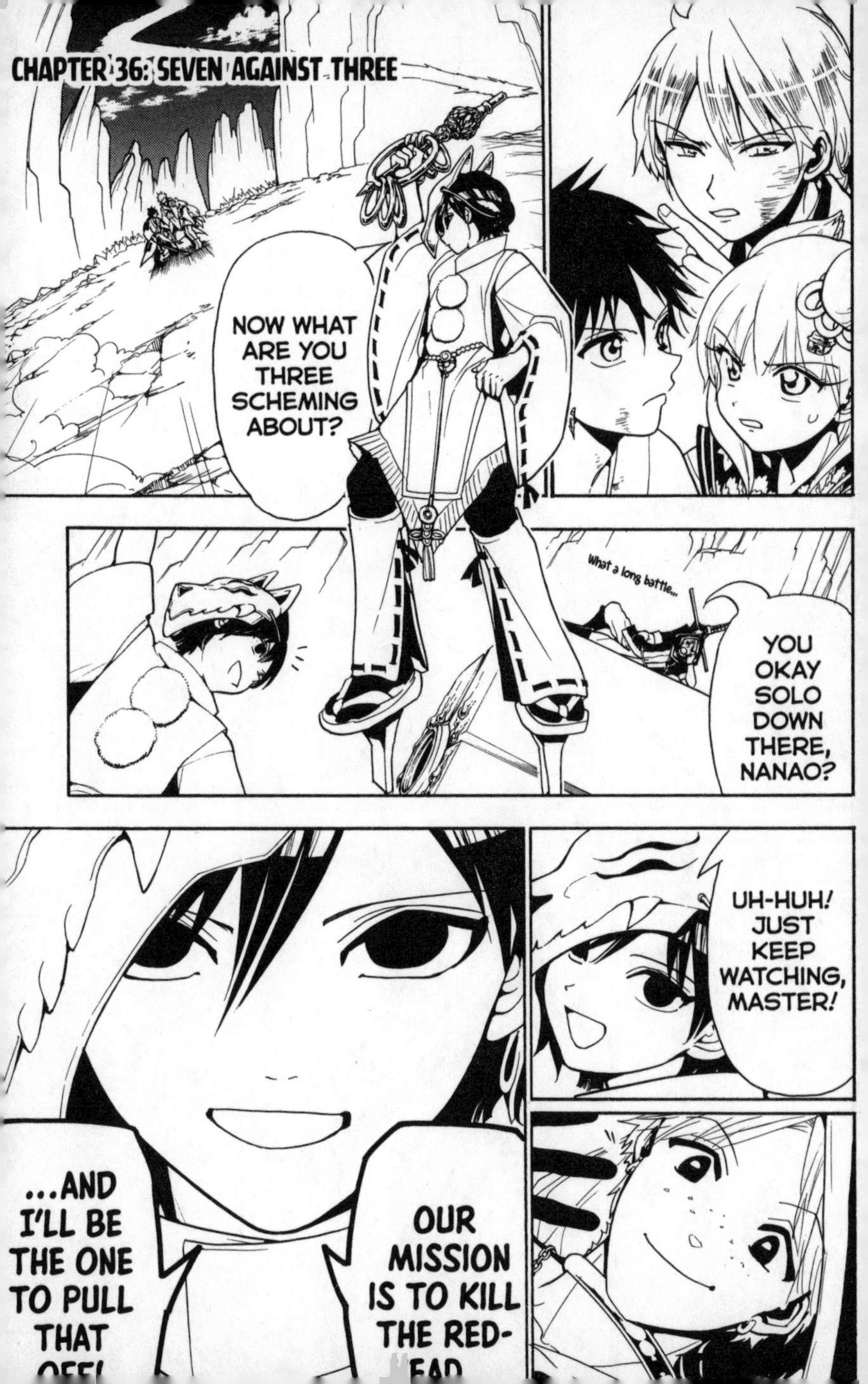
CHAPTER 36: SEVEN AGAINST THREE
NOW WHAT ARE YOU THREE SCHEMING ABOUT?
What a long battle...
YOU OKAY SOLO DOWN THERE, NANAO?
UH-HUH! JUST KEEP WATCHING, MASTER!
OUR MISSION IS TO KILL THE RED-
...AND I'LL BE THE ONE TO PULL THAT

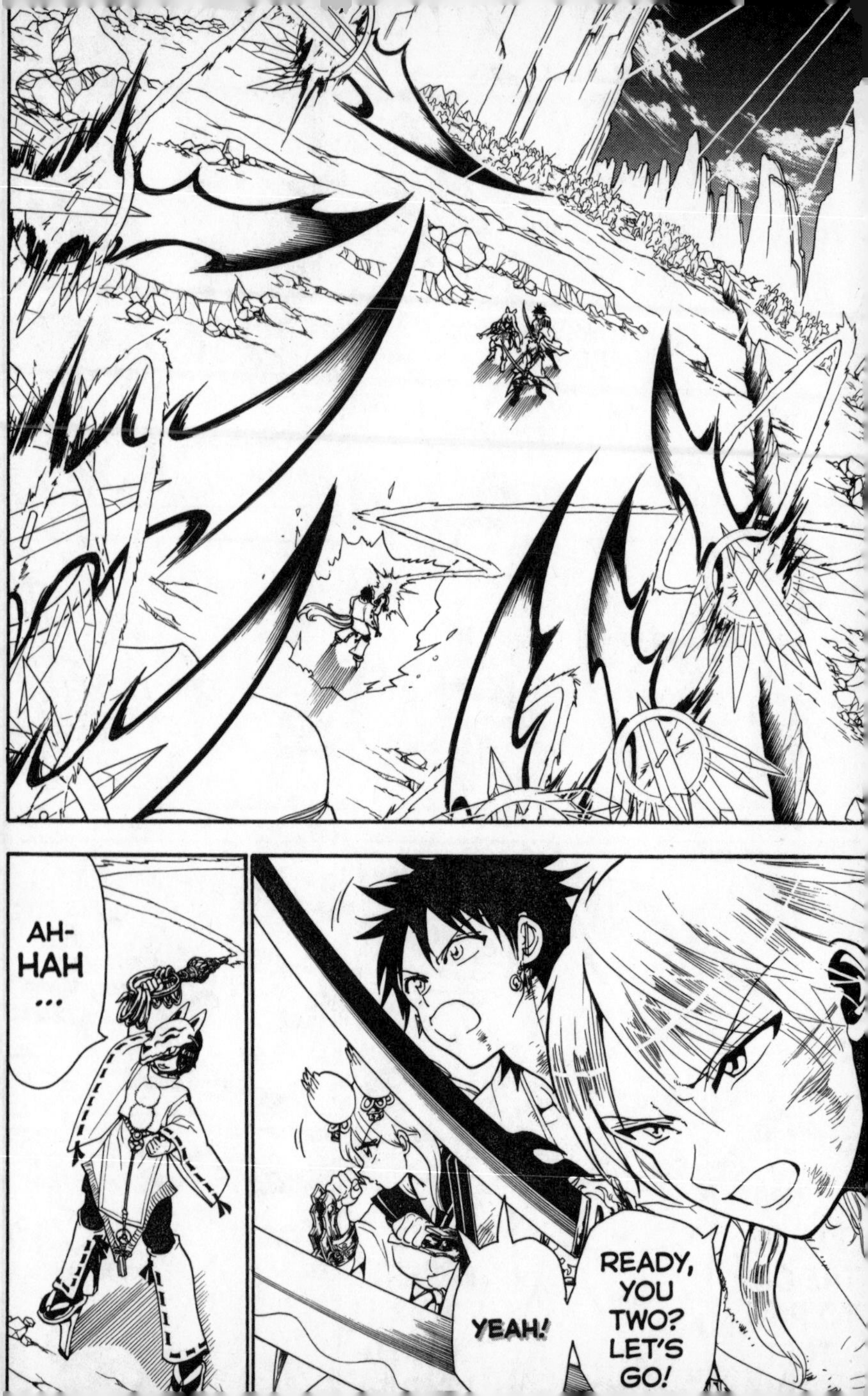
READY, YOU TWO? LET'S GO!
YEAH!
AH-HAH ...

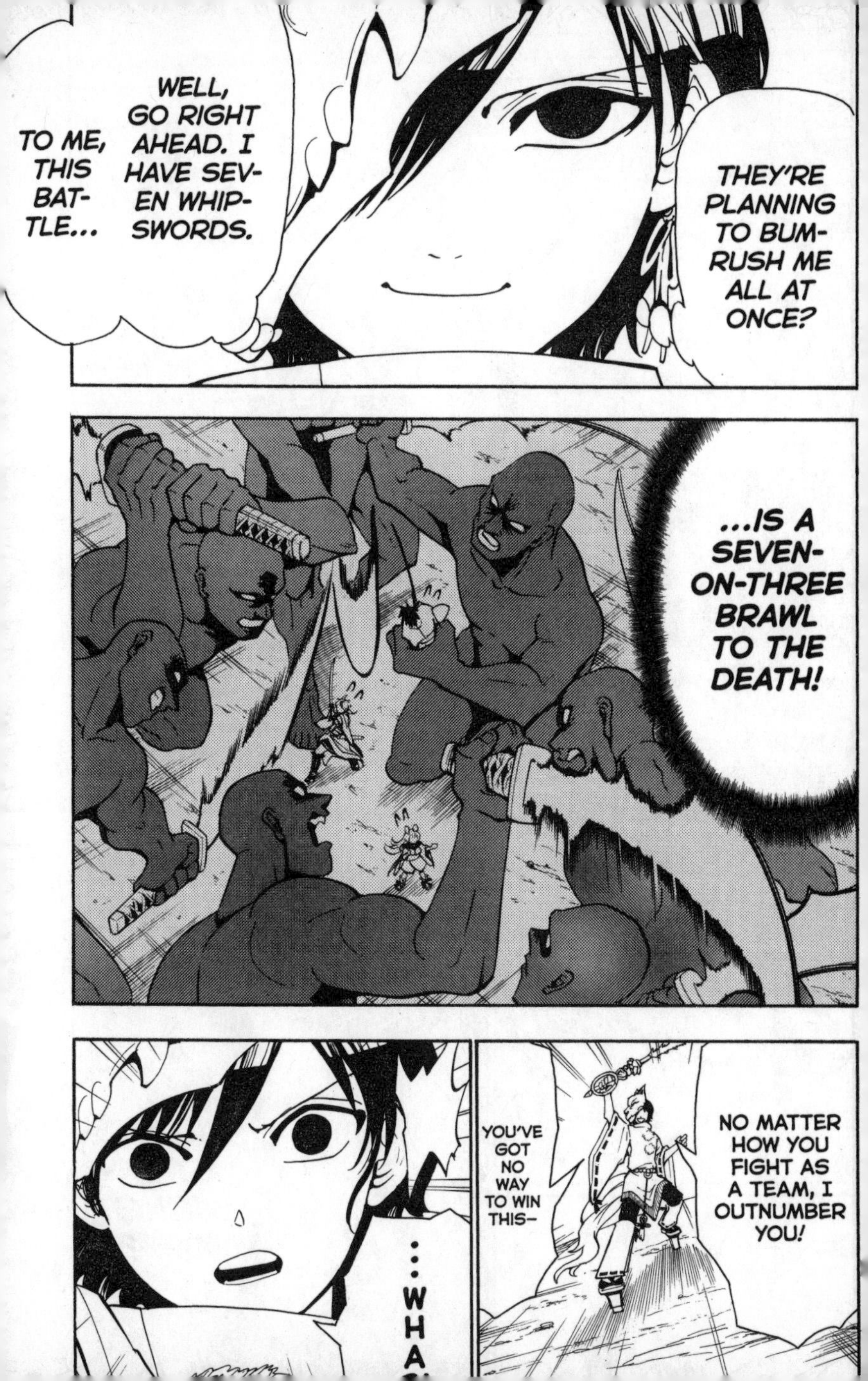
THEY'RE PLANNING TO BUM-RUSH ME ALL AT ONCE?
WELL, GO RIGHT AHEAD. I HAVE SEVEN WHIP-SWORDS.
TO ME, THIS BATTLE...
...IS A SEVEN-ON-THREE BRAWL TO THE DEATH!
NO MATTER HOW YOU FIGHT AS A TEAM, I OUTNUMBER YOU!
YOU'VE GOT NO WAY TO WIN THIS—
...WHA

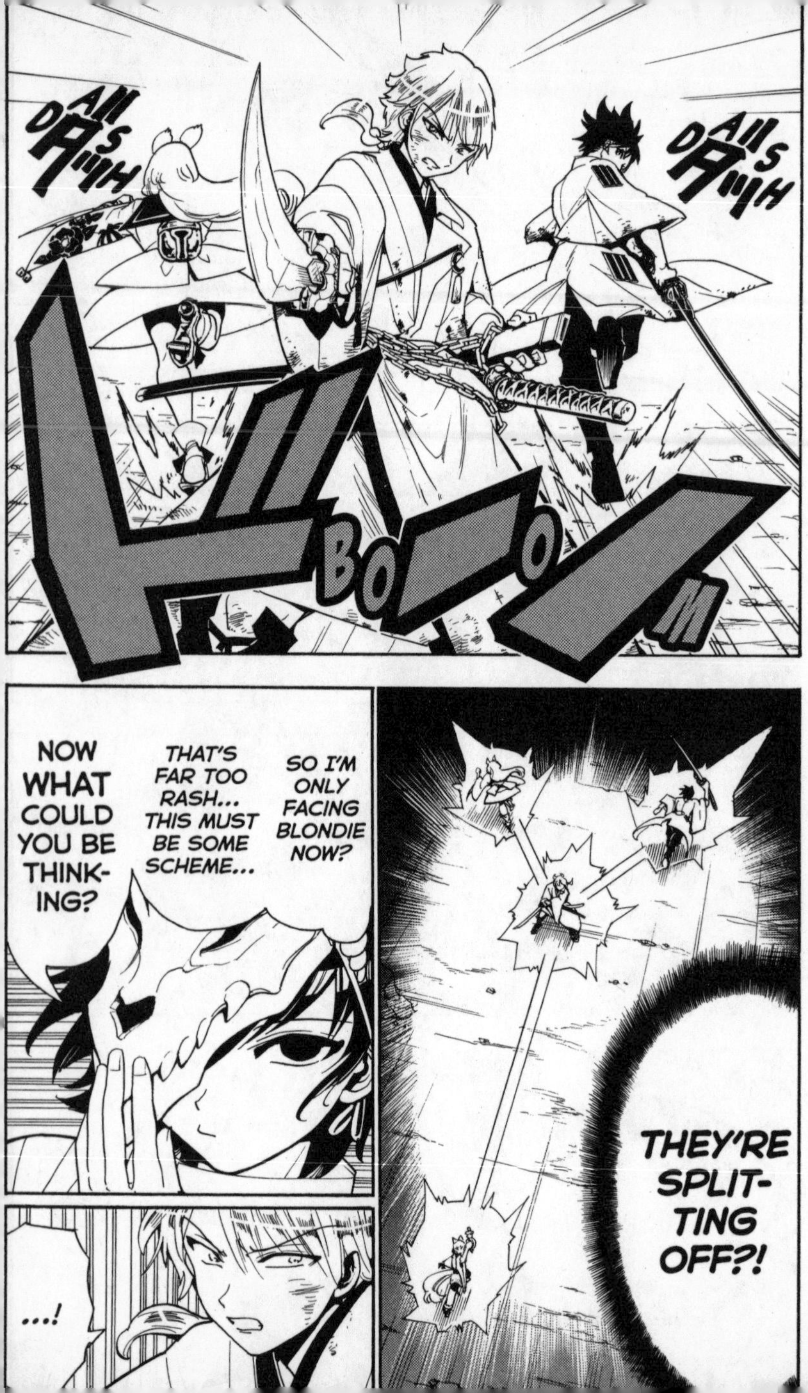
DASH
DASH
BOOM
THEY'RE SPLIT-TING OFF?!
SO I'M ONLY FACING BLONDIE NOW?
THAT'S FAR TOO RASH... THIS MUST BE SOME SCHEME...
NOW WHAT COULD YOU BE THINK-ING?
...!

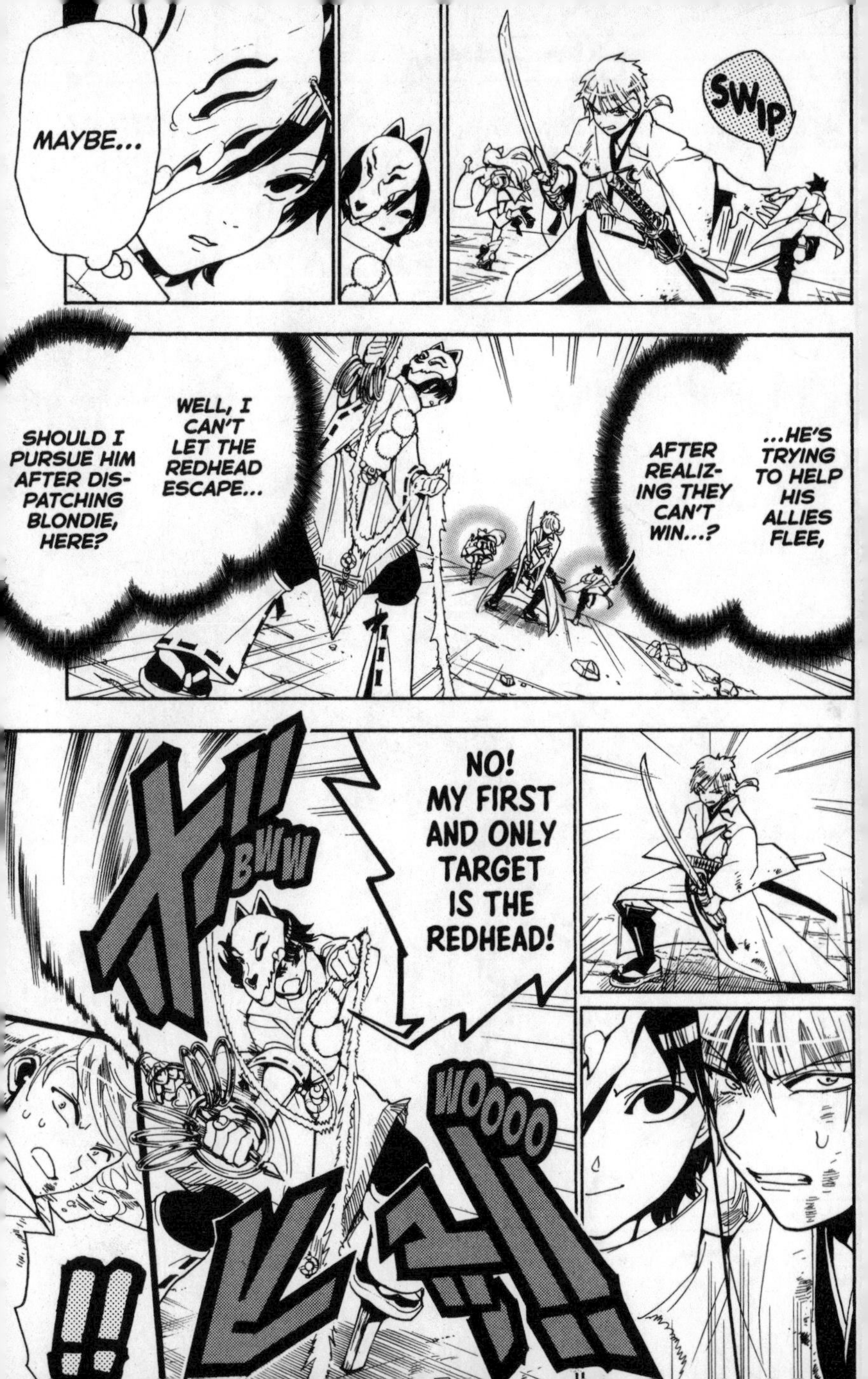
SWIP
MAYBE...
...HE'S TRYING TO HELP HIS ALLIES FLEE,
AFTER REALIZING THEY CAN'T WIN...?
WELL, I CAN'T LET THE REDHEAD ESCAPE...
SHOULD I PURSUE HIM AFTER DISPATCHING BLONDIE, HERE?
NO! MY FIRST AND ONLY TARGET IS THE REDHEAD!
BWW
WOOOO
!!

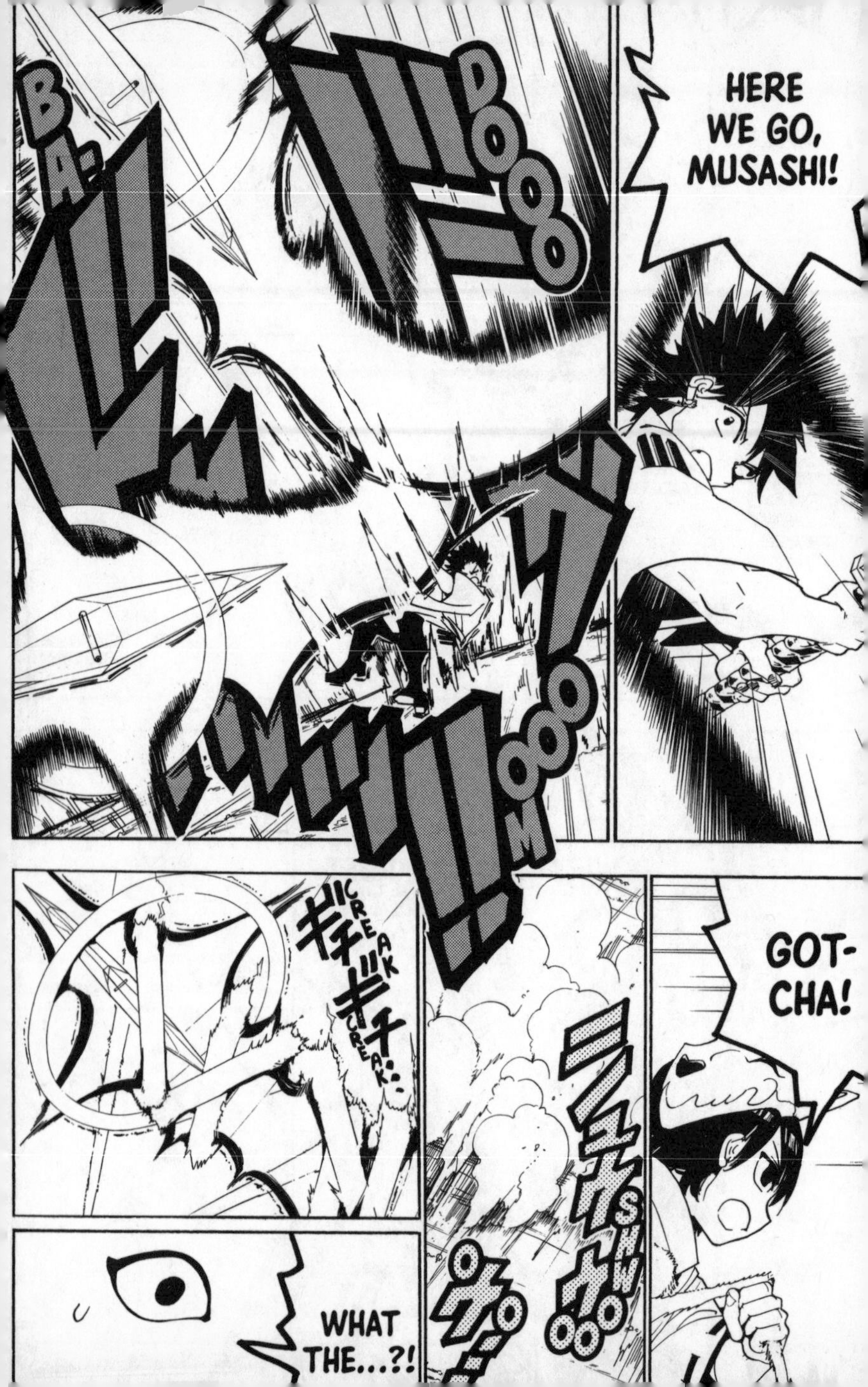
HERE WE GO, MUSASHI!
BA-
DOOOO
OOOOM
GOT-CHA!
SHW...
CREAK
CREAK...
WHAT THE...?!

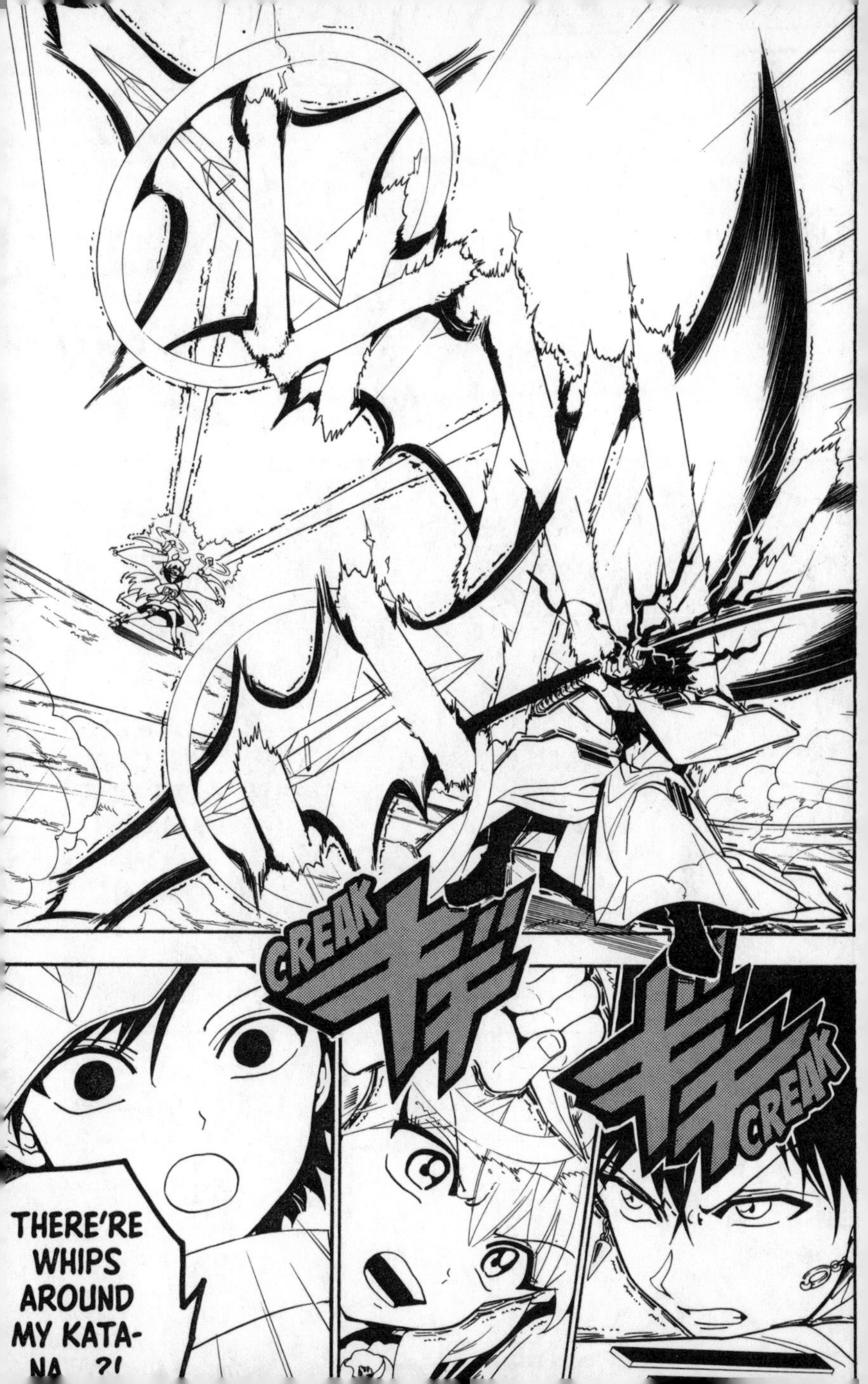
ギ
CREAK
CREAK
ギ
THERE'RE WHIPS AROUND MY KATA-NA...?!

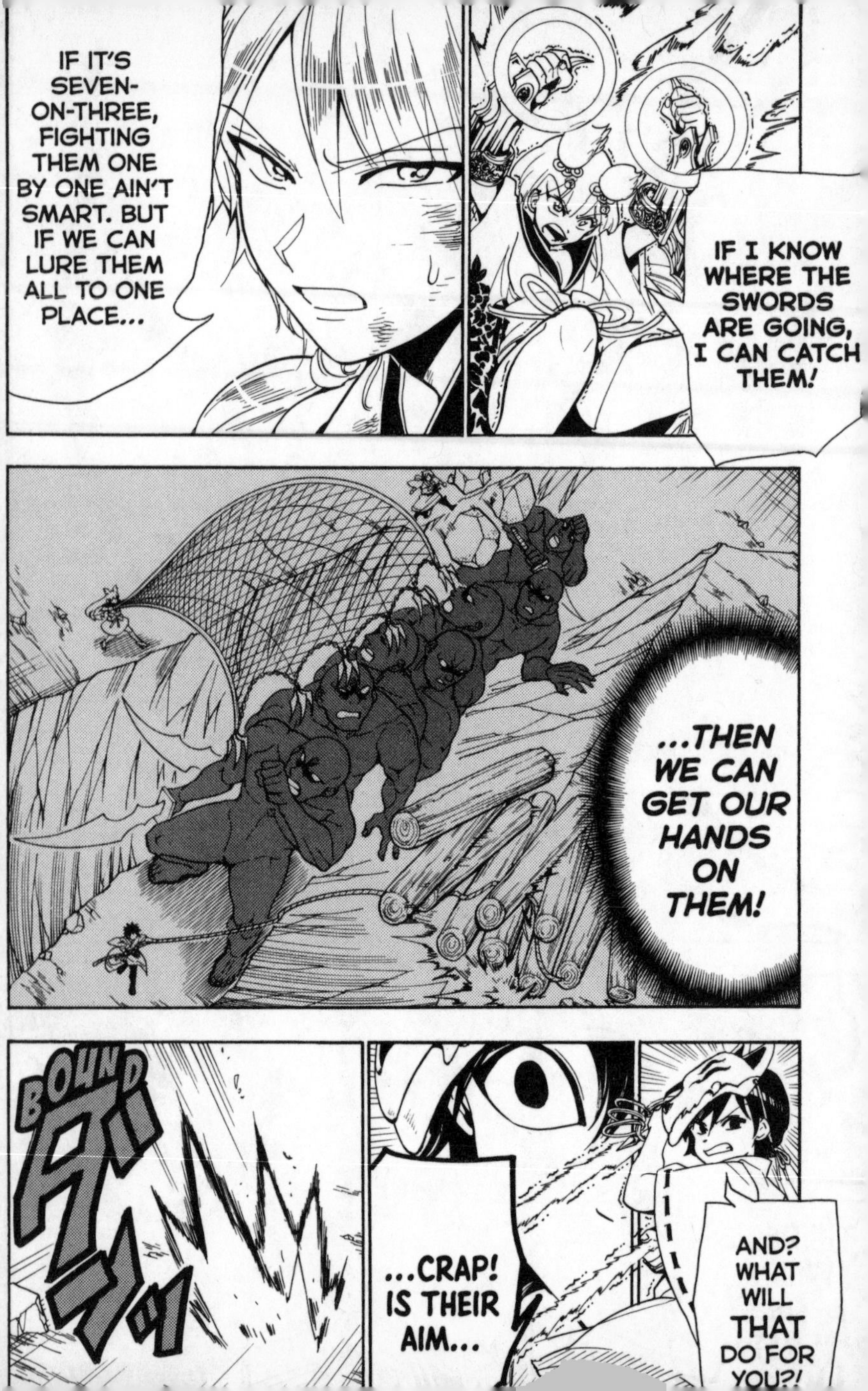
IF I KNOW WHERE THE SWORDS ARE GOING, I CAN CATCH THEM!
IF IT'S SEVEN-ON-THREE, FIGHTING THEM ONE BY ONE AIN'T SMART. BUT IF WE CAN LURE THEM ALL TO ONE PLACE...
...THEN WE CAN GET OUR HANDS ON THEM!
AND? WHAT WILL THAT DO FOR YOU?!
...CRAP! IS THEIR AIM...
BOUND

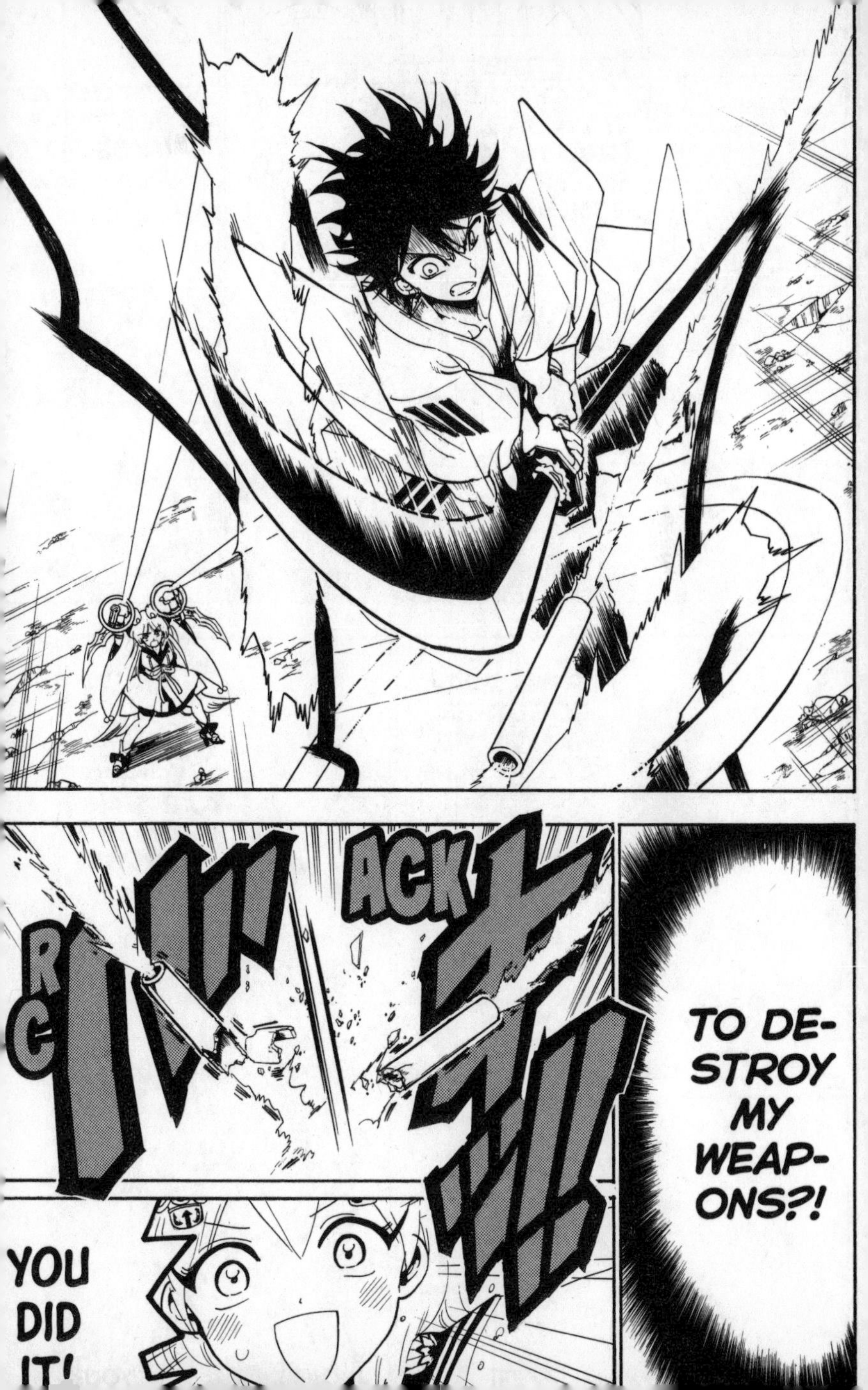
TO DE-
STROY
MY
WEAP-
ONS?!
CRACK
YOU
DID
IT!

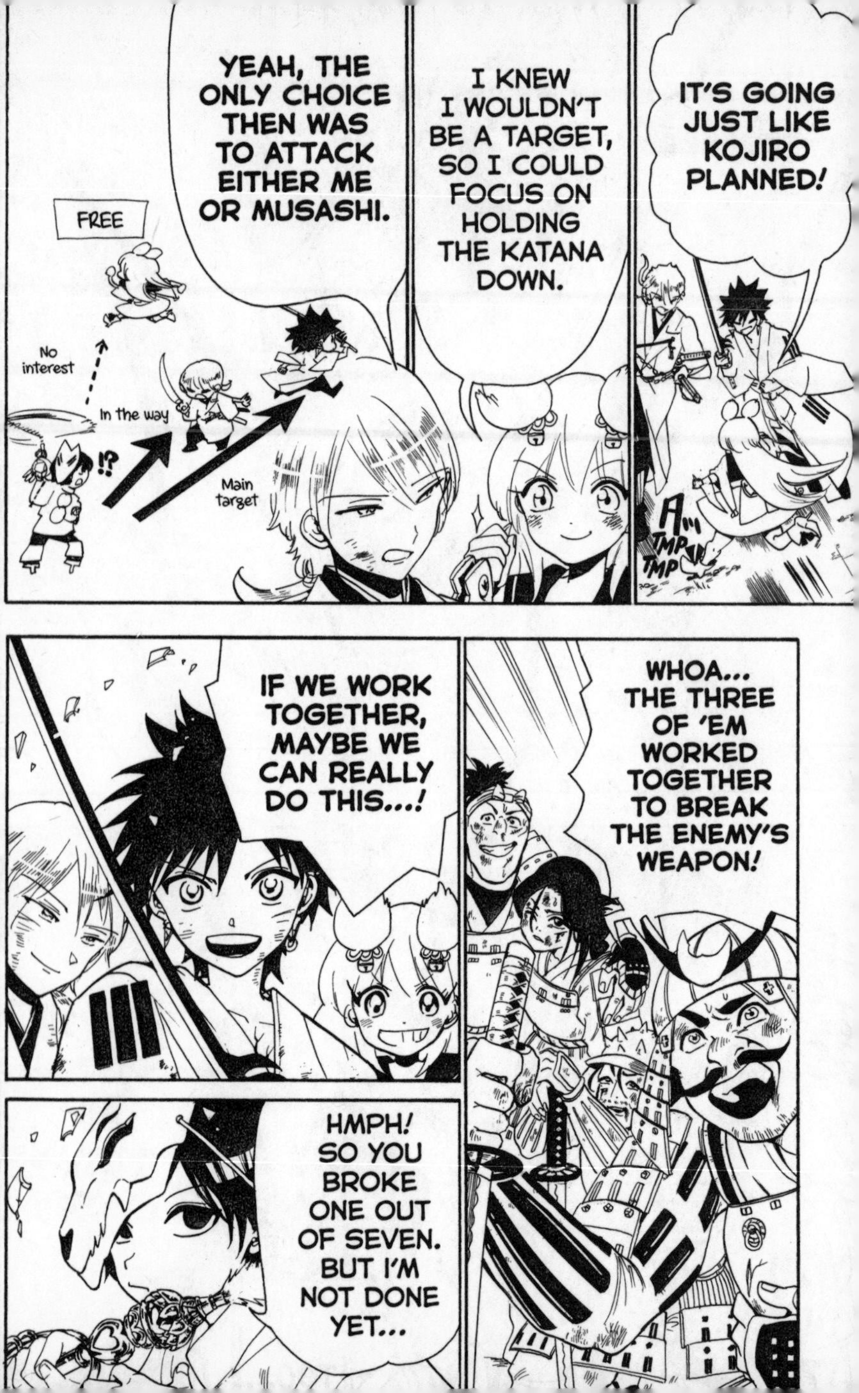
IT'S GOING JUST LIKE KOJIRO PLANNED!
TMP TMP
I KNEW I WOULDN'T BE A TARGET, SO I COULD FOCUS ON HOLDING THE KATANA DOWN.
YEAH, THE ONLY CHOICE THEN WAS TO ATTACK EITHER ME OR MUSASHI.
FREE
No interest
In the way
Main target
!?
WHOA... THE THREE OF 'EM WORKED TOGETHER TO BREAK THE ENEMY'S WEAPON!
IF WE WORK TOGETHER, MAYBE WE CAN REALLY DO THIS...!
HMPH! SO YOU BROKE ONE OUT OF SEVEN. BUT I'M NOT DONE YET...

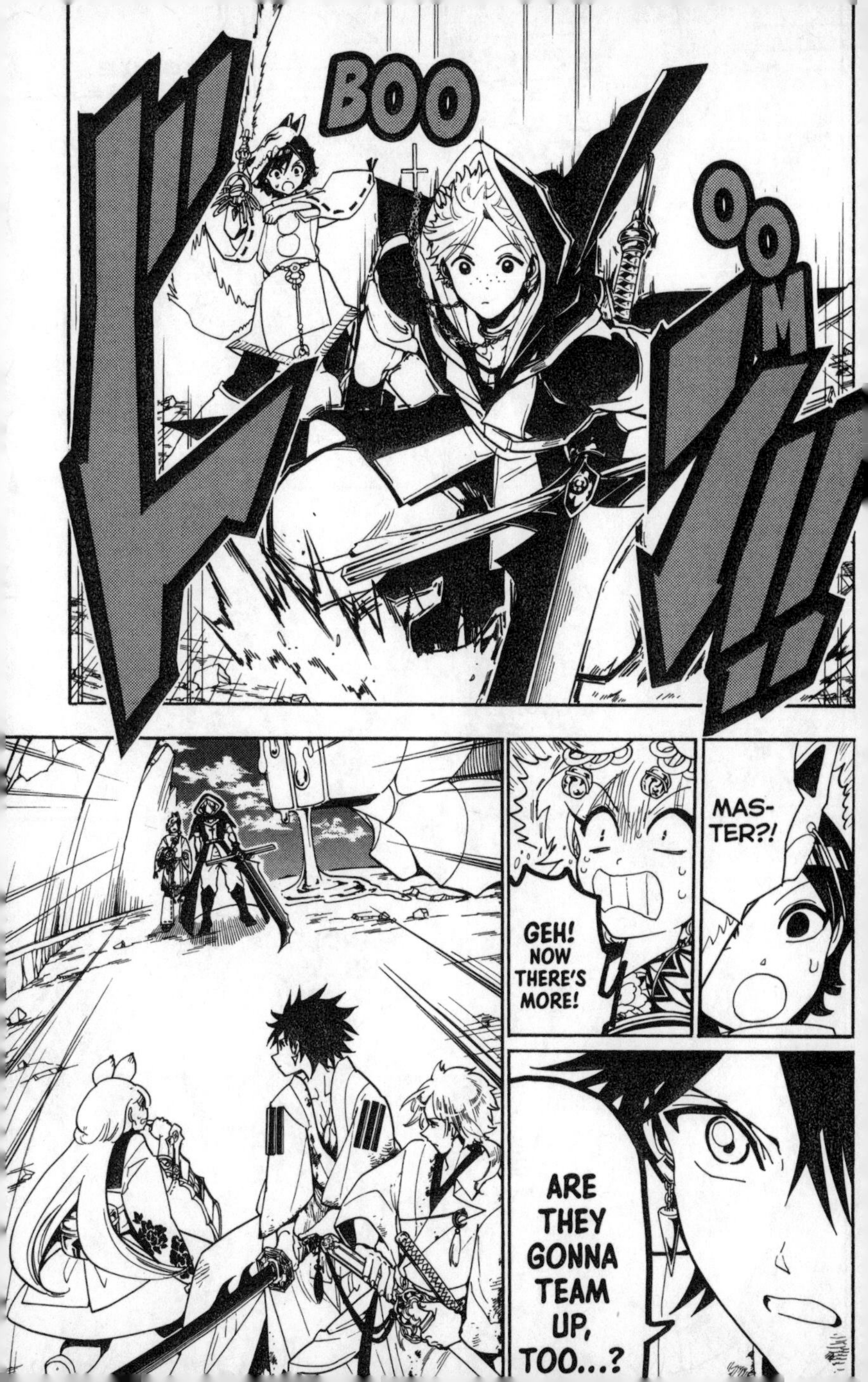
BOOOOM!!
MAS- TER?!
GEH! NOW THERE'S MORE!
ARE THEY GONNA TEAM UP, TOO...?

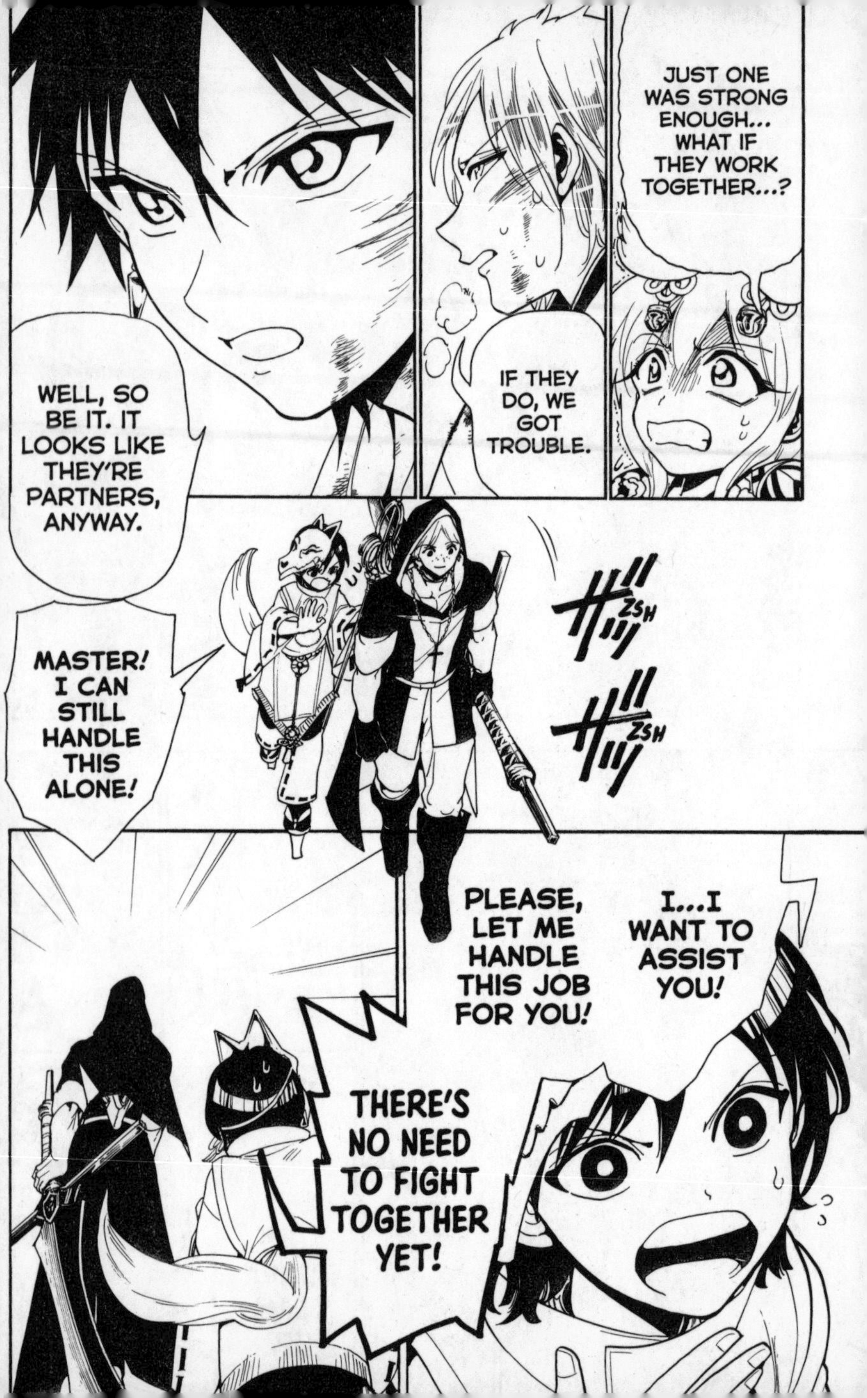
JUST ONE WAS STRONG ENOUGH... WHAT IF THEY WORK TOGETHER...?
IF THEY DO, WE GOT TROUBLE.
WELL, SO BE IT. IT LOOKS LIKE THEY'RE PARTNERS, ANYWAY.
ZSH
ZSH
MASTER! I CAN STILL HANDLE THIS ALONE!
I...I WANT TO ASSIST YOU!
PLEASE, LET ME HANDLE THIS JOB FOR YOU!
THERE'S NO NEED TO FIGHT TOGETHER YET!

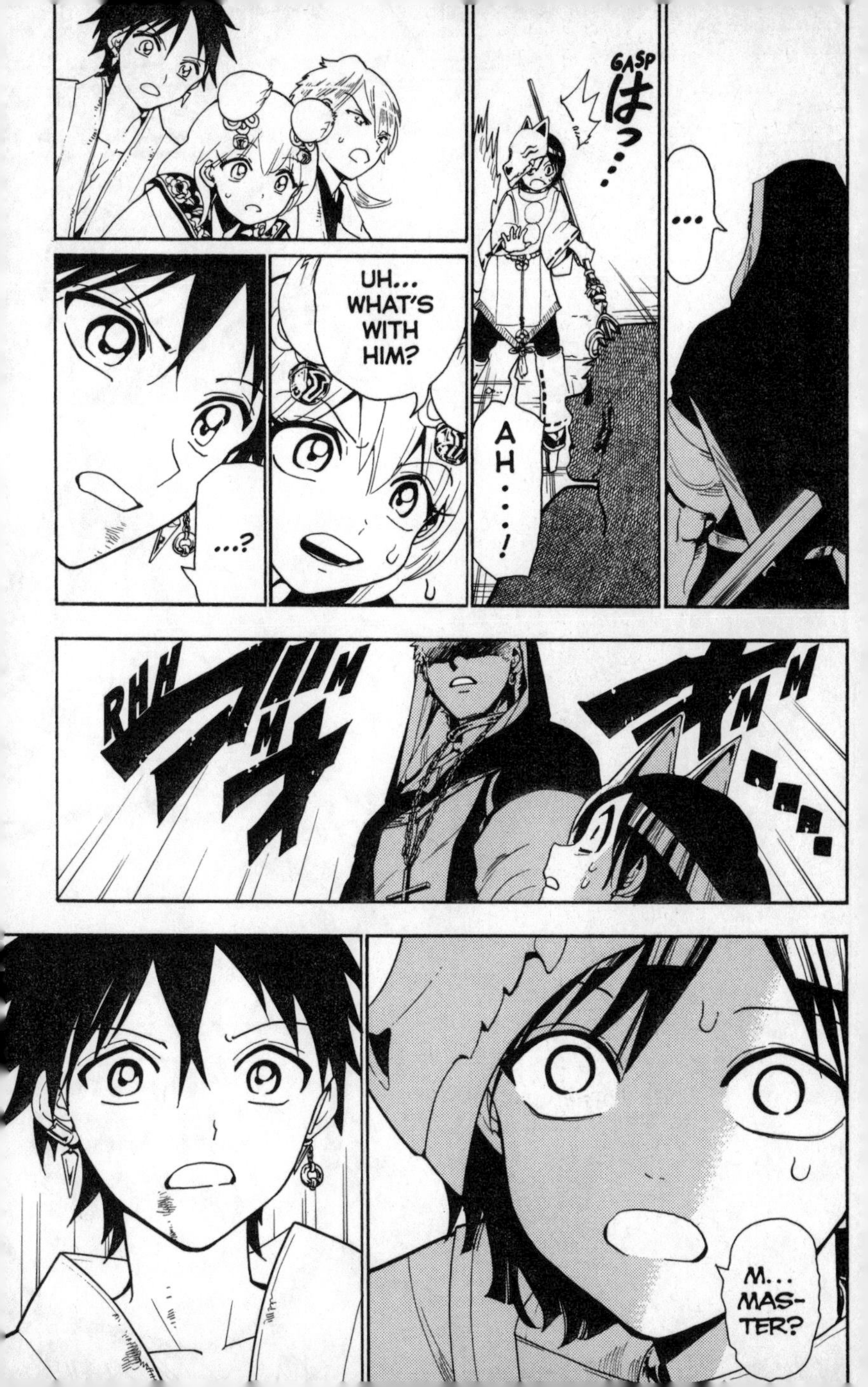
...
GASP
はっ...
AH...!
UH... WHAT'S WITH HIM?
...?
RHHMMM
M...
M... MAS-TER?

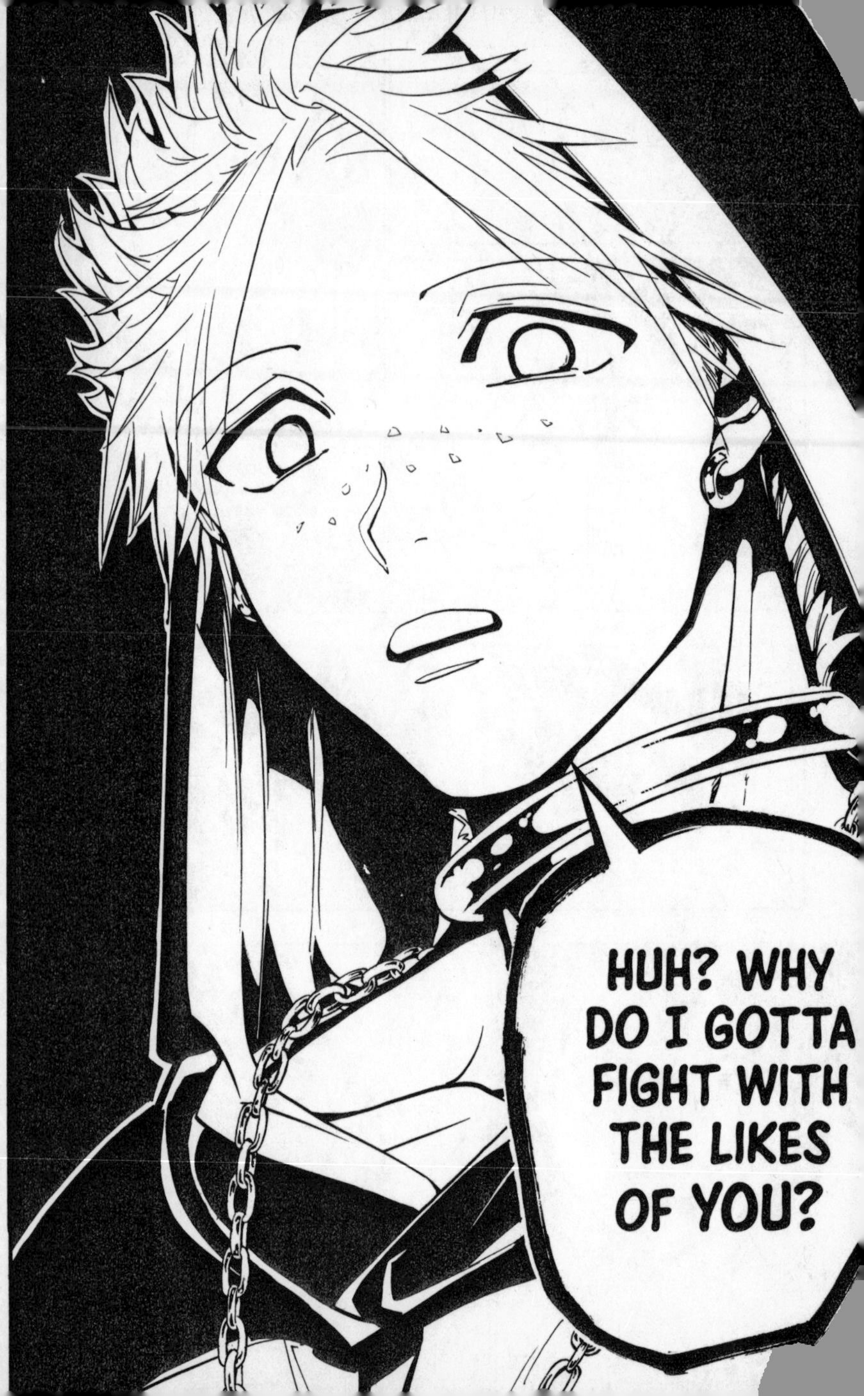
HUH? WHY DO I GOTTA FIGHT WITH THE LIKES OF YOU?

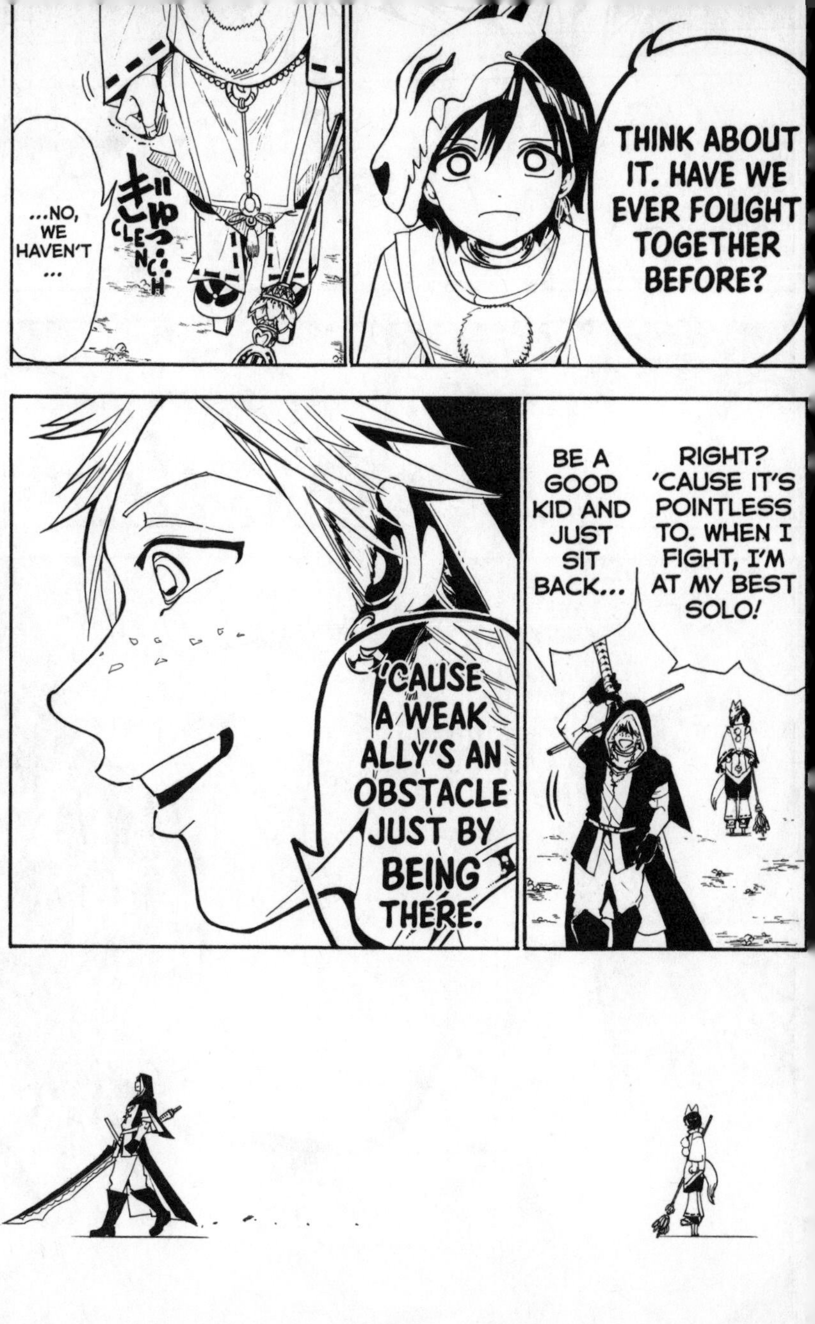
THINK ABOUT IT. HAVE WE EVER FOUGHT TOGETHER BEFORE?
ぎゅっ CLENCH
...NO, WE HAVEN'T ...
RIGHT? 'CAUSE IT'S POINTLESS TO. WHEN I FIGHT, I'M AT MY BEST SOLO!
BE A GOOD KID AND JUST SIT BACK...
'CAUSE A WEAK ALLY'S AN OBSTACLE JUST BY BEING THERE.

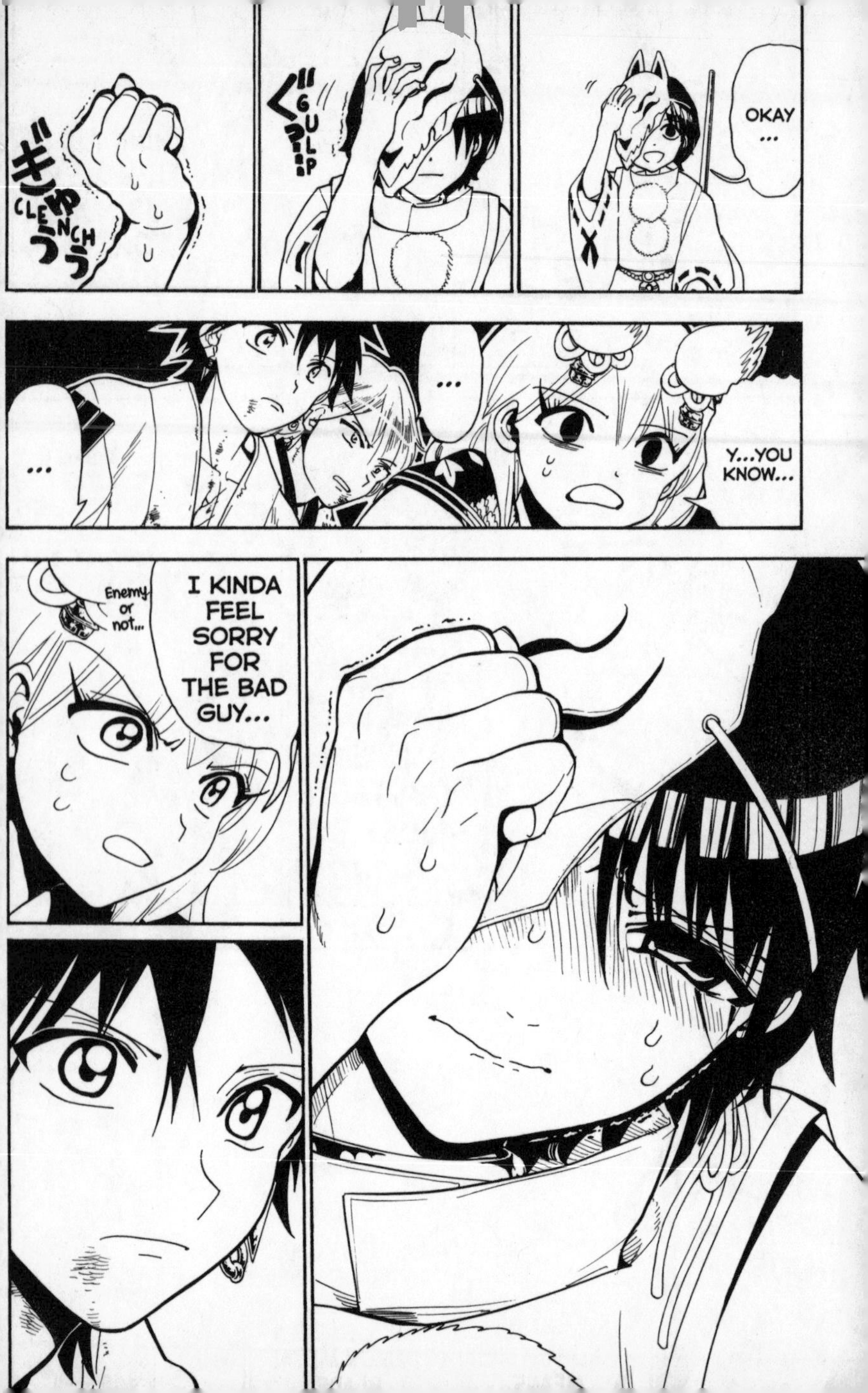
OKAY ...
GULP
CLENCH
Y...YOU KNOW...
...
...
I KINDA FEEL SORRY FOR THE BAD GUY...
Enemy or not...

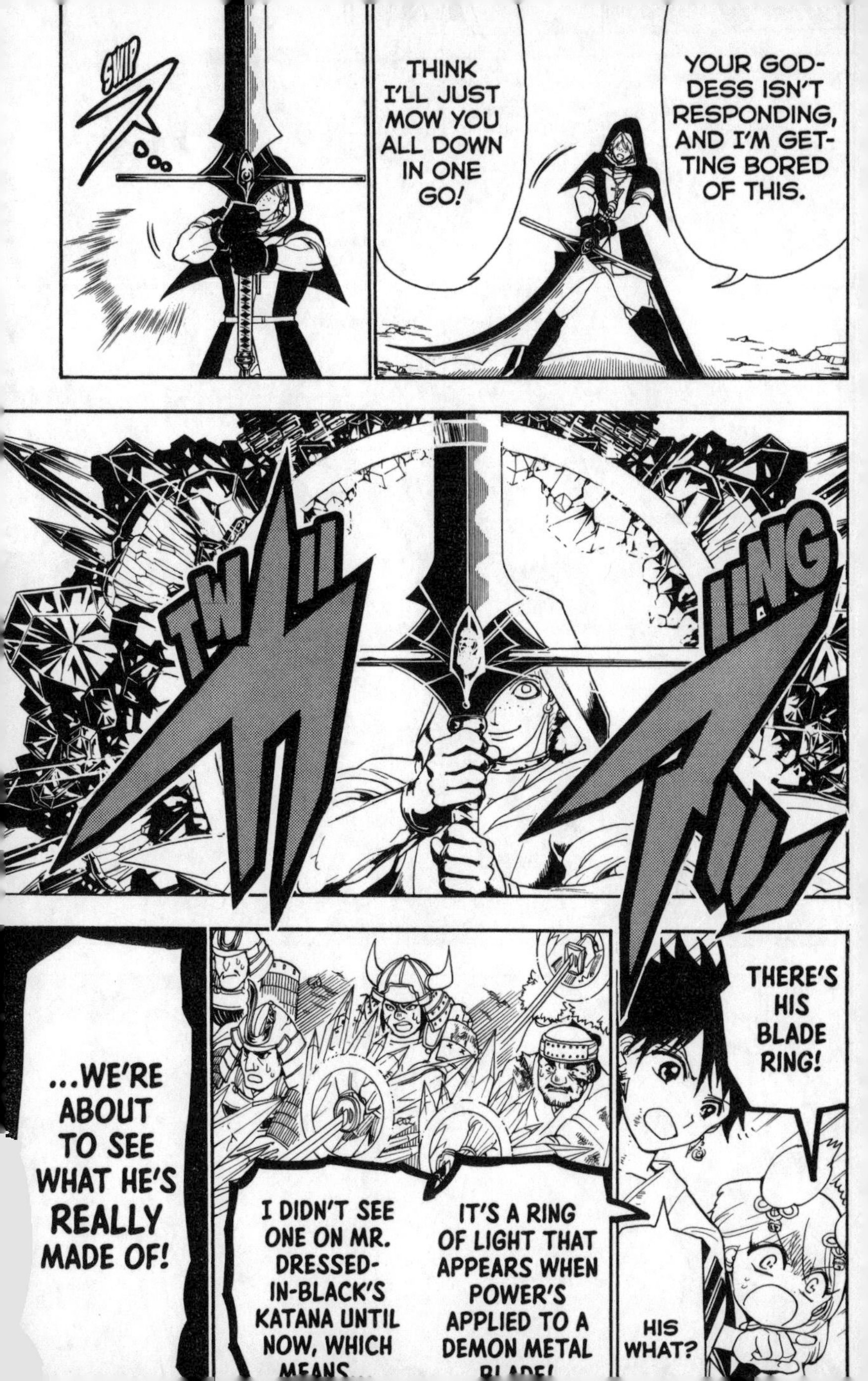
YOUR GOD-DESS ISN'T RESPONDING, AND I'M GET-TING BORED OF THIS.
THINK I'LL JUST MOW YOU ALL DOWN IN ONE GO!
SWIP
TWIIING
THERE'S HIS BLADE RING!
HIS WHAT?
IT'S A RING OF LIGHT THAT APPEARS WHEN POWER'S APPLIED TO A DEMON METAL
I DIDN'T SEE ONE ON MR. DRESSED-IN-BLACK'S KATANA UNTIL NOW, WHICH
...WE'RE ABOUT TO SEE WHAT HE'S REALLY MADE OF!

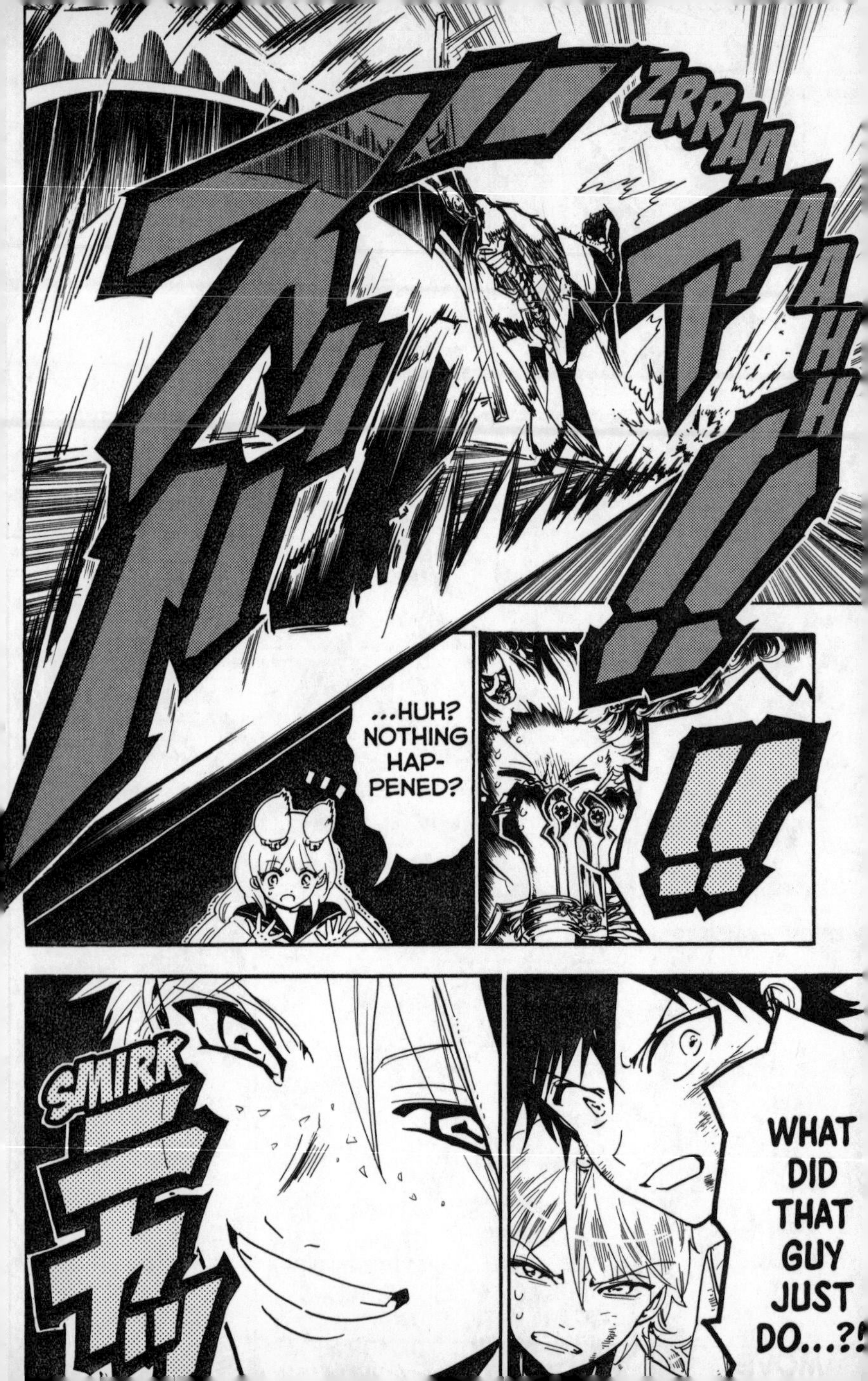
ZRRAAAAAHHH
!!
...HUH? NOTHING HAP-PENED?
WHAT DID THAT GUY JUST DO...?!
SMIRK

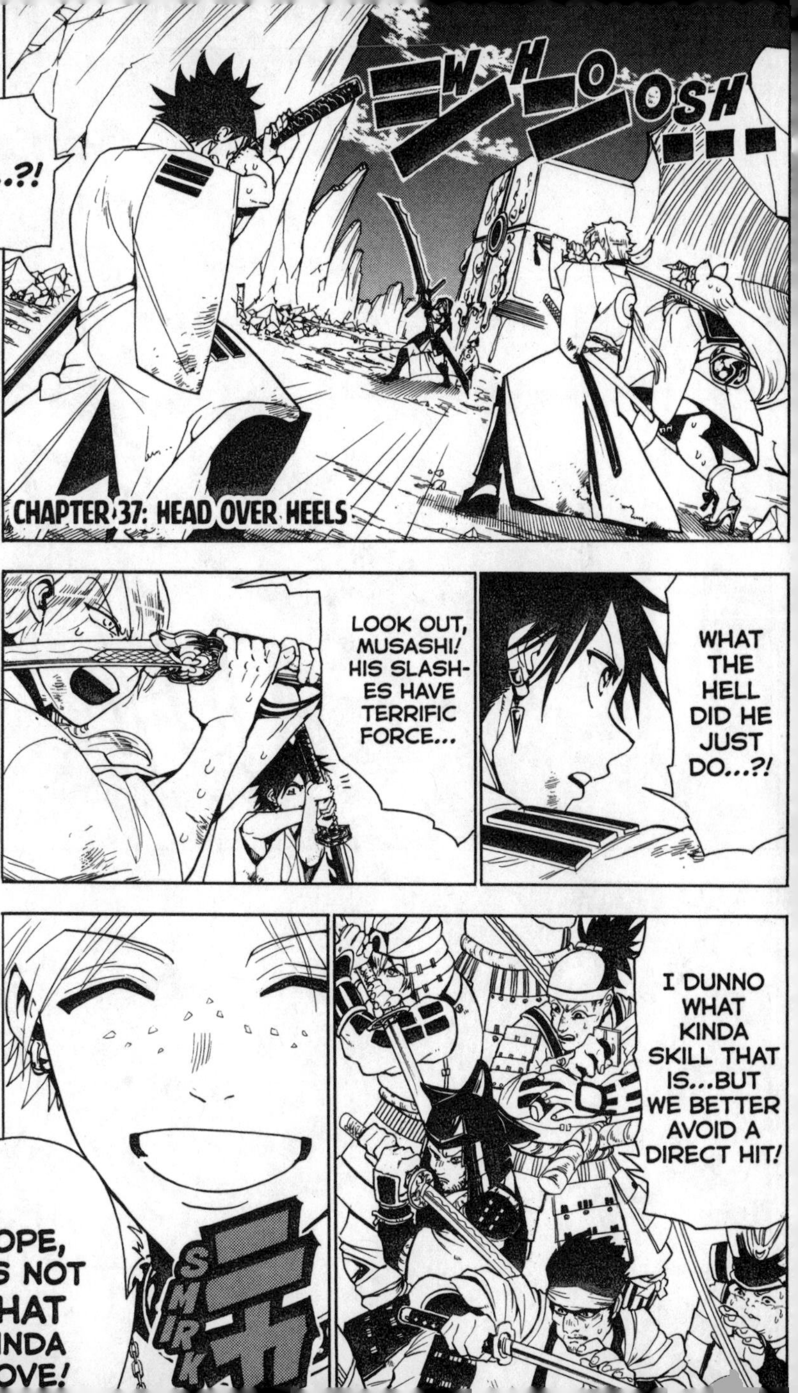
WHOOOSH
...?!
CHAPTER 37: HEAD OVER HEELS
WHAT THE HELL DID HE JUST DO...?!
LOOK OUT, MUSASHI! HIS SLASH-ES HAVE TERRIFIC FORCE...
I DUNNO WHAT KINDA SKILL THAT IS...BUT WE BETTER AVOID A DIRECT HIT!
SMIRK
NOPE, IT'S NOT THAT KINDA MOVE!

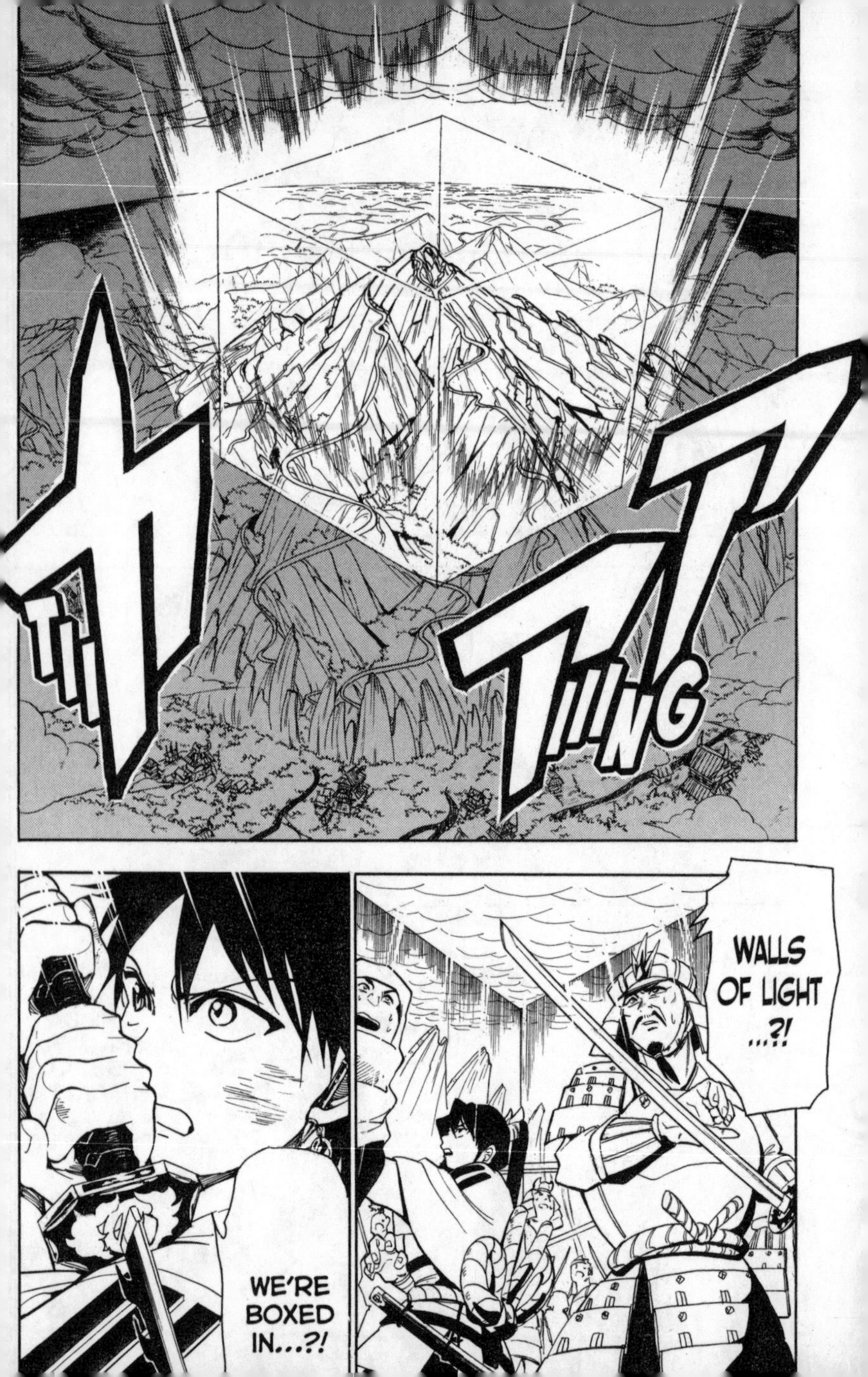
TIIIIING
WALLS OF LIGHT ...?!
WE'RE BOXED IN...?!

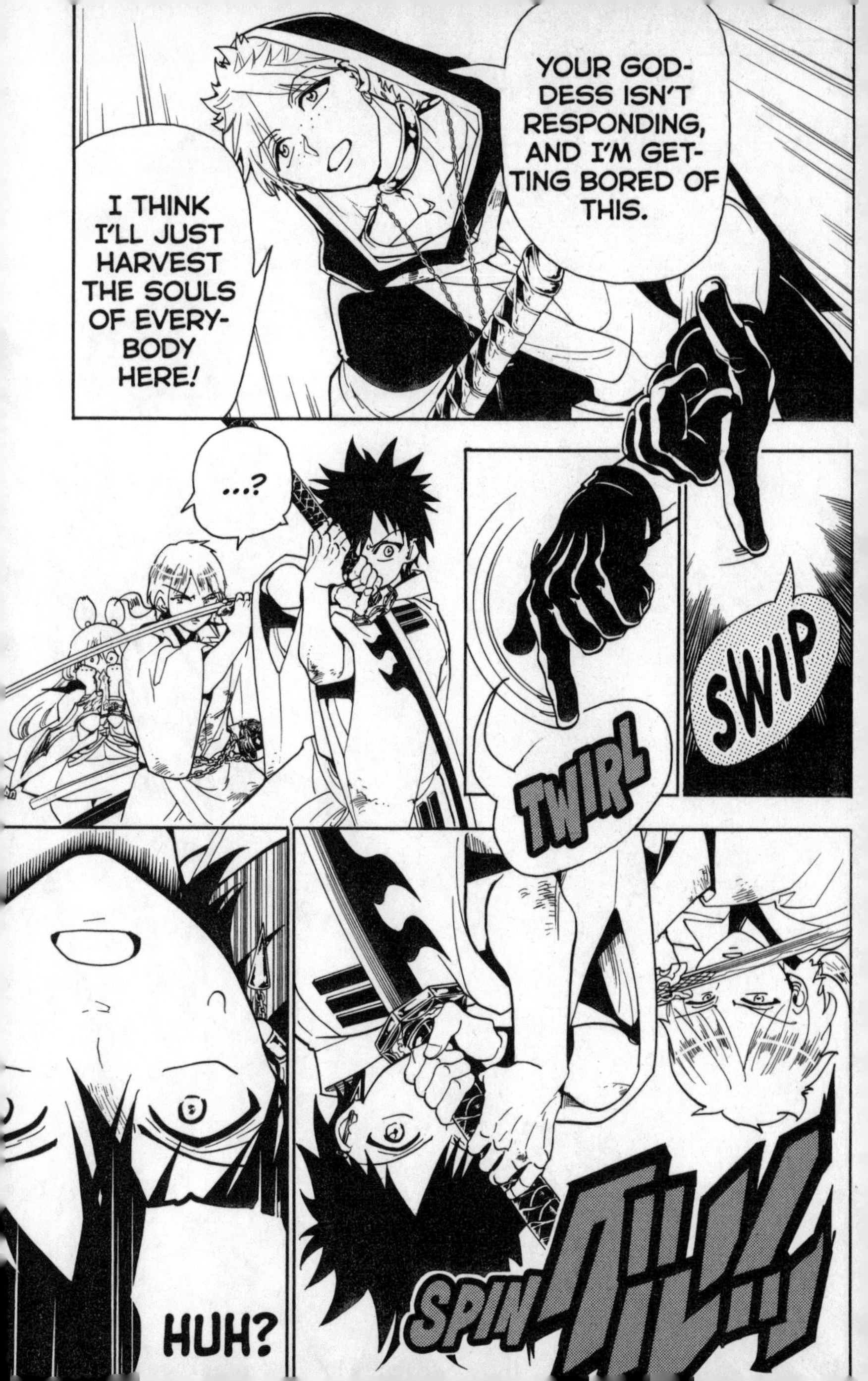

YOUR GOD-DESS ISN'T RESPONDING, AND I'M GET-TING BORED OF THIS.
I THINK I'LL JUST HARVEST THE SOULS OF EVERY-BODY HERE!
SWIP
TWIRL
...?
SPIN
HUH?

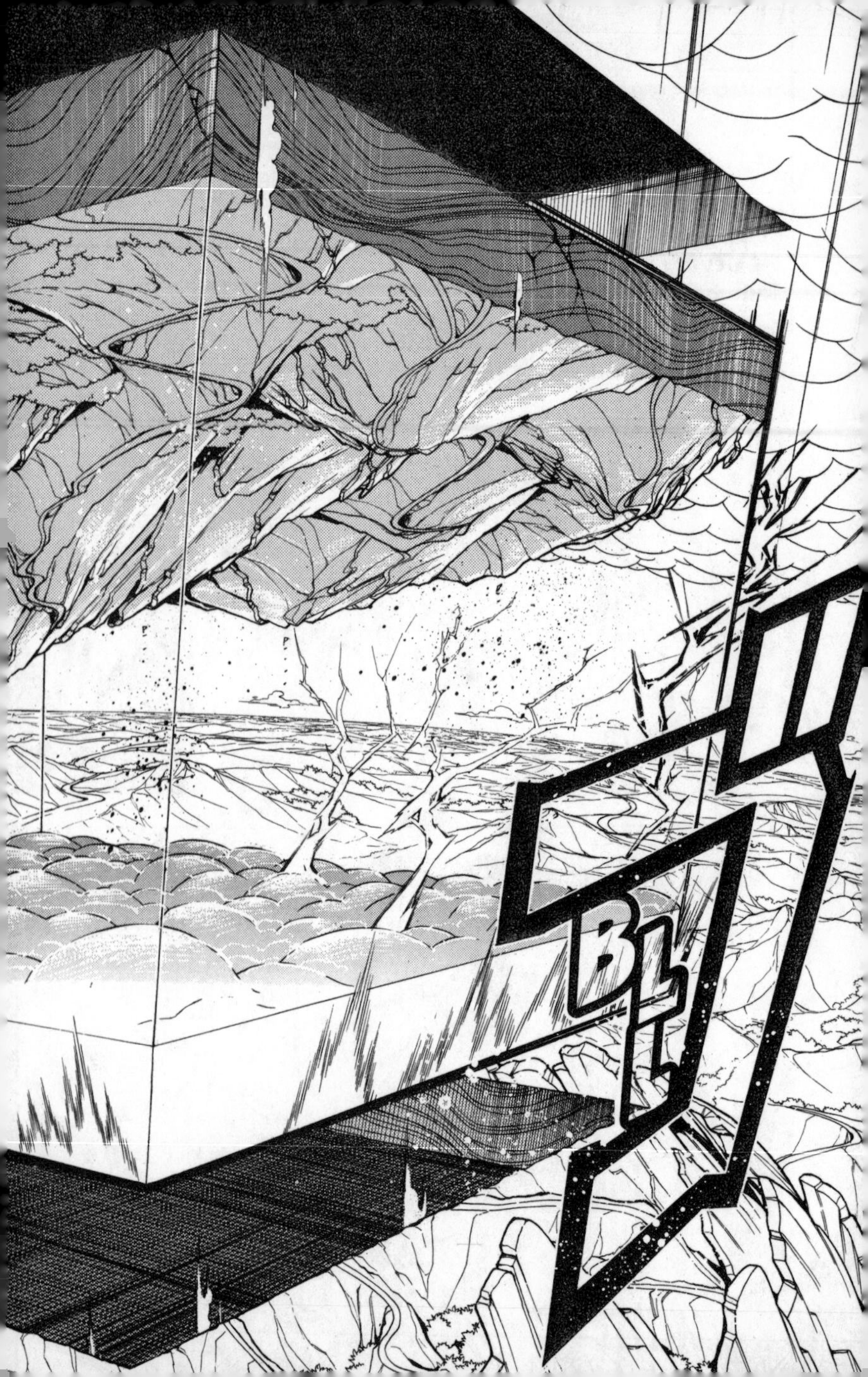
BLL

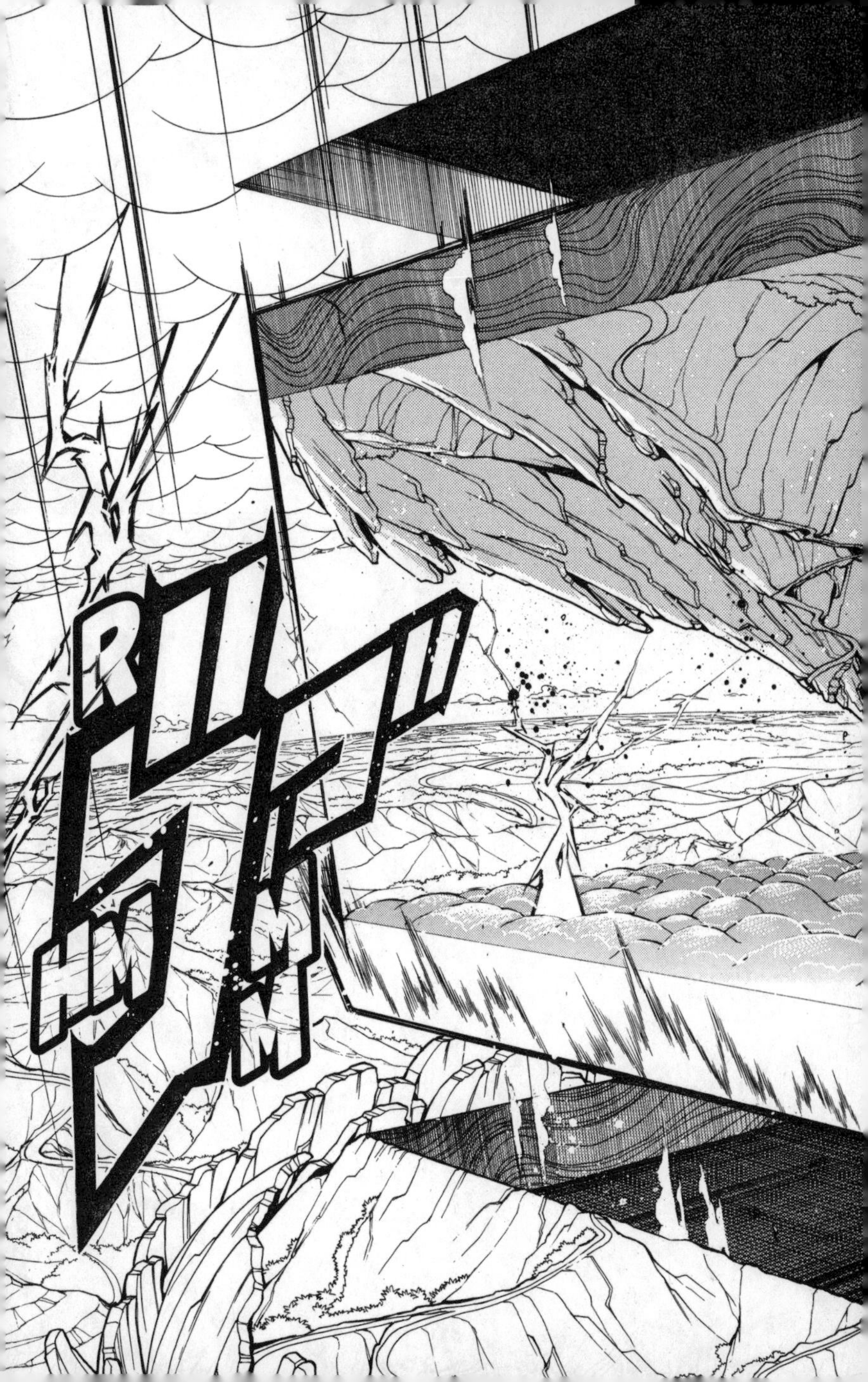

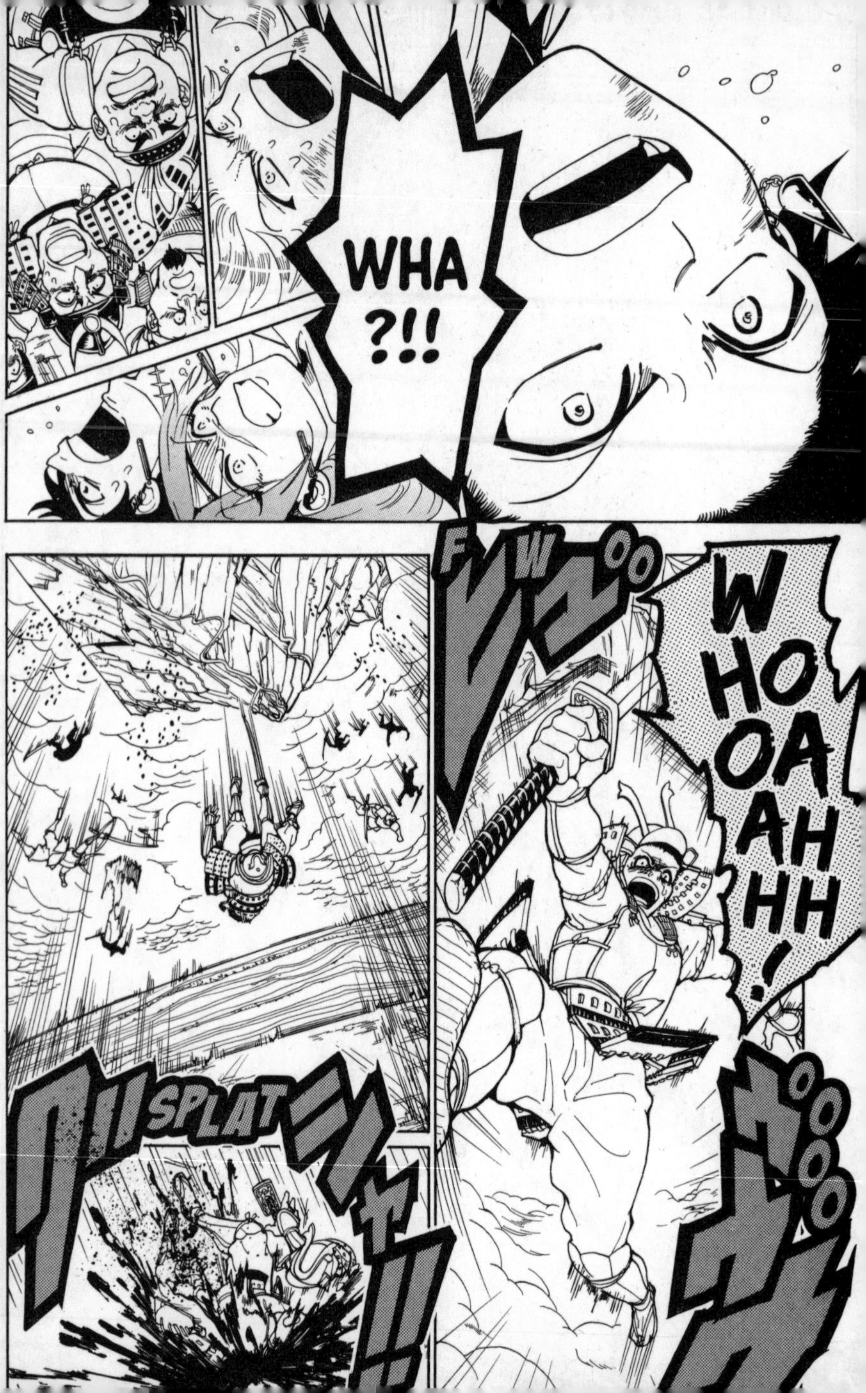
WHA ?!!
FWOO
WHOOAAAHHH!
SPLAT

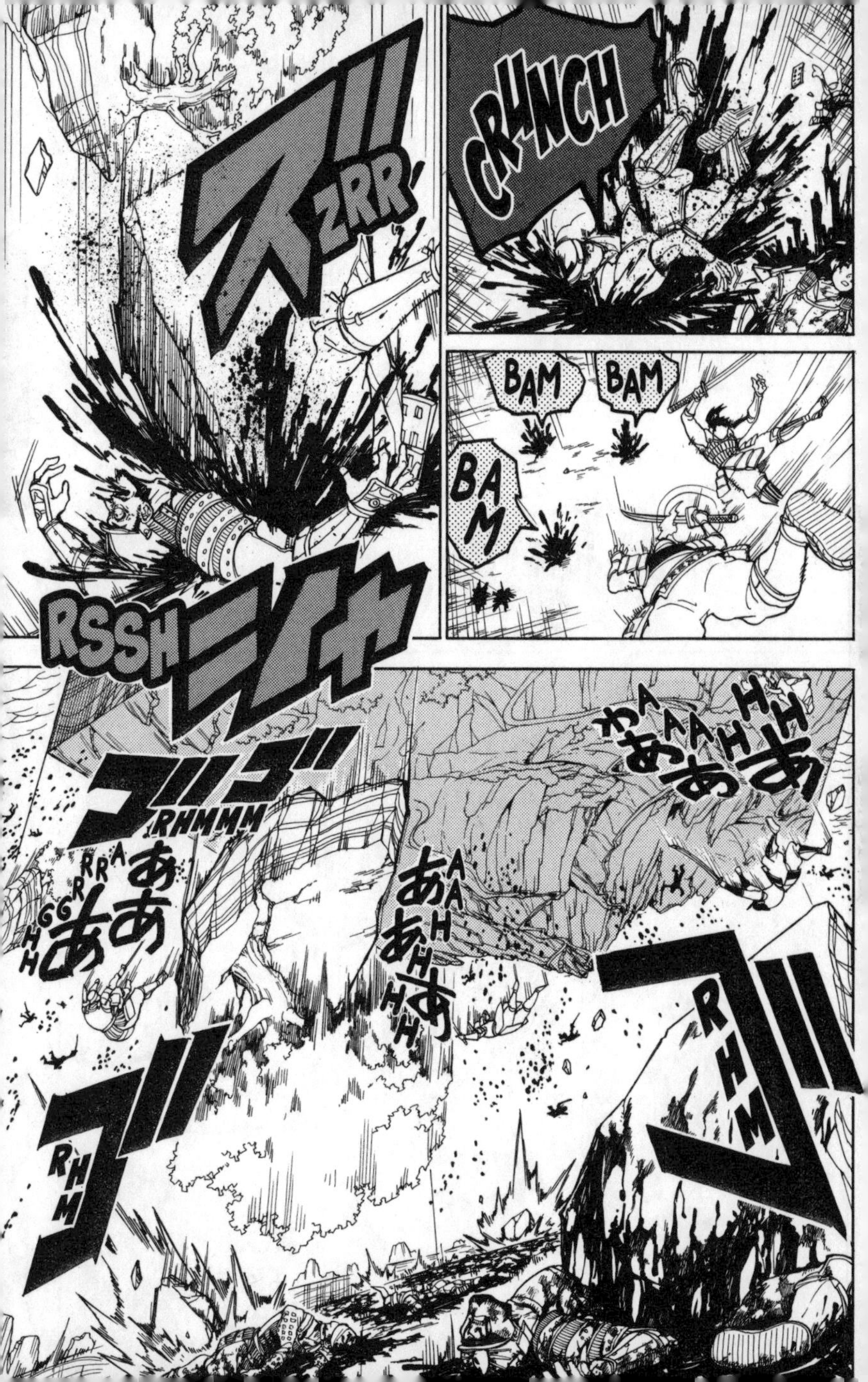
CRUNCH
BAM
BAM
BAM
ZRR
RSSH
AAAHHHH
RHMMMM
AAHHHHH
RHM
RHM

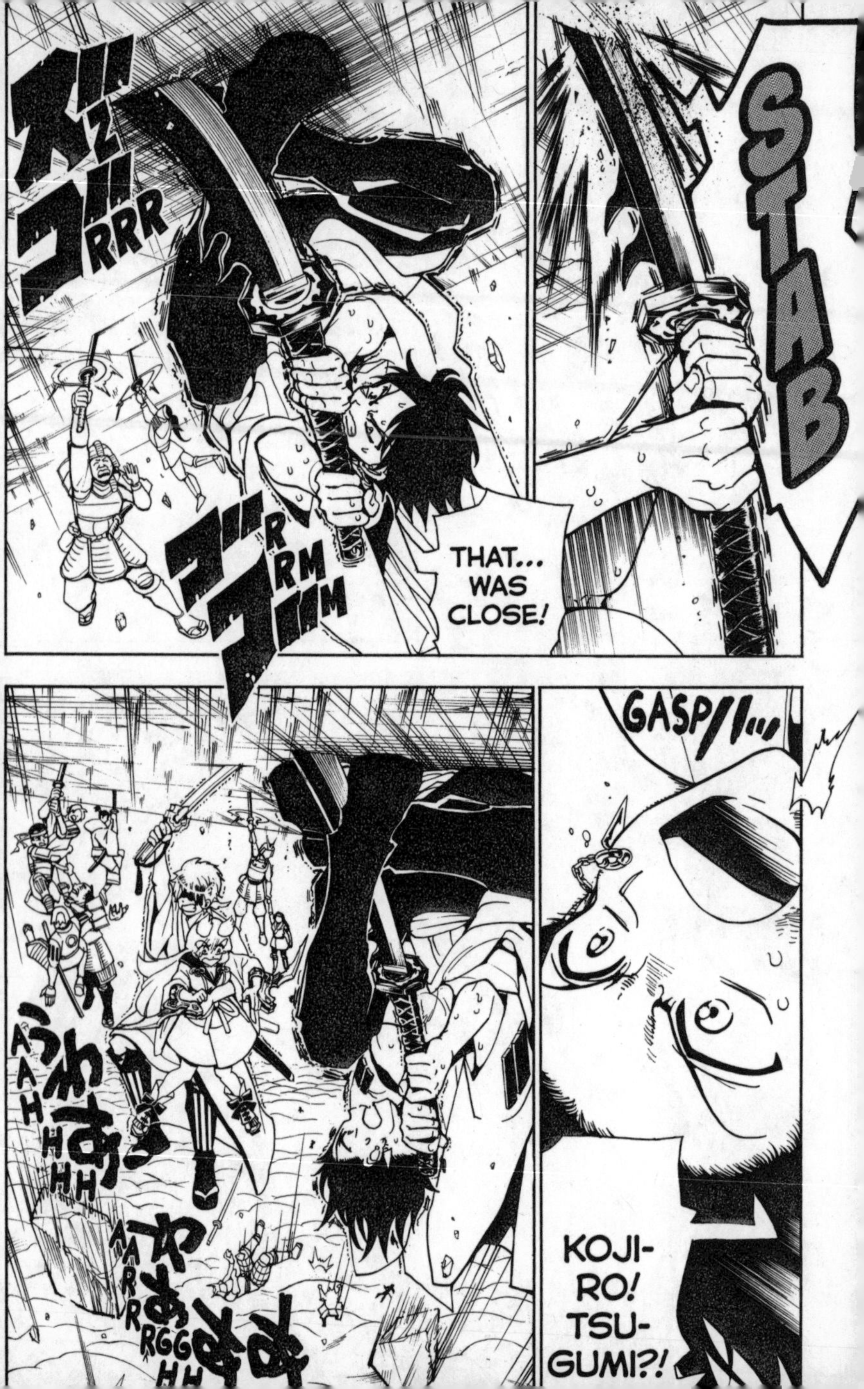
STAB
RRRR
RRMMMM
THAT... WAS CLOSE!
GASP/!...
KOJI-RO! TSU-GUMI?!
AAHHHHH
AARRRGGHH

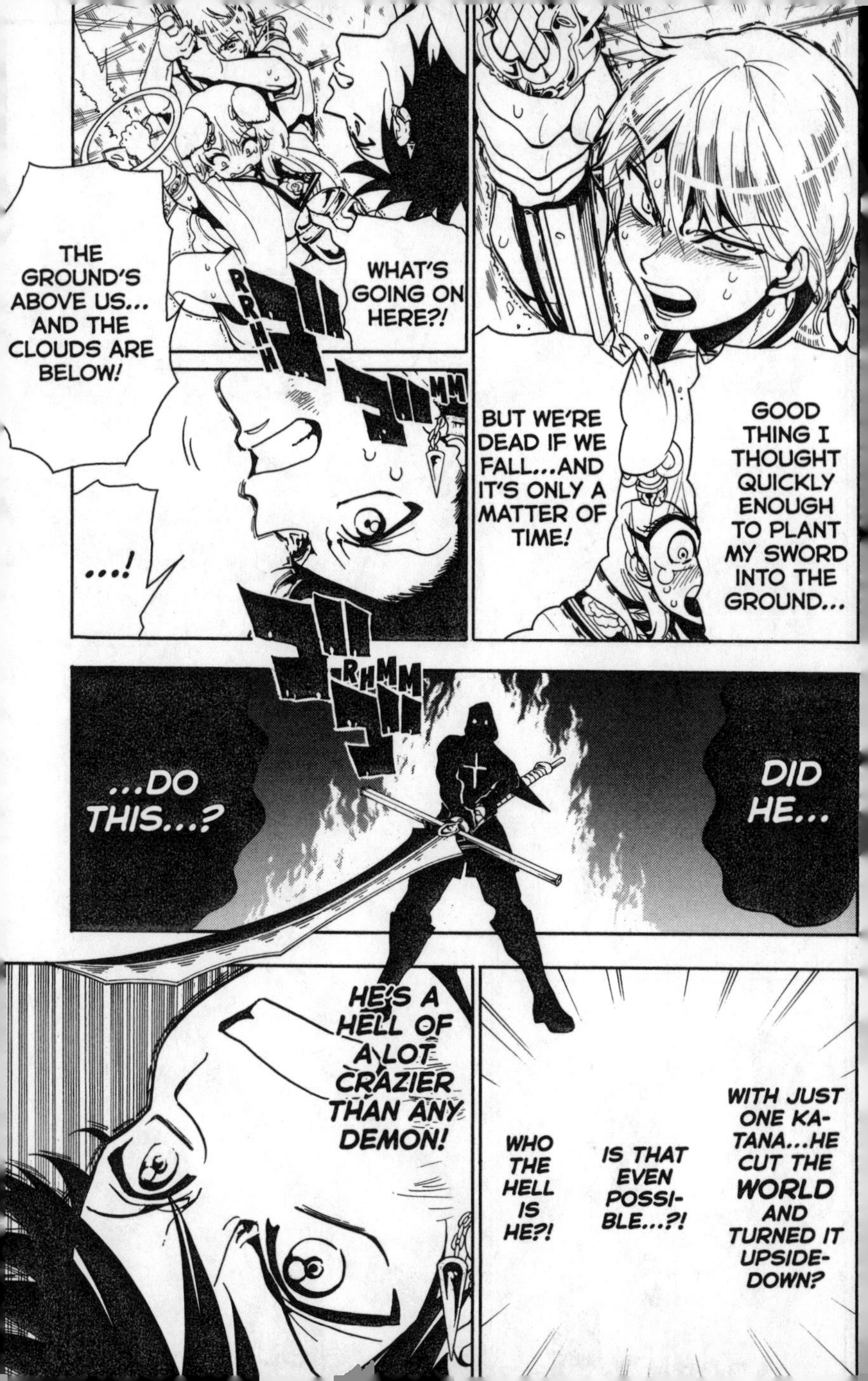
GOOD THING I THOUGHT QUICKLY ENOUGH TO PLANT MY SWORD INTO THE GROUND...
BUT WE'RE DEAD IF WE FALL...AND IT'S ONLY A MATTER OF TIME!
WHAT'S GOING ON HERE?!
THE GROUND'S ABOVE US... AND THE CLOUDS ARE BELOW!
RRHH
MM
...!
DID HE...
...DO THIS...?
-RHMMM
WITH JUST ONE KATANA...HE CUT THE WORLD AND TURNED IT UPSIDE-DOWN?
IS THAT EVEN POSSIBLE...?!
WHO THE HELL IS HE?!
HE'S A HELL OF A LOT CRAZIER THAN ANY DEMON!

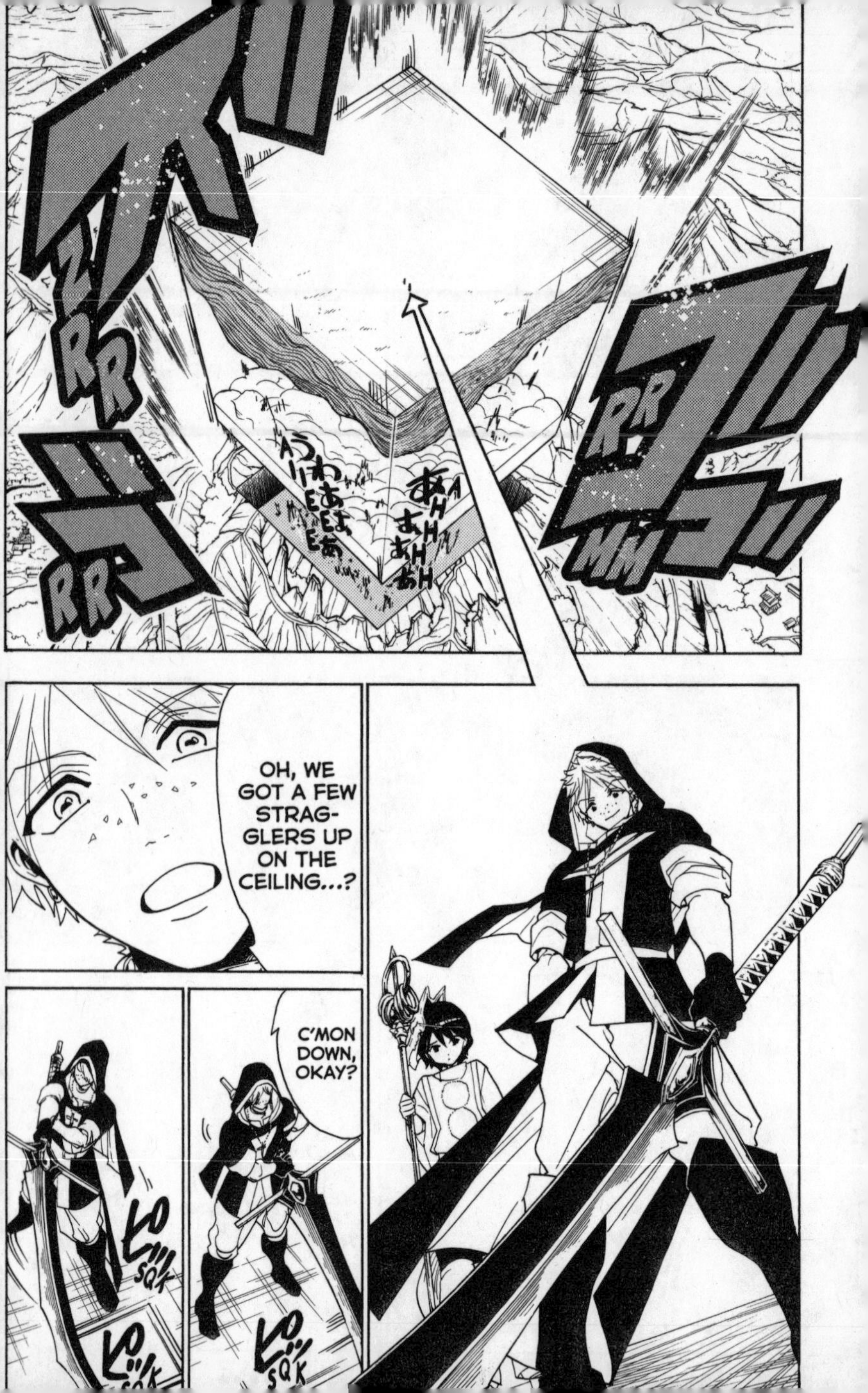
OH, WE GOT A FEW STRAG-GLERS UP ON THE CEILING...?
C'MON DOWN, OKAY?
SQK
SQK

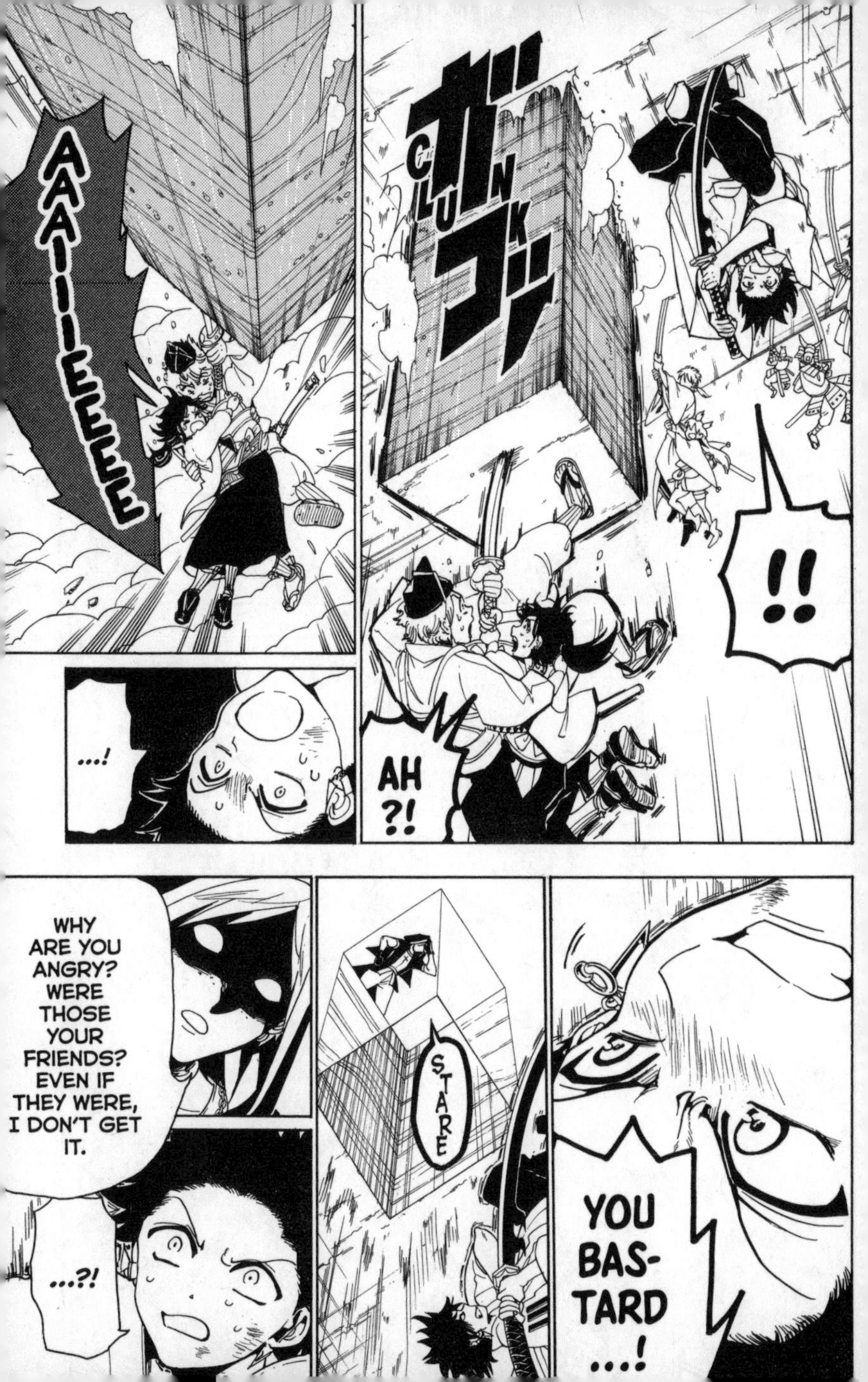
CLUNK
!!
AH ?!
AAAIIIEEEE
...!
YOU BASTARD ...!
STARE
WHY ARE YOU ANGRY? WERE THOSE YOUR FRIENDS? EVEN IF THEY WERE, I DON'T GET IT.
...?!

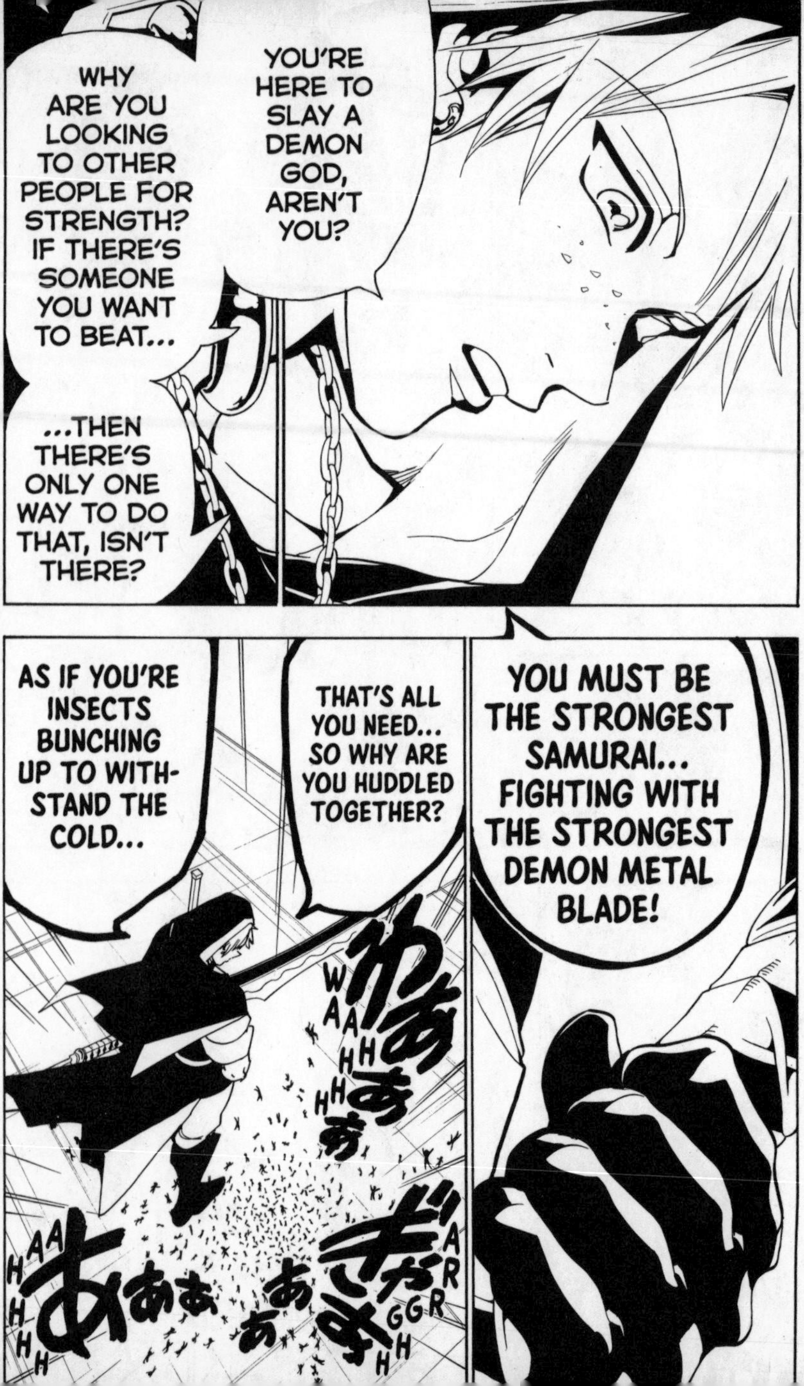
YOU'RE HERE TO SLAY A DEMON GOD, AREN'T YOU?
WHY ARE YOU LOOKING TO OTHER PEOPLE FOR STRENGTH? IF THERE'S SOMEONE YOU WANT TO BEAT...
...THEN THERE'S ONLY ONE WAY TO DO THAT, ISN'T THERE?
YOU MUST BE THE STRONGEST SAMURAI... FIGHTING WITH THE STRONGEST DEMON METAL BLADE!
THAT'S ALL YOU NEED... SO WHY ARE YOU HUDDLED TOGETHER?
AS IF YOU'RE INSECTS BUNCHING UP TO WITH-STAND THE COLD...
WAAHHHH
ARRGGHH
AAHHHHH

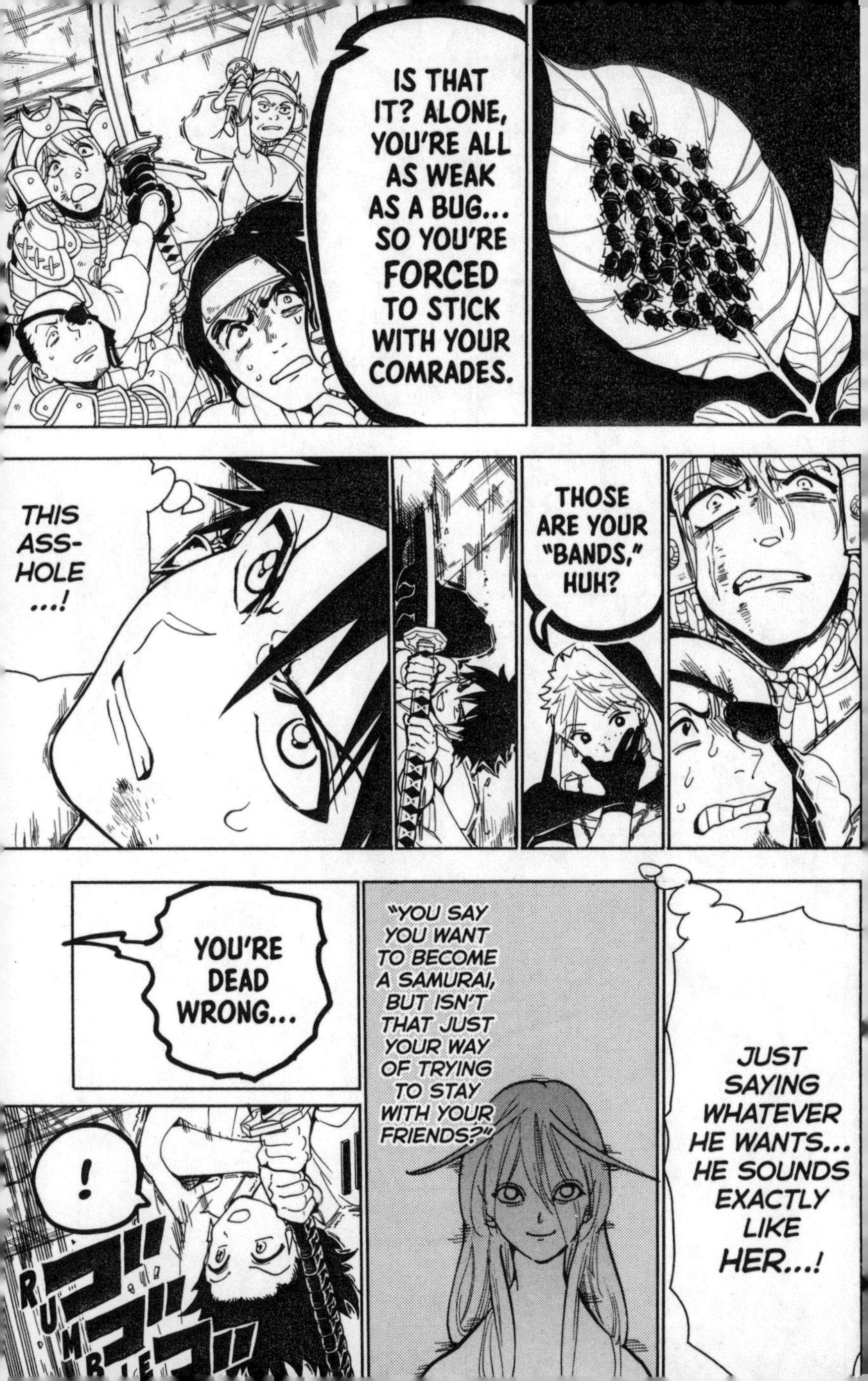
IS THAT IT? ALONE, YOU'RE ALL AS WEAK AS A BUG... SO YOU'RE FORCED TO STICK WITH YOUR COMRADES.
THOSE ARE YOUR "BANDS," HUH?
THIS ASS-HOLE ...!
JUST SAYING WHATEVER HE WANTS... HE SOUNDS EXACTLY LIKE HER...!
"YOU SAY YOU WANT TO BECOME A SAMURAI, BUT ISN'T THAT JUST YOUR WAY OF TRYING TO STAY WITH YOUR FRIENDS?"
YOU'RE DEAD WRONG...
!
RUMBLE

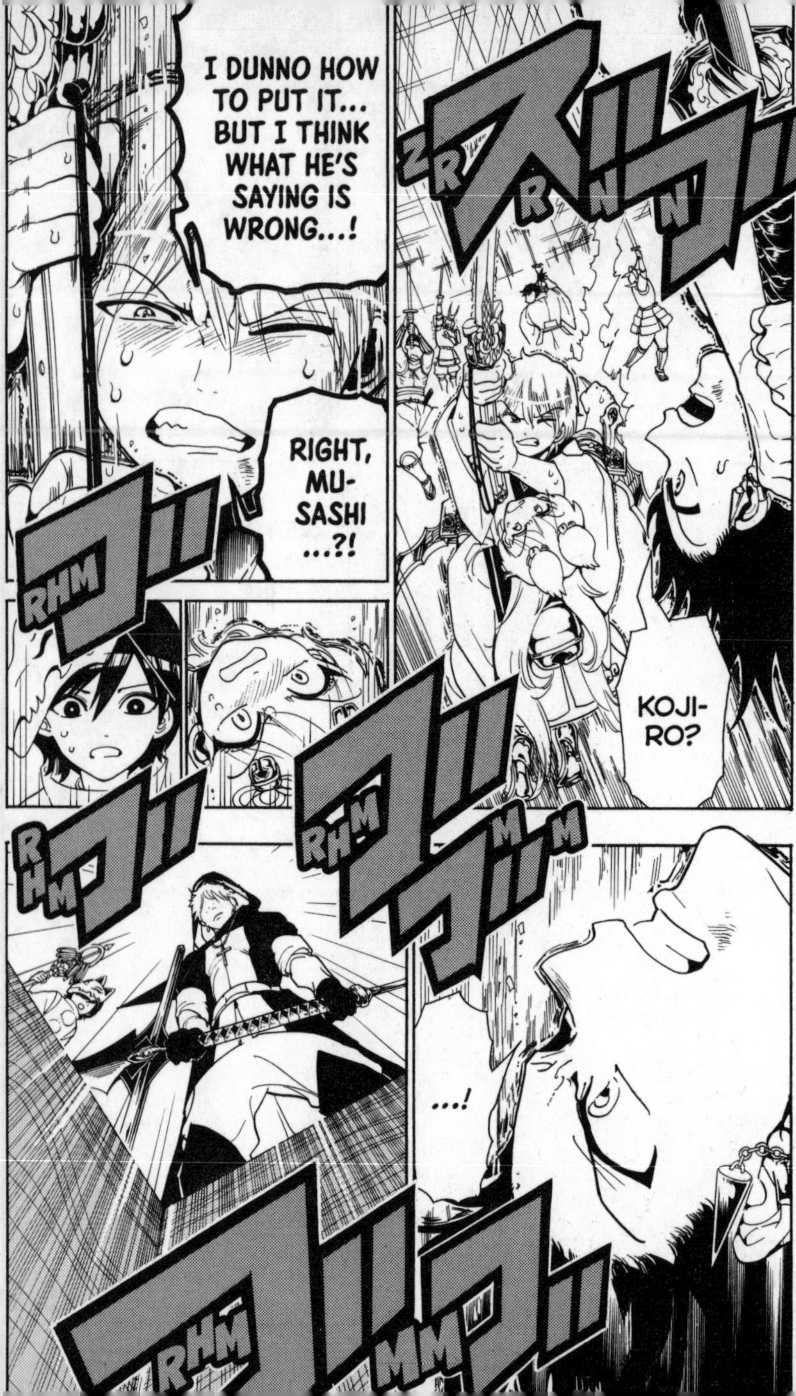
ZRRNN
KOJI-RO?
I DUNNO HOW TO PUT IT... BUT I THINK WHAT HE'S SAYING IS WRONG...!
RIGHT, MU-SASHI ...?!
RHM
RHM
RHM
MMM
...!
RHMMM

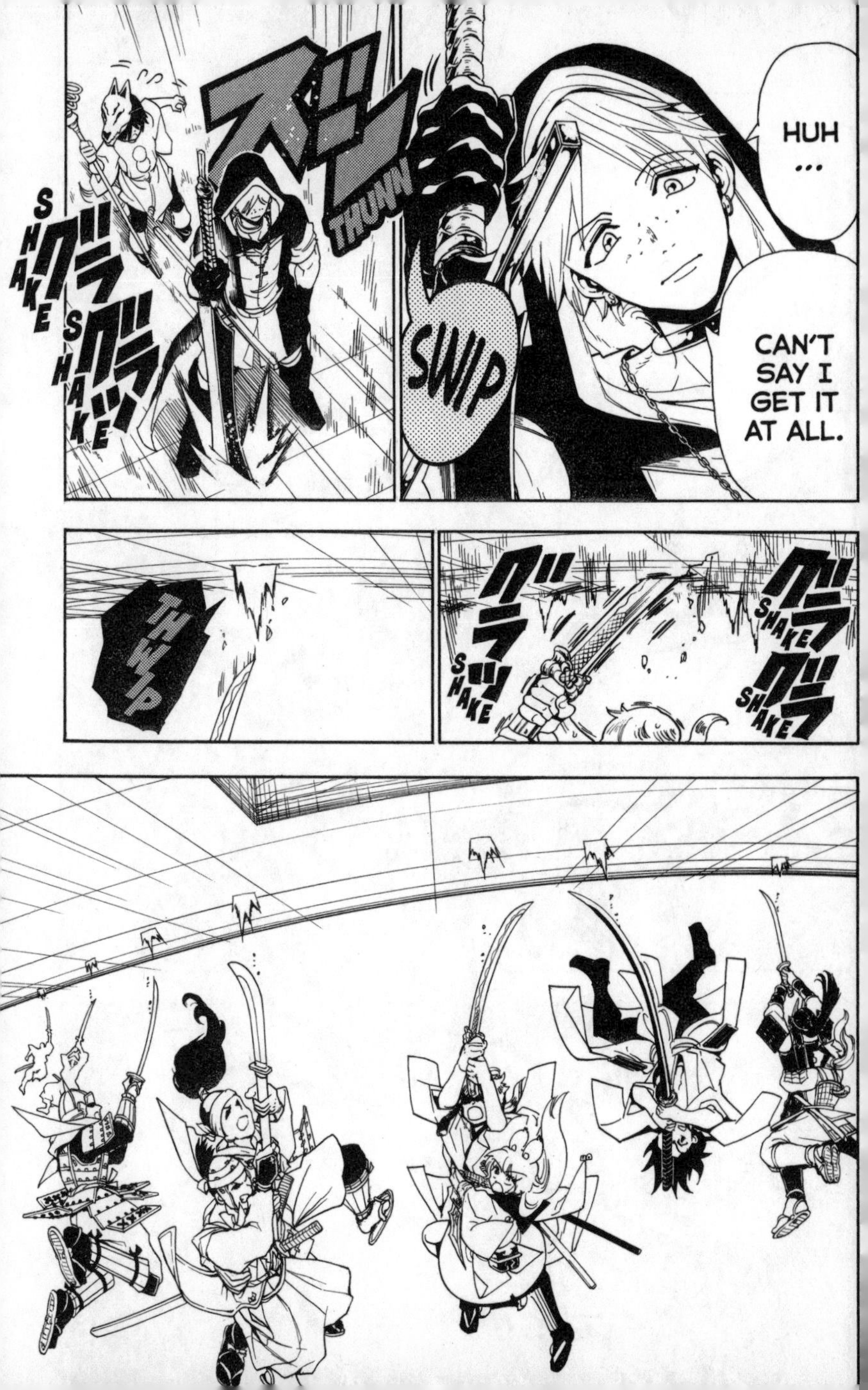
HUH ...
CAN'T SAY I GET IT AT ALL.
SWIP
THUNN
SHAKE
SHAKE
SHAKE
SHAKE
SHAKE
SHAKE
THWIP

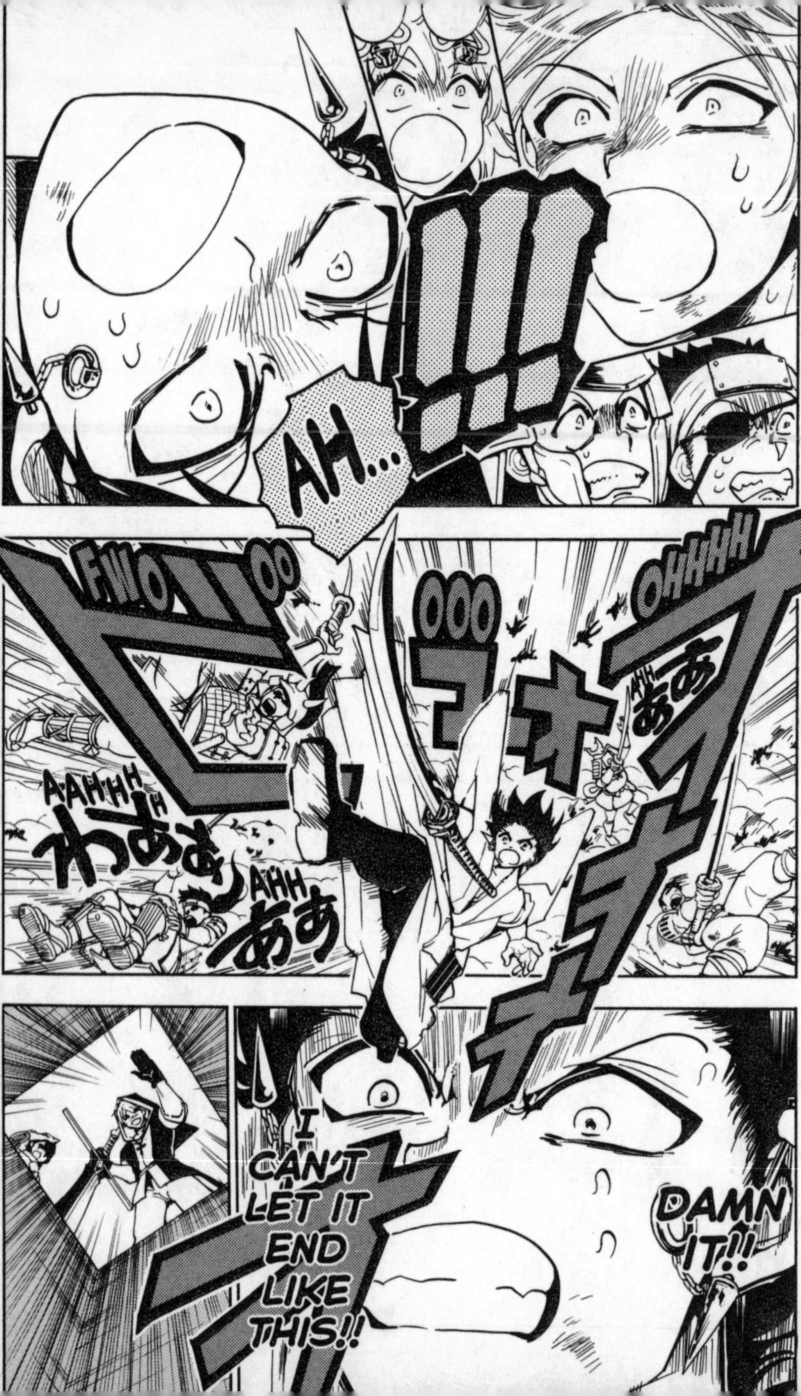
!!
AH...
OHHHH
OOO
OO
AHH
ああ
AAHHHH
わあぁ
AHH
ああ
DAMN IT!!
I CAN'T LET IT END LIKE THIS!!

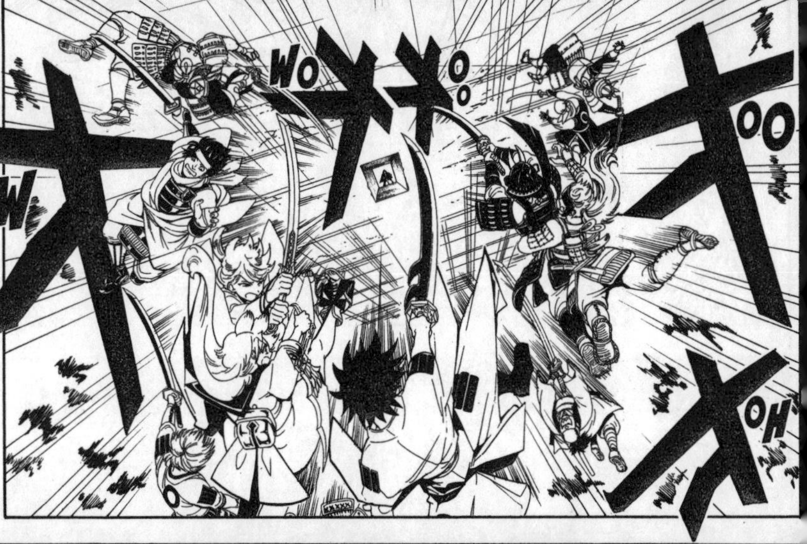
FW
WO
OO
OO
OH
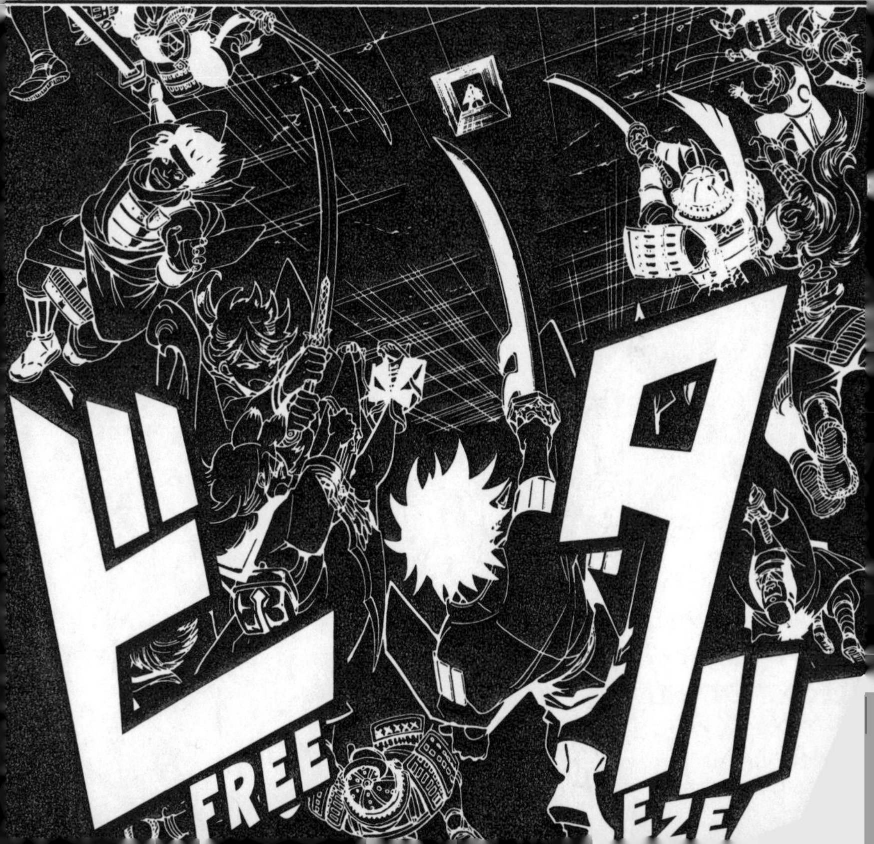
FREE
EZE

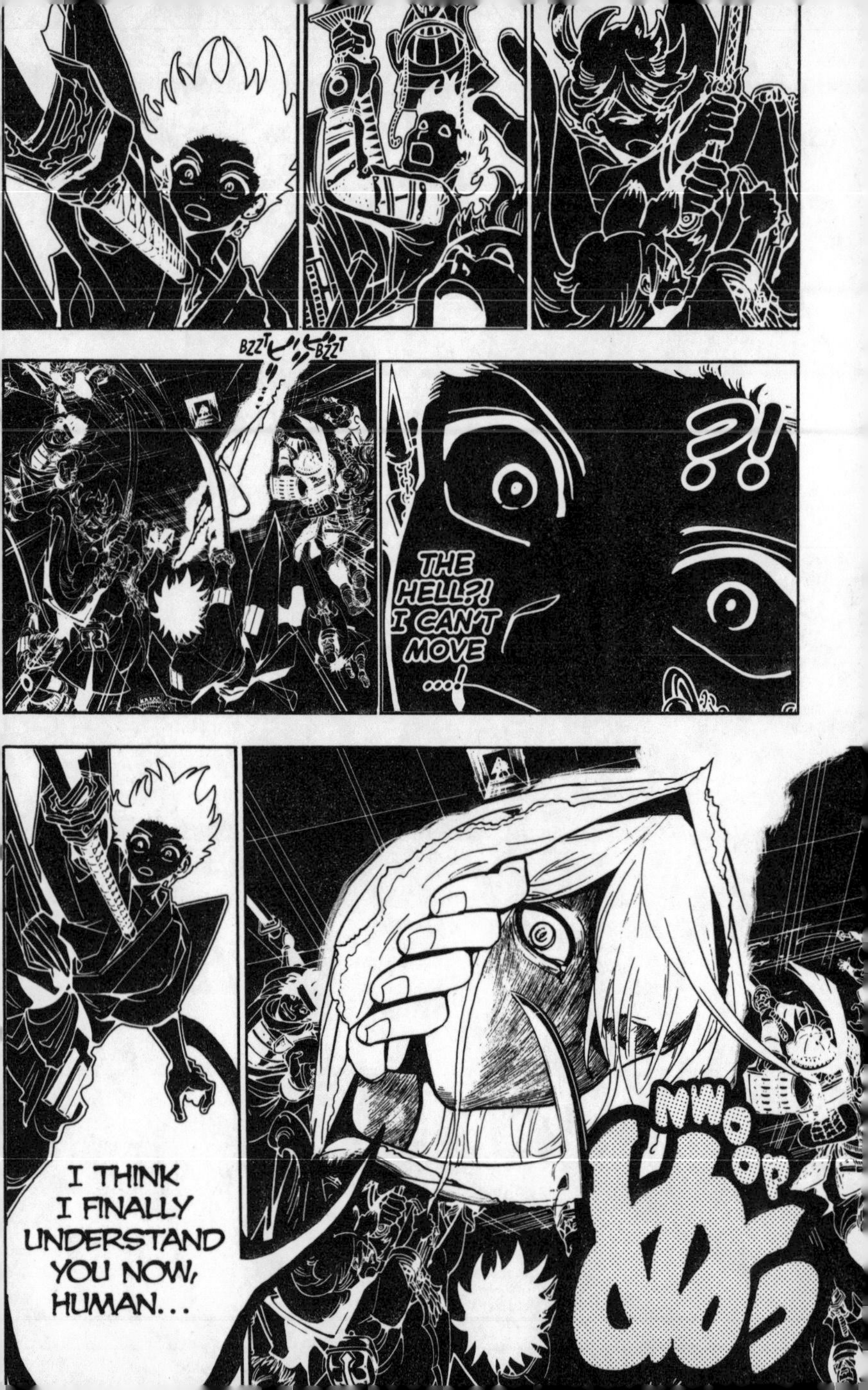
?!
THE HELL?! I CAN'T MOVE ...!
BZZT ビッ
ビッ BZZT
NWOOP
I THINK I FINALLY UNDERSTAND YOU NOW, HUMAN...

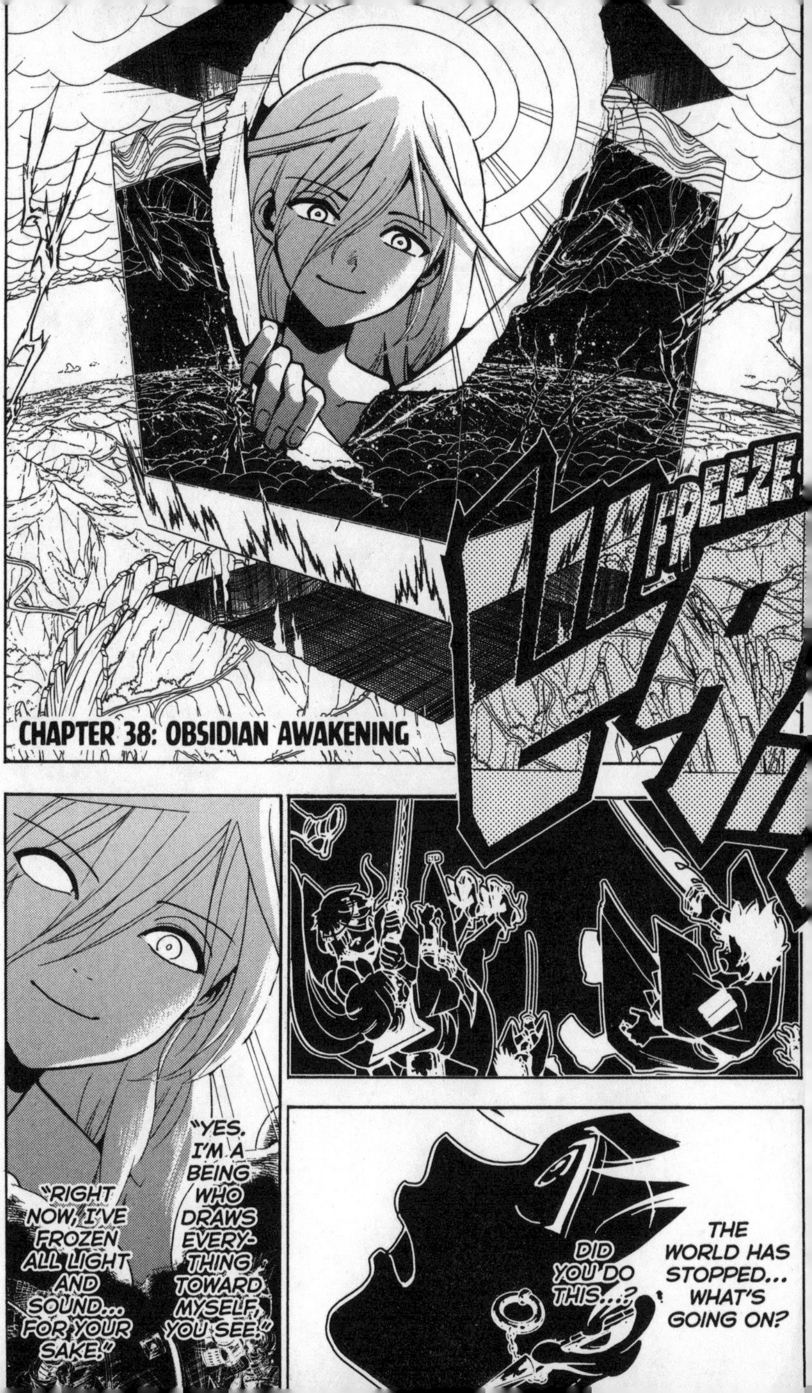
CHAPTER 38: OBSIDIAN AWAKENING
FREEZE
THE WORLD HAS STOPPED... WHAT'S GOING ON?
DID YOU DO THIS...?
"YES. I'M A BEING WHO DRAWS EVERYTHING TOWARD MYSELF, YOU SEE."
"RIGHT NOW, I'VE FROZEN ALL LIGHT AND SOUND... FOR YOUR SAKE."

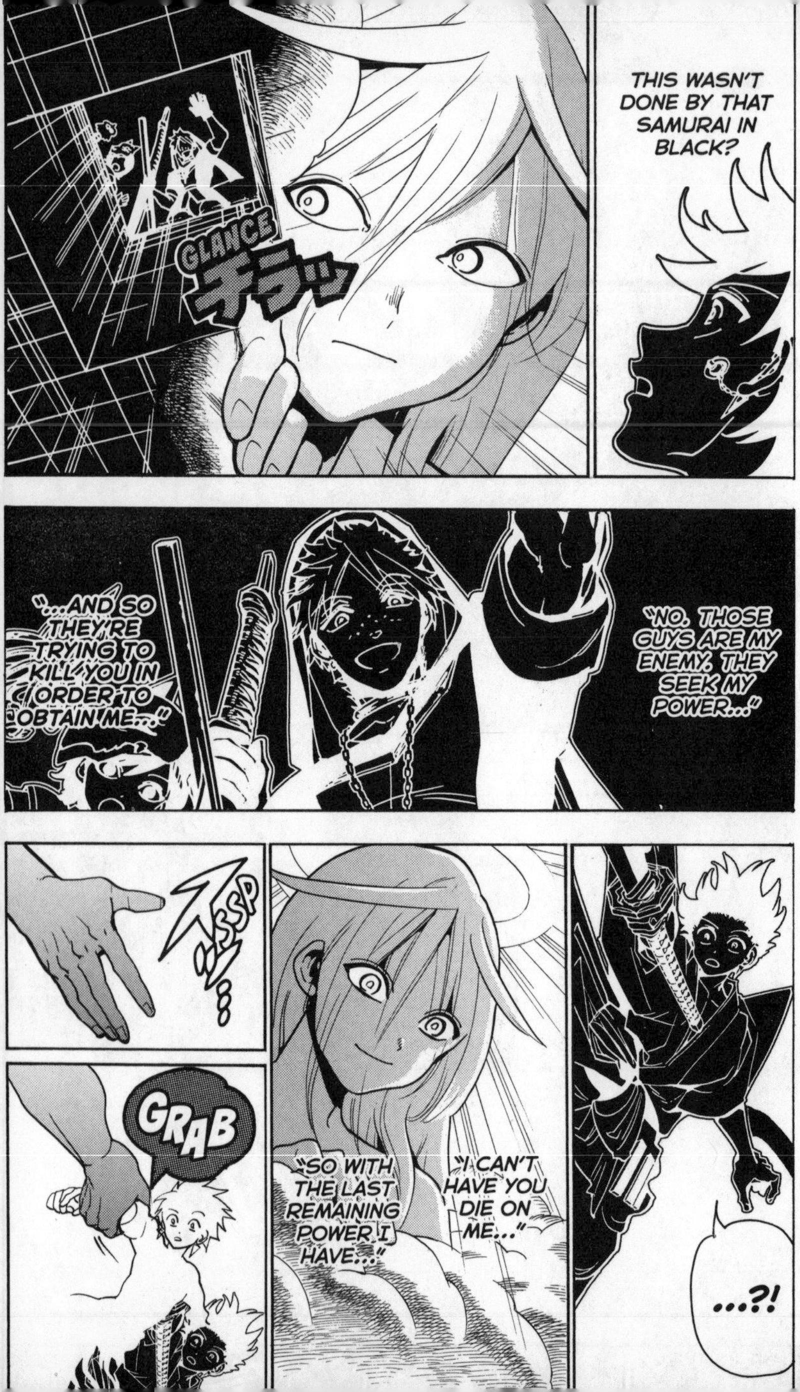
THIS WASN'T DONE BY THAT SAMURAI IN BLACK?
GLANCE
"NO. THOSE GUYS ARE MY ENEMY. THEY SEEK MY POWER..."
"...AND SO THEY'RE TRYING TO KILL YOU IN ORDER TO OBTAIN ME..."
...?!
"I CAN'T HAVE YOU DIE ON ME..."
"SO WITH THE LAST REMAINING POWER I HAVE..."
ZSSP
GRAB

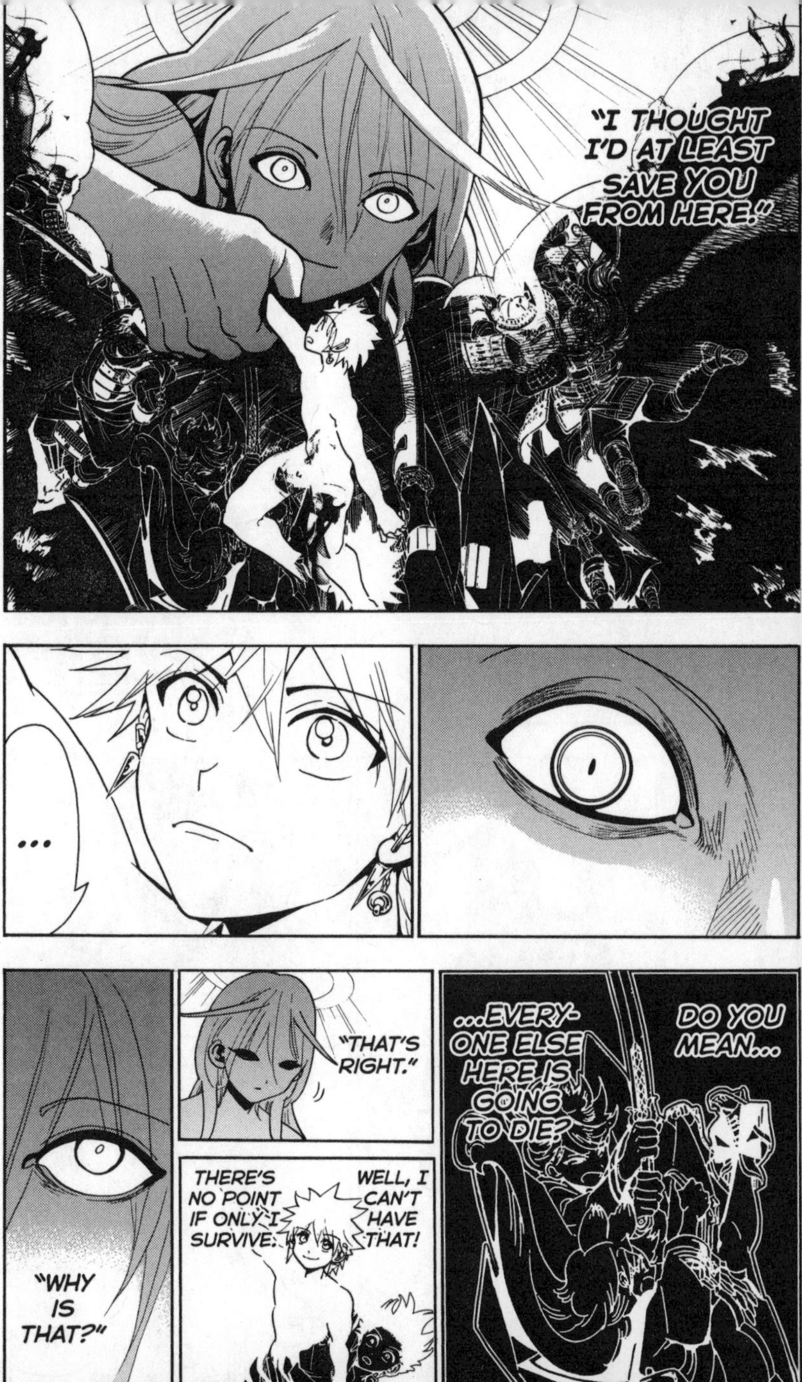
"I THOUGHT I'D AT LEAST SAVE YOU FROM HERE."
...
DO YOU MEAN...
...EVERY-ONE ELSE HERE IS GOING TO DIE?
"THAT'S RIGHT."
WELL, I CAN'T HAVE THAT!
THERE'S NO POINT IF ONLY I SURVIVE.
"WHY IS THAT?"

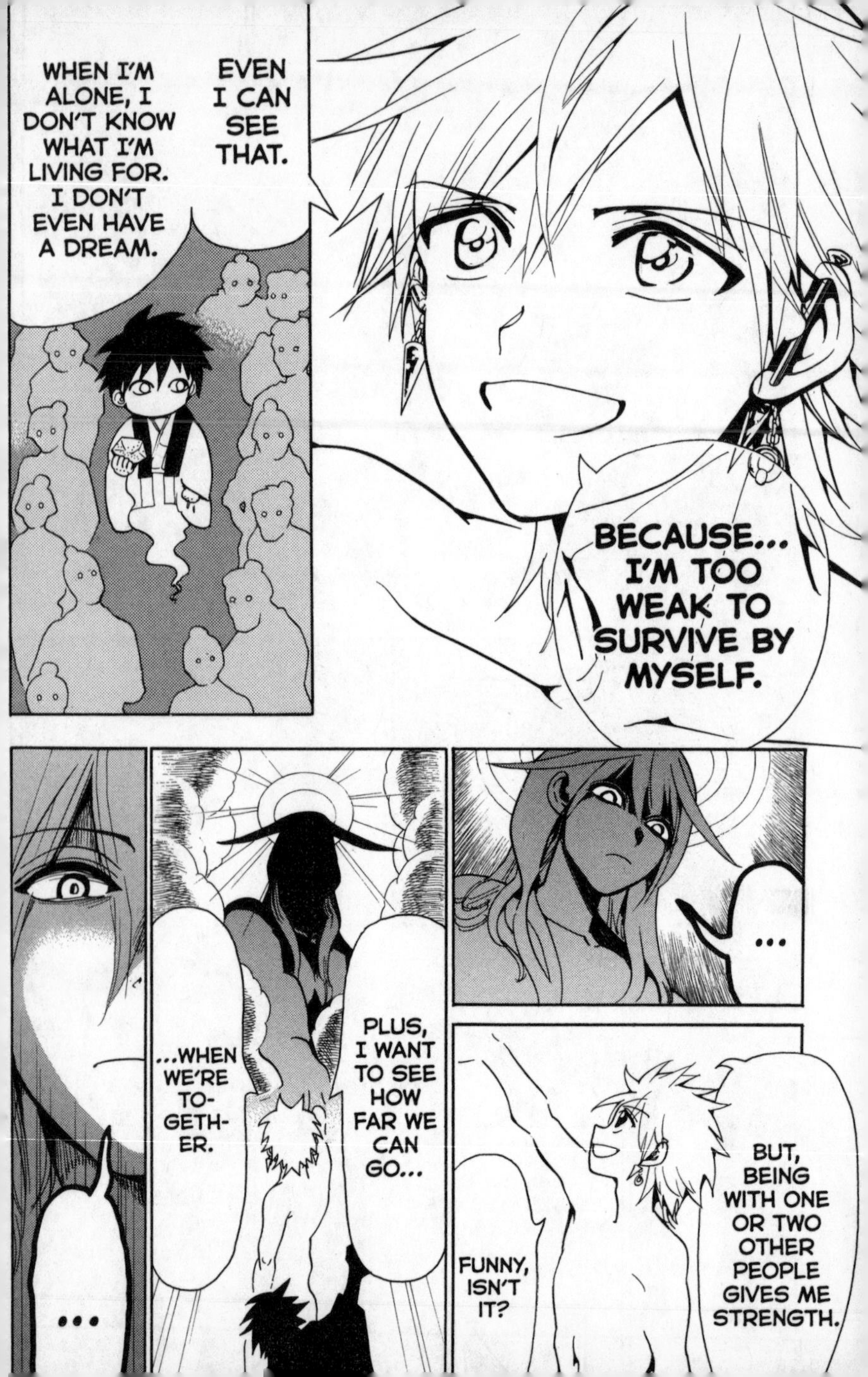
EVEN I CAN SEE THAT.
WHEN I'M ALONE, I DON'T KNOW WHAT I'M LIVING FOR. I DON'T EVEN HAVE A DREAM.
BECAUSE... I'M TOO WEAK TO SURVIVE BY MYSELF.
...
BUT, BEING WITH ONE OR TWO OTHER PEOPLE GIVES ME STRENGTH.
FUNNY, ISN'T IT?
PLUS, I WANT TO SEE HOW FAR WE CAN GO...
...WHEN WE'RE TO-GETH-ER.
...

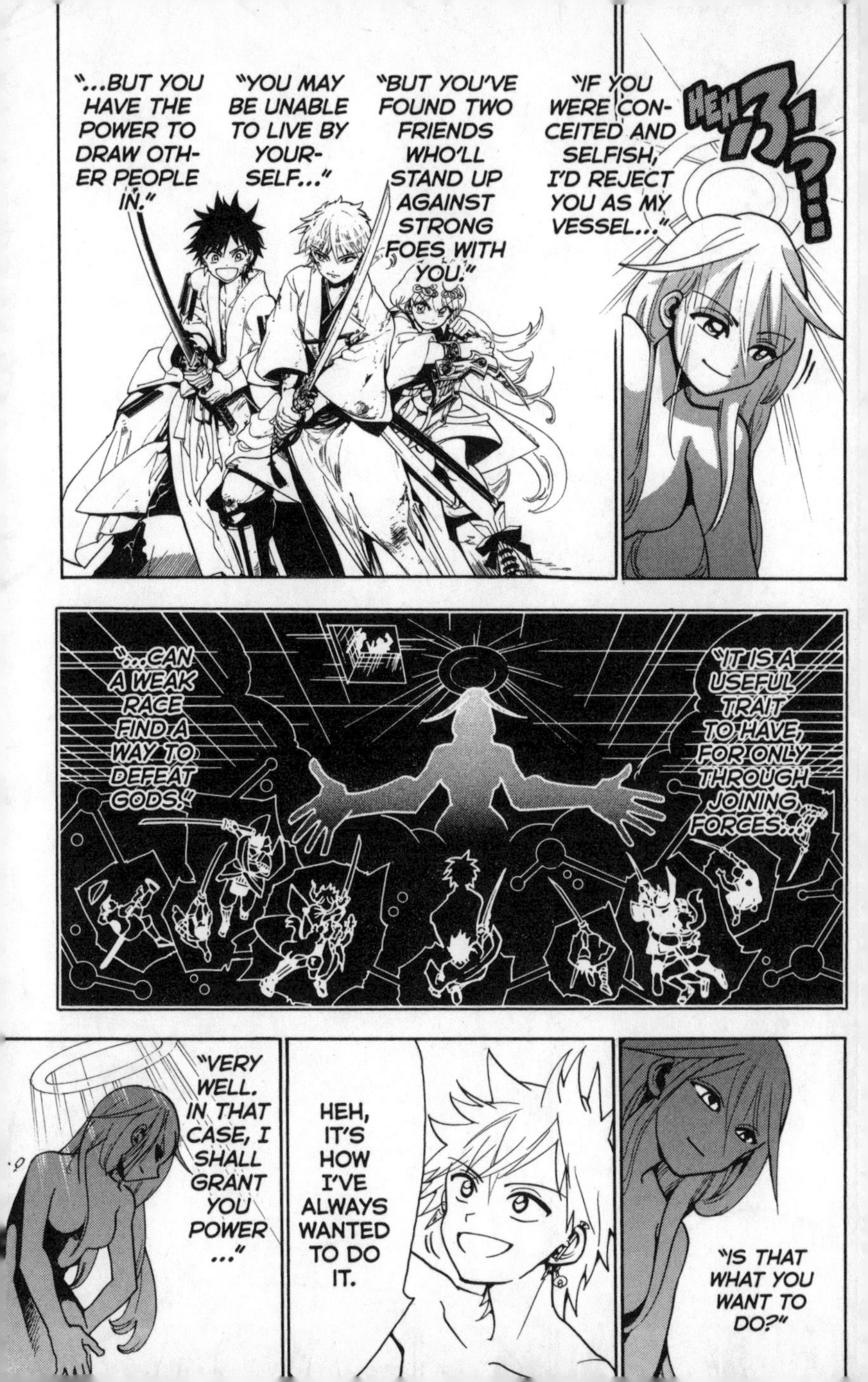
HEH
"IF YOU WERE CONCEITED AND SELFISH, I'D REJECT YOU AS MY VESSEL..."
"BUT YOU'VE FOUND TWO FRIENDS WHO'LL STAND UP AGAINST STRONG FOES WITH YOU."
"YOU MAY BE UNABLE TO LIVE BY YOURSELF..."
"...BUT YOU HAVE THE POWER TO DRAW OTHER PEOPLE IN."
"IT IS A USEFUL TRAIT TO HAVE, FOR ONLY THROUGH JOINING FORCES..."
"...CAN A WEAK RACE FIND A WAY TO DEFEAT GODS."
"IS THAT WHAT YOU WANT TO DO?"
HEH, IT'S HOW I'VE ALWAYS WANTED TO DO IT.
"VERY WELL. IN THAT CASE, I SHALL GRANT YOU POWER ..."

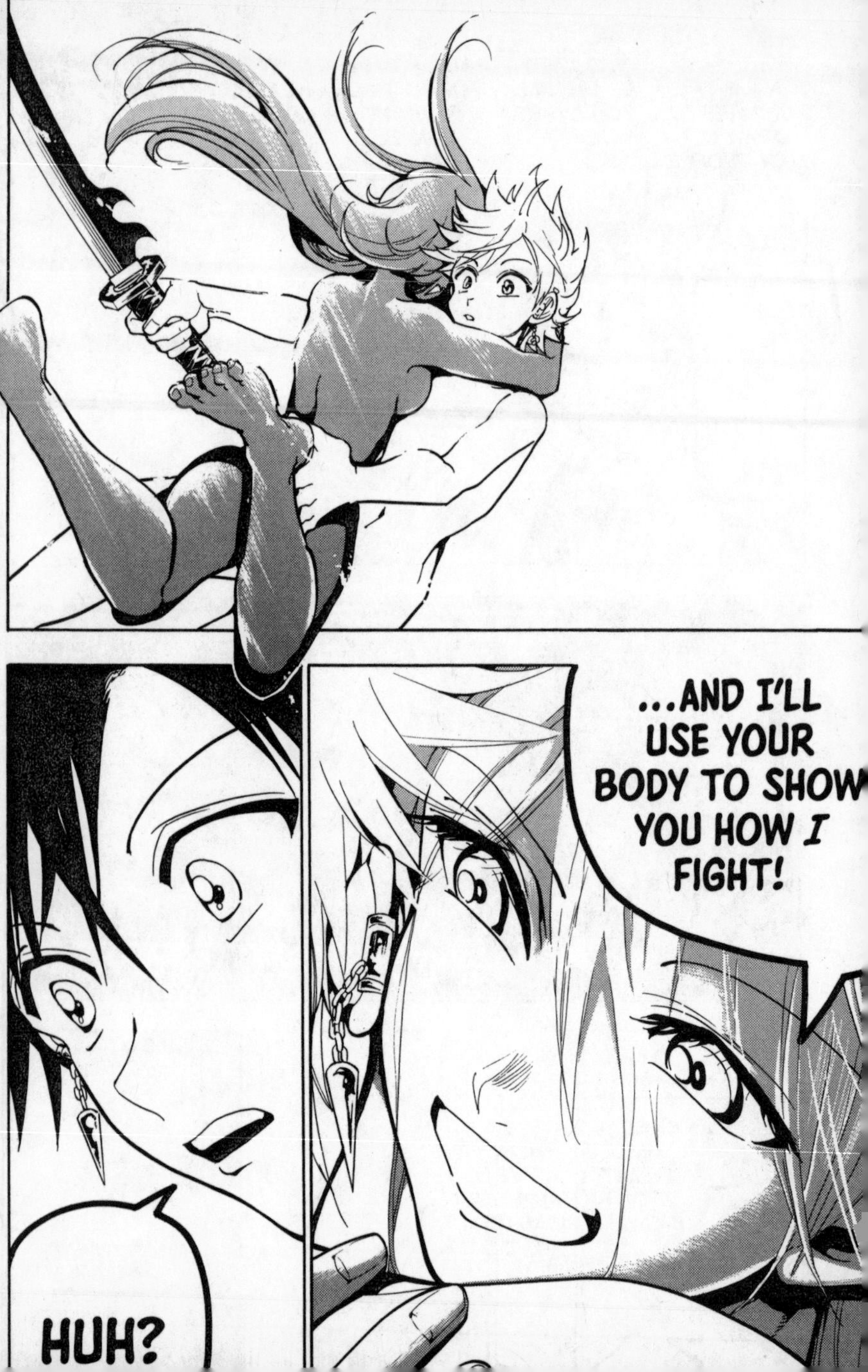
...AND I'LL USE YOUR BODY TO SHOW YOU HOW *I* FIGHT!
HUH?

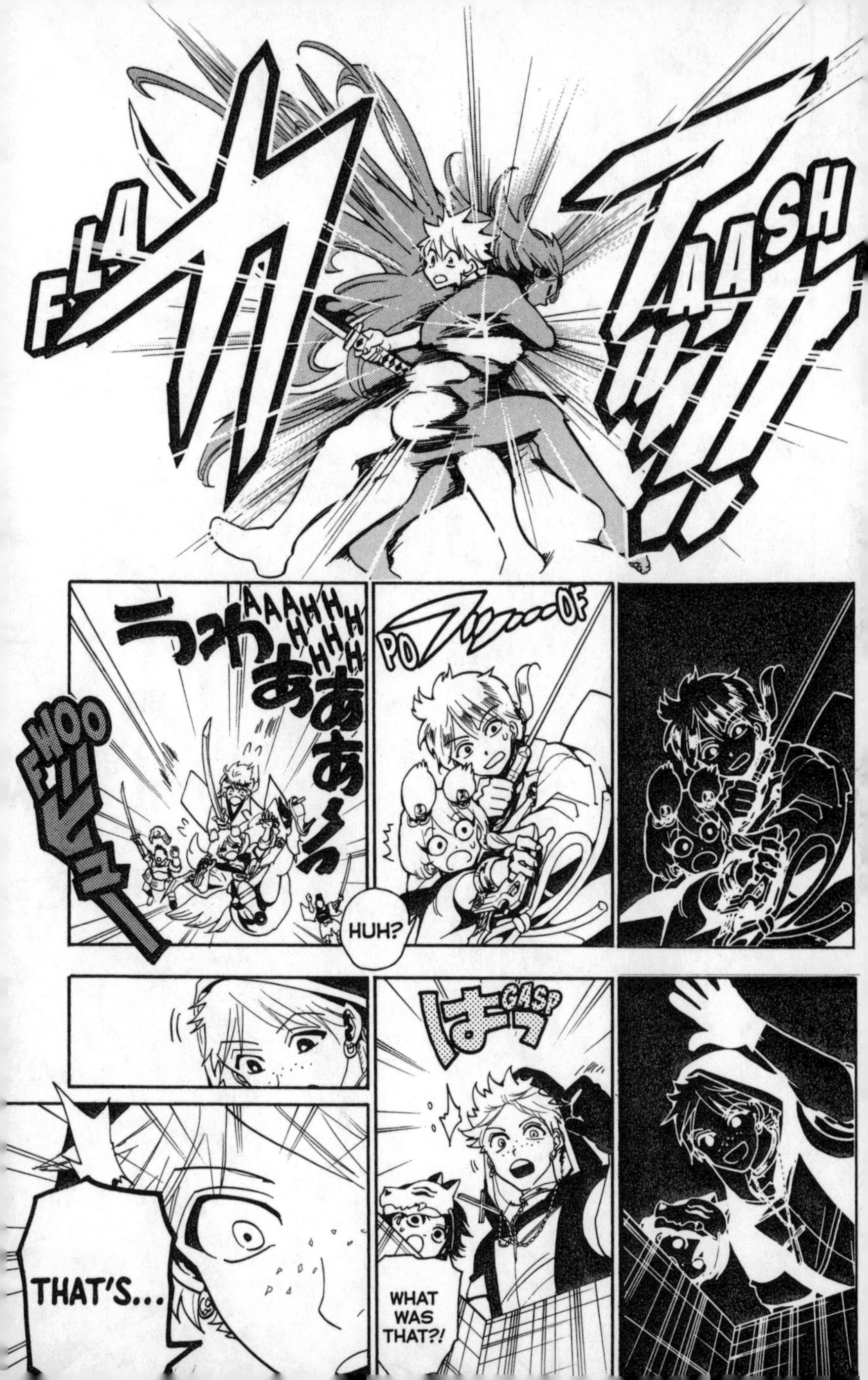
FLAAASH
POFOF
HUH?
うっわあああ〜っ
AAAHHHHHHHHH
ヒュ
FWOO
はっ
GASP
WHAT WAS THAT?!
THAT'S...

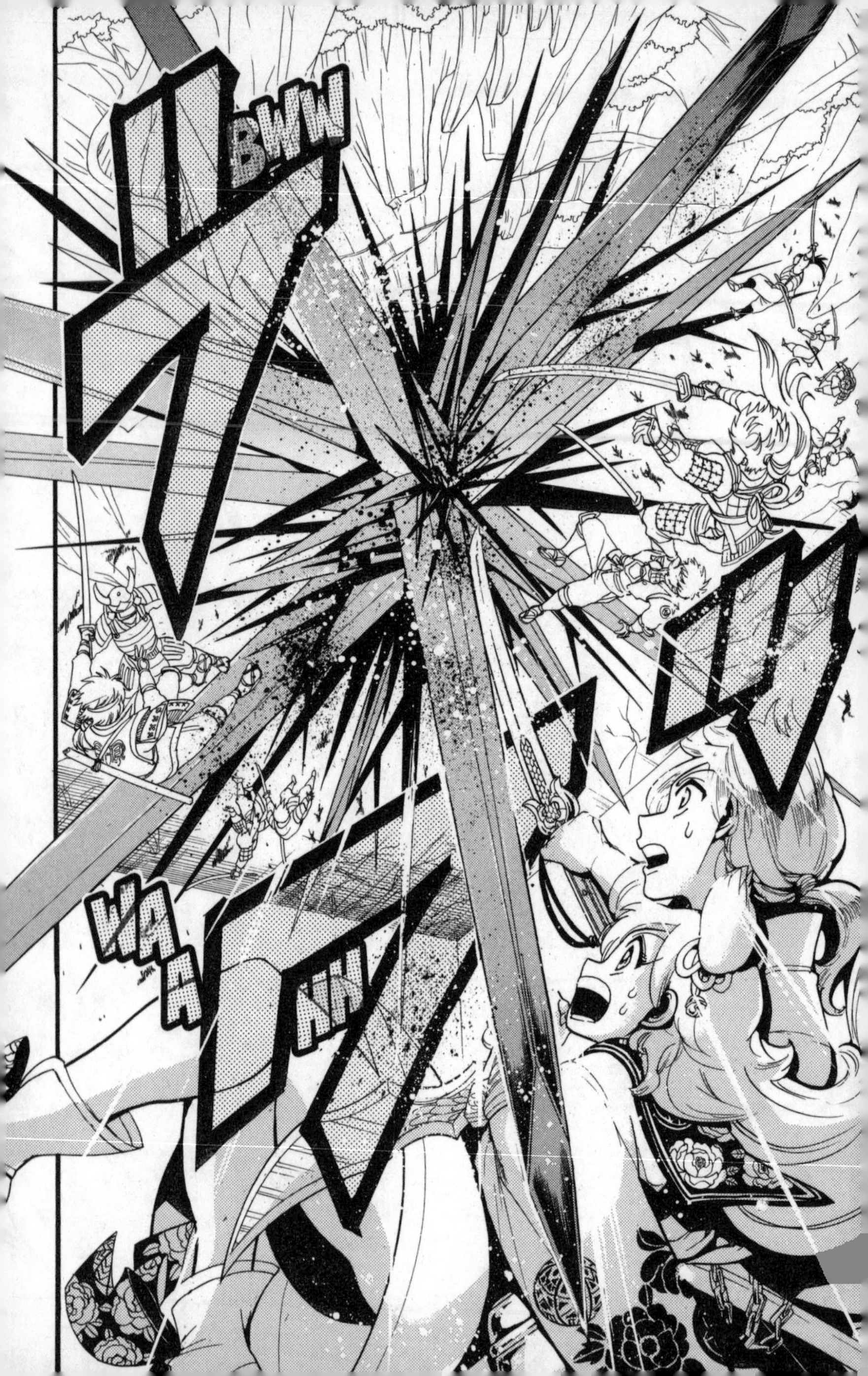
BWW
WAAAHH

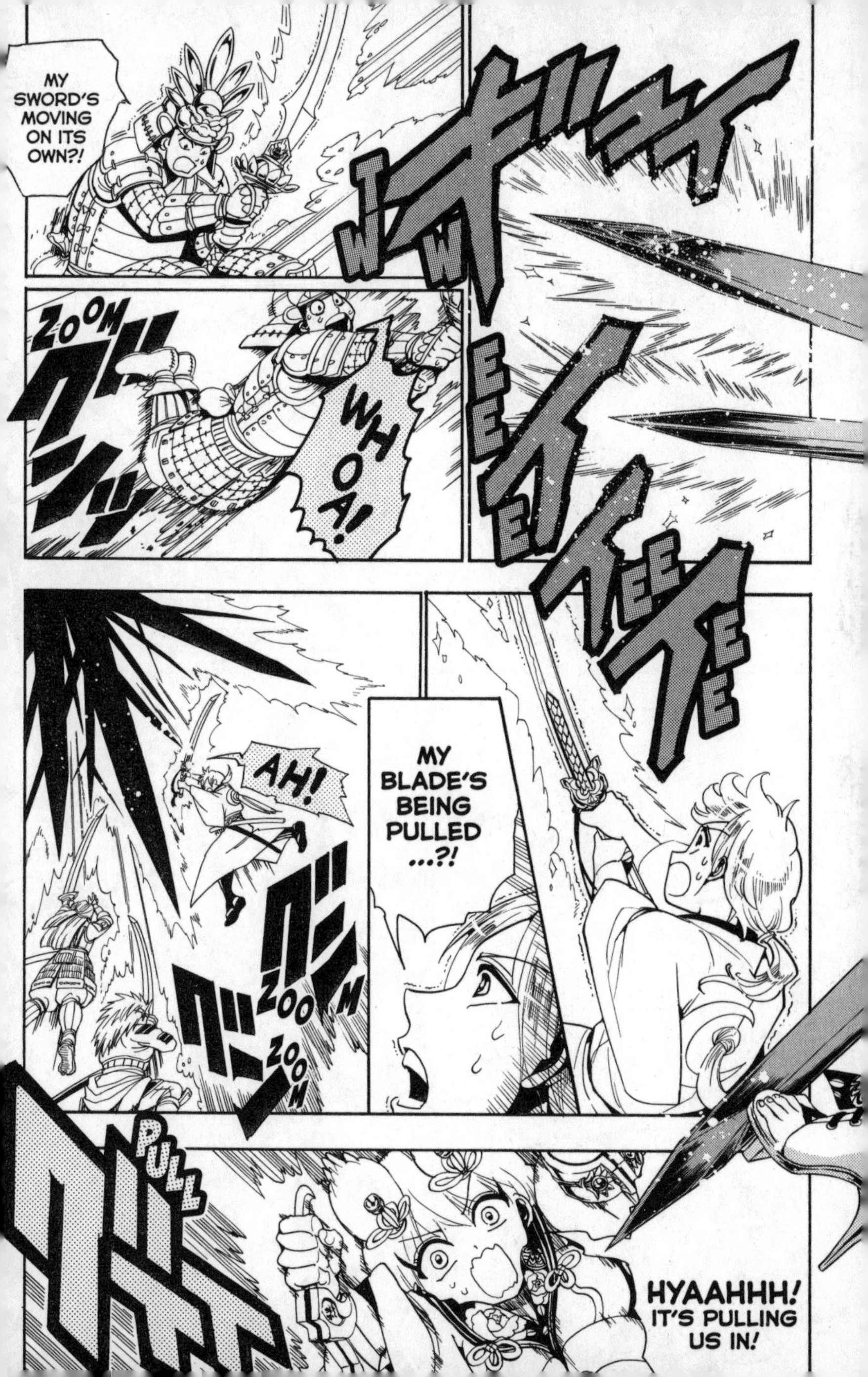

TWWEEE
TEEEE
MY SWORD'S MOVING ON ITS OWN?!
ZOOM
WHOA!
MY BLADE'S BEING PULLED...?!
AH!
ZOOM
ZOOM
PULL
HYAAHHH! IT'S PULLING US IN!

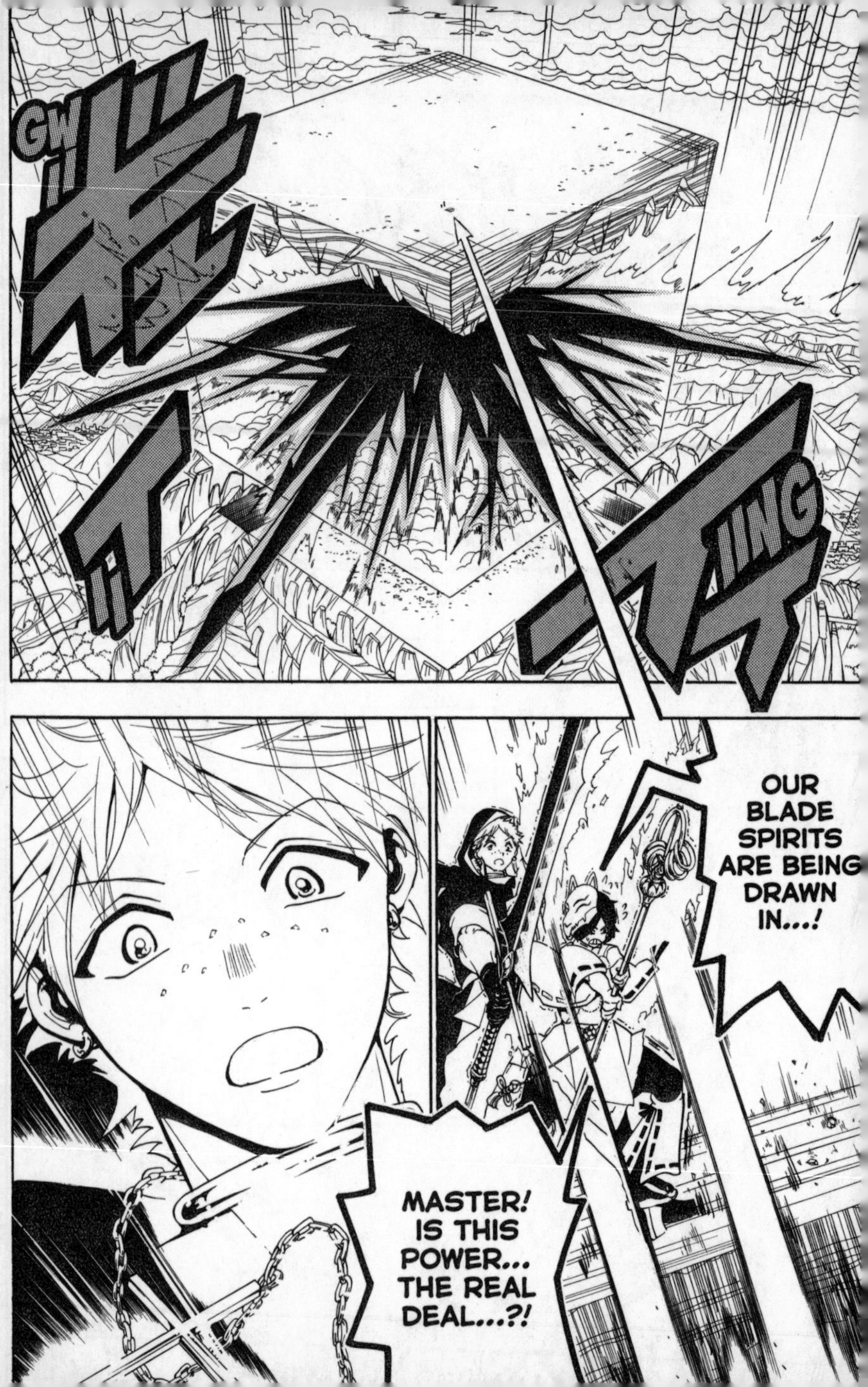
GW
IING
OUR BLADE SPIRITS ARE BEING DRAWN IN...!
MASTER! IS THIS POWER... THE REAL DEAL...?!

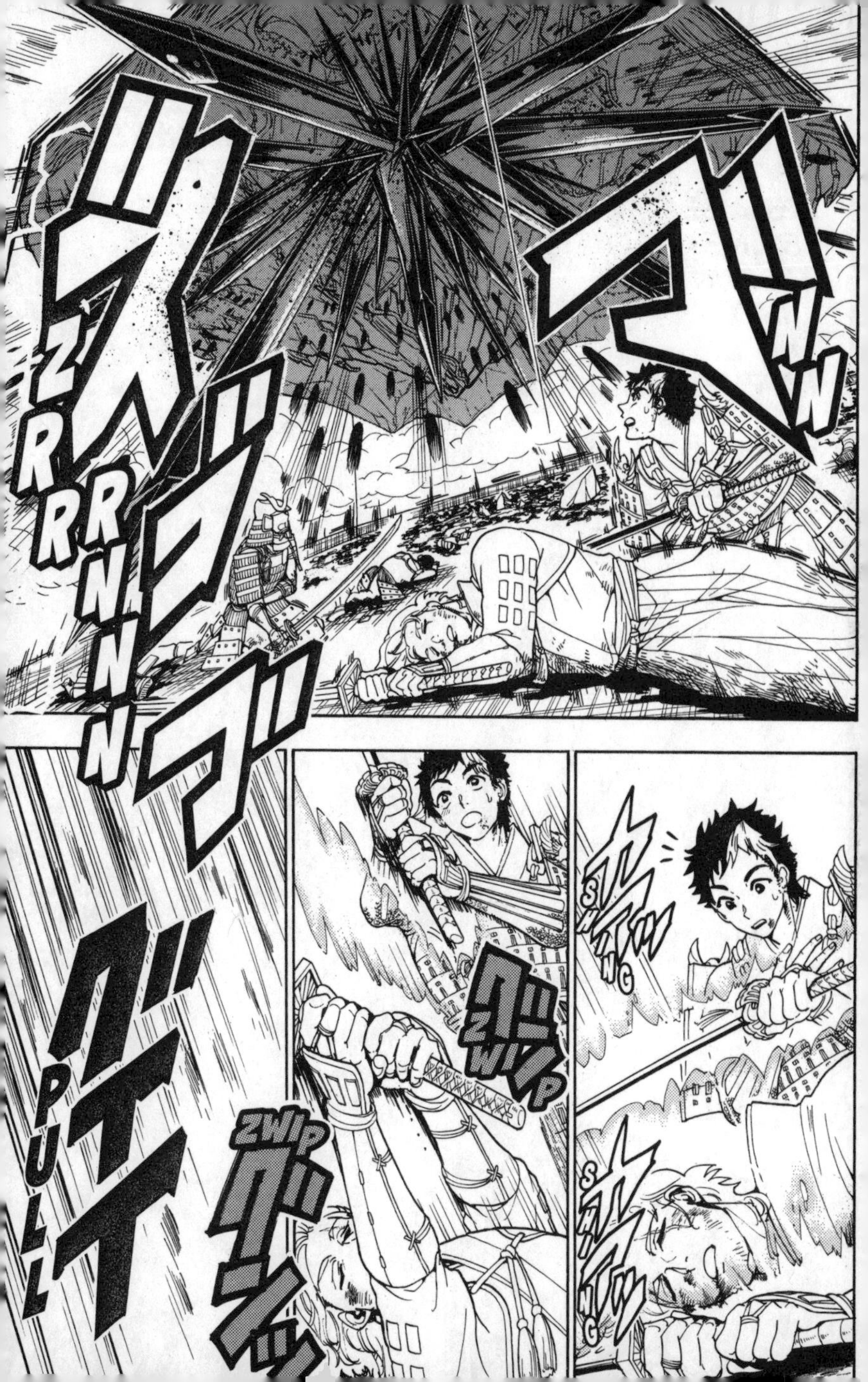
ZRRRNNNN
SHING
ZWIP
PULL
ZWIP
SHING

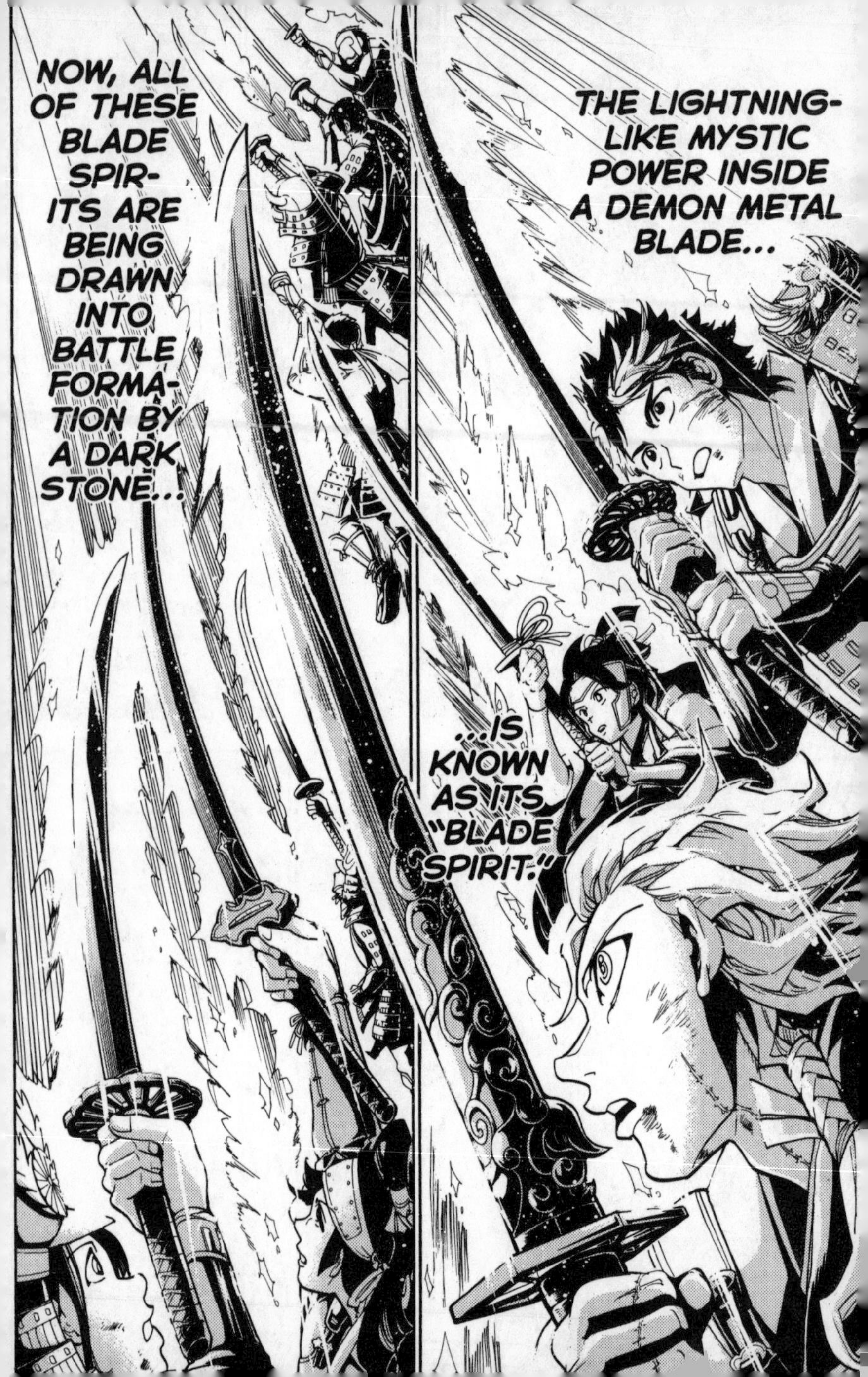
THE LIGHTNING-LIKE MYSTIC POWER INSIDE A DEMON METAL BLADE...
...IS KNOWN AS ITS "BLADE SPIRIT."
NOW, ALL OF THESE BLADE SPIR-ITS ARE BEING DRAWN INTO BATTLE FORMA-TION BY A DARK STONE...

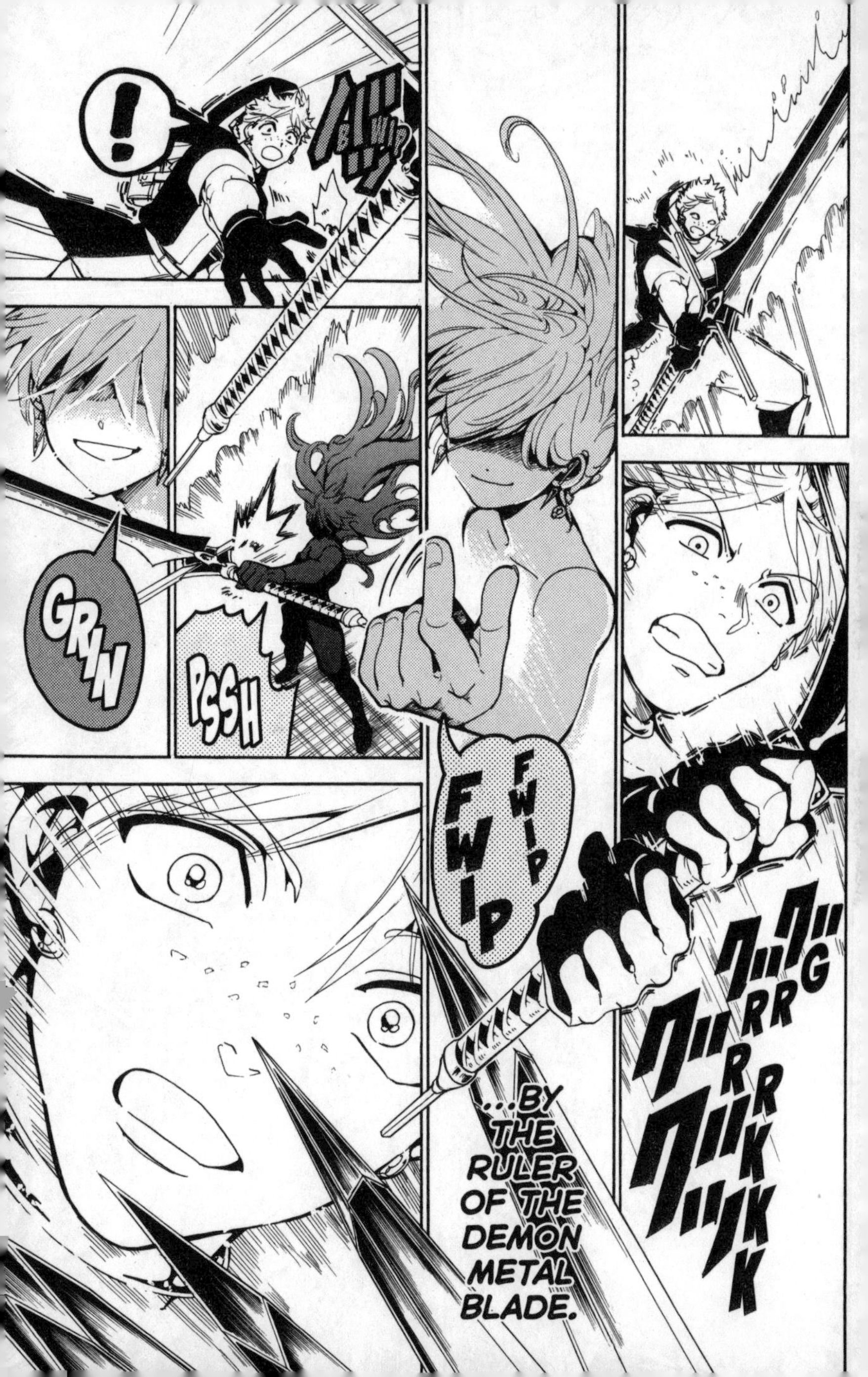
FWIP FWIP
!
BWIP
GRIN
PSSH
GRRRRRKKK
...BY THE RULER OF THE DEMON METAL BLADE.

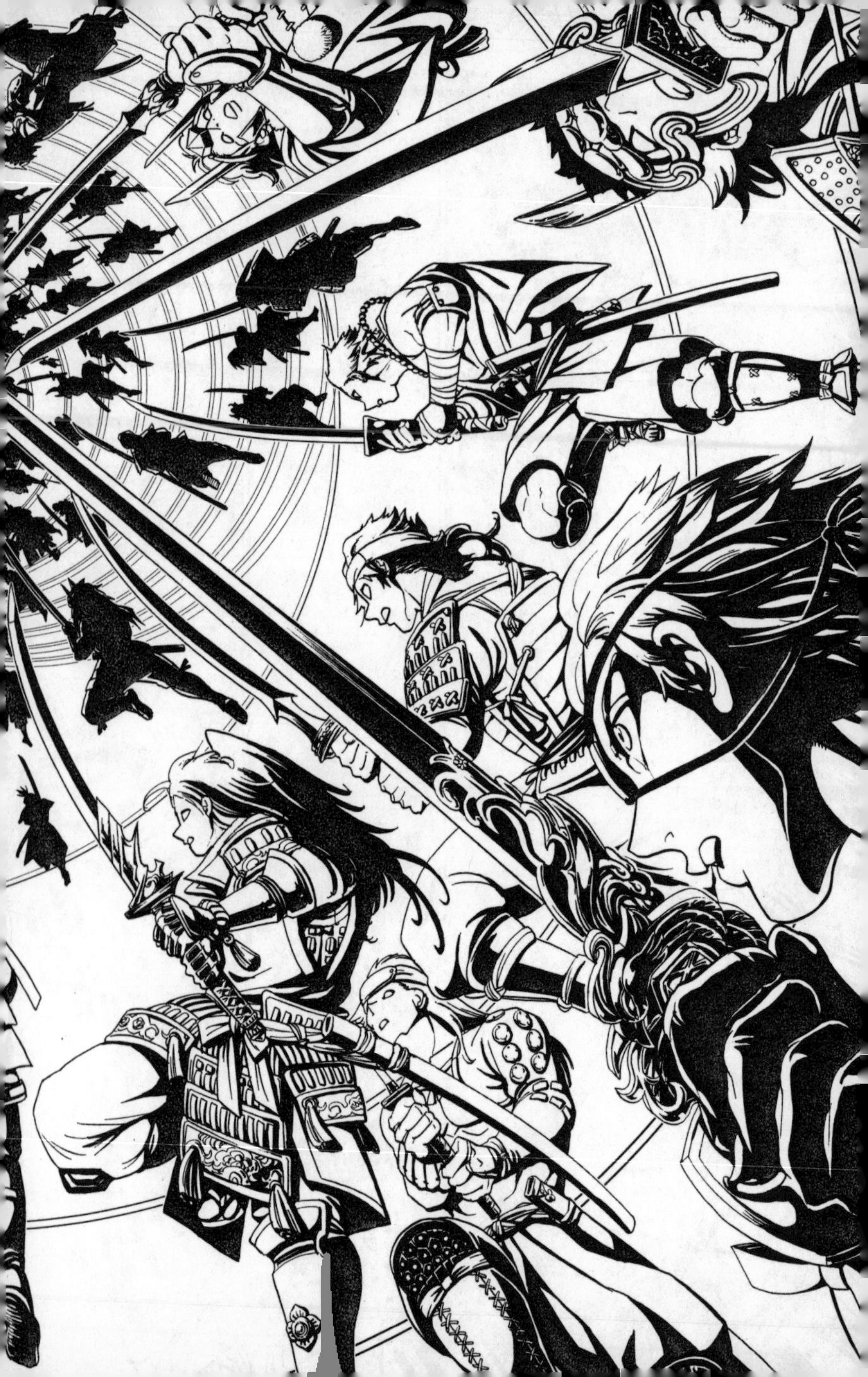

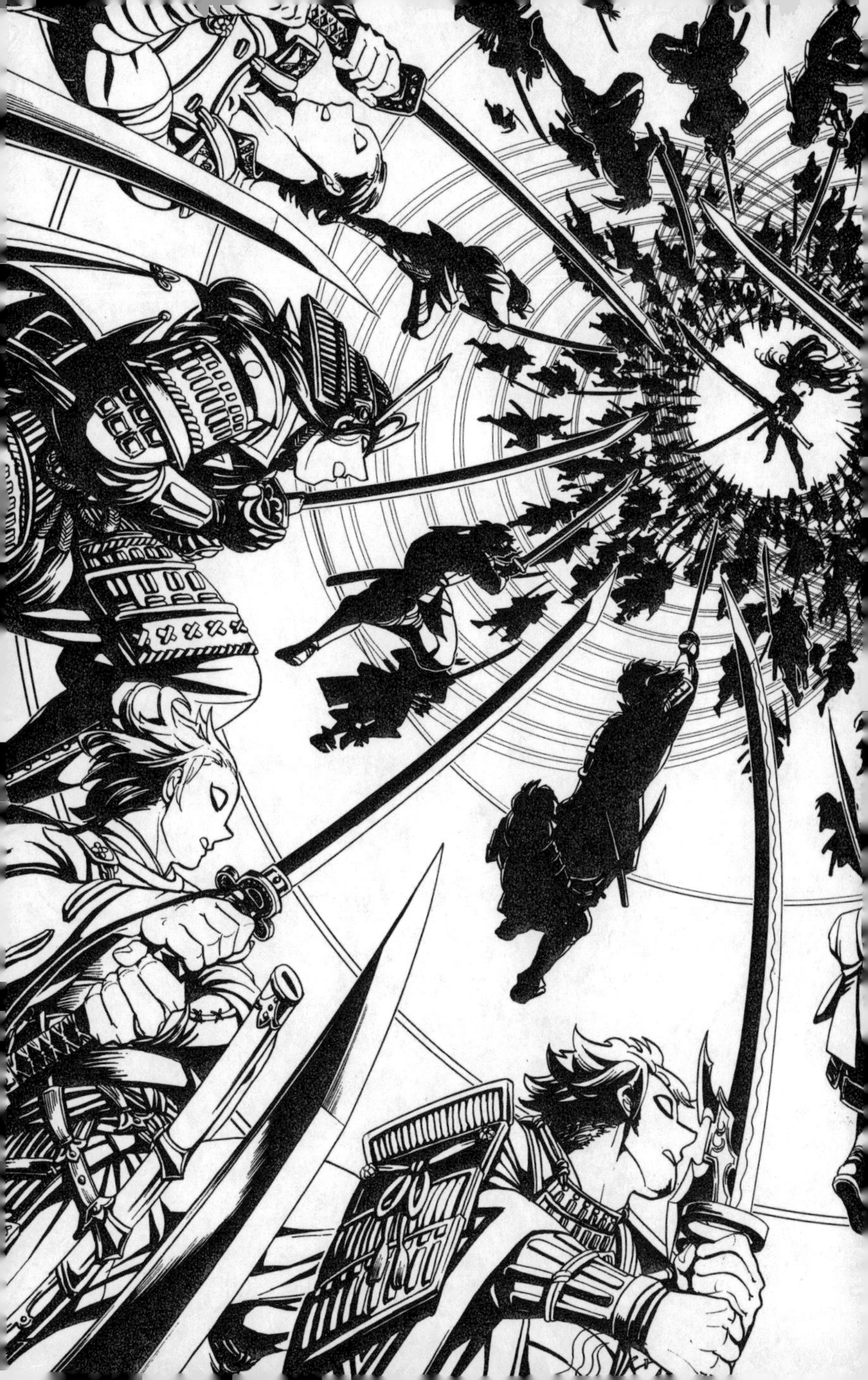

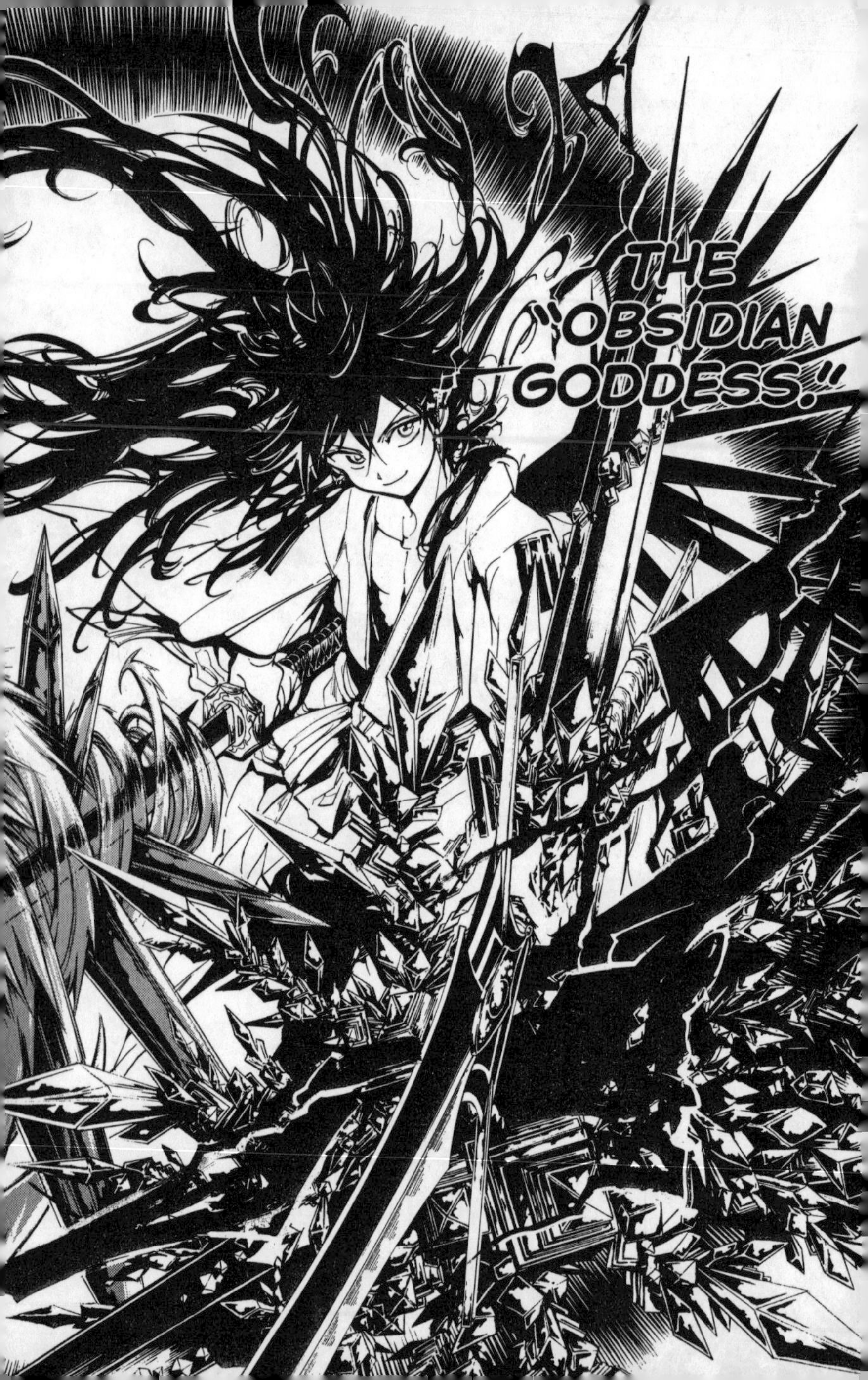
THE "OBSIDIAN GODDESS."

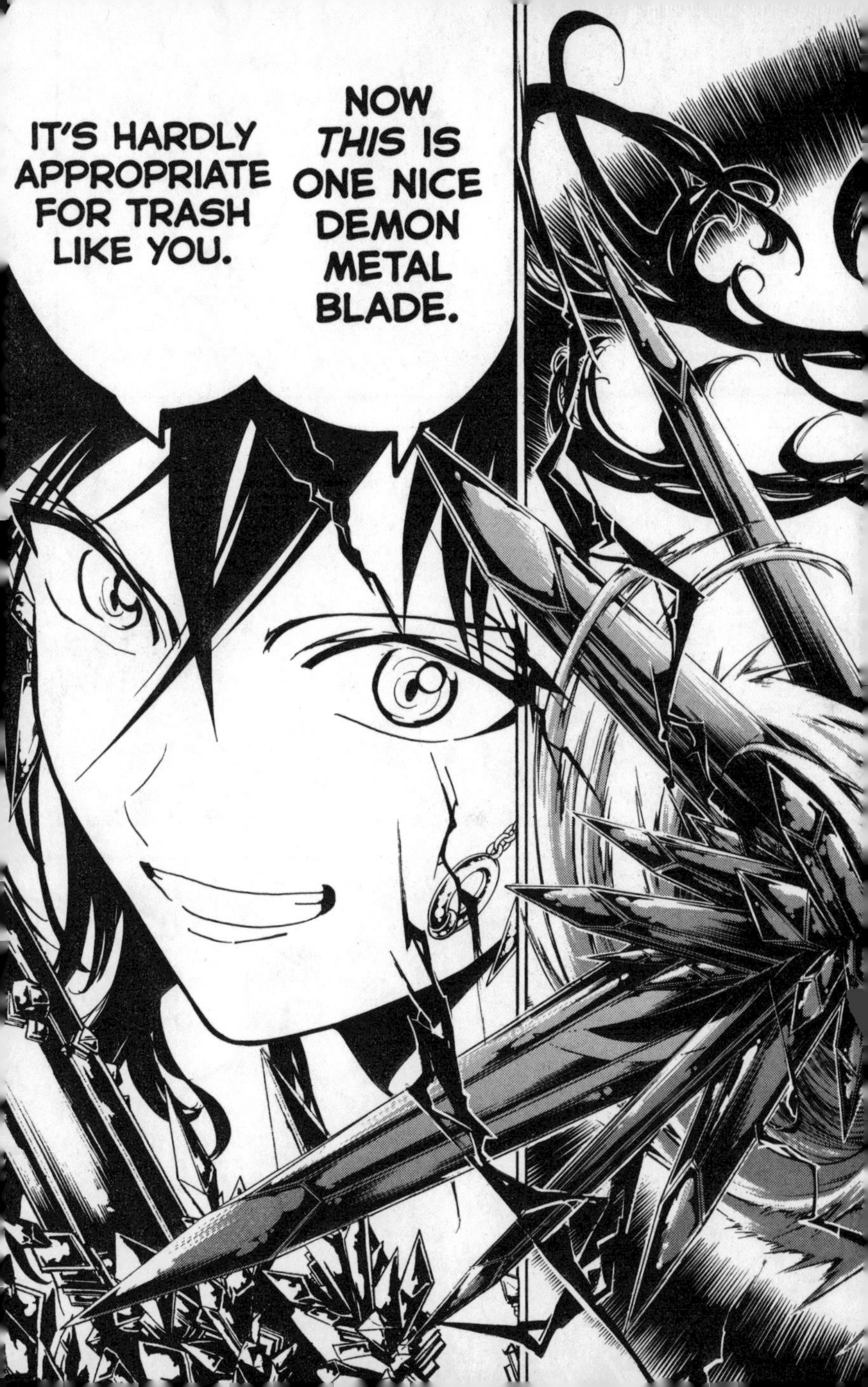
NOW *THIS* IS ONE NICE DEMON METAL BLADE.
IT'S HARDLY APPROPRIATE FOR TRASH LIKE YOU.

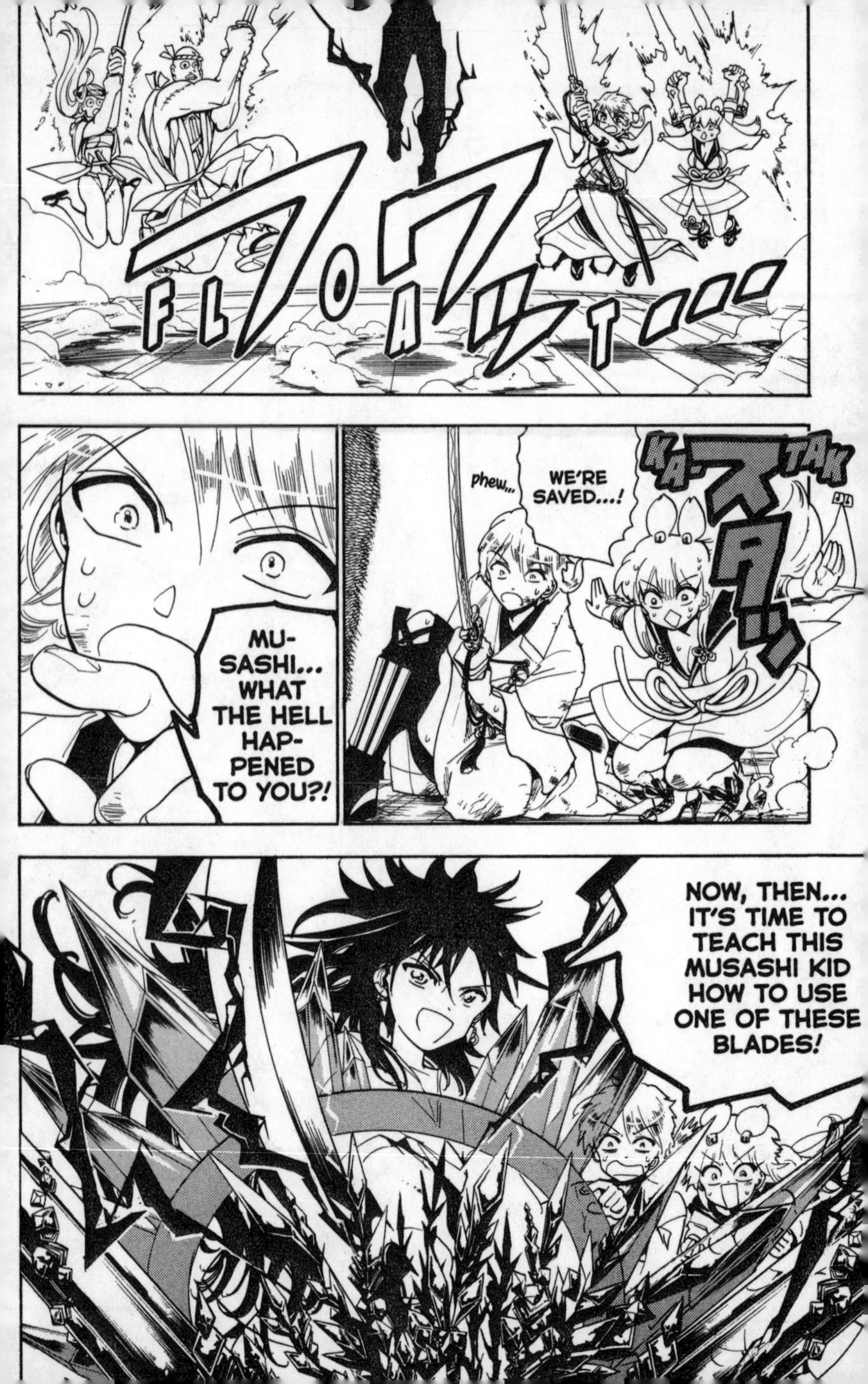
FLOAT...
TAK
phew...
WE'RE SAVED...!
MU-SASHI... WHAT THE HELL HAP-PENED TO YOU?!
NOW, THEN... IT'S TIME TO TEACH THIS MUSASHI KID HOW TO USE ONE OF THESE BLADES!

ORIENT

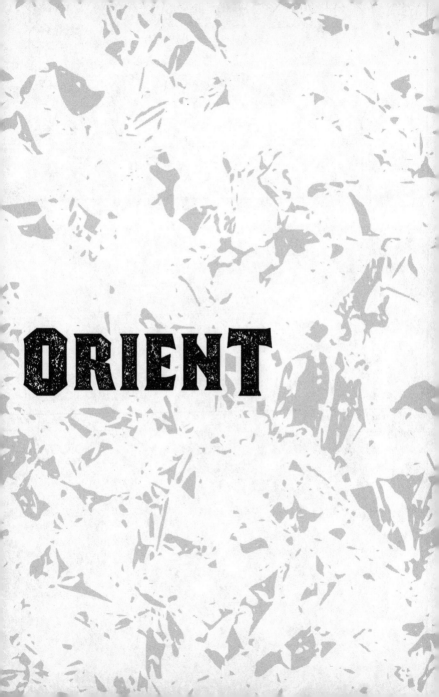

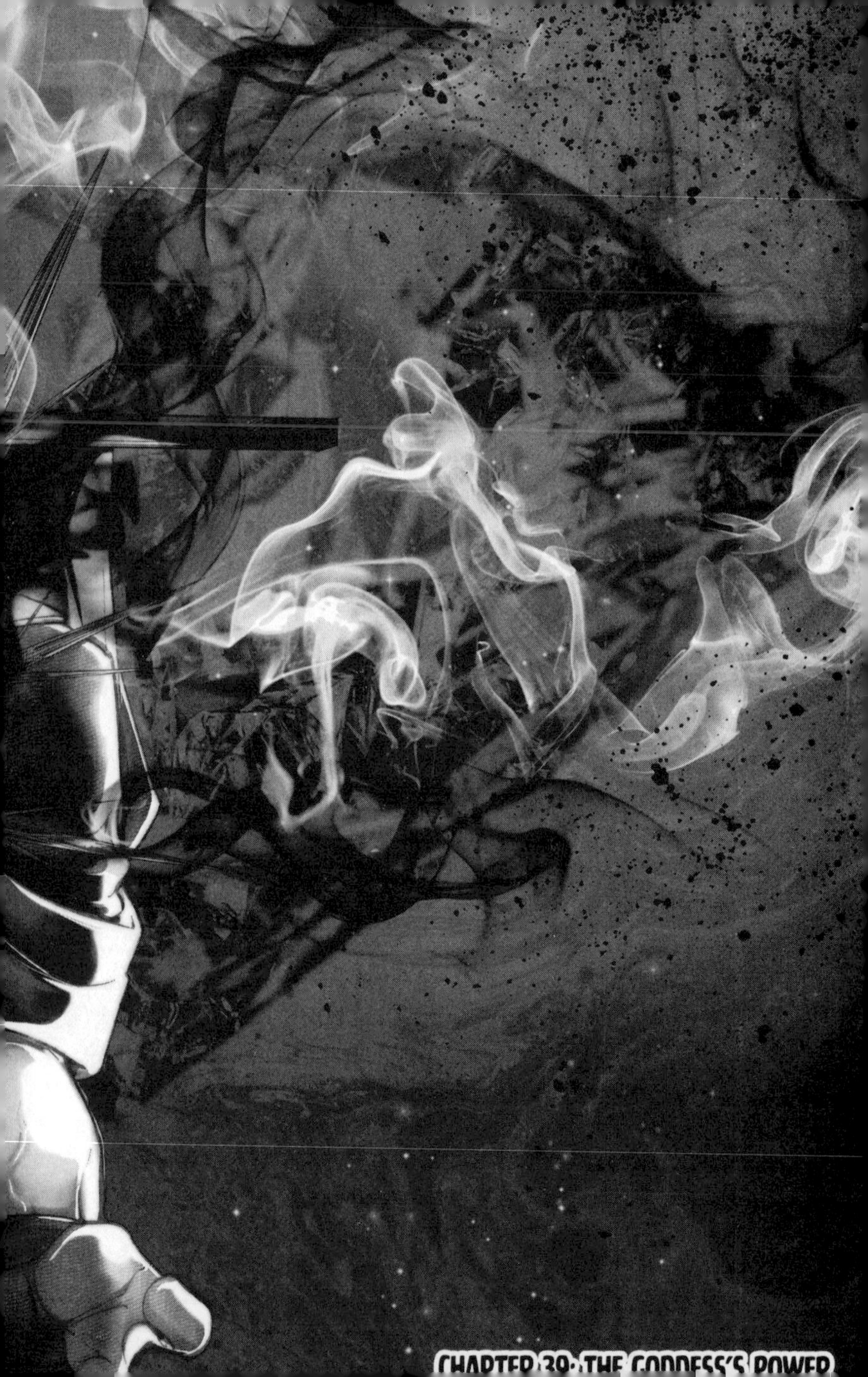
CHAPTER 39: THE GODDESS'S POWER

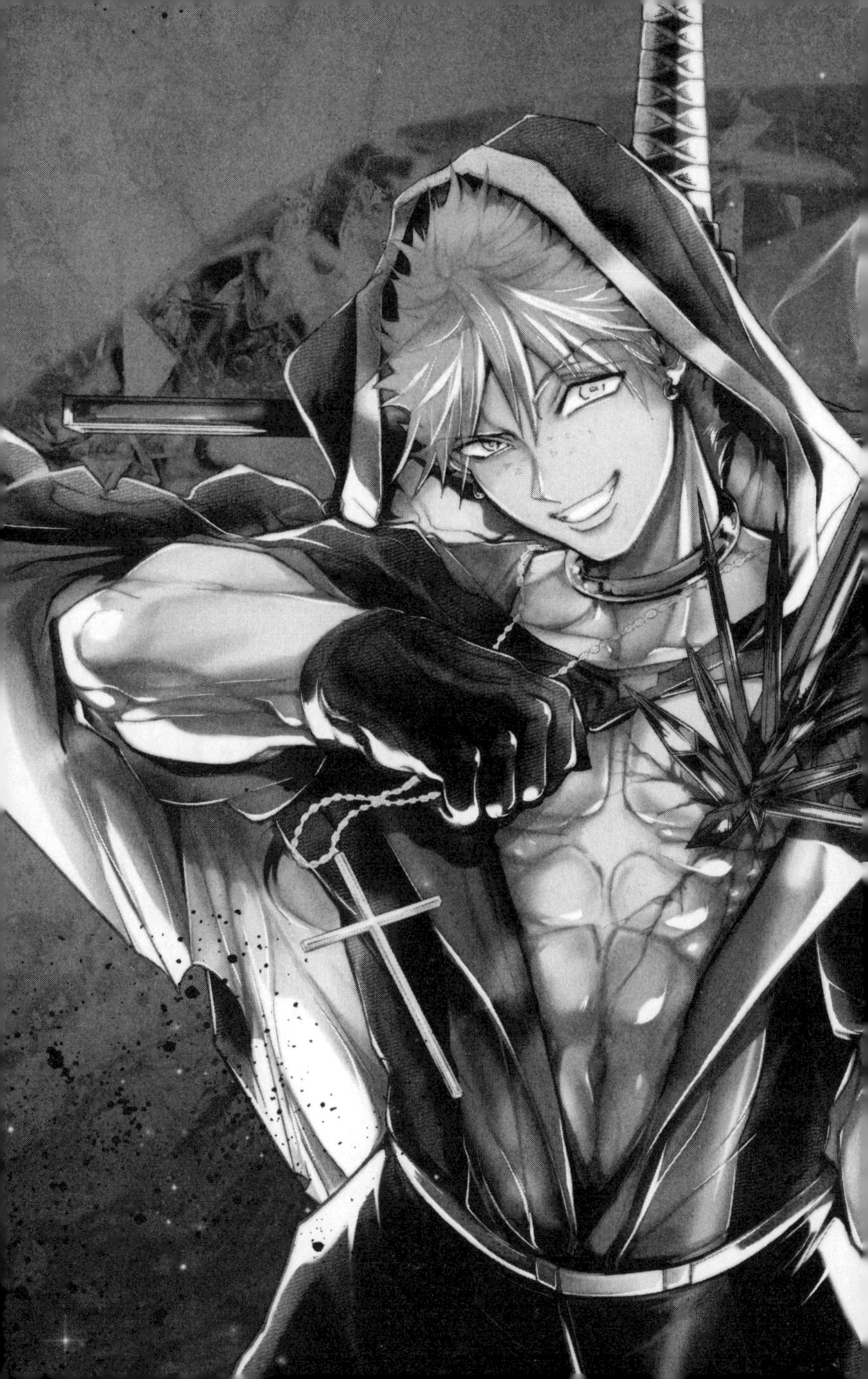

ORIENT

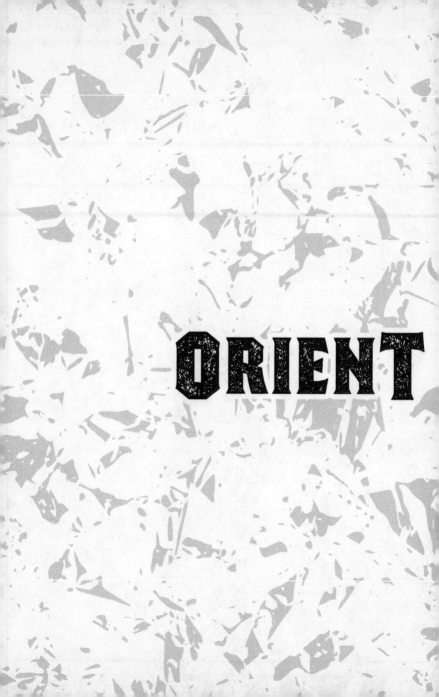

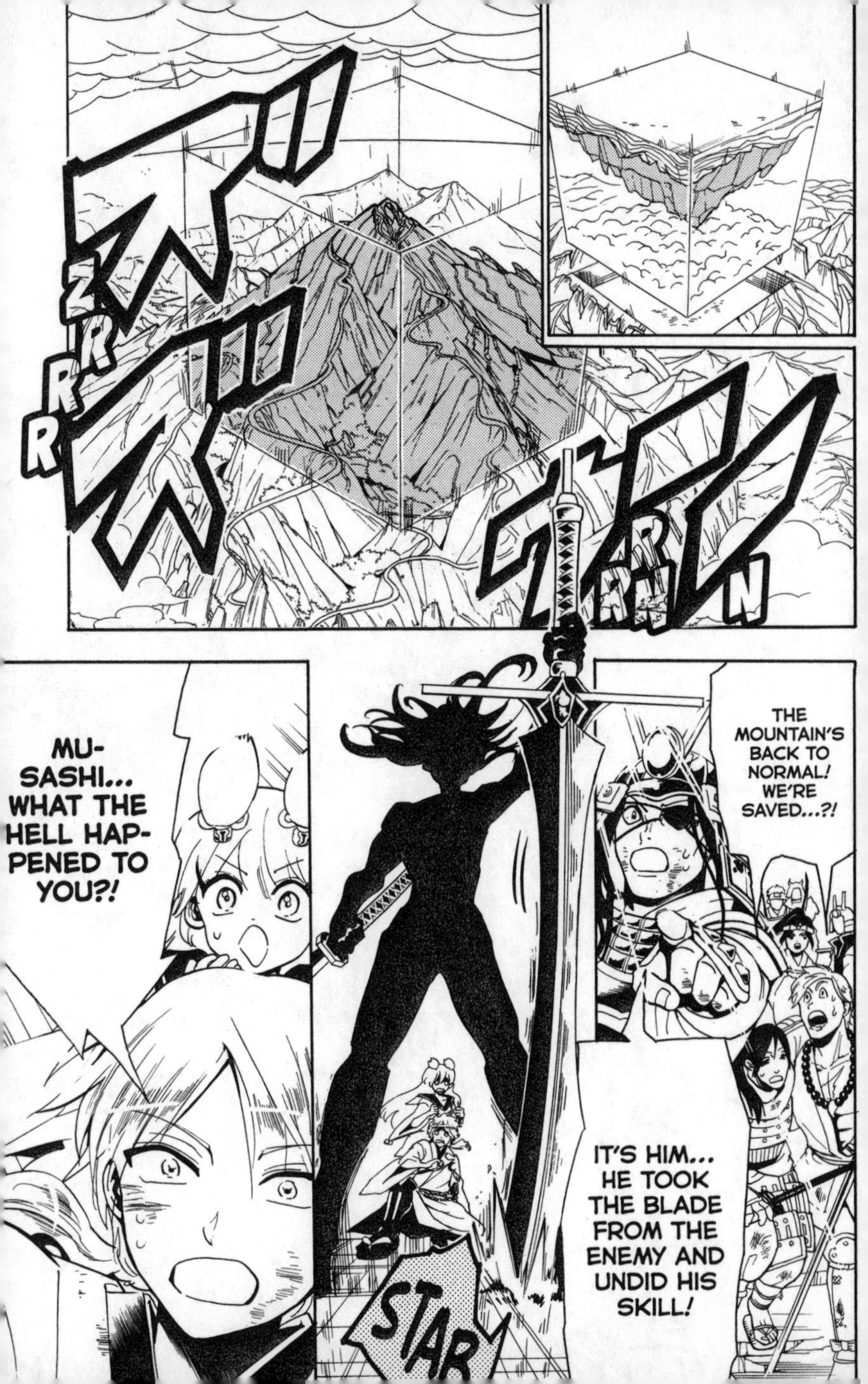
ZRRN
ZRRR
THE MOUNTAIN'S BACK TO NORMAL! WE'RE SAVED...?!
IT'S HIM... HE TOOK THE BLADE FROM THE ENEMY AND UNDID HIS SKILL!
MU-SASHI... WHAT THE HELL HAP-PENED TO YOU?!
STAR

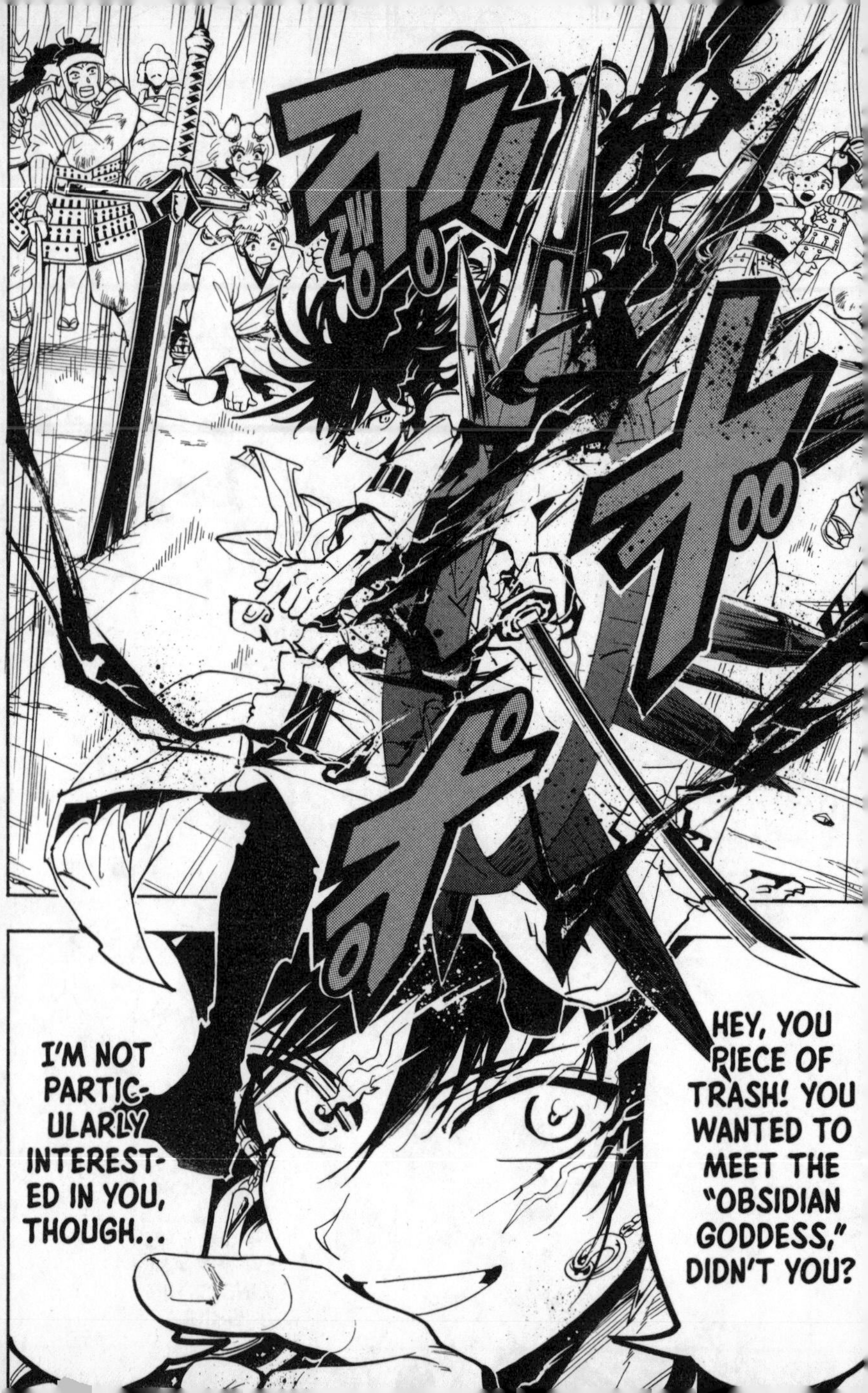
ZWOOO
HEY, YOU PIECE OF TRASH! YOU WANTED TO MEET THE "OBSIDIAN GODDESS," DIDN'T YOU?
I'M NOT PARTIC-ULARLY INTEREST-ED IN YOU, THOUGH...

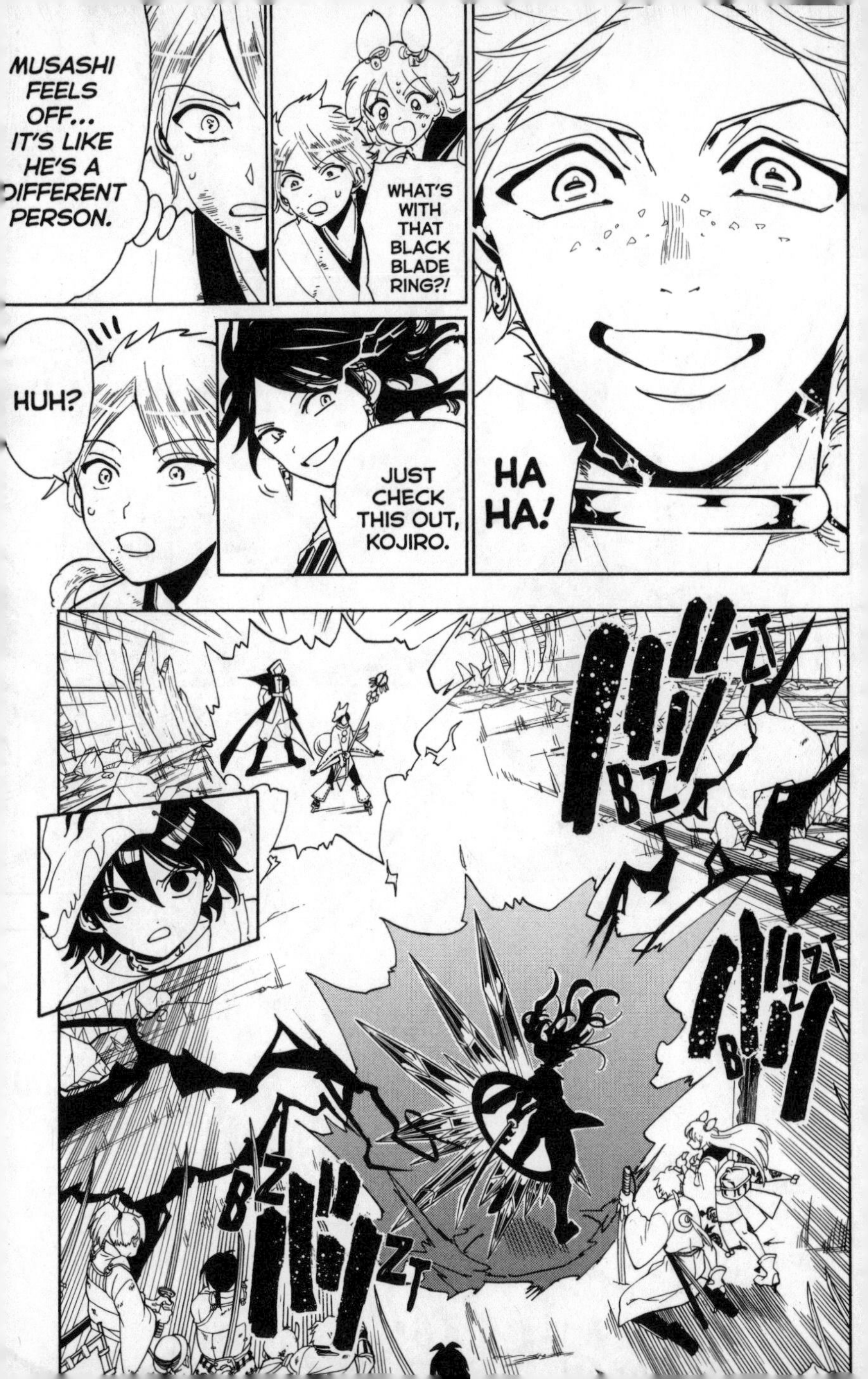
HA HA!
WHAT'S WITH THAT BLACK BLADE RING?!
MUSASHI FEELS OFF... IT'S LIKE HE'S A DIFFERENT PERSON.
JUST CHECK THIS OUT, KOJIRO.
HUH?
BZZT
BZZT
BZZT

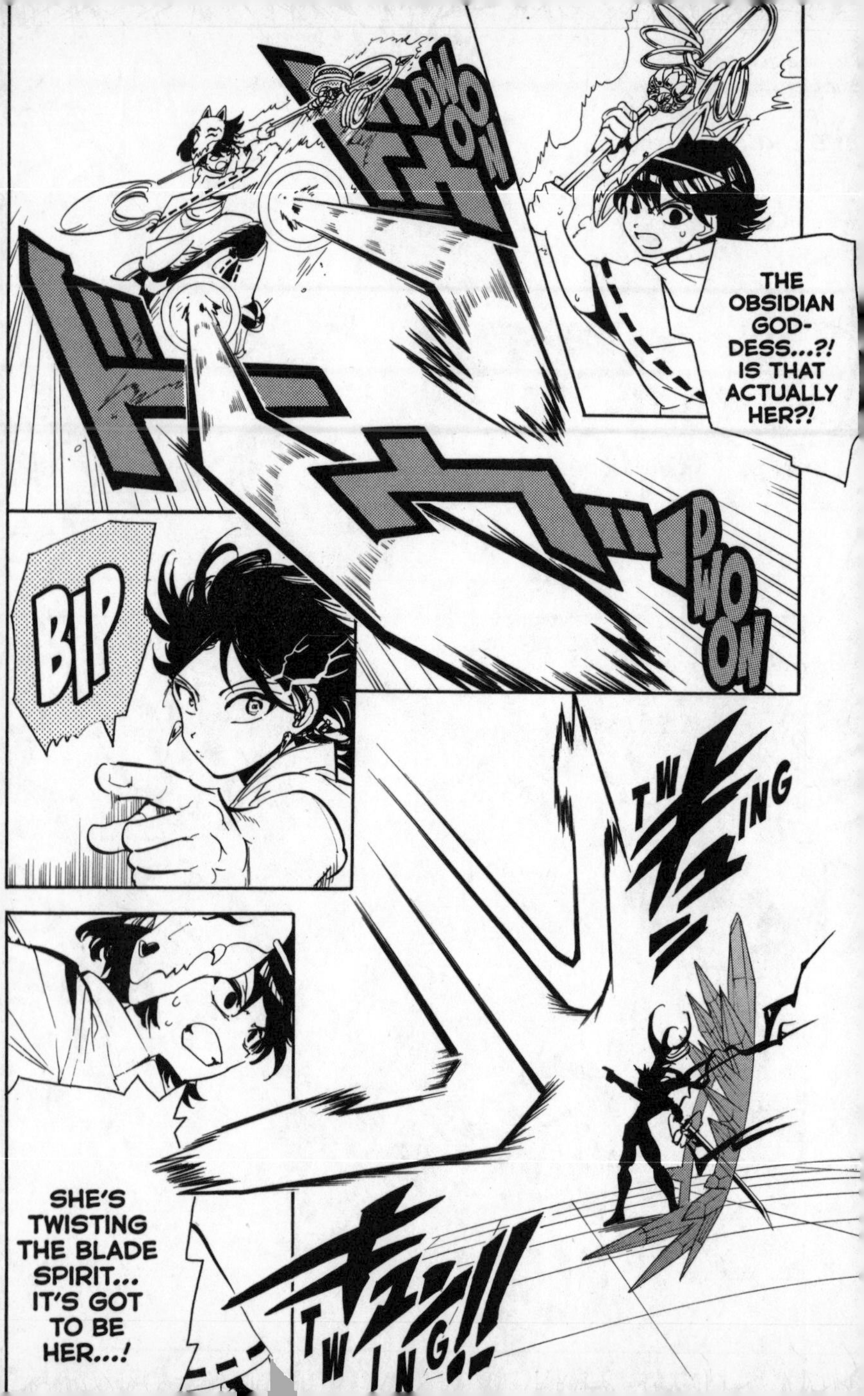
DWOON
THE OBSIDIAN GOD-DESS...?! IS THAT ACTUALLY HER?!
DWOON
BIP
TWING
TWING!!
SHE'S TWISTING THE BLADE SPIRIT... IT'S GOT TO BE HER...!

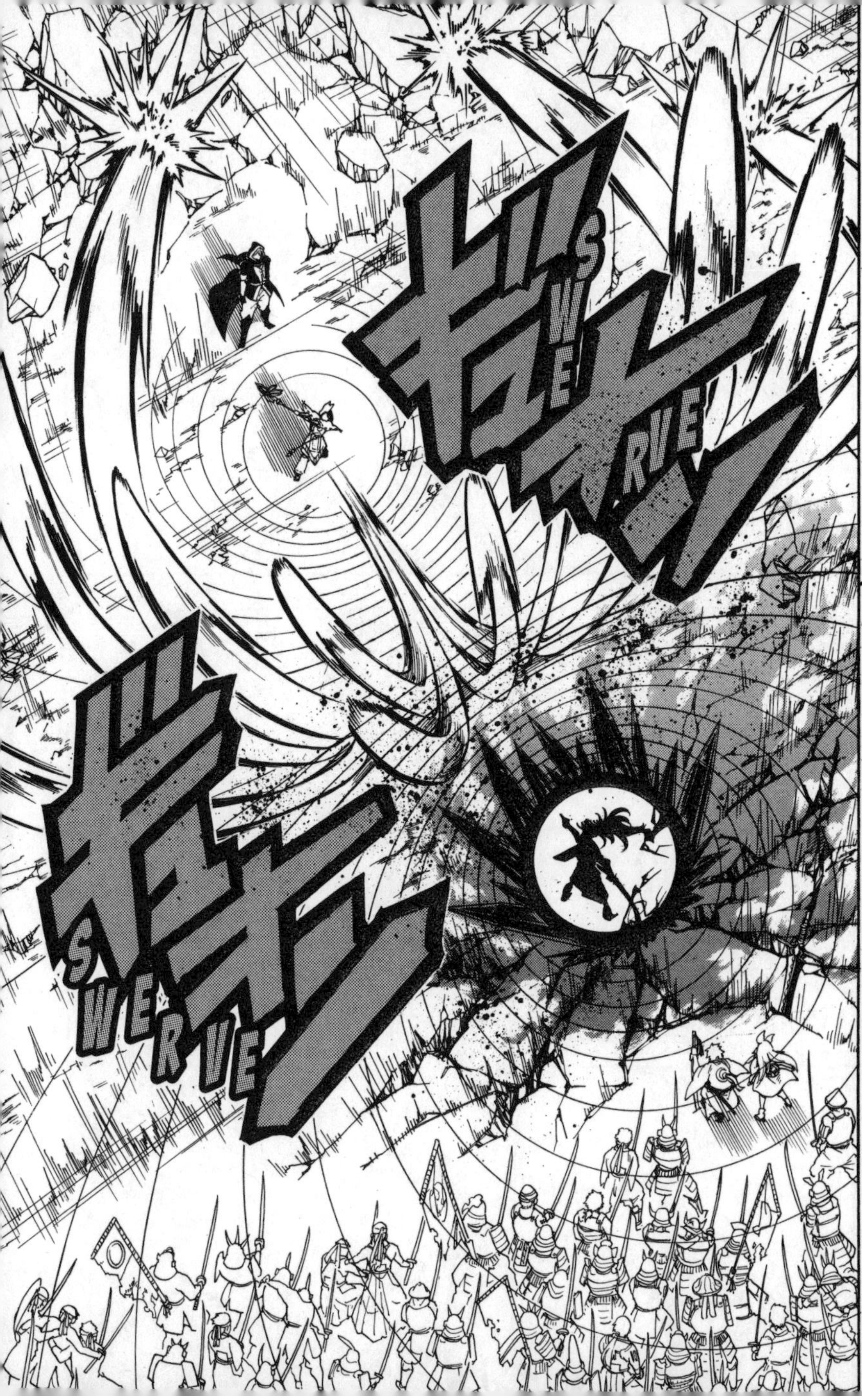
SWERVE
SWERVE

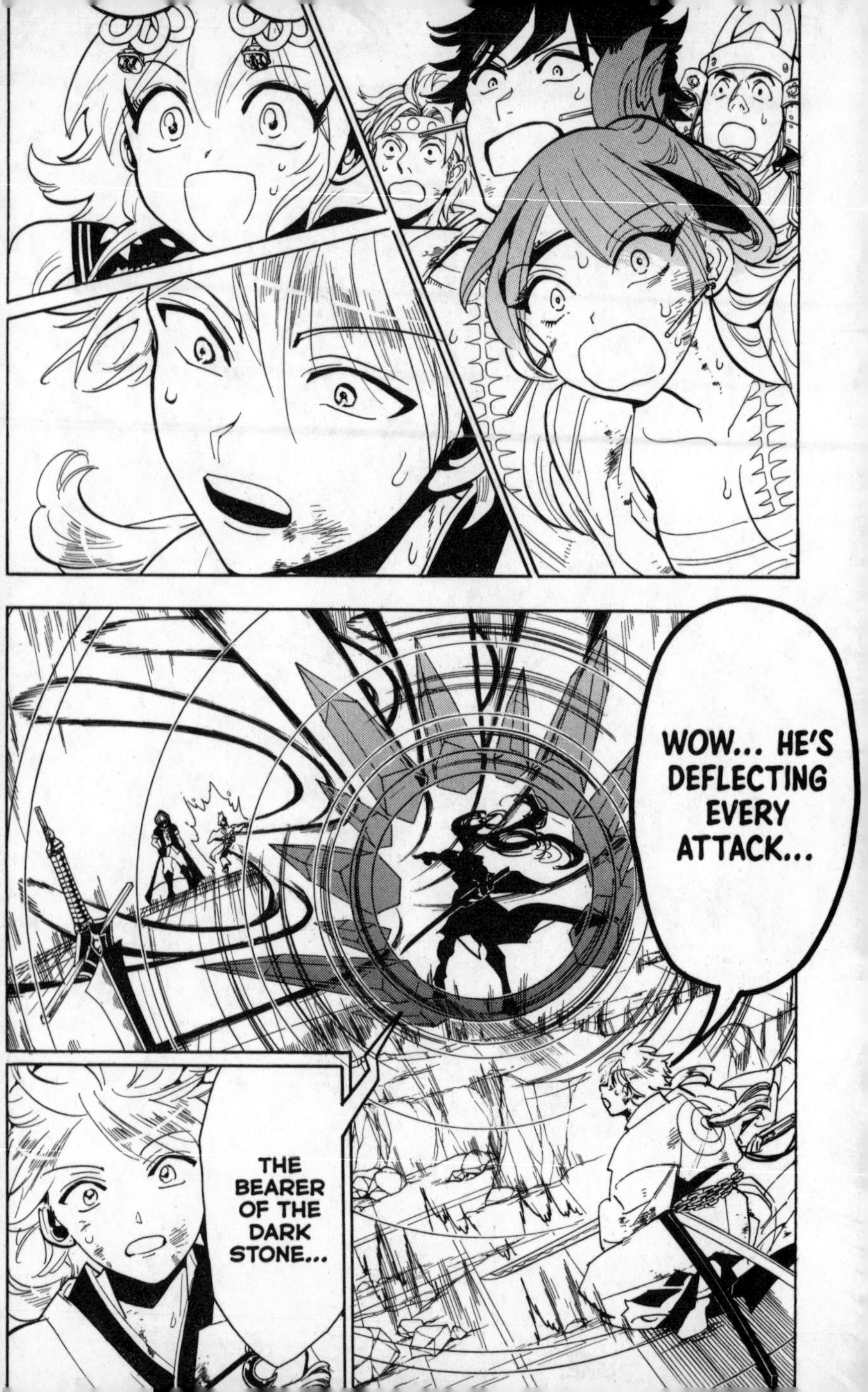
WOW... HE'S DEFLECTING EVERY ATTACK...
THE BEARER OF THE DARK STONE...

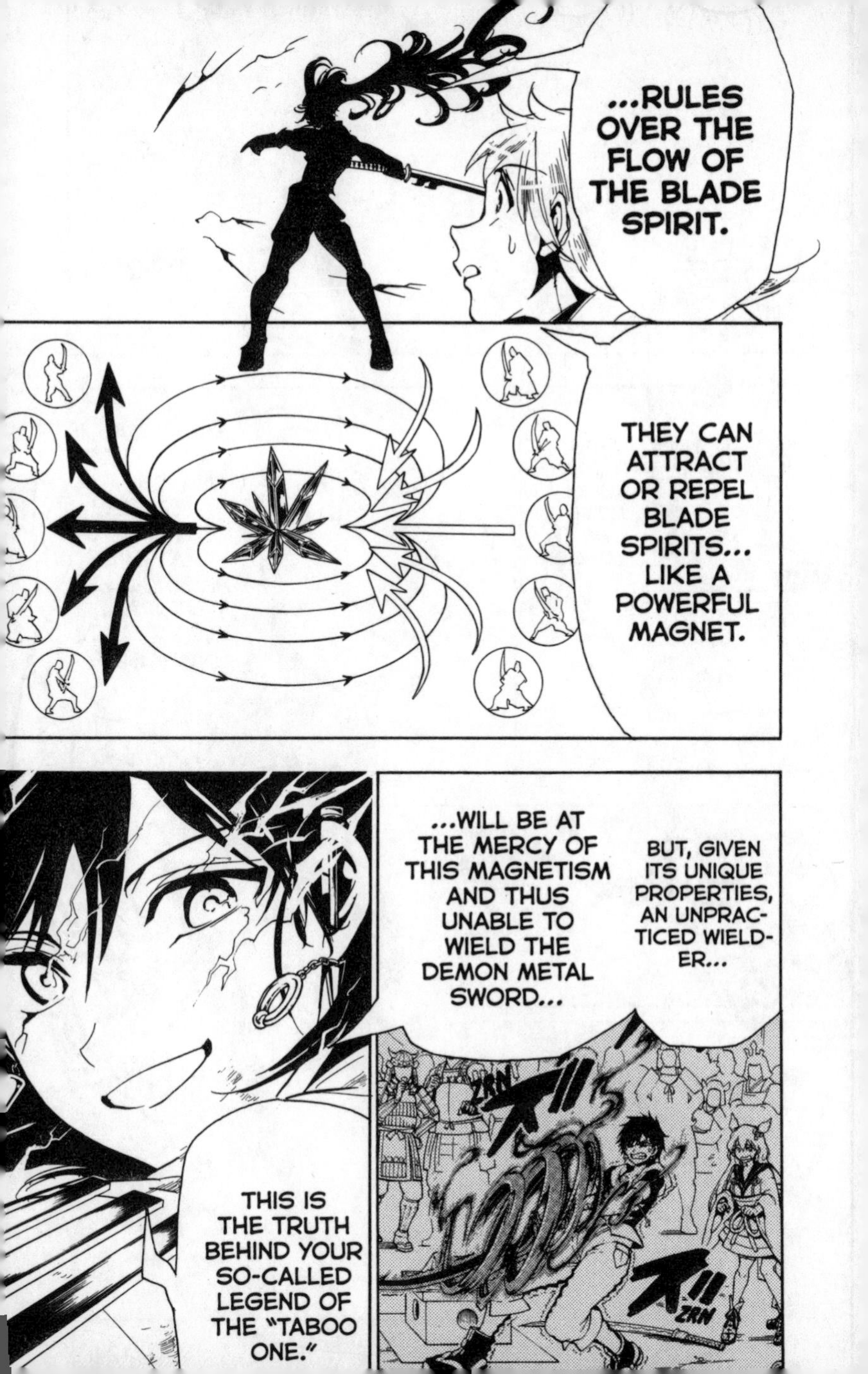
...RULES OVER THE FLOW OF THE BLADE SPIRIT.
THEY CAN ATTRACT OR REPEL BLADE SPIRITS... LIKE A POWERFUL MAGNET.
BUT, GIVEN ITS UNIQUE PROPERTIES, AN UNPRAC-TICED WIELD-ER...
...WILL BE AT THE MERCY OF THIS MAGNETISM AND THUS UNABLE TO WIELD THE DEMON METAL SWORD...
ZRN
ZRN
THIS IS THE TRUTH BEHIND YOUR SO-CALLED LEGEND OF THE "TABOO ONE."

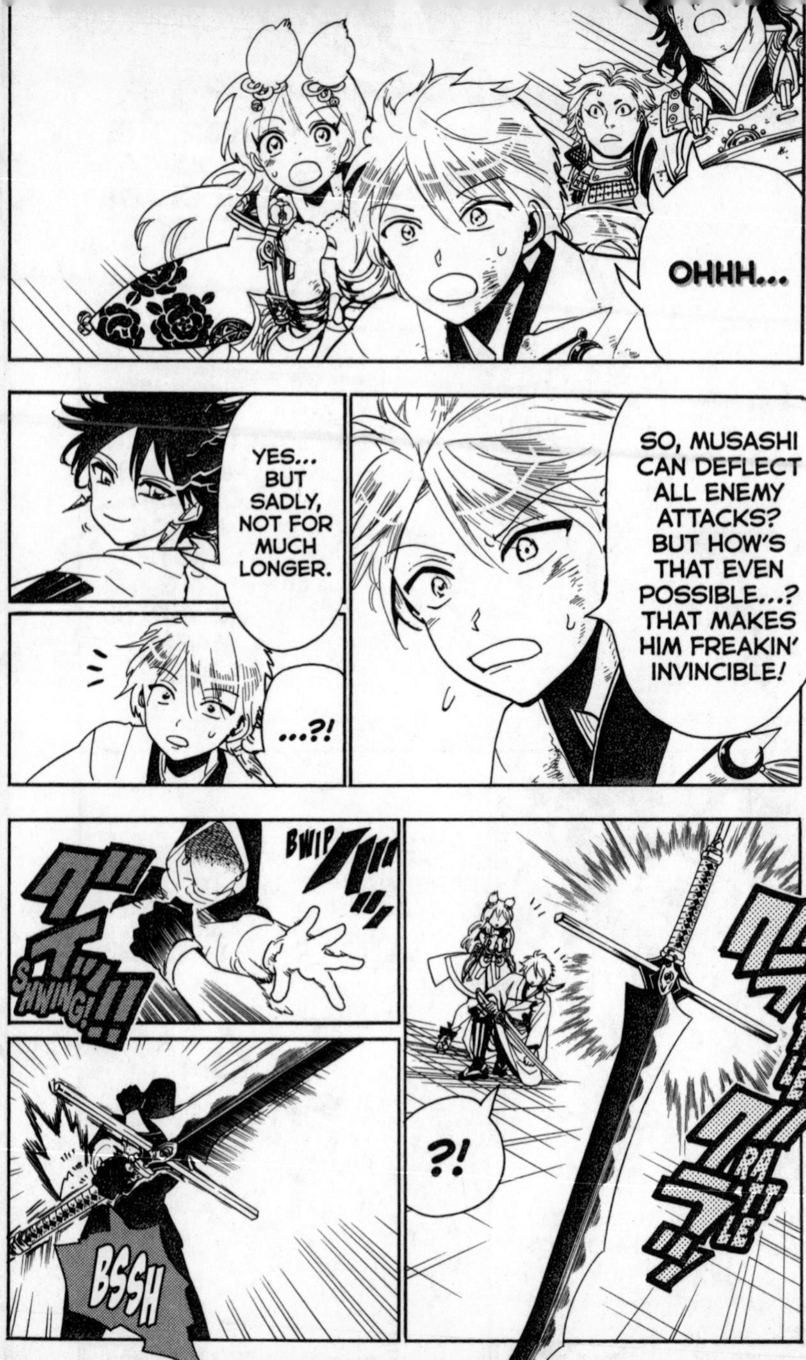
OHHH...
SO, MUSASHI CAN DEFLECT ALL ENEMY ATTACKS? BUT HOW'S THAT EVEN POSSIBLE...? THAT MAKES HIM FREAKIN' INVINCIBLE!
YES... BUT SADLY, NOT FOR MUCH LONGER.
...?!
RATTLE
RATTLE
?!
BWIP
SHWING!!
BSSH

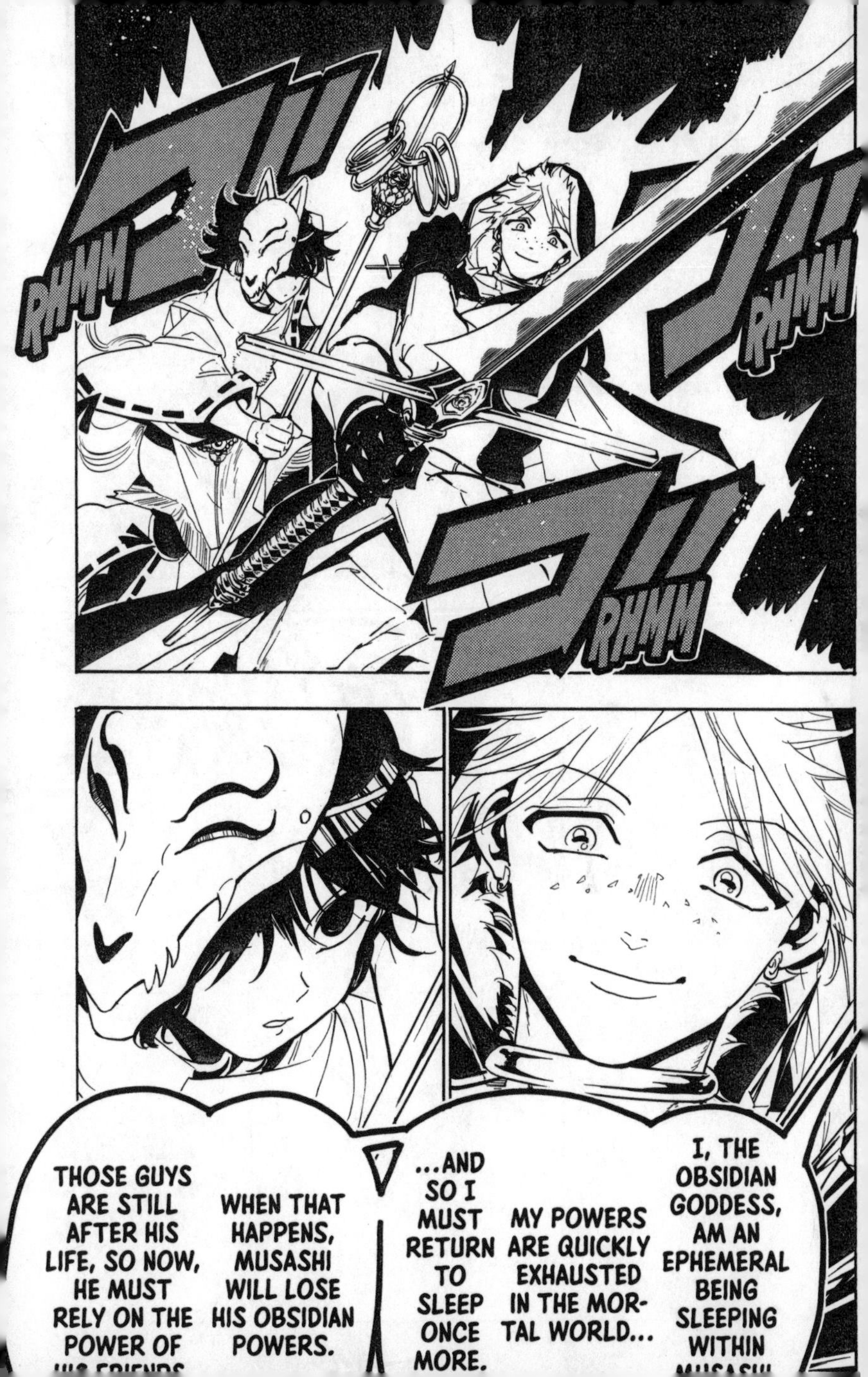
RHMM
RHMM
RHMM
I, THE OBSIDIAN GODDESS, AM AN EPHEMERAL BEING SLEEPING WITHIN
MY POWERS ARE QUICKLY EXHAUSTED IN THE MOR-TAL WORLD...
...AND SO I MUST RETURN TO SLEEP ONCE MORE.
WHEN THAT HAPPENS, MUSASHI WILL LOSE HIS OBSIDIAN POWERS.
THOSE GUYS ARE STILL AFTER HIS LIFE, SO NOW, HE MUST RELY ON THE POWER OF

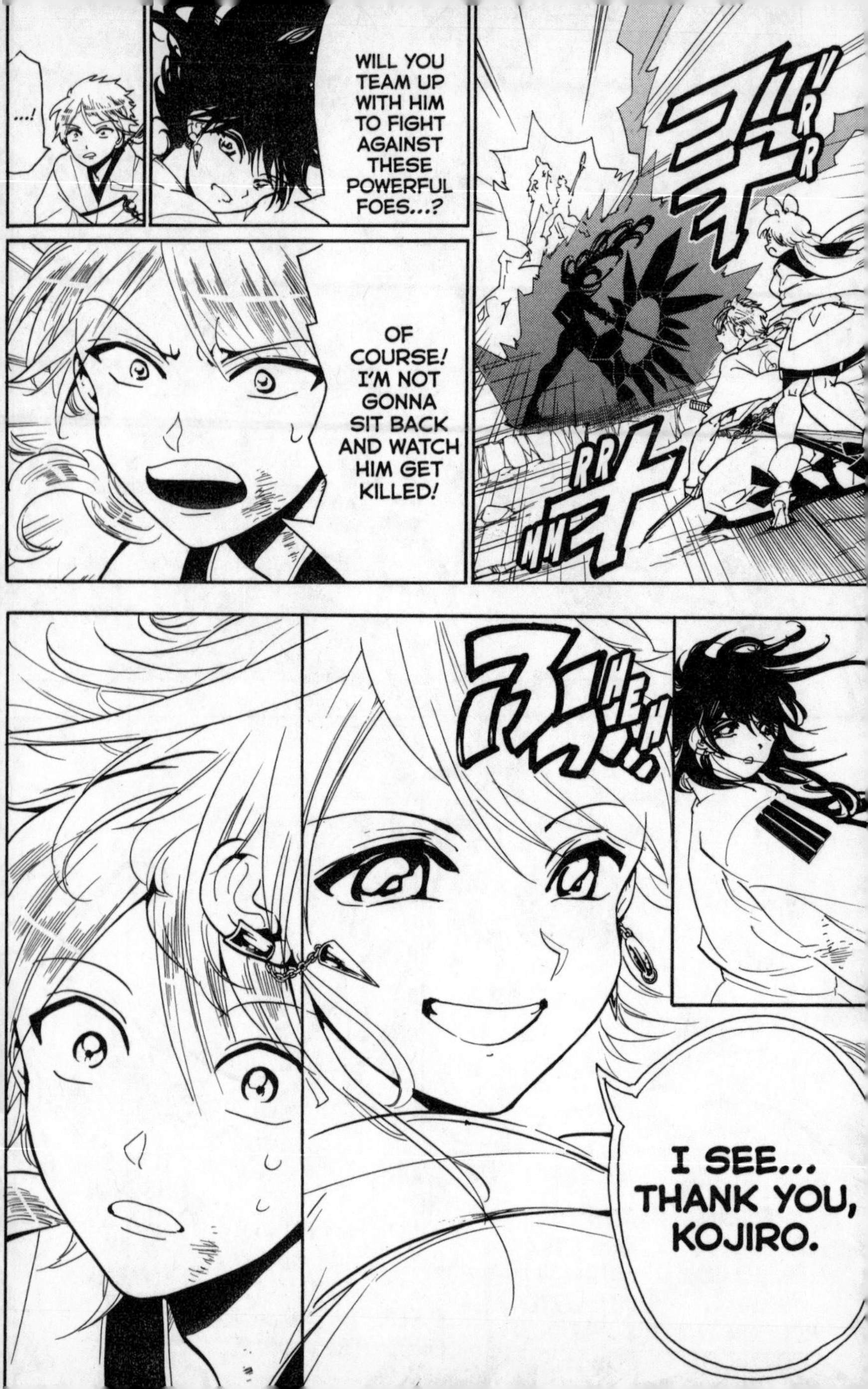
VRRR
RRMM
WILL YOU TEAM UP WITH HIM TO FIGHT AGAINST THESE POWERFUL FOES...?
...!
OF COURSE! I'M NOT GONNA SIT BACK AND WATCH HIM GET KILLED!
HEH!!
I SEE... THANK YOU, KOJIRO.

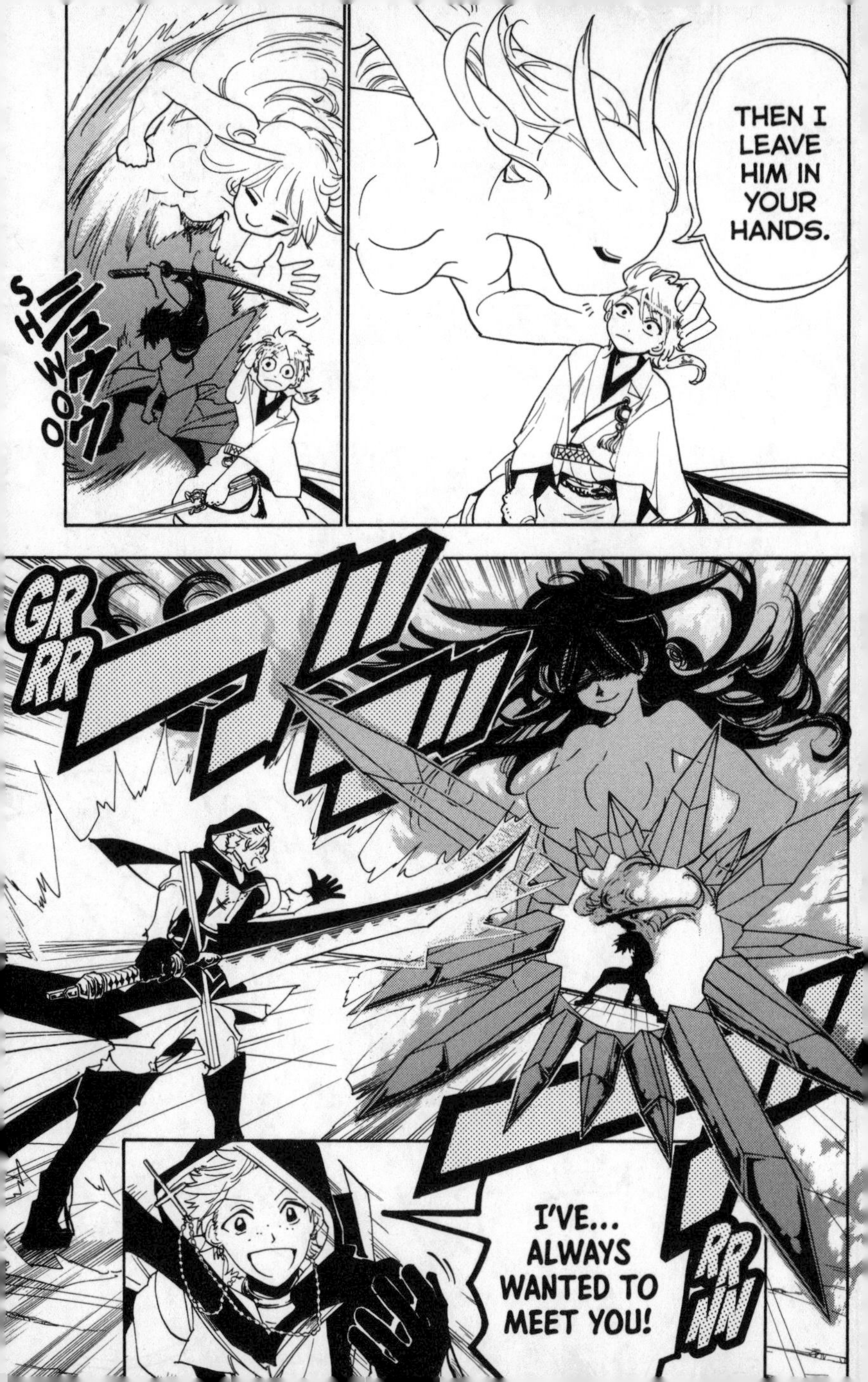
THEN I LEAVE HIM IN YOUR HANDS.
SHWOOO
GR RR
RR RN
I'VE... ALWAYS WANTED TO MEET YOU!

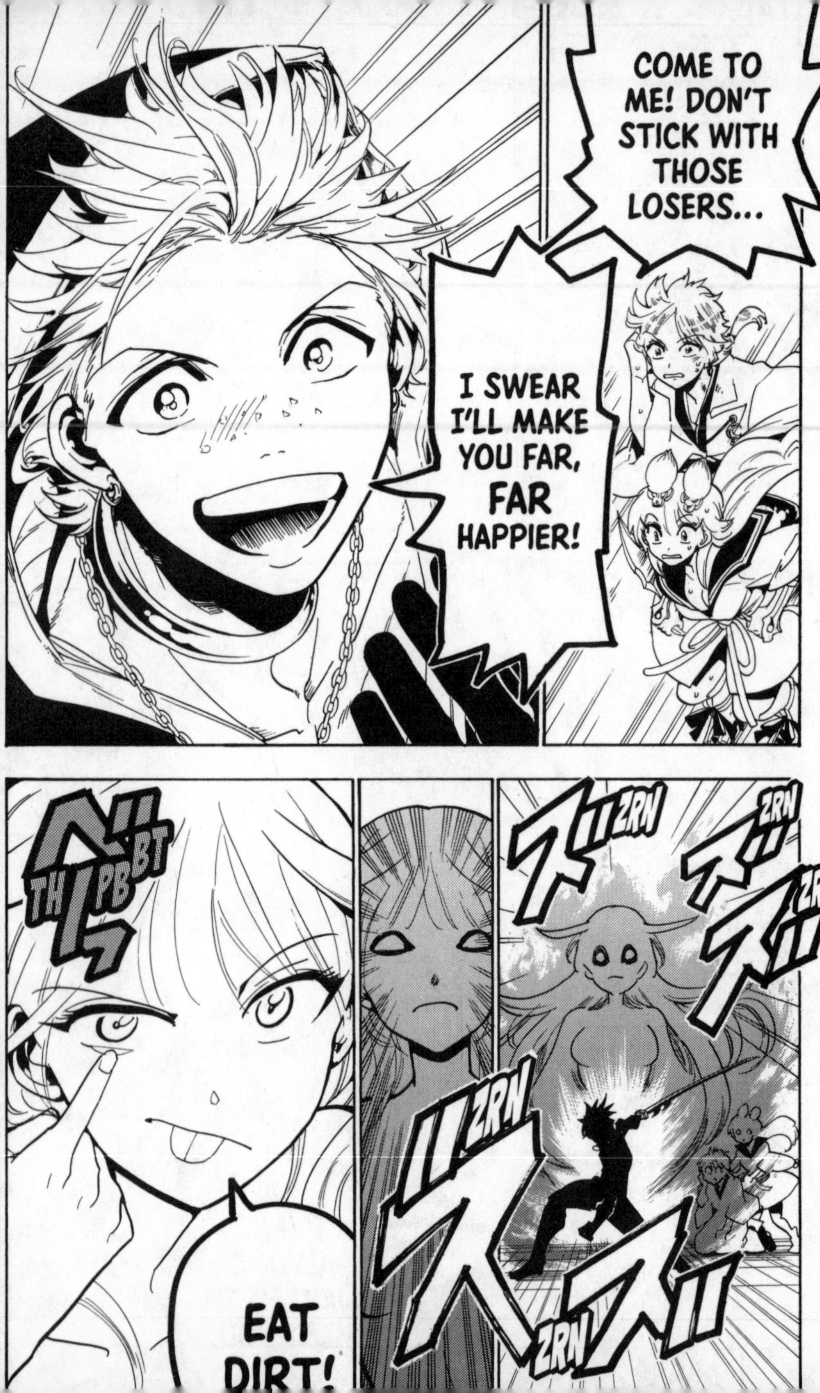
COME TO ME! DON'T STICK WITH THOSE LOSERS...
I SWEAR I'LL MAKE YOU FAR, FAR HAPPIER!
ZRN
ZRN
ZRN
ZRN
ZRN
THPBBT
EAT DIRT!

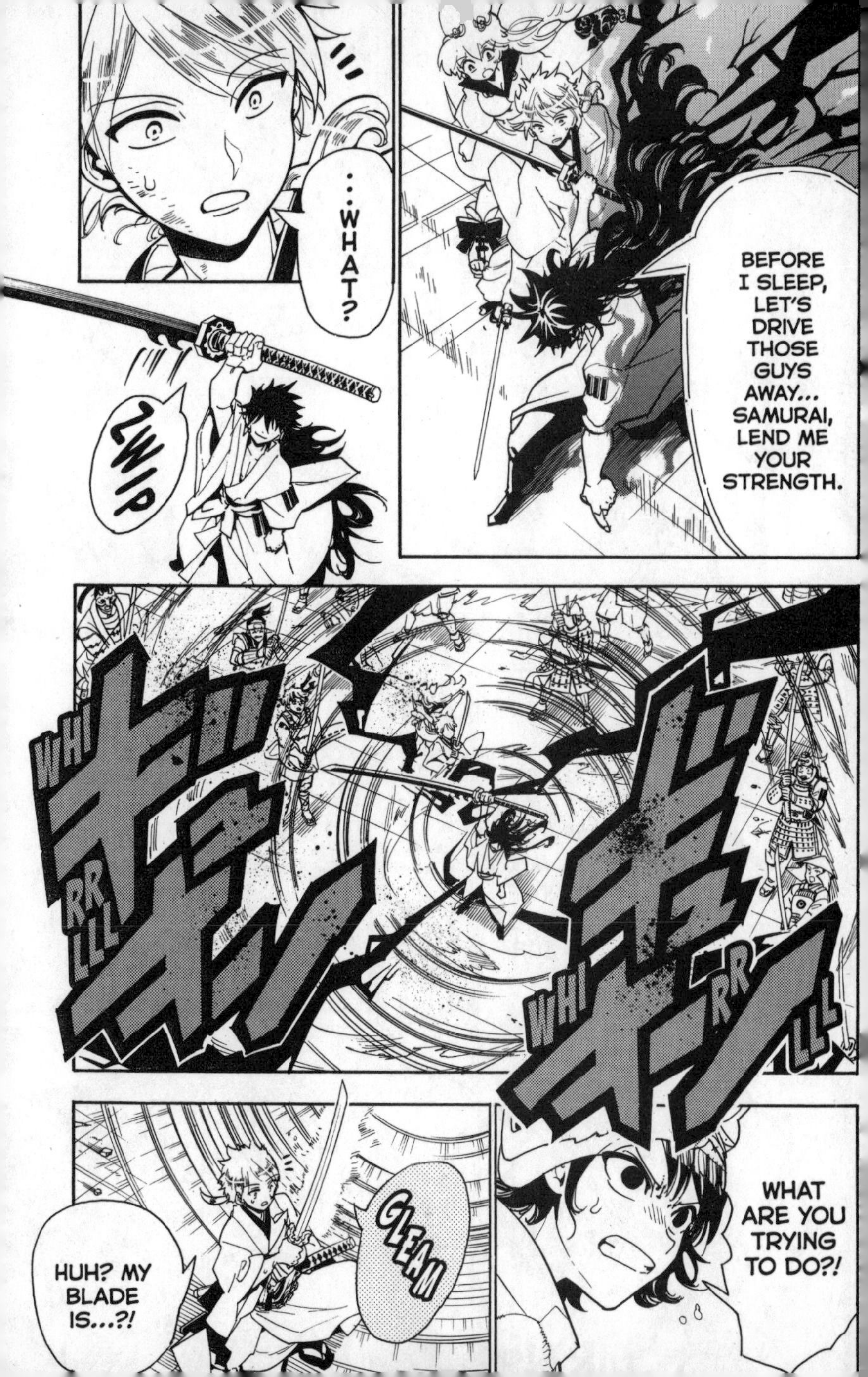
BEFORE I SLEEP, LET'S DRIVE THOSE GUYS AWAY... SAMURAI, LEND ME YOUR STRENGTH.
...WHAT?
ZWIP
WHIRRLLL
WHIRRLLL
WHAT ARE YOU TRYING TO DO?!
GLEAM
HUH? MY BLADE IS...?!

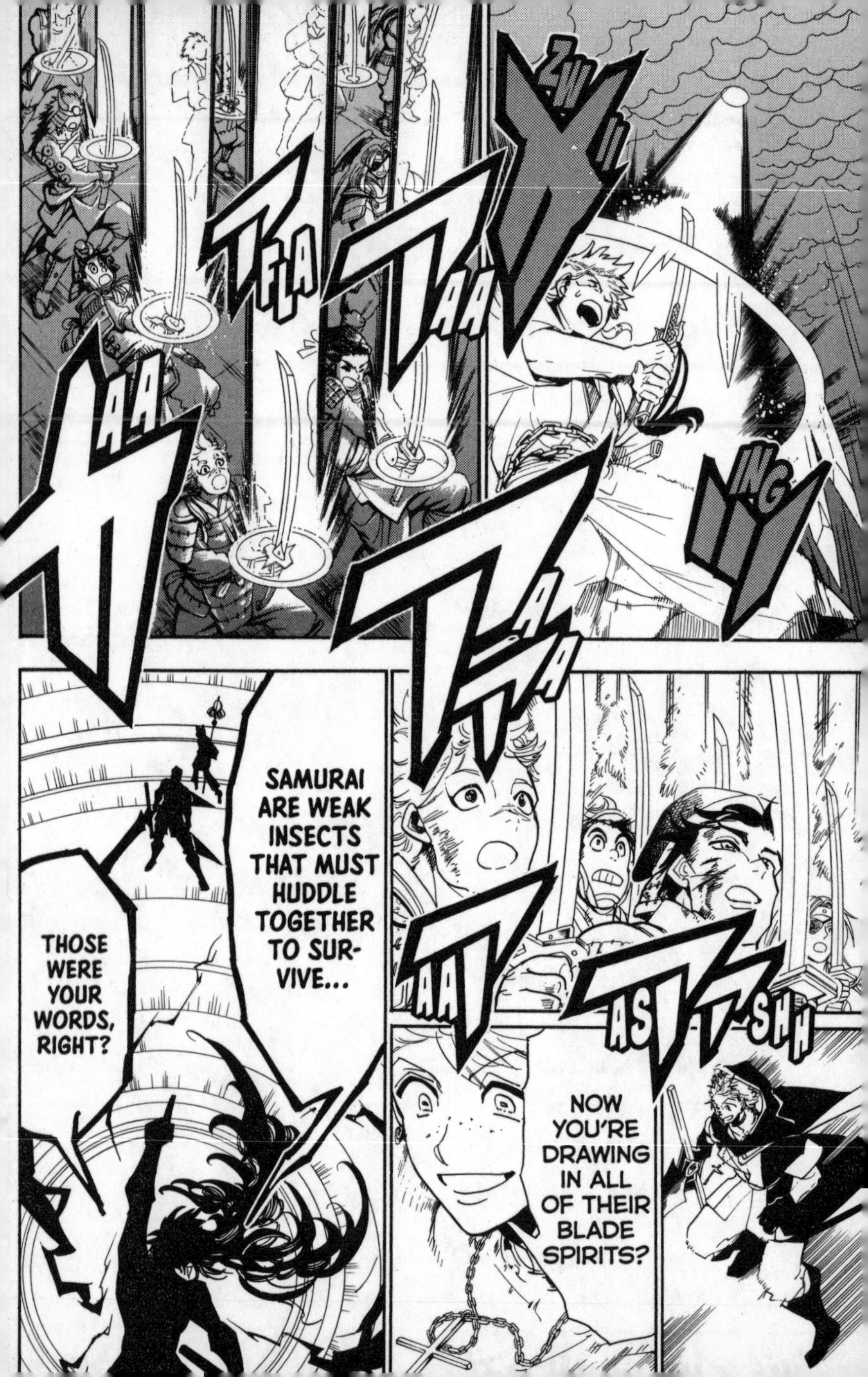
NOW YOU'RE DRAWING IN ALL OF THEIR BLADE SPIRITS?
SAMURAI ARE WEAK INSECTS THAT MUST HUDDLE TOGETHER TO SUR-VIVE...
THOSE WERE YOUR WORDS, RIGHT?

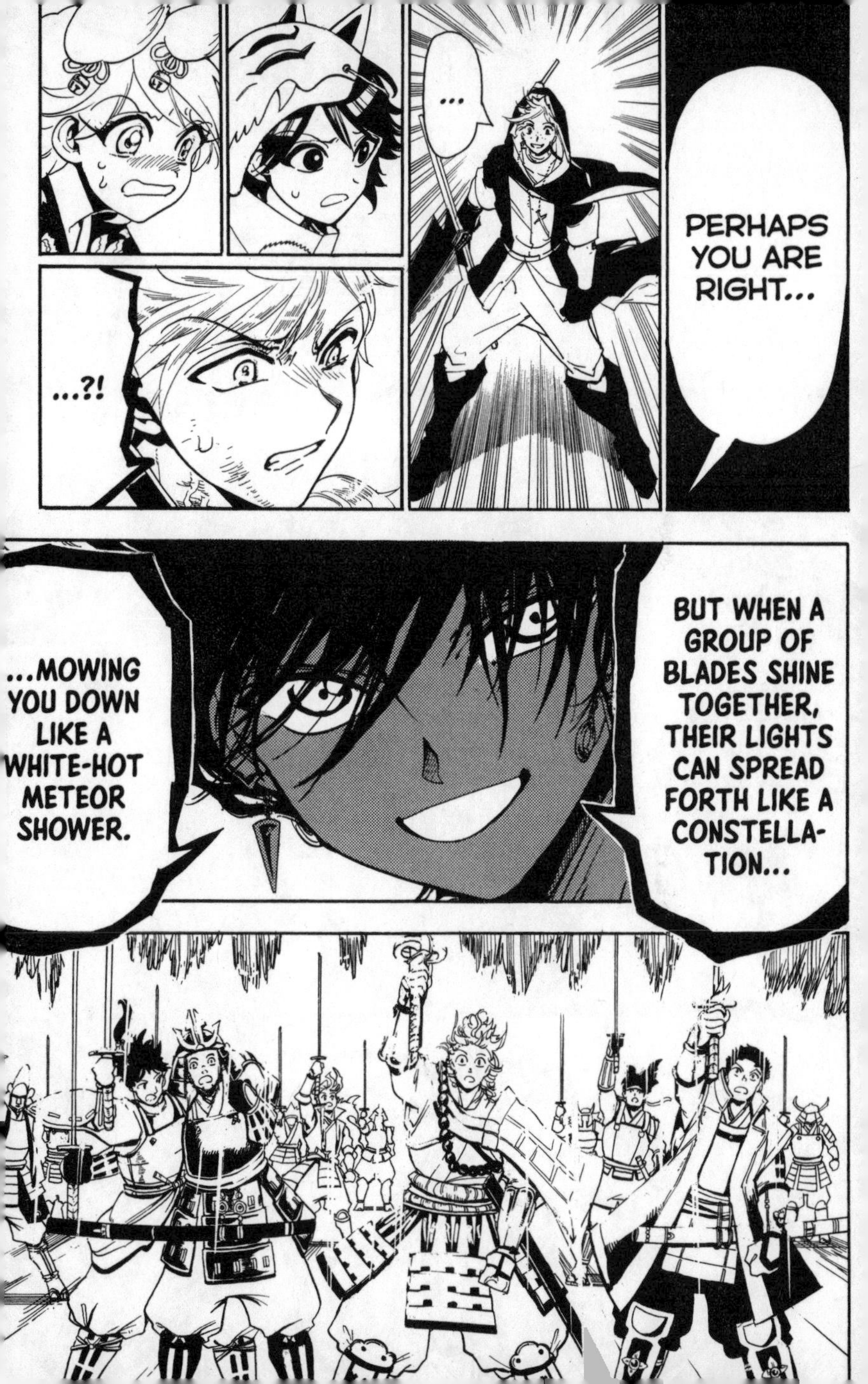
PERHAPS YOU ARE RIGHT...
...
...?!
BUT WHEN A GROUP OF BLADES SHINE TOGETHER, THEIR LIGHTS CAN SPREAD FORTH LIKE A CONSTELLA-TION...
...MOWING YOU DOWN LIKE A WHITE-HOT METEOR SHOWER.

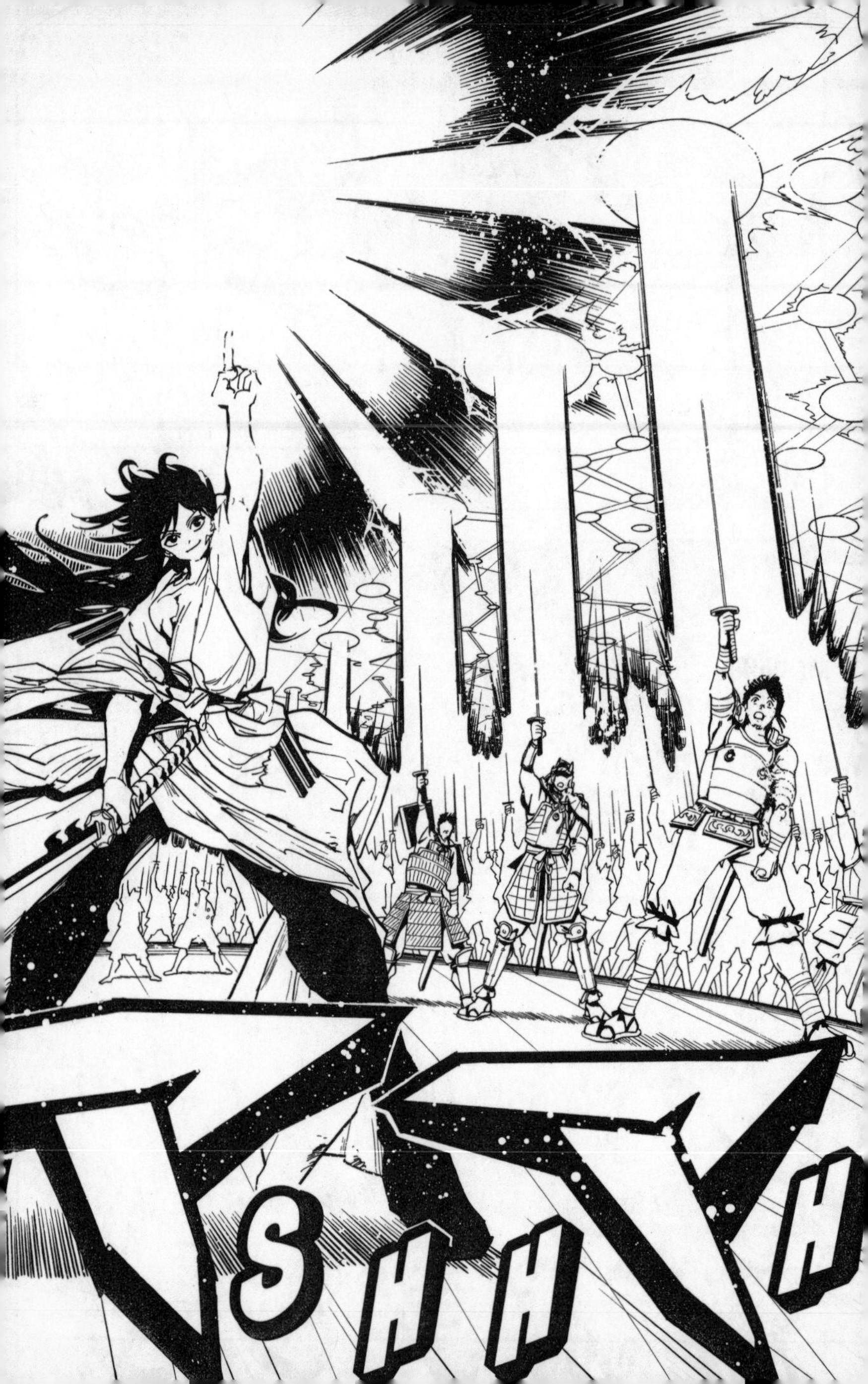
SHHH

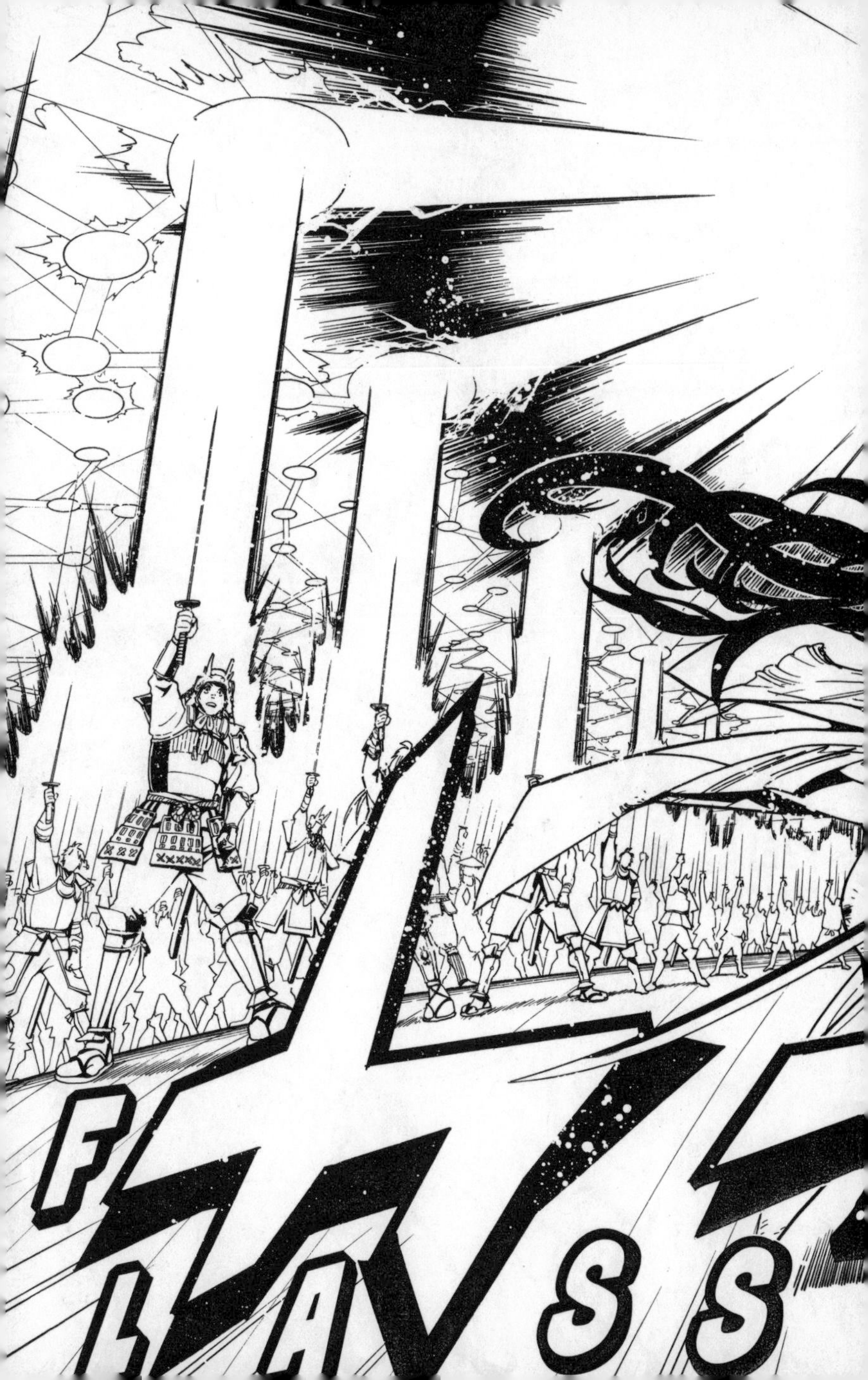
FLASS

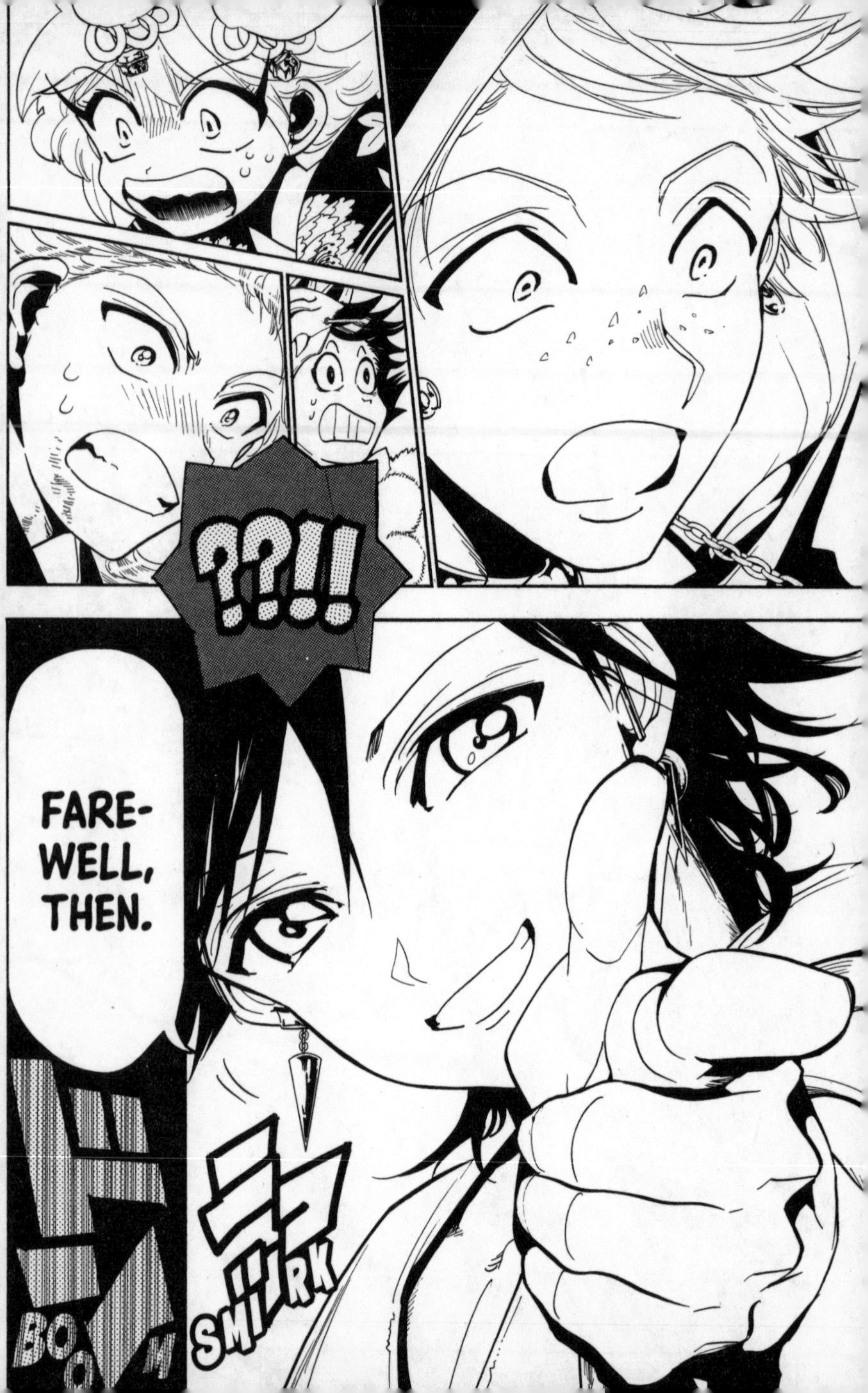
??!!
FARE-WELL, THEN.
SMIRK

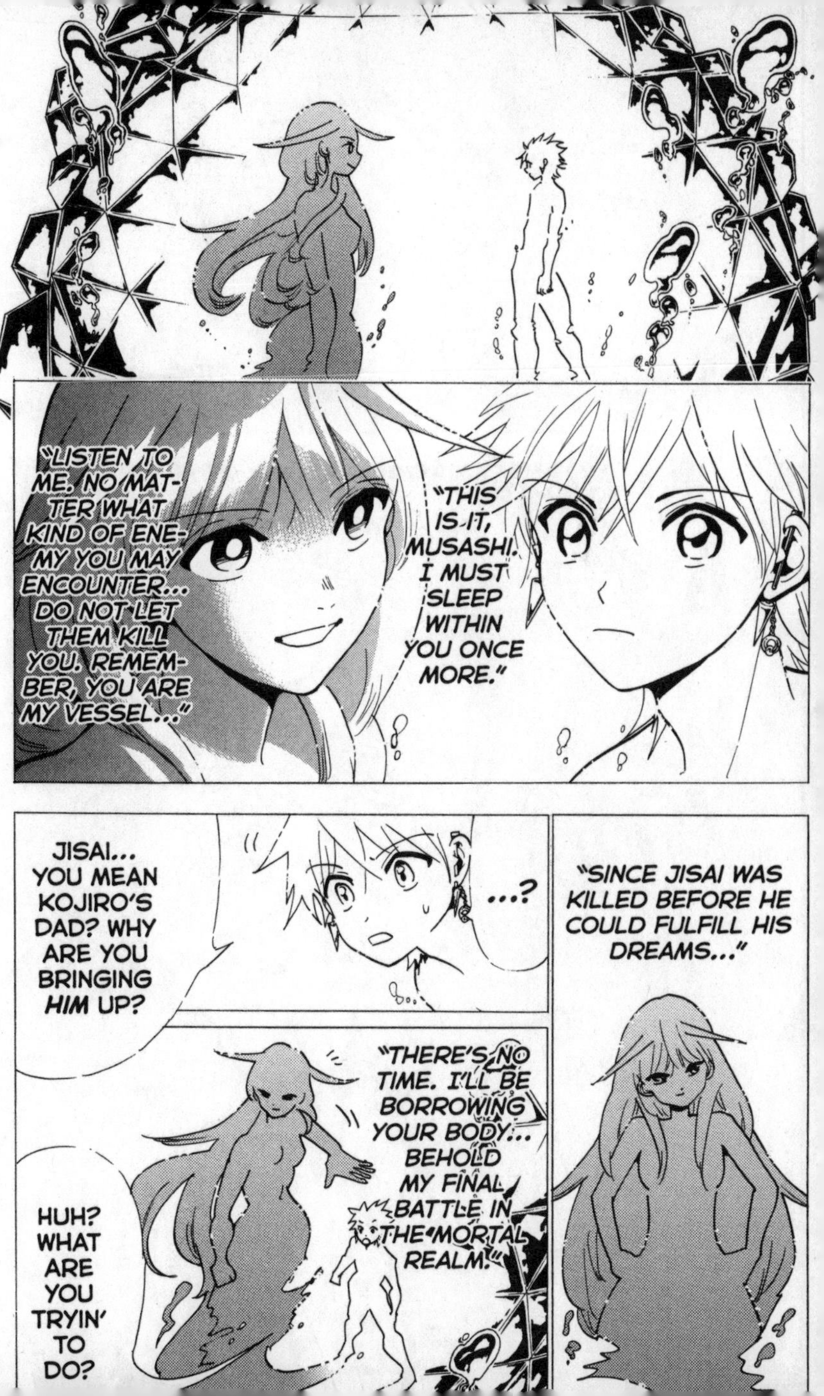
"THIS IS IT, MUSASHI. I MUST SLEEP WITHIN YOU ONCE MORE."
"LISTEN TO ME. NO MATTER WHAT KIND OF ENEMY YOU MAY ENCOUNTER... DO NOT LET THEM KILL YOU. REMEMBER, YOU ARE MY VESSEL..."
"SINCE JISAI WAS KILLED BEFORE HE COULD FULFILL HIS DREAMS..."
...?
JISAI... YOU MEAN KOJIRO'S DAD? WHY ARE YOU BRINGING *HIM* UP?
"THERE'S NO TIME. I'LL BE BORROWING YOUR BODY... BEHOLD MY FINAL BATTLE IN THE MORTAL REALM."
HUH? WHAT ARE YOU TRYIN' TO DO?

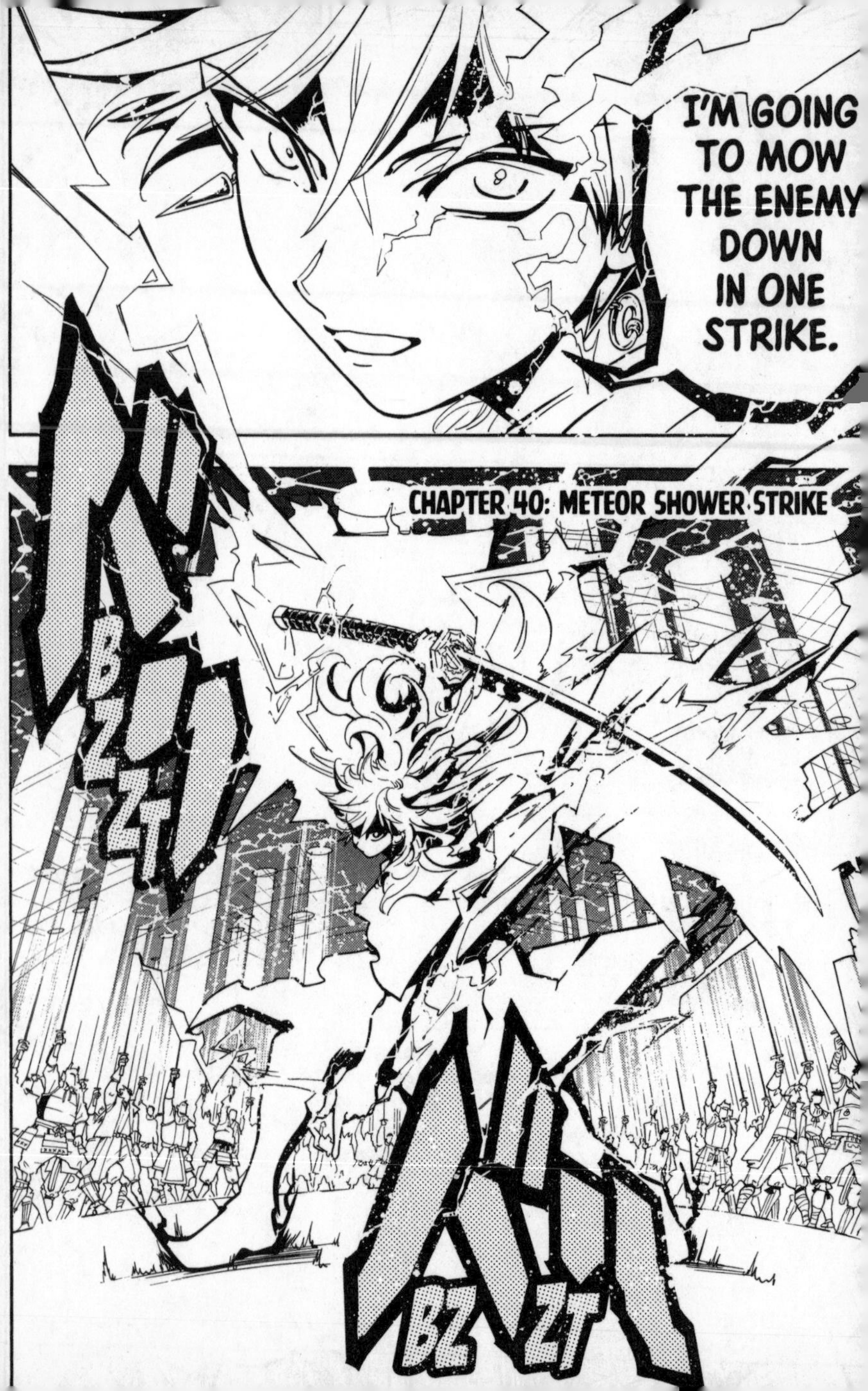
I'M GOING TO MOW THE ENEMY DOWN IN ONE STRIKE.
BZZT
CHAPTER 40: METEOR SHOWER STRIKE
BZ ZT

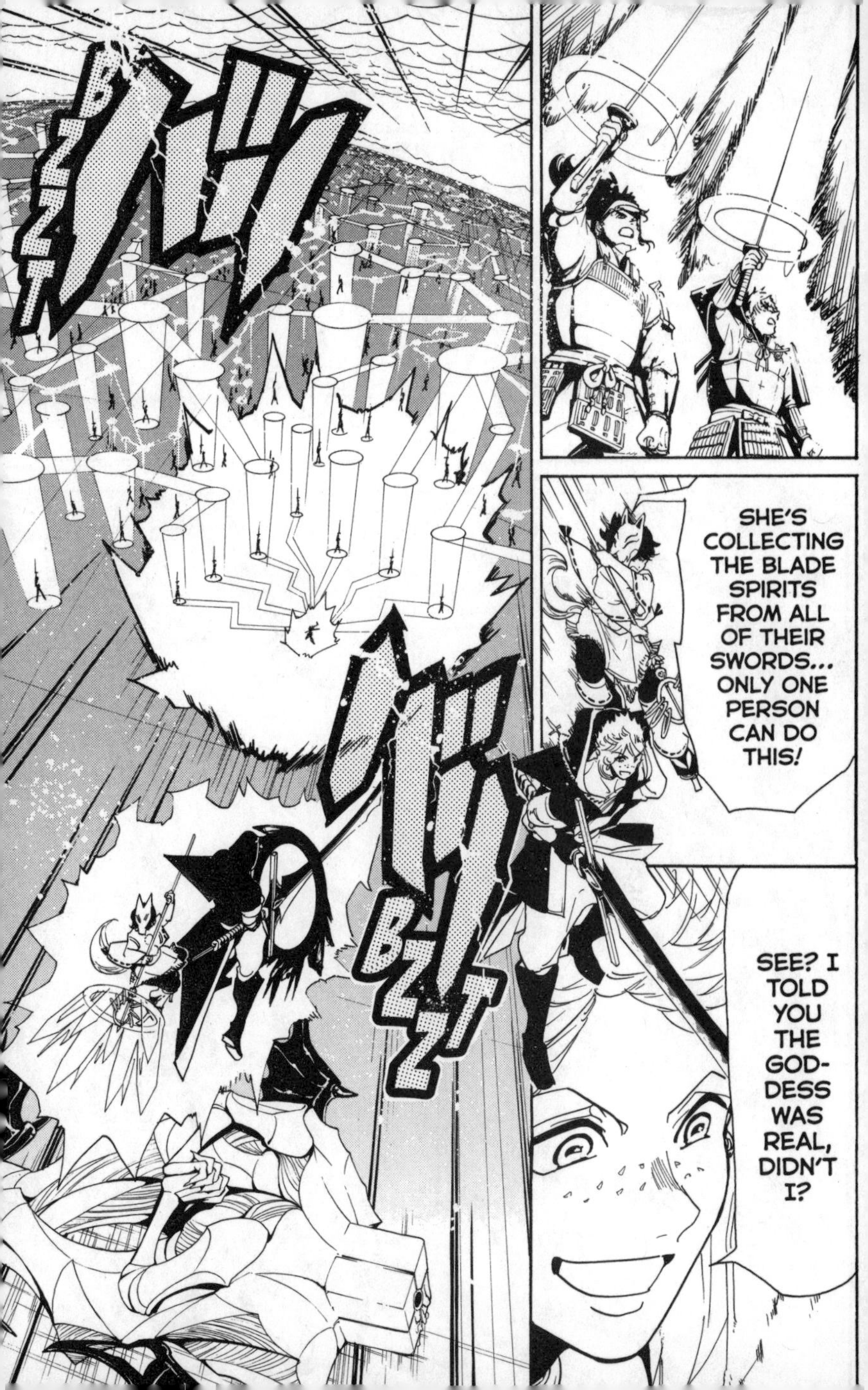
SHE'S COLLECTING THE BLADE SPIRITS FROM ALL OF THEIR SWORDS... ONLY ONE PERSON CAN DO THIS!
SEE? I TOLD YOU THE GOD-DESS WAS REAL, DIDN'T I?

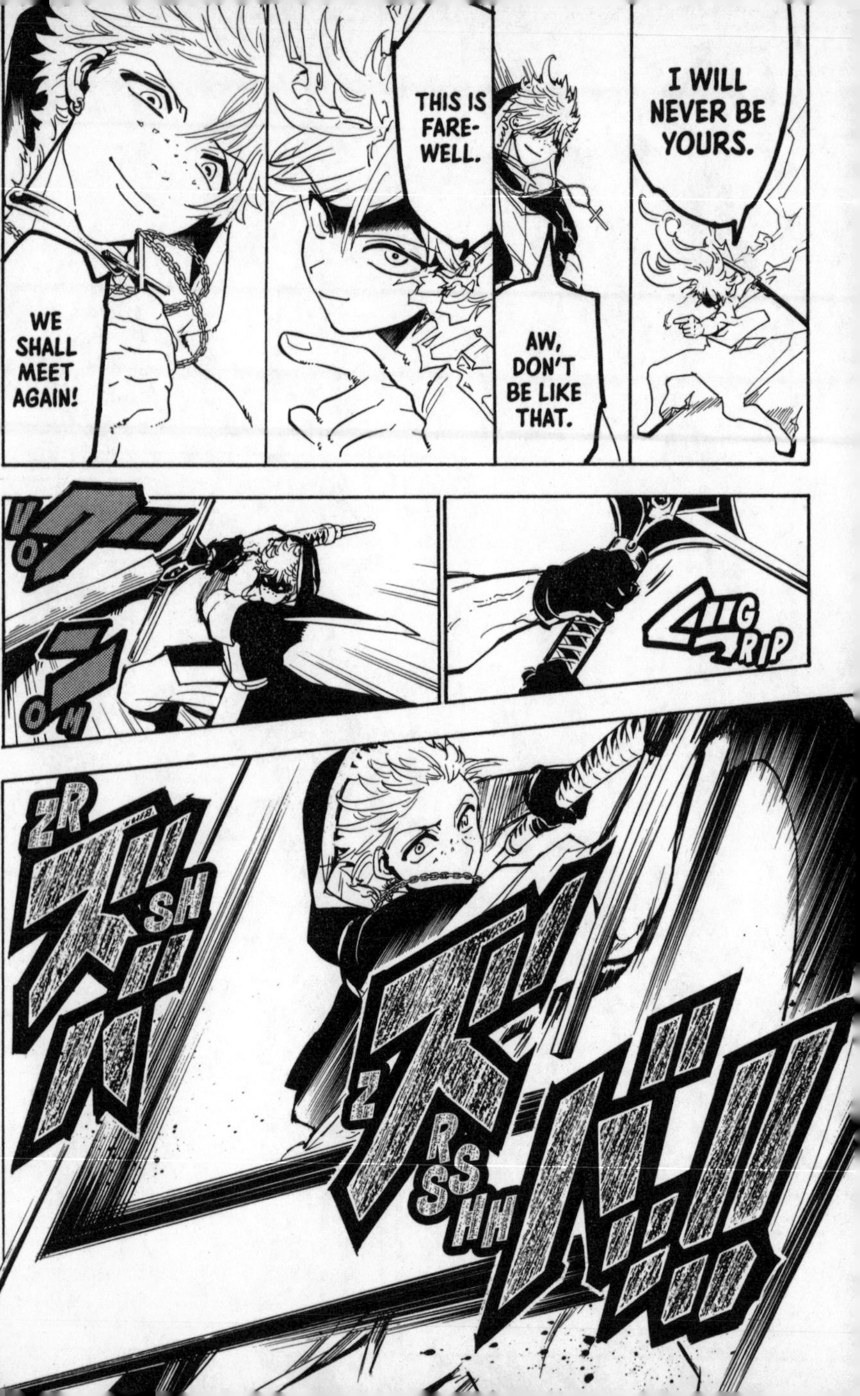
I WILL NEVER BE YOURS.
AW, DON'T BE LIKE THAT.
THIS IS FARE-WELL.
WE SHALL MEET AGAIN!
GRIP
VOOM
ZRSSHH
ZRSH

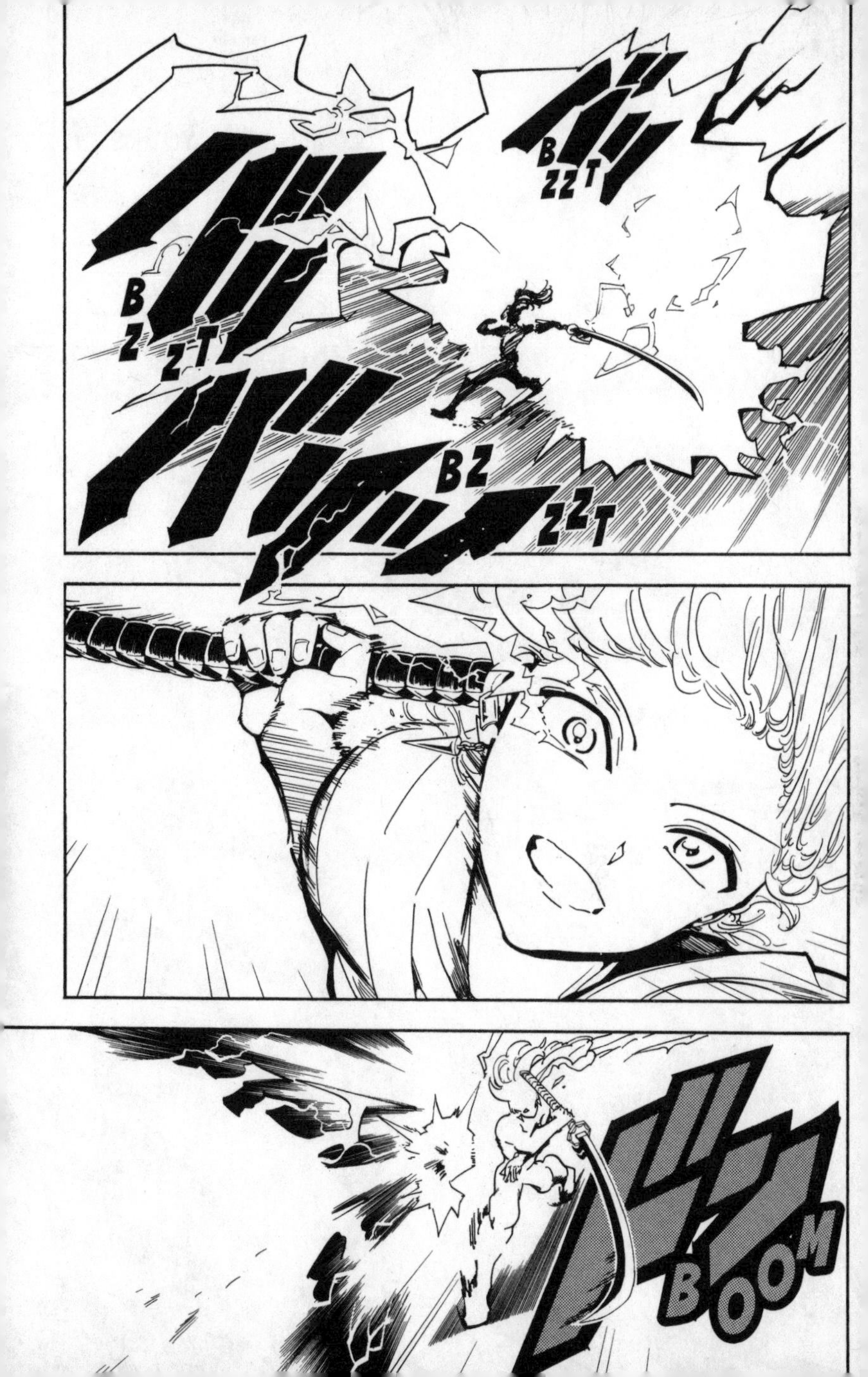
BZZT
BZZT
BZZZT
BOOM

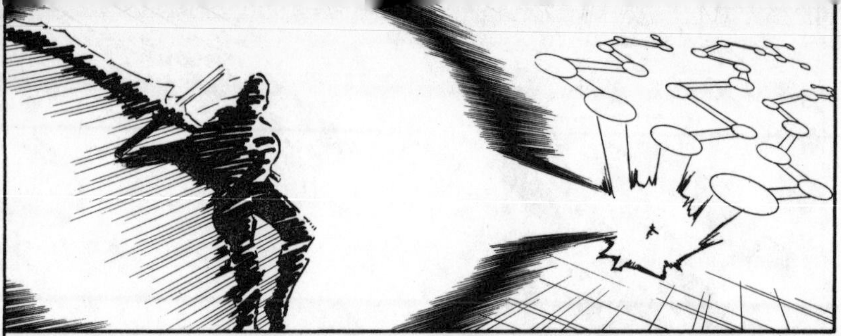

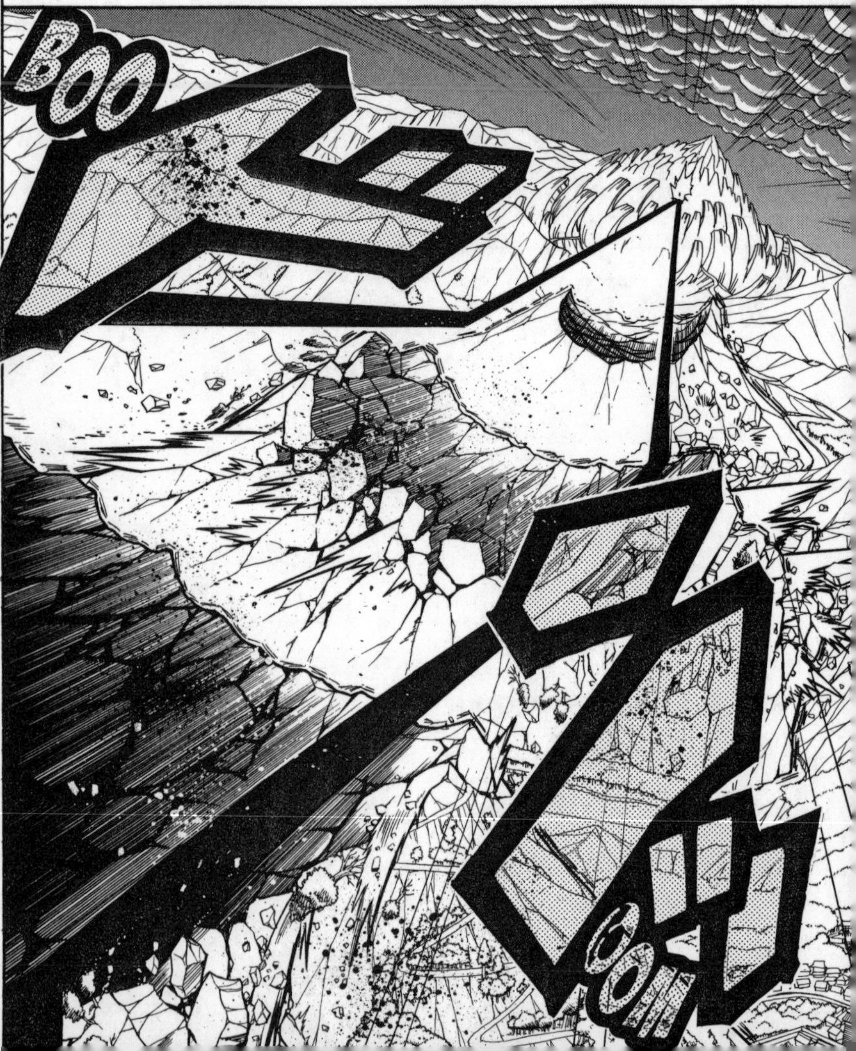
BOO

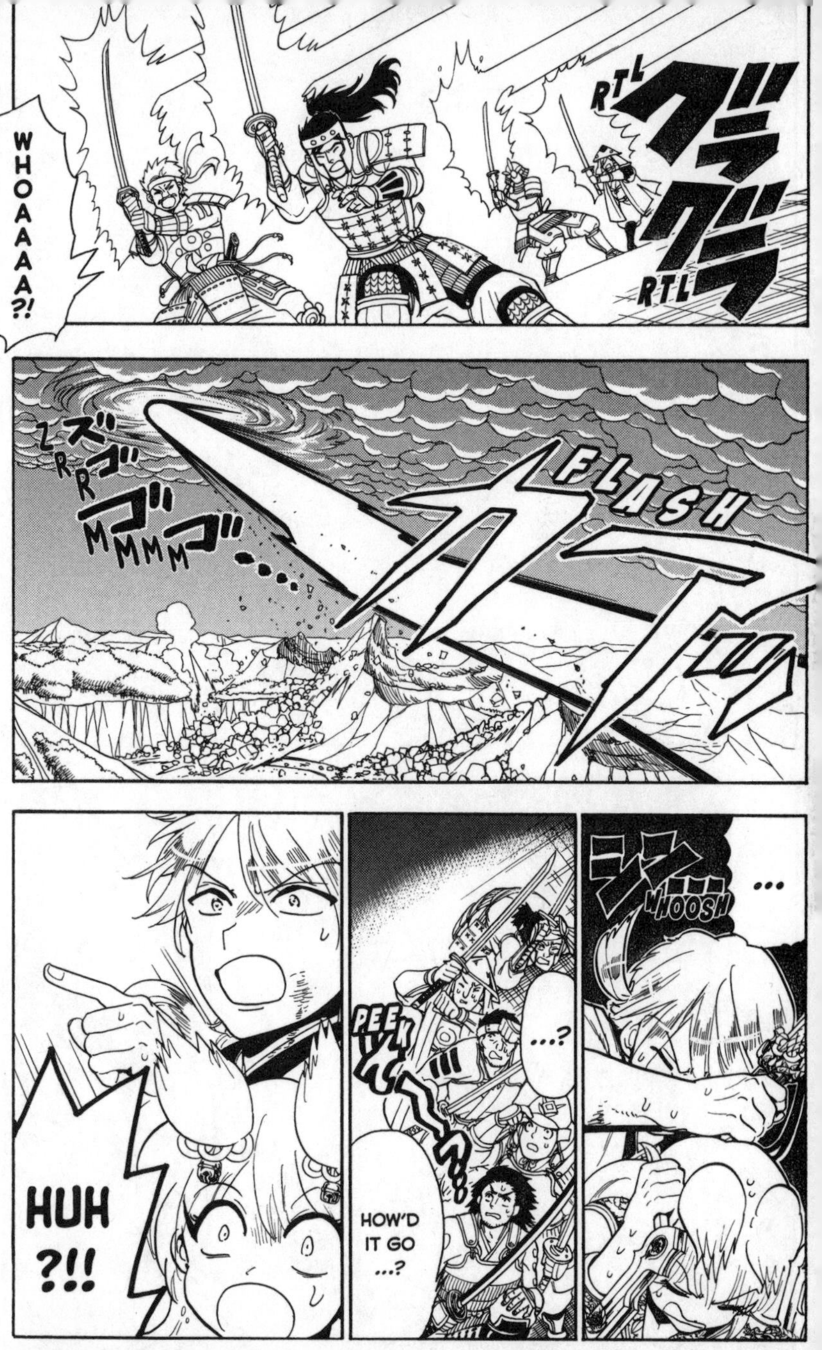

グラグラ
RTL
RTL
WHOAAAAA?!
FLASH
ズゴゴゴ
ZRR
MMMM
シン…
WHOOSH
…
…?
PEEK
HOW'D IT GO …?
HUH ?!!

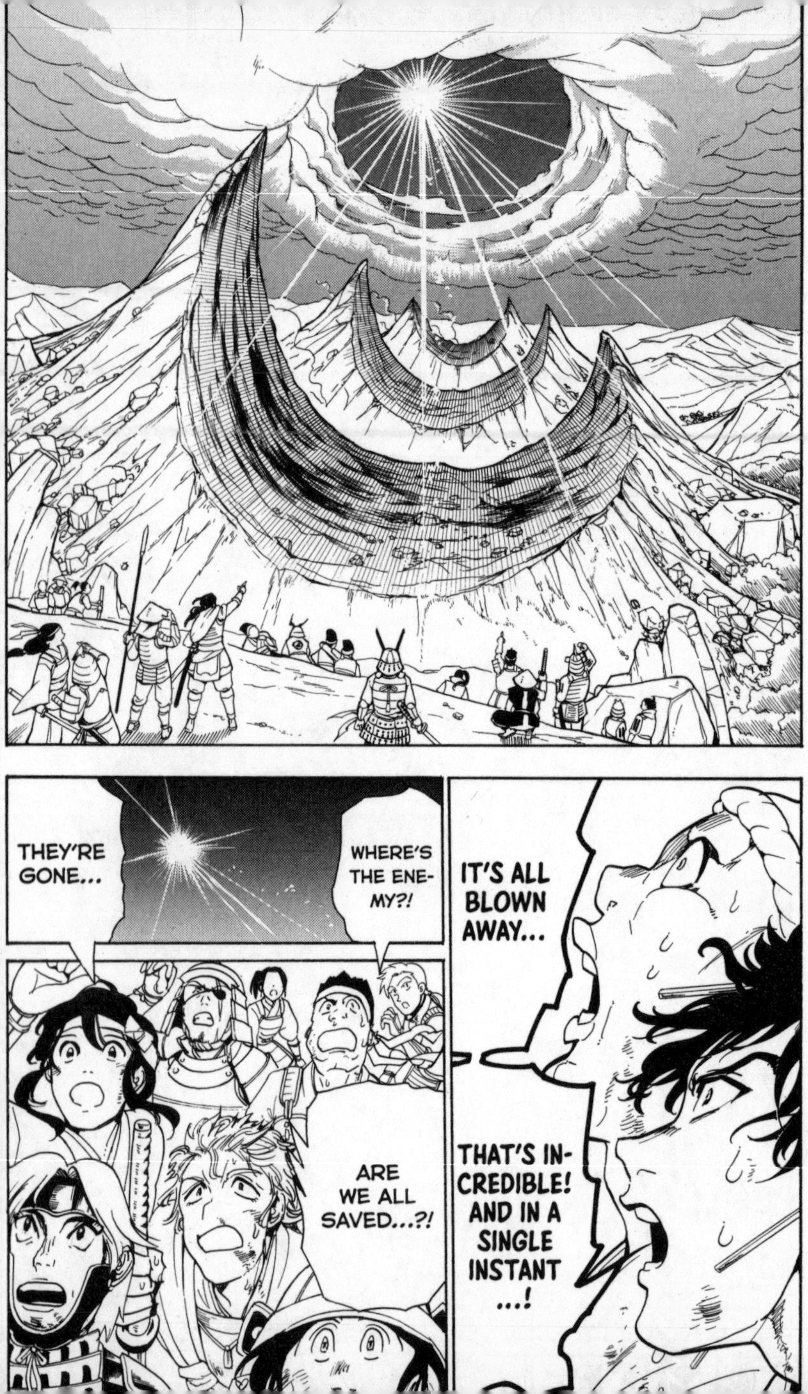
IT'S ALL BLOWN AWAY...
THAT'S IN-CREDIBLE! AND IN A SINGLE INSTANT ...!
WHERE'S THE ENE-MY?!
THEY'RE GONE...
ARE WE ALL SAVED...?!

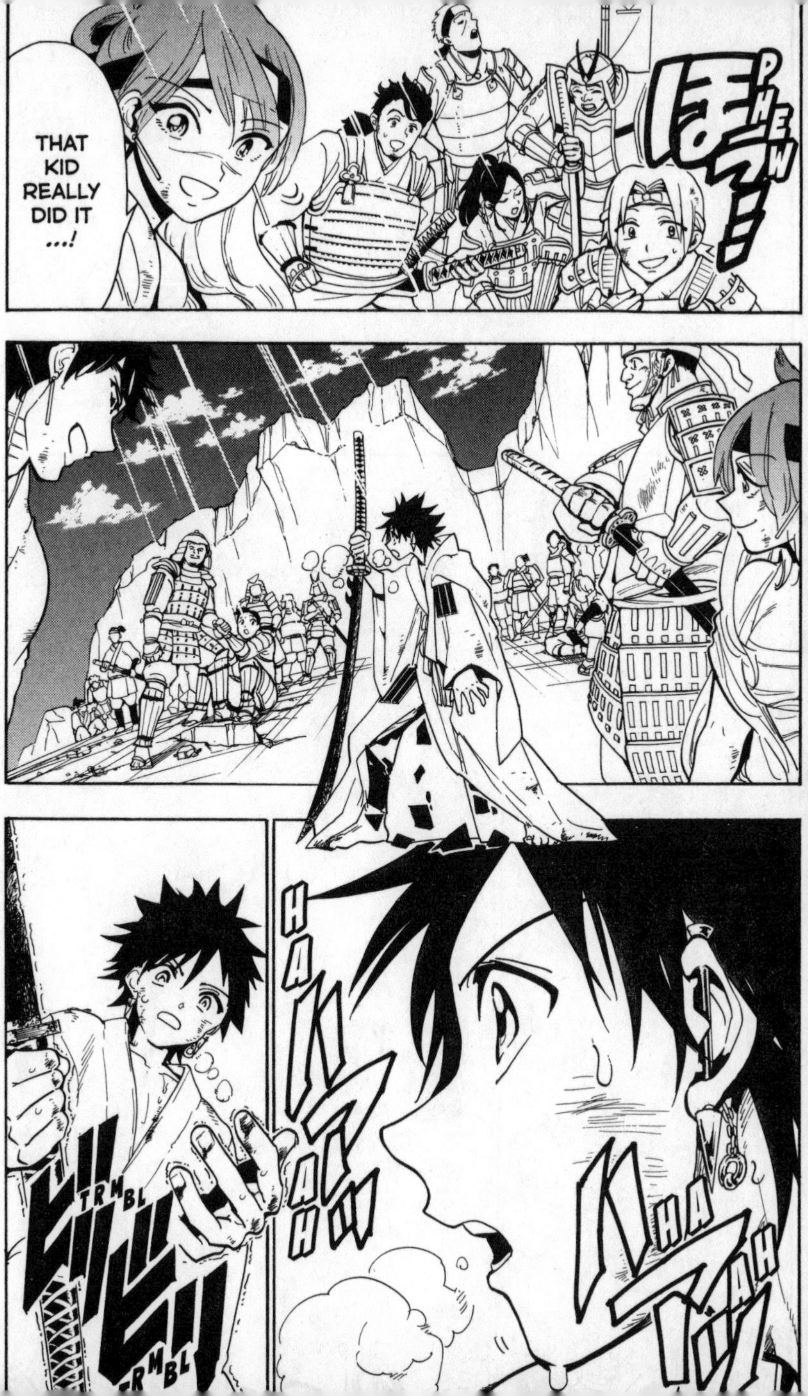
PHEW
THAT KID REALLY DID IT ...!
HA AH AH
HA AH AH
TRMBL
TRMBL

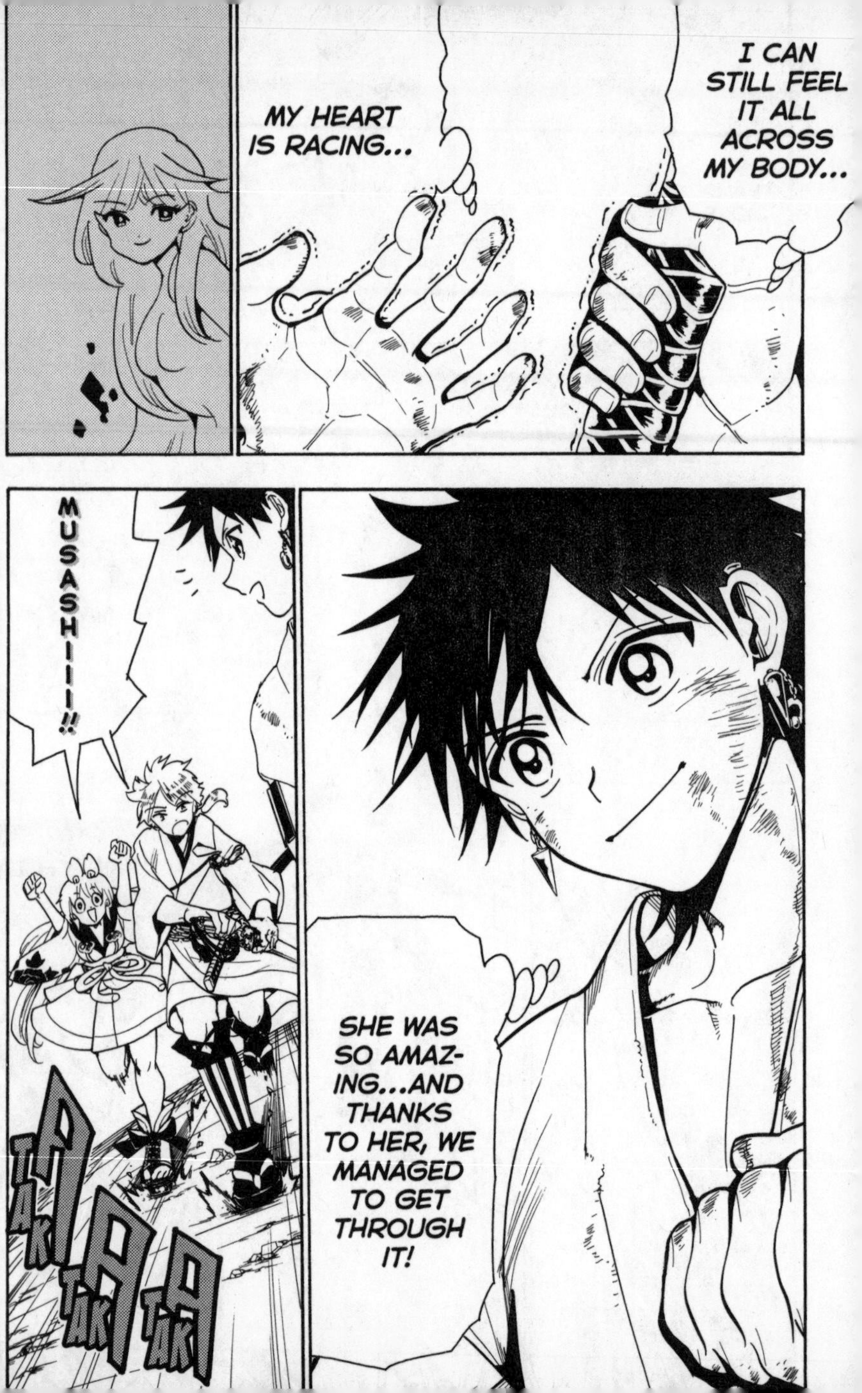
I CAN STILL FEEL IT ALL ACROSS MY BODY...
MY HEART IS RACING...
SHE WAS SO AMAZ-ING...AND THANKS TO HER, WE MANAGED TO GET THROUGH IT!
MUSASHIIII!!
TAK TAK TAK

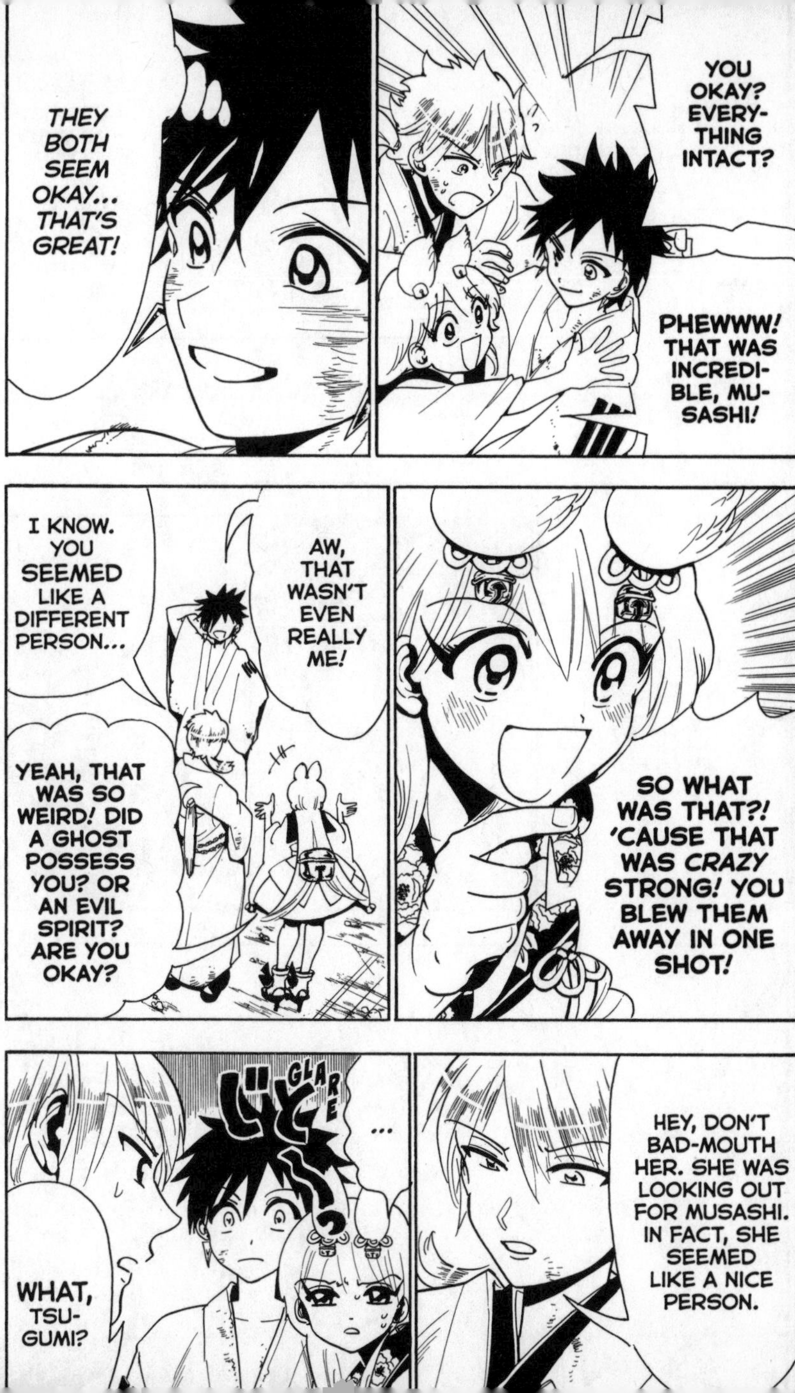
YOU OKAY? EVERYTHING INTACT?
PHEWWW! THAT WAS INCREDIBLE, MUSASHI!
THEY BOTH SEEM OKAY... THAT'S GREAT!
SO WHAT WAS THAT?! 'CAUSE THAT WAS CRAZY STRONG! YOU BLEW THEM AWAY IN ONE SHOT!
AW, THAT WASN'T EVEN REALLY ME!
I KNOW. YOU SEEMED LIKE A DIFFERENT PERSON...
YEAH, THAT WAS SO WEIRD! DID A GHOST POSSESS YOU? OR AN EVIL SPIRIT? ARE YOU OKAY?
HEY, DON'T BAD-MOUTH HER. SHE WAS LOOKING OUT FOR MUSASHI. IN FACT, SHE SEEMED LIKE A NICE PERSON.
GLARE
...
WHAT, TSUGUMI?

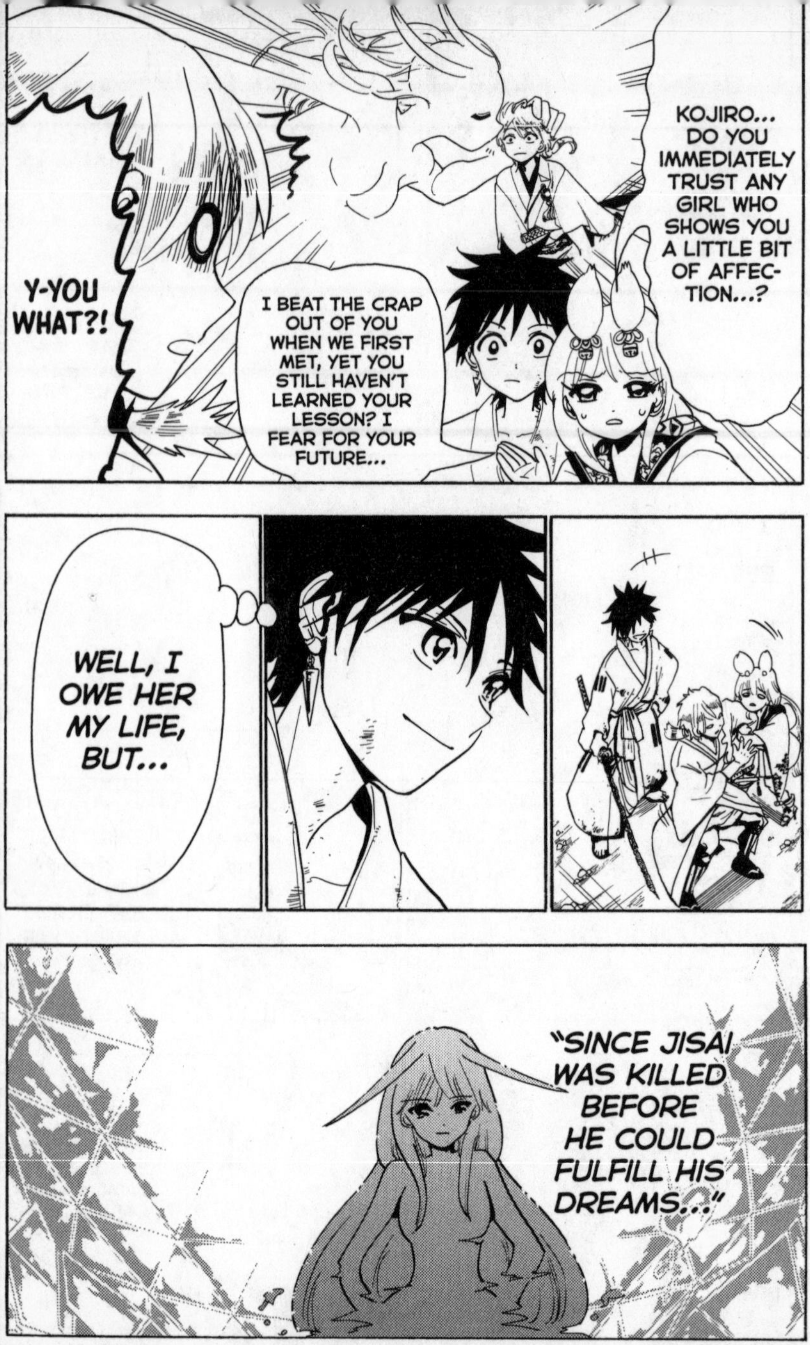
KOJIRO... DO YOU IMMEDIATELY TRUST ANY GIRL WHO SHOWS YOU A LITTLE BIT OF AFFEC-TION...?
I BEAT THE CRAP OUT OF YOU WHEN WE FIRST MET, YET YOU STILL HAVEN'T LEARNED YOUR LESSON? I FEAR FOR YOUR FUTURE...
Y-YOU WHAT?!
WELL, I OWE HER MY LIFE, BUT...
"SINCE JISAI WAS KILLED BEFORE HE COULD FULFILL HIS DREAMS..."

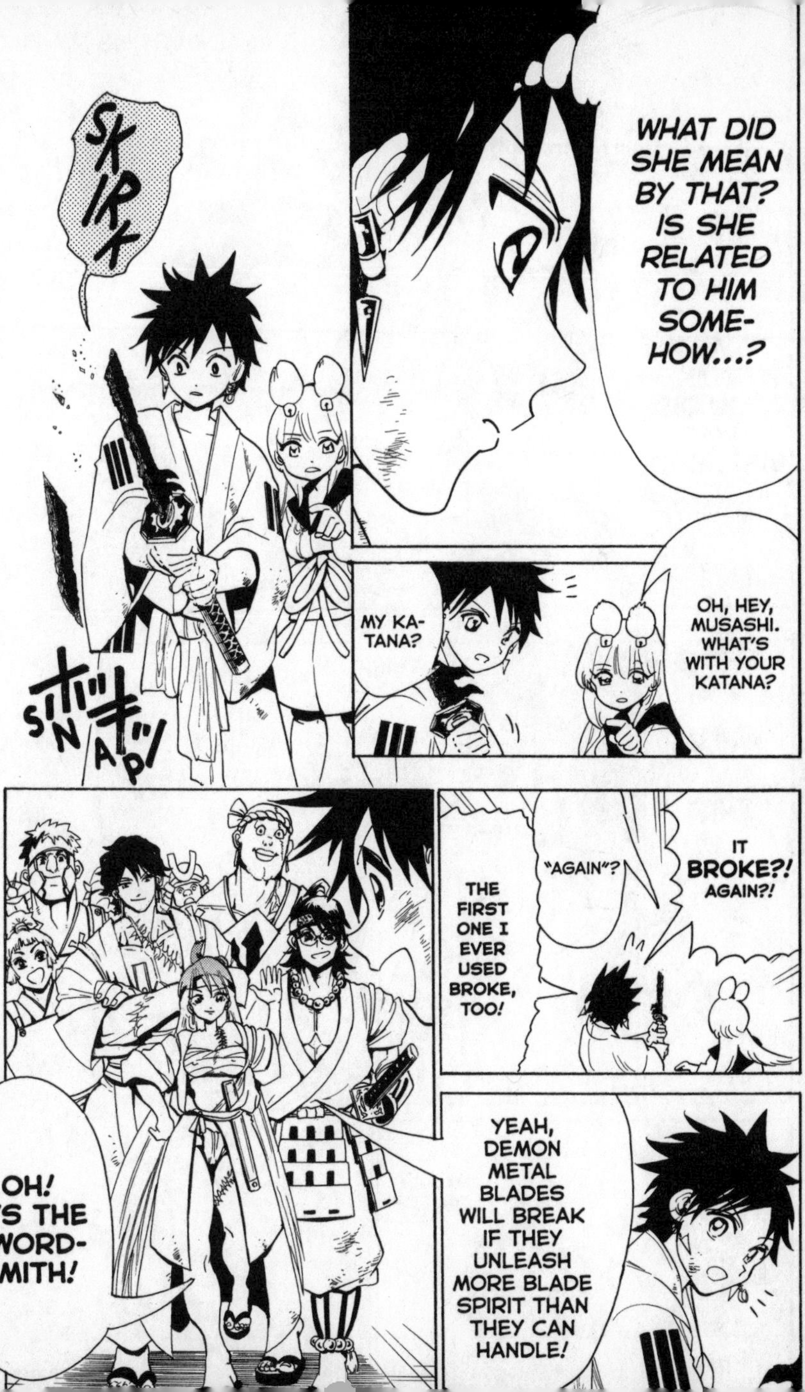
WHAT DID SHE MEAN BY THAT? IS SHE RELATED TO HIM SOME-HOW...?
OH, HEY, MUSASHI. WHAT'S WITH YOUR KATANA?
MY KA-TANA?
SKIRK
SNAP
IT BROKE?! AGAIN?!
"AGAIN"?
THE FIRST ONE I EVER USED BROKE, TOO!
YEAH, DEMON METAL BLADES WILL BREAK IF THEY UNLEASH MORE BLADE SPIRIT THAN THEY CAN HANDLE!
OH! IT'S THE SWORD-SMITH!

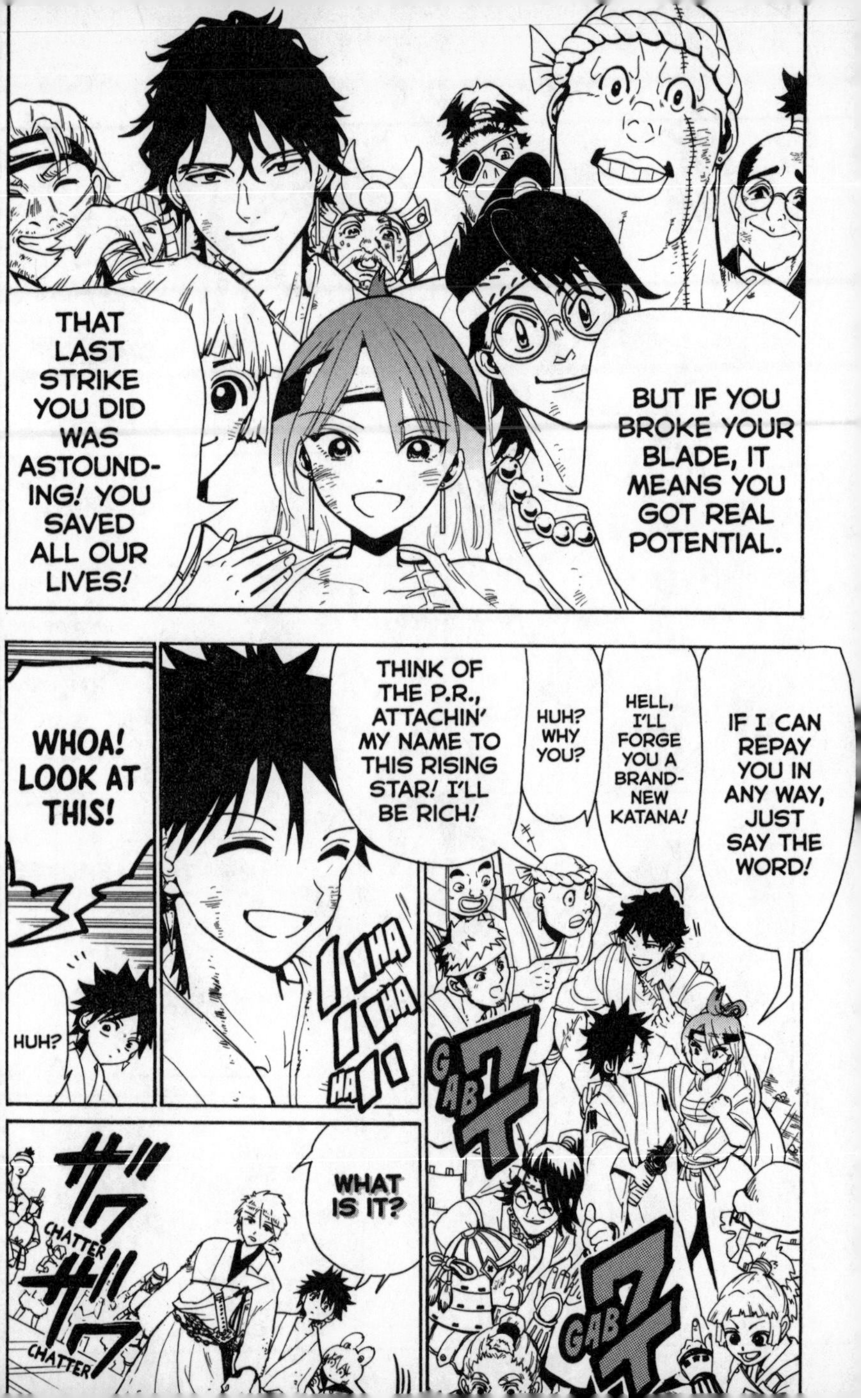
BUT IF YOU BROKE YOUR BLADE, IT MEANS YOU GOT REAL POTENTIAL.
THAT LAST STRIKE YOU DID WAS ASTOUNDING! YOU SAVED ALL OUR LIVES!
IF I CAN REPAY YOU IN ANY WAY, JUST SAY THE WORD!
HELL, I'LL FORGE YOU A BRAND-NEW KATANA!
HUH? WHY YOU?
THINK OF THE P.R., ATTACHIN' MY NAME TO THIS RISING STAR! I'LL BE RICH!
GABI
GABI
HA HA HA HA
WHOA! LOOK AT THIS!
HUH?
WHAT IS IT?
CHATTER
CHATTER

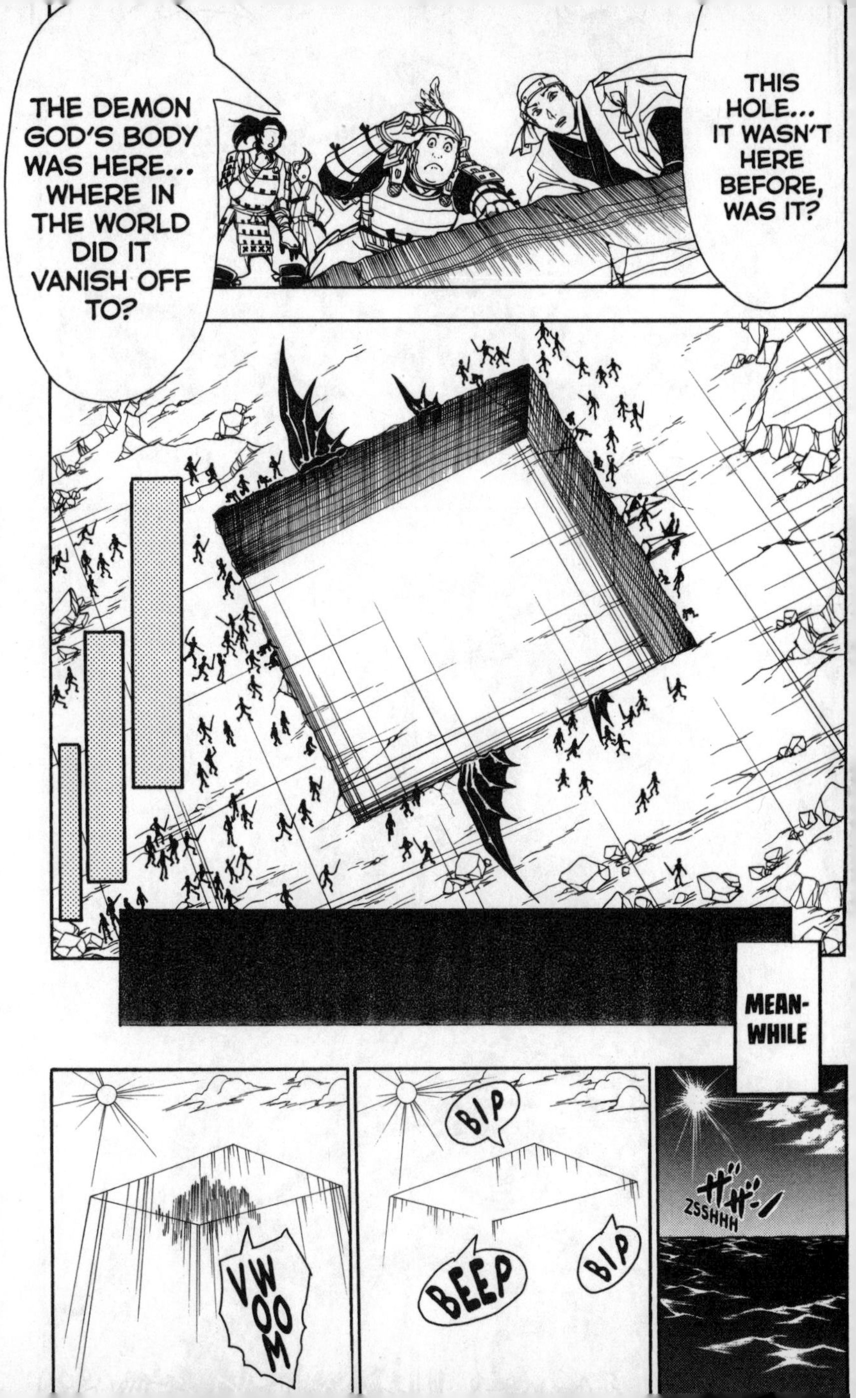
THIS HOLE... IT WASN'T HERE BEFORE, WAS IT?
THE DEMON GOD'S BODY WAS HERE... WHERE IN THE WORLD DID IT VANISH OFF TO?
MEAN-WHILE
ザザーン
ZSSHHH
BIP
BIP
BEEP
VWOOM

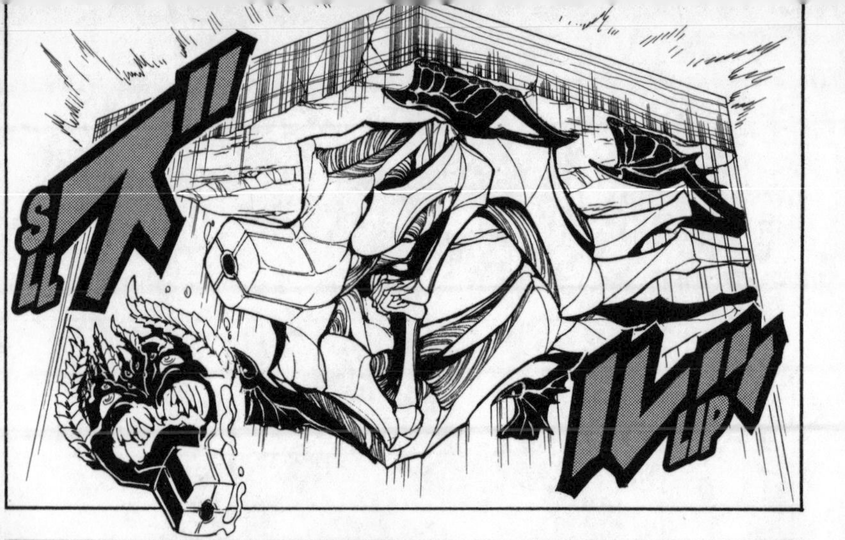
SLL
LIP
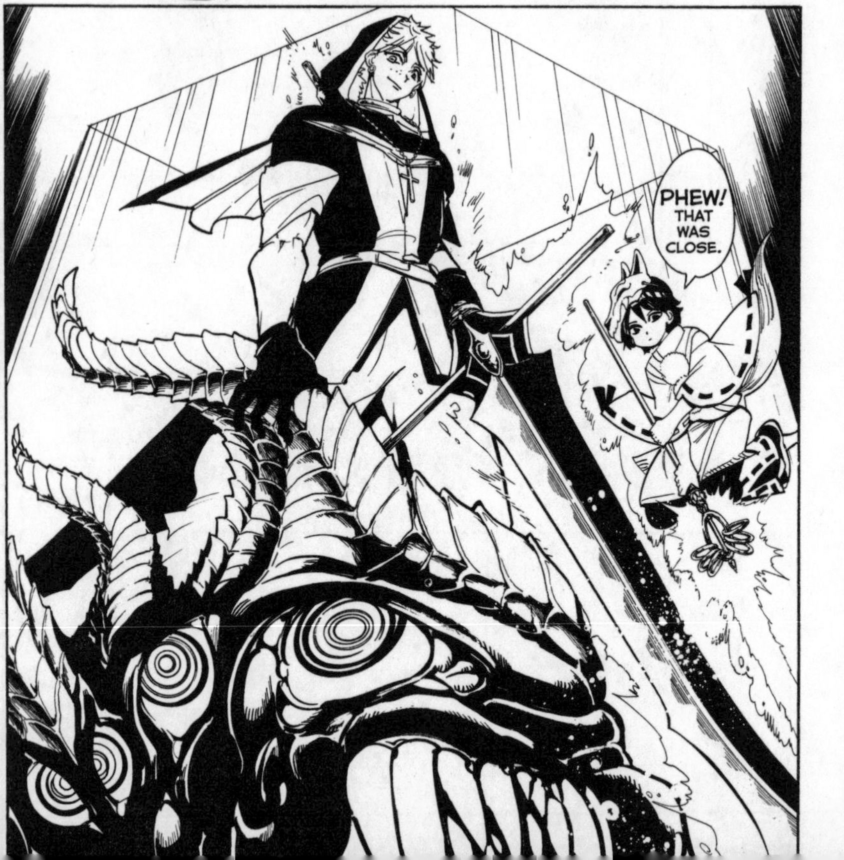
PHEW! THAT WAS CLOSE.

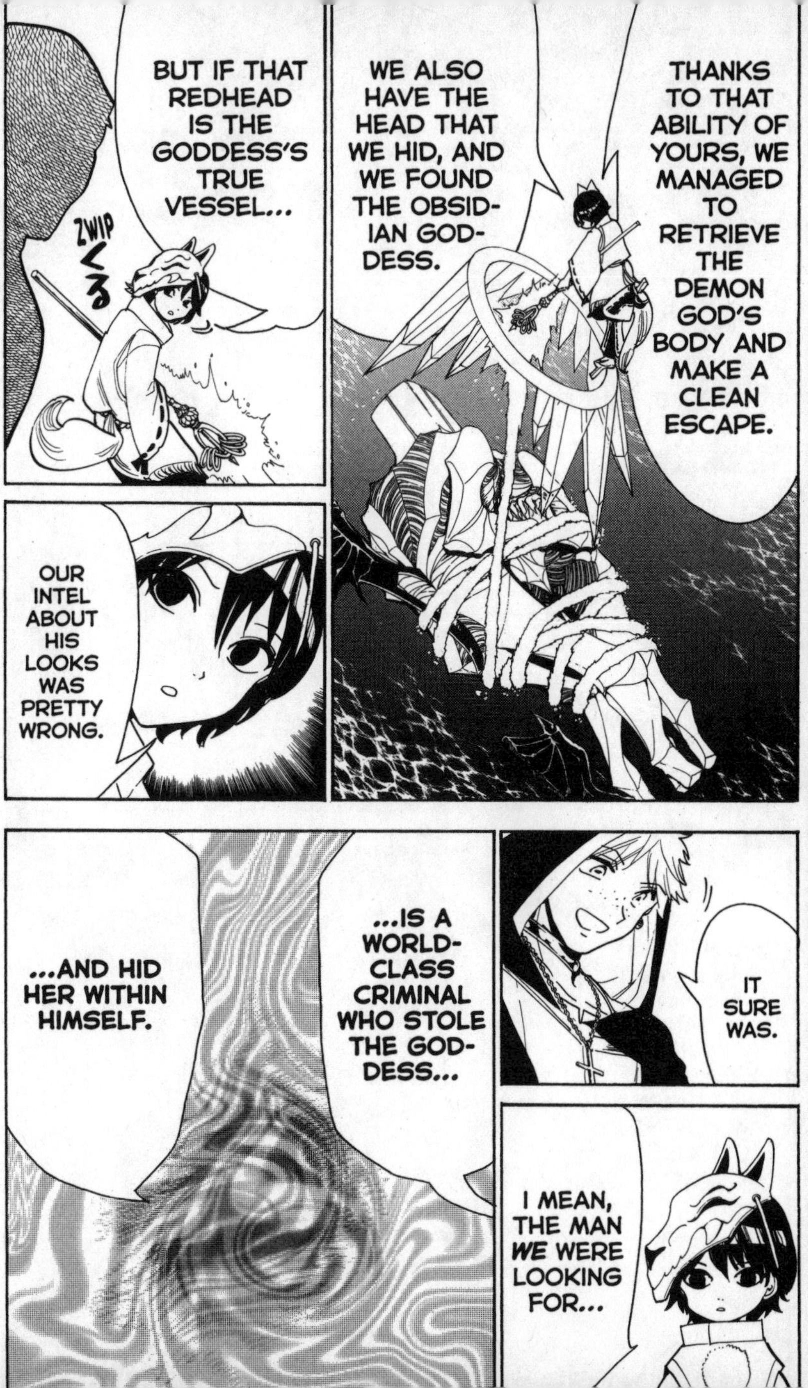
THANKS TO THAT ABILITY OF YOURS, WE MANAGED TO RETRIEVE THE DEMON GOD'S BODY AND MAKE A CLEAN ESCAPE.
WE ALSO HAVE THE HEAD THAT WE HID, AND WE FOUND THE OBSID-IAN GOD-DESS.
BUT IF THAT REDHEAD IS THE GODDESS'S TRUE VESSEL...
ZWIP
くる
OUR INTEL ABOUT HIS LOOKS WAS PRETTY WRONG.
IT SURE WAS.
I MEAN, THE MAN *WE* WERE LOOKING FOR...
...IS A WORLD-CLASS CRIMINAL WHO STOLE THE GOD-DESS...
...AND HID HER WITHIN HIMSELF.

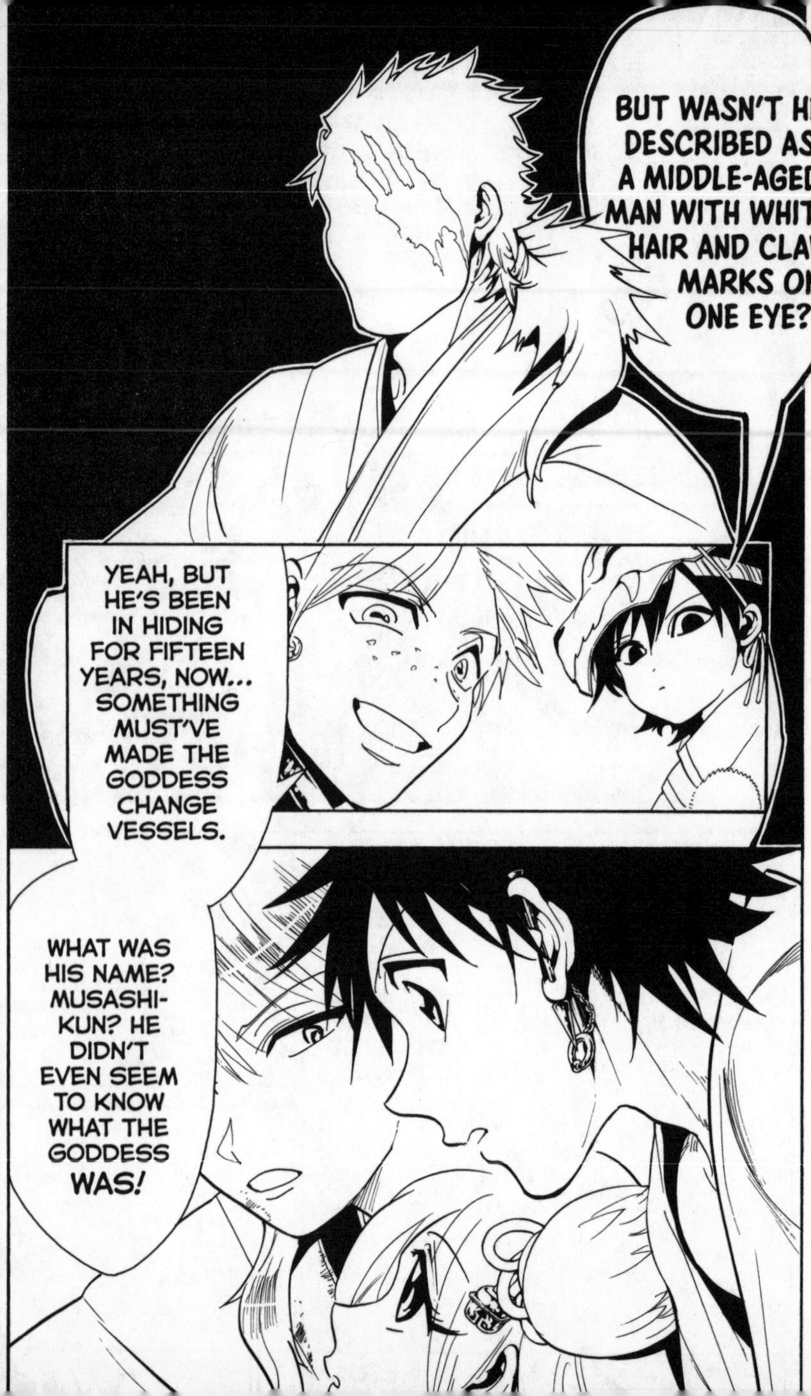
BUT WASN'T HE DESCRIBED AS A MIDDLE-AGED MAN WITH WHITE HAIR AND CLAW MARKS ON ONE EYE?
YEAH, BUT HE'S BEEN IN HIDING FOR FIFTEEN YEARS, NOW... SOMETHING MUST'VE MADE THE GODDESS CHANGE VESSELS.
WHAT WAS HIS NAME? MUSASHI-KUN? HE DIDN'T EVEN SEEM TO KNOW WHAT THE GODDESS WAS!

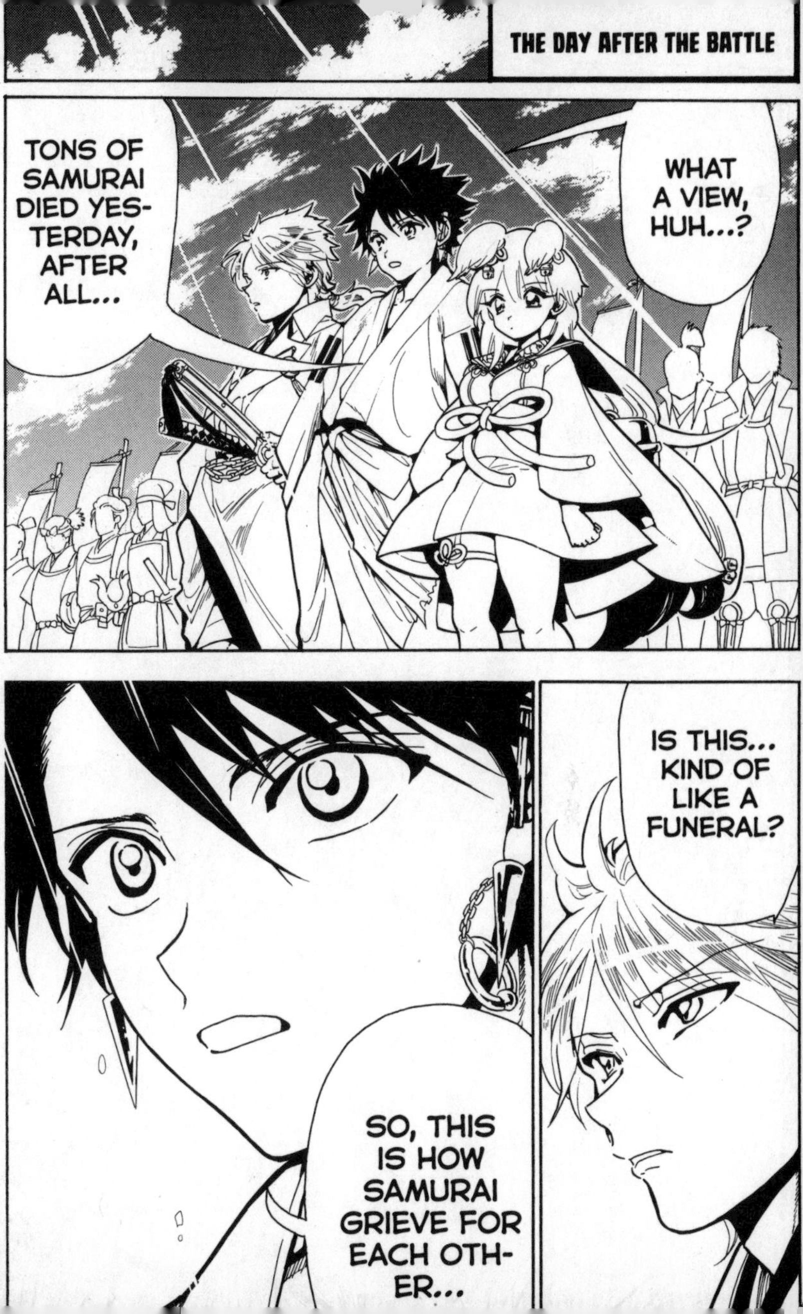
THE DAY AFTER THE BATTLE
WHAT A VIEW, HUH...?
TONS OF SAMURAI DIED YES-TERDAY, AFTER ALL...
IS THIS... KIND OF LIKE A FUNERAL?
SO, THIS IS HOW SAMURAI GRIEVE FOR EACH OTH-ER...

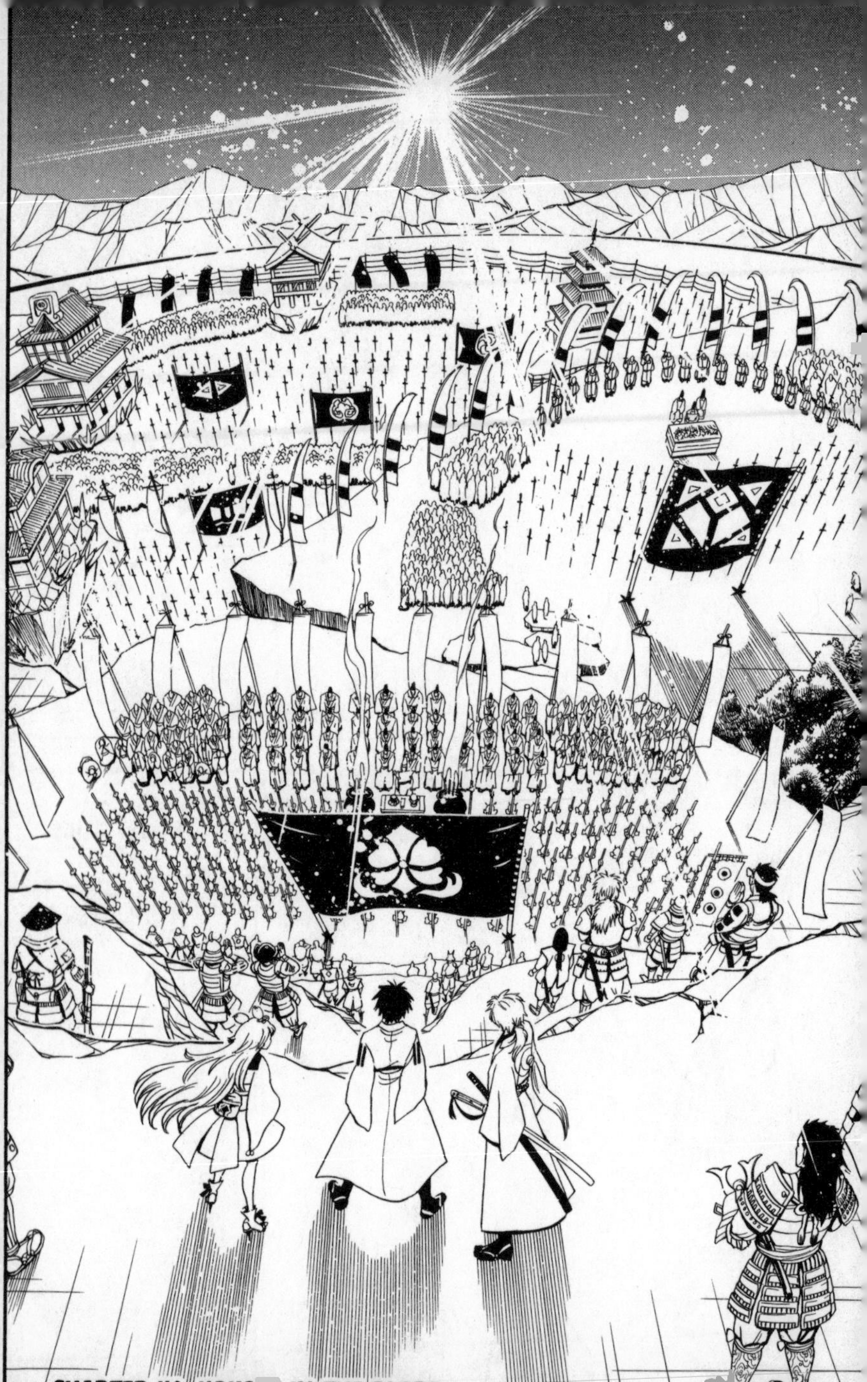

CHAPTER 41: VOWS IN THE BLADE

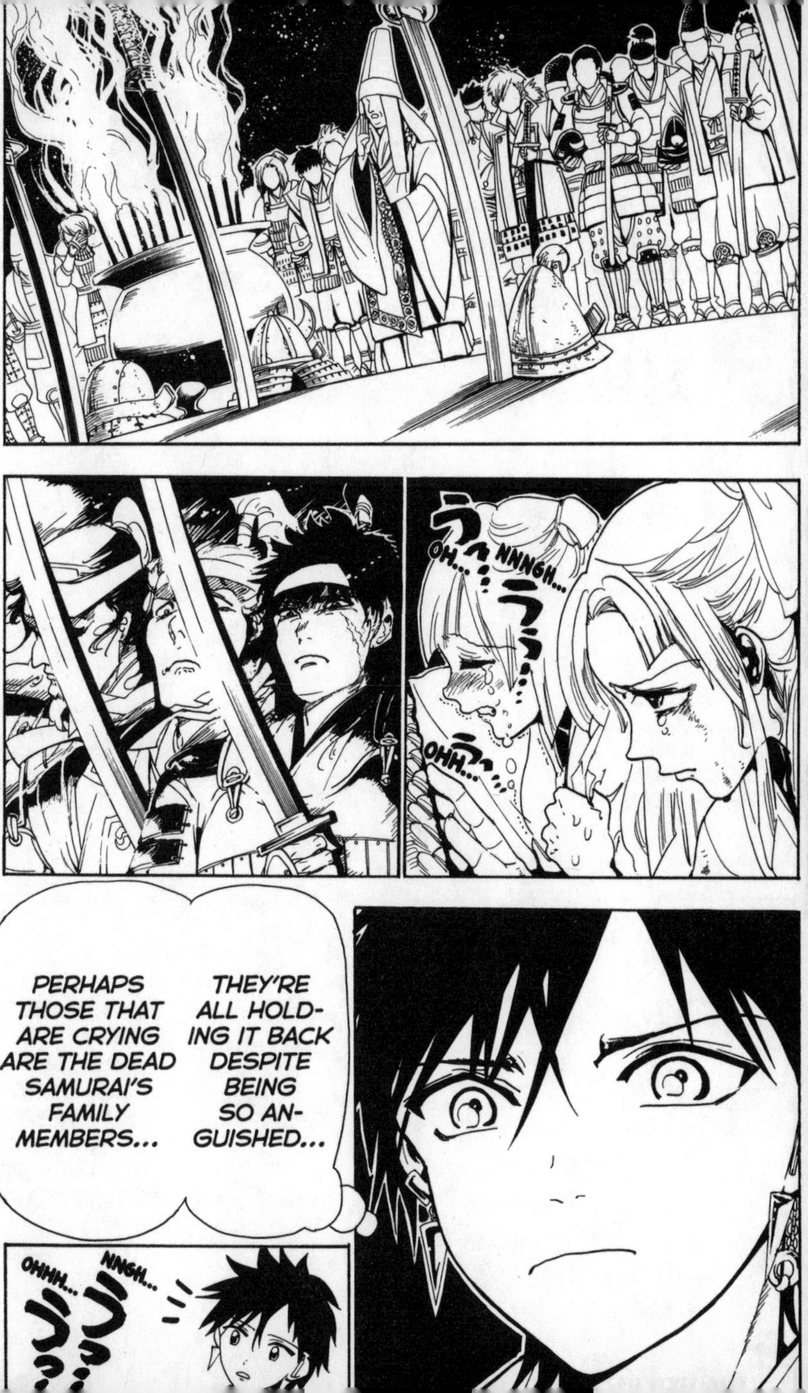
OH...
NNNGH...
OHH...
PERHAPS THOSE THAT ARE CRYING ARE THE DEAD SAMURAI'S FAMILY MEMBERS...
THEY'RE ALL HOLDING IT BACK DESPITE BEING SO ANGUISHED...
OHHH...
NNGH...

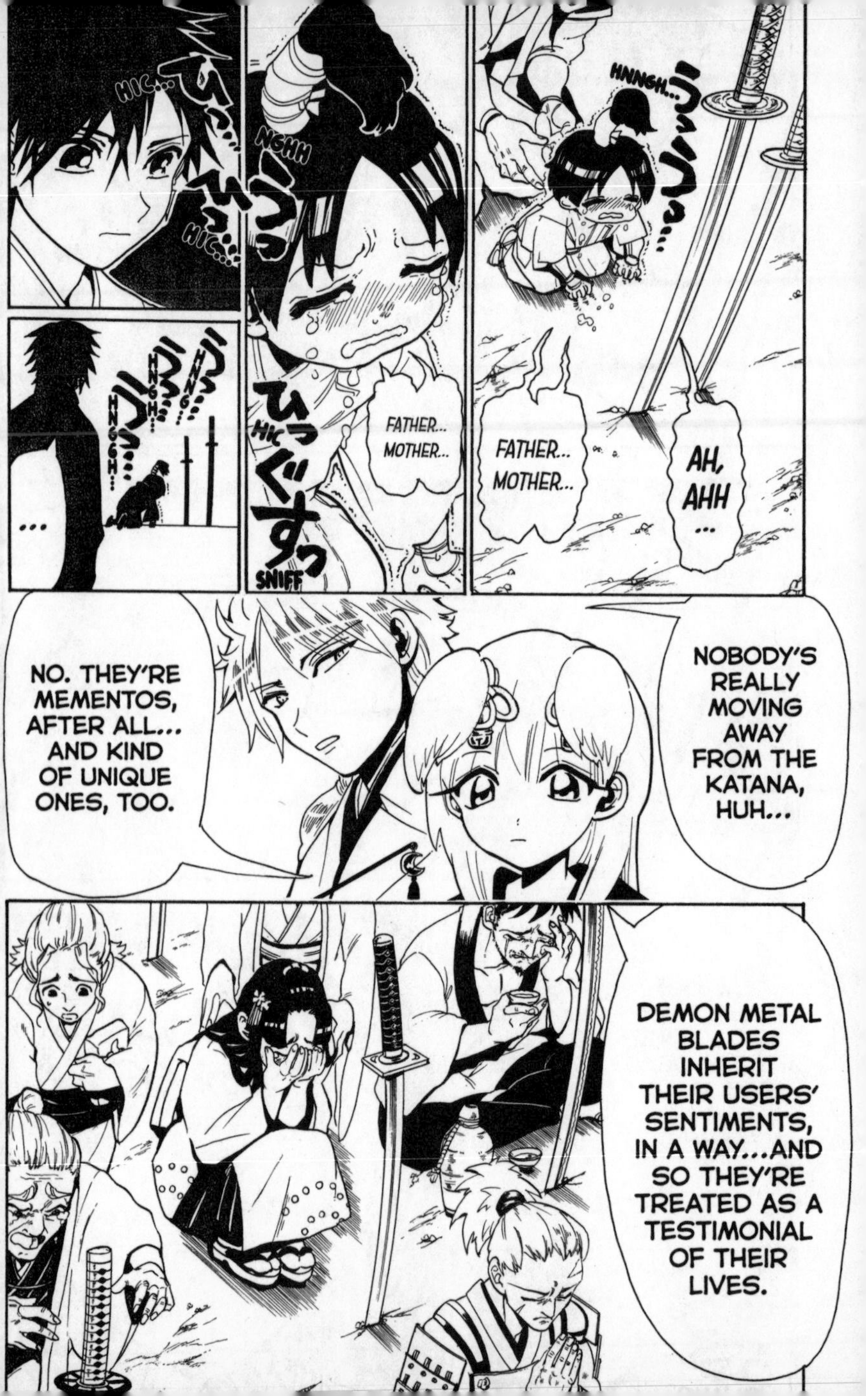
HNNGH...
AH, AHH...
FATHER... MOTHER...
NGHH
FATHER... MOTHER...
HIC
SNIFF
HIC...
HIC...
HNNG...
HNGGH...
HNGGH...
...
NOBODY'S REALLY MOVING AWAY FROM THE KATANA, HUH...
NO. THEY'RE MEMENTOS, AFTER ALL... AND KIND OF UNIQUE ONES, TOO.
DEMON METAL BLADES INHERIT THEIR USERS' SENTIMENTS, IN A WAY...AND SO THEY'RE TREATED AS A TESTIMONIAL OF THEIR LIVES.

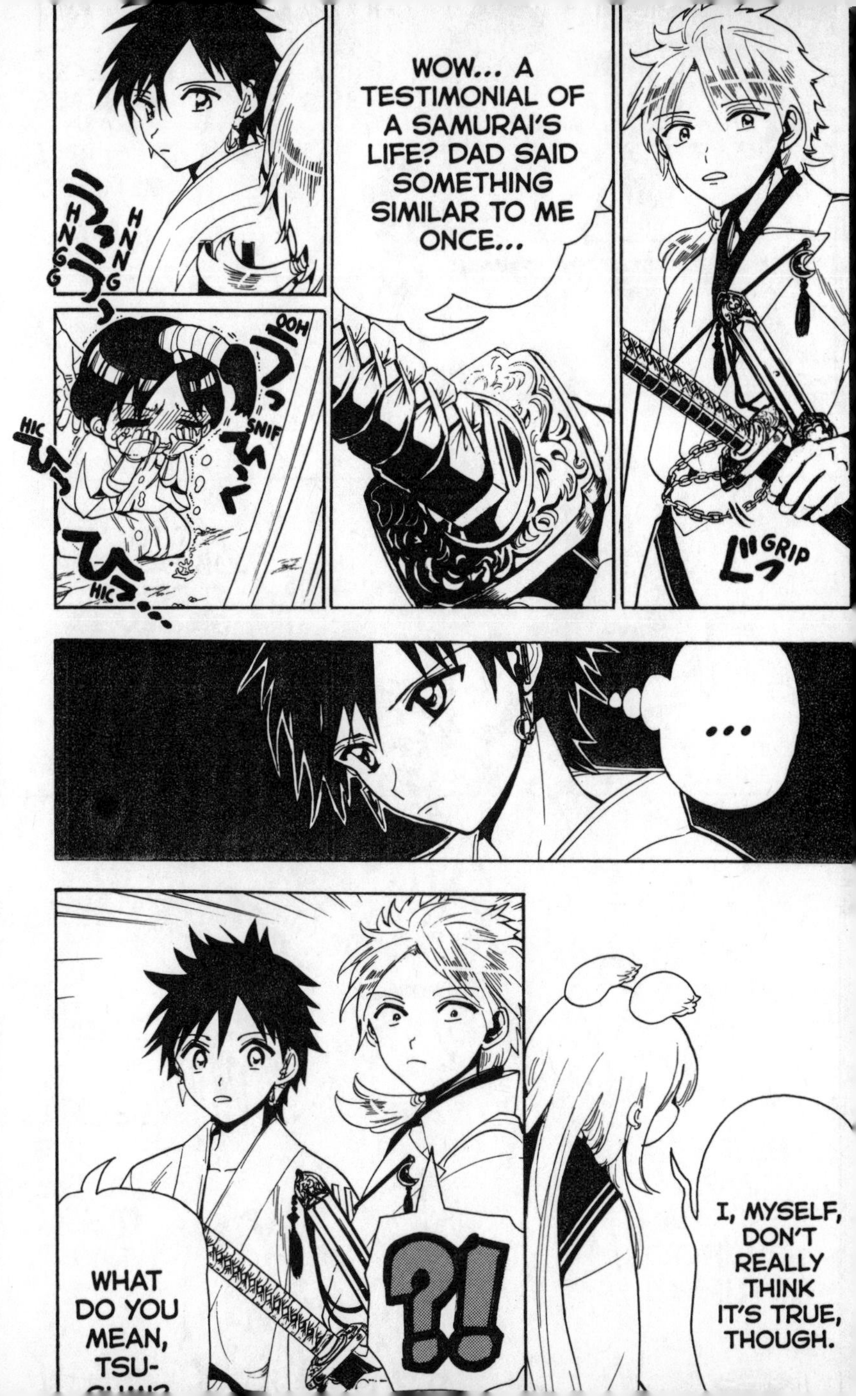
GRIP
WOW... A TESTIMONIAL OF A SAMURAI'S LIFE? DAD SAID SOMETHING SIMILAR TO ME ONCE...
HNNG
HNNG
OOH
SNIF
HIC
HIC
...
I, MYSELF, DON'T REALLY THINK IT'S TRUE, THOUGH.
?!
WHAT DO YOU MEAN, TSU-

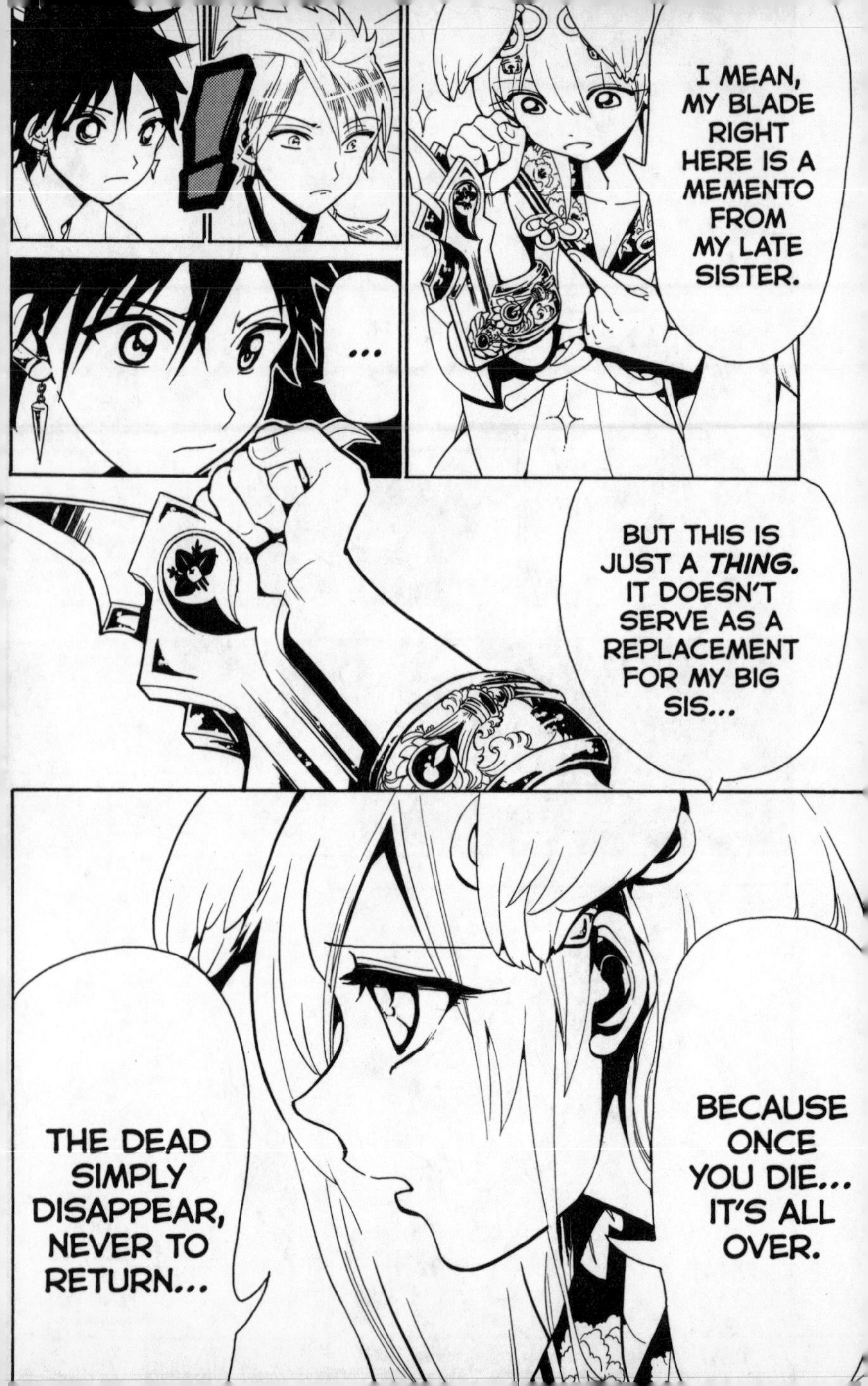
I MEAN, MY BLADE RIGHT HERE IS A MEMENTO FROM MY LATE SISTER.
...
BUT THIS IS JUST A *THING.* IT DOESN'T SERVE AS A REPLACEMENT FOR MY BIG SIS...
BECAUSE ONCE YOU DIE... IT'S ALL OVER.
THE DEAD SIMPLY DISAPPEAR, NEVER TO RETURN...

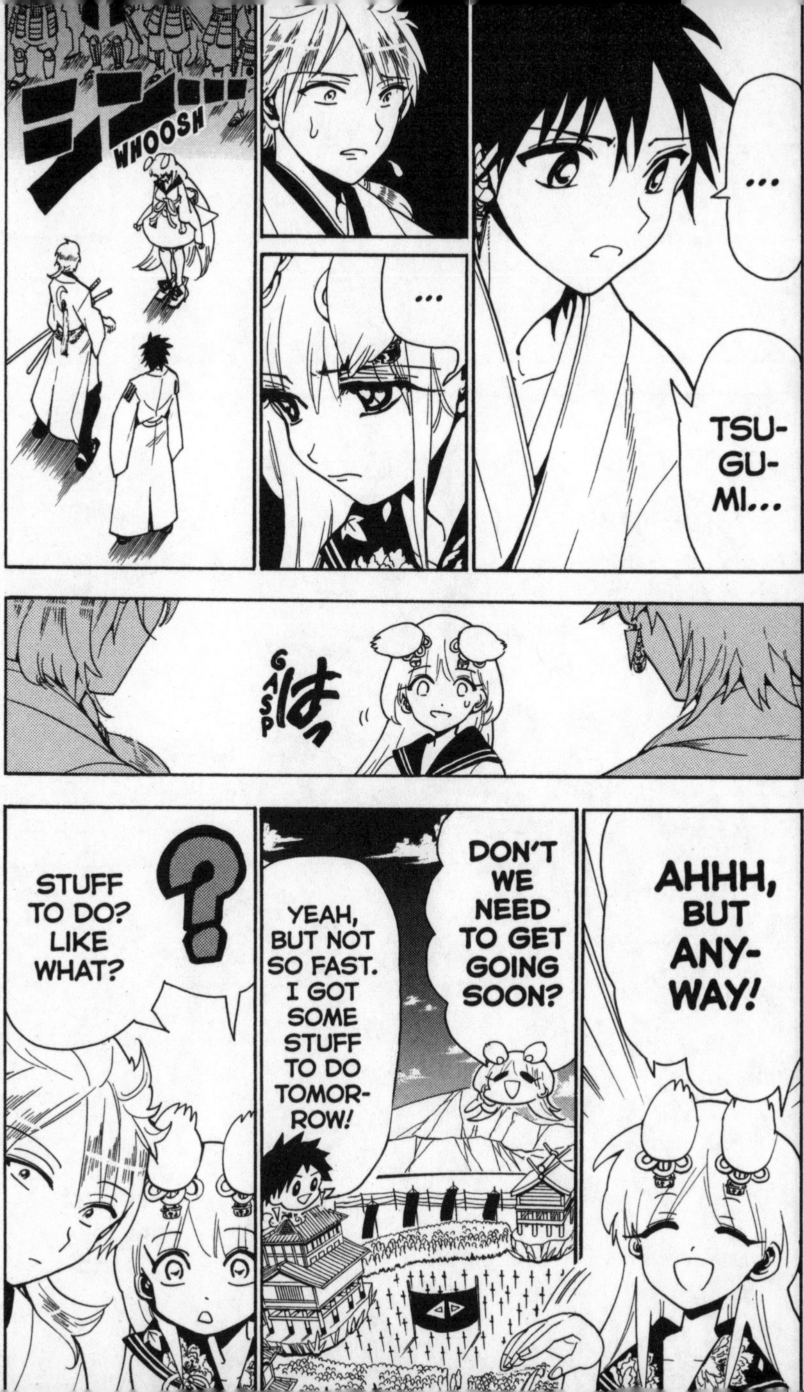
...
TSU-GU-MI...
...
WHOOSH
GASP
AHHH, BUT ANY-WAY!
DON'T WE NEED TO GET GOING SOON?
YEAH, BUT NOT SO FAST. I GOT SOME STUFF TO DO TOMORROW!
STUFF TO DO? LIKE WHAT?
?

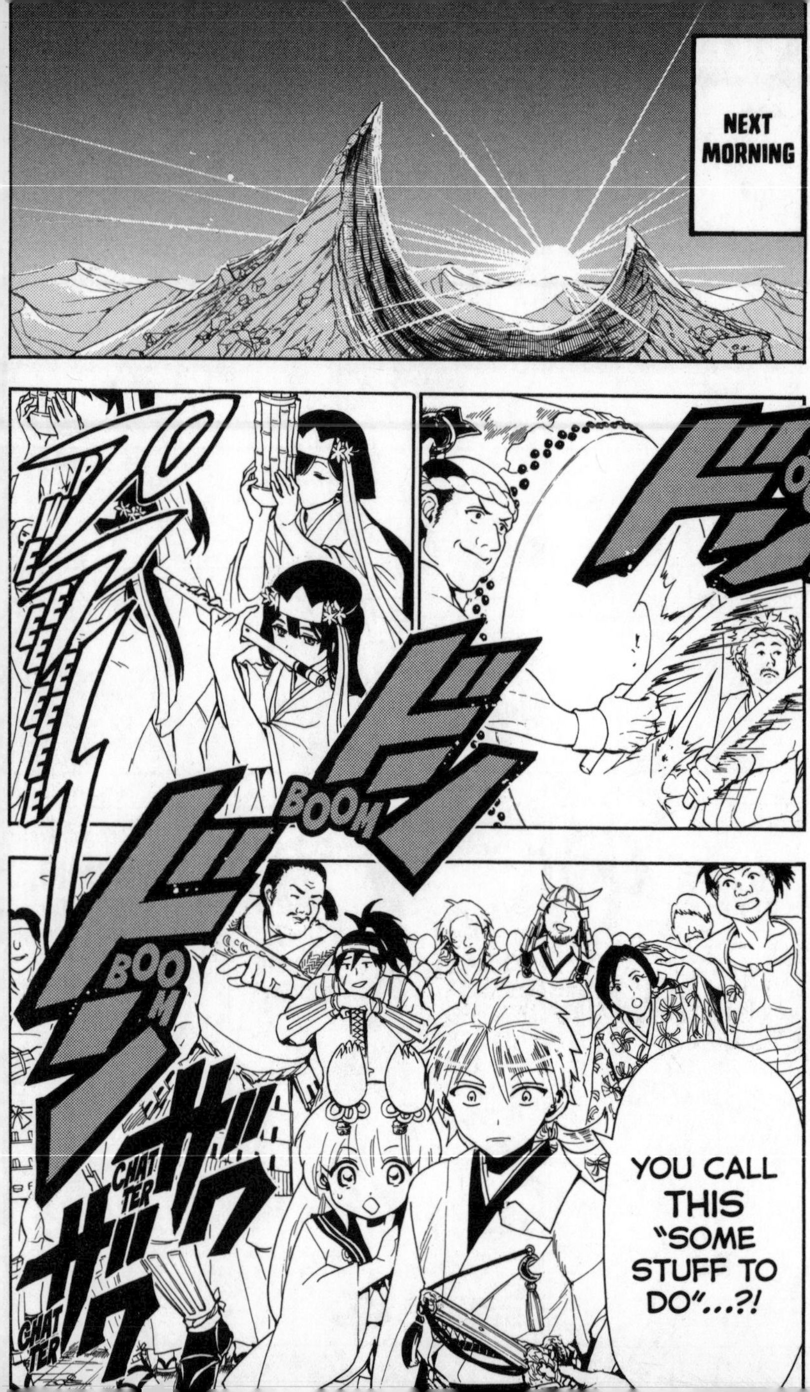
NEXT MORNING
BOOM
PWEEEEEEEEEEE
BOOM
BOOM
YOU CALL THIS "SOME STUFF TO DO"...?!
CHATTER
CHATTER

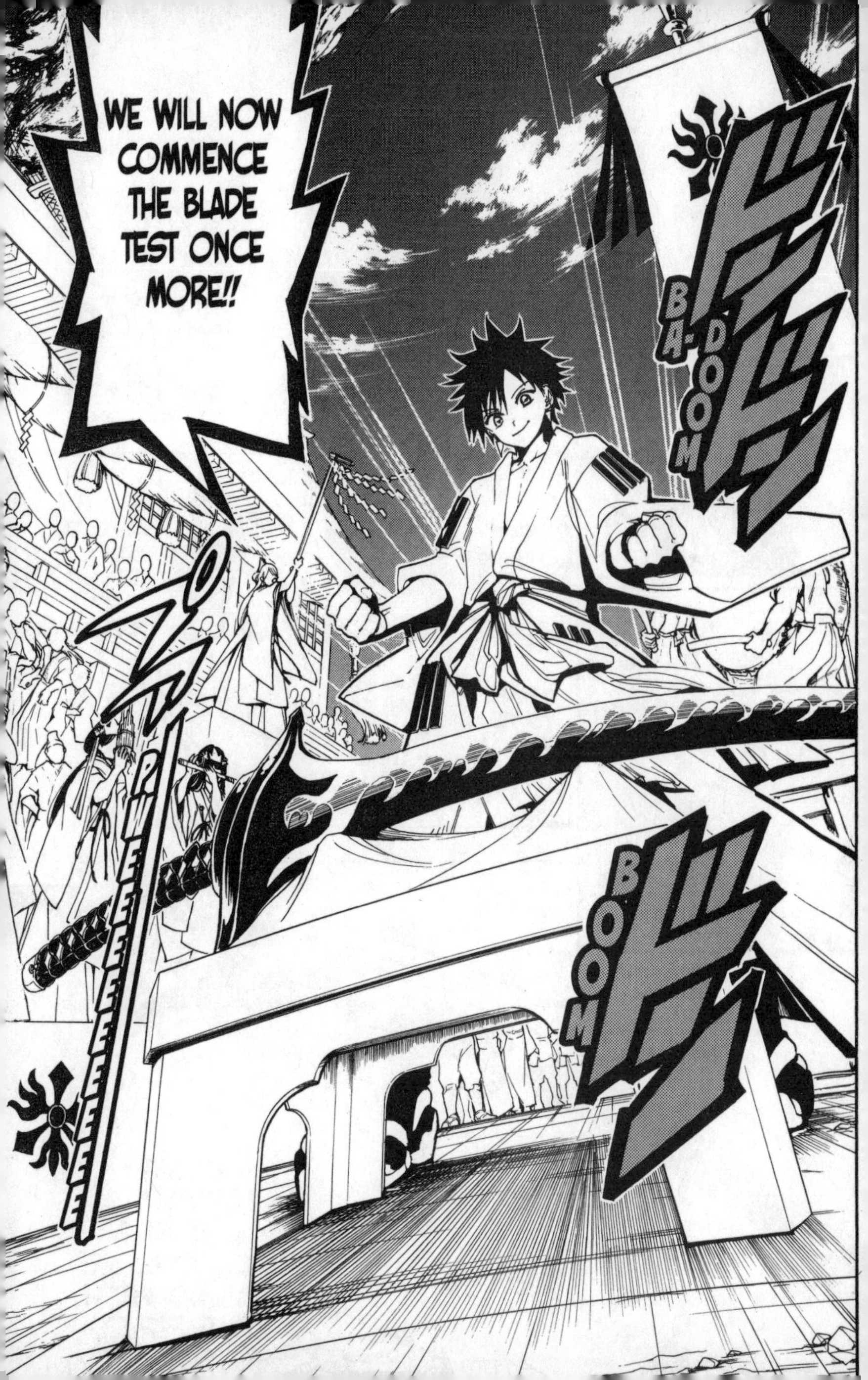
BA-DOOM
WE WILL NOW COMMENCE THE BLADE TEST ONCE MORE!!
BOOM
PWEEEEEEEEEEEE

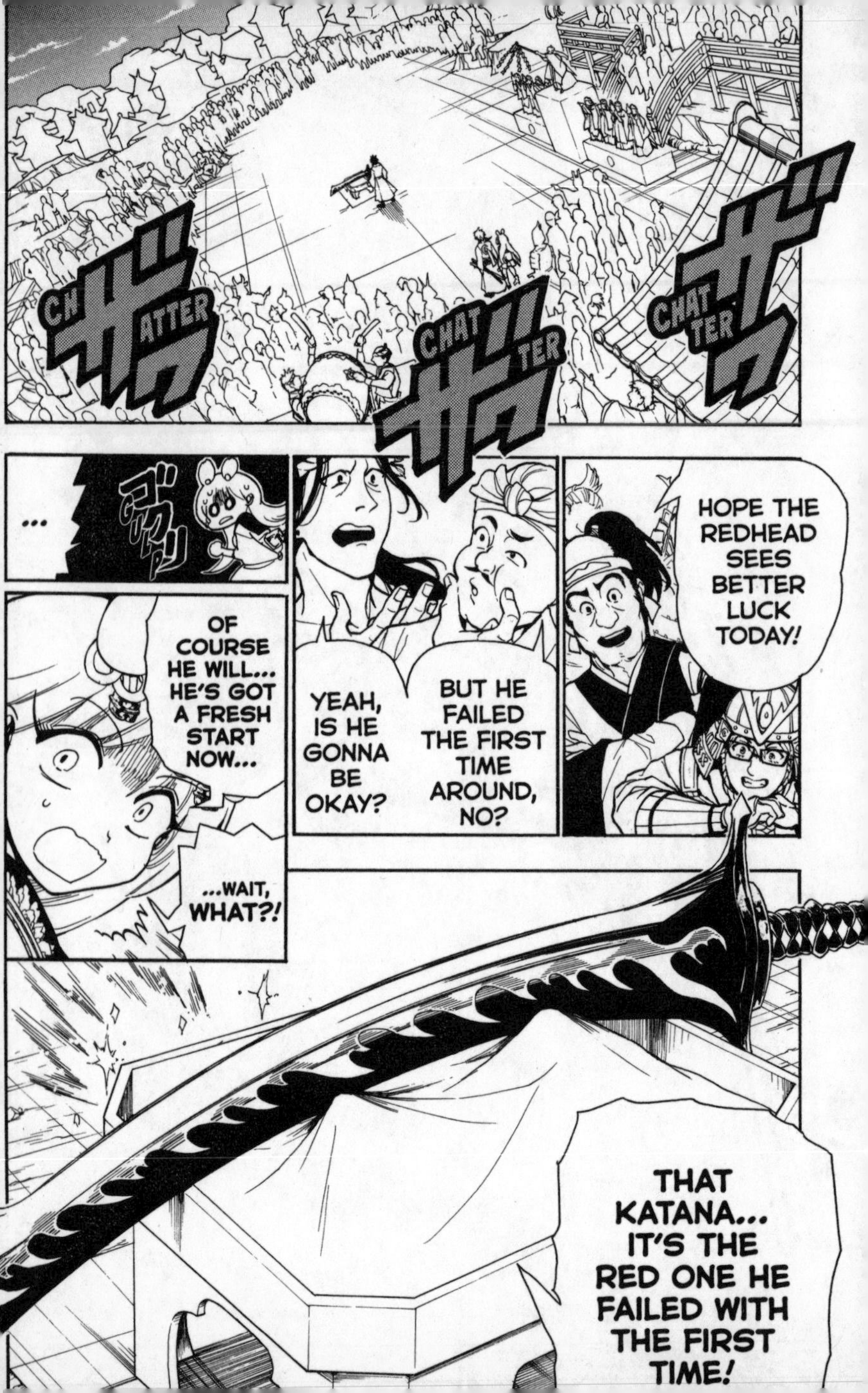
CHAT TER
CHAT TER
CH ATTER
HOPE THE REDHEAD SEES BETTER LUCK TODAY!
BUT HE FAILED THE FIRST TIME AROUND, NO?
YEAH, IS HE GONNA BE OKAY?
...
GULP
OF COURSE HE WILL... HE'S GOT A FRESH START NOW...
...WAIT, WHAT?!
THAT KATANA... IT'S THE RED ONE HE FAILED WITH THE FIRST TIME!

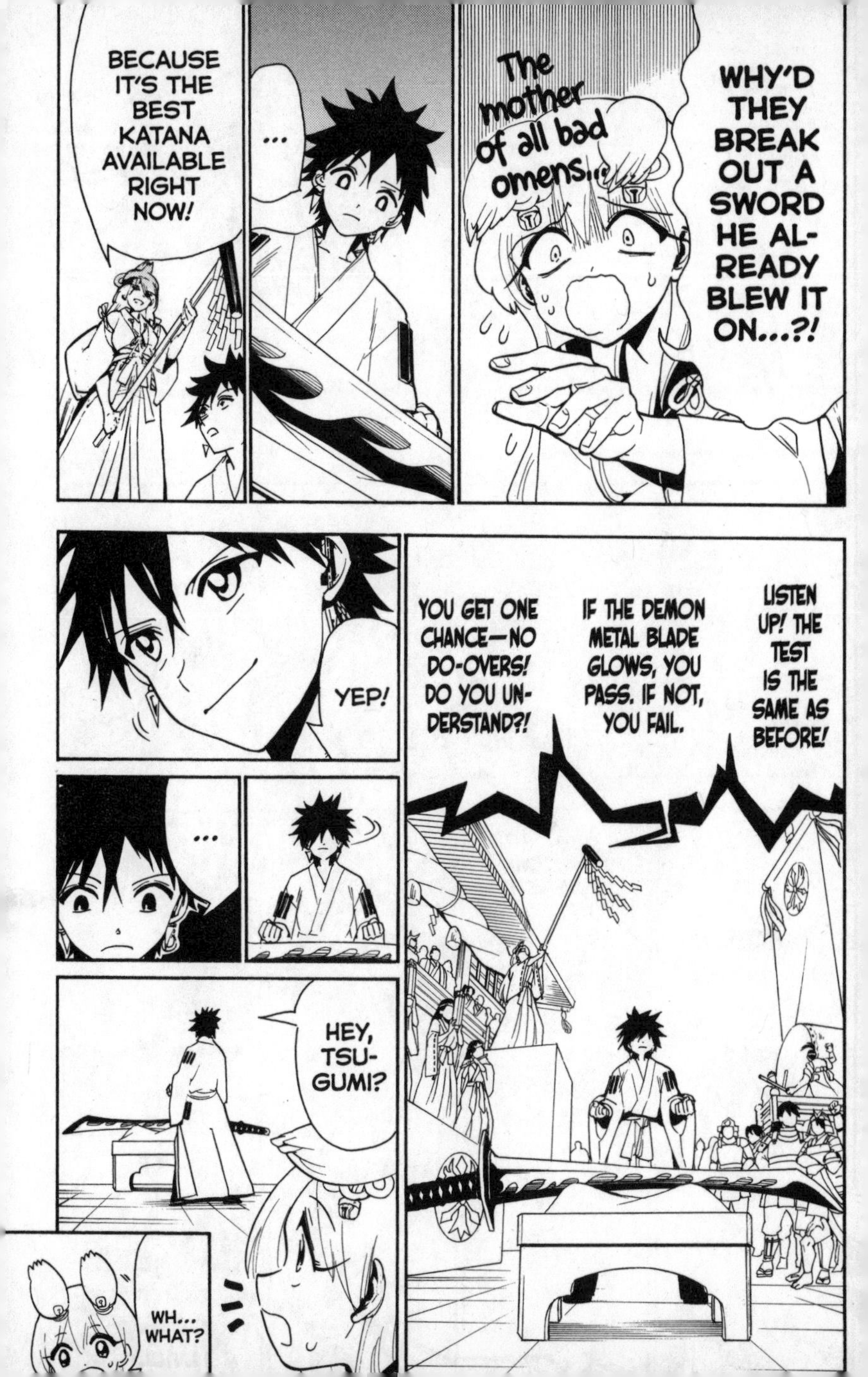
WHY'D THEY BREAK OUT A SWORD HE ALREADY BLEW IT ON...?!
The mother of all bad omens...
...
BECAUSE IT'S THE BEST KATANA AVAILABLE RIGHT NOW!
LISTEN UP! THE TEST IS THE SAME AS BEFORE!
IF THE DEMON METAL BLADE GLOWS, YOU PASS. IF NOT, YOU FAIL.
YOU GET ONE CHANCE—NO DO-OVERS! DO YOU UNDERSTAND?!
YEP!
...
HEY, TSUGUMI?
WH... WHAT?

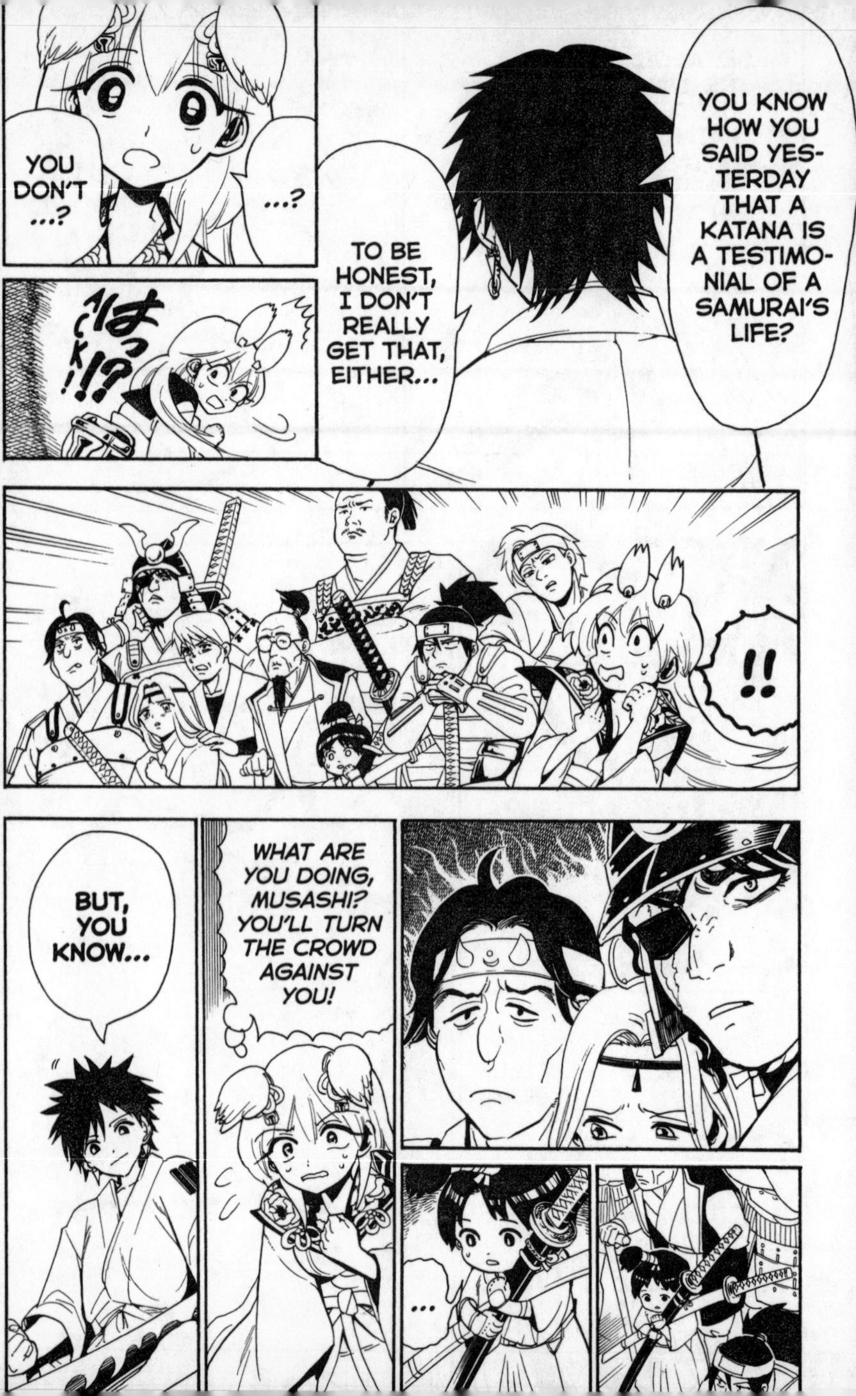
YOU KNOW HOW YOU SAID YES-TERDAY THAT A KATANA IS A TESTIMO-NIAL OF A SAMURAI'S LIFE?
TO BE HONEST, I DON'T REALLY GET THAT, EITHER...
...?
YOU DON'T ...?
はっ
HACK!!?
!!
...
WHAT ARE YOU DOING, MUSASHI? YOU'LL TURN THE CROWD AGAINST YOU!
BUT, YOU KNOW...

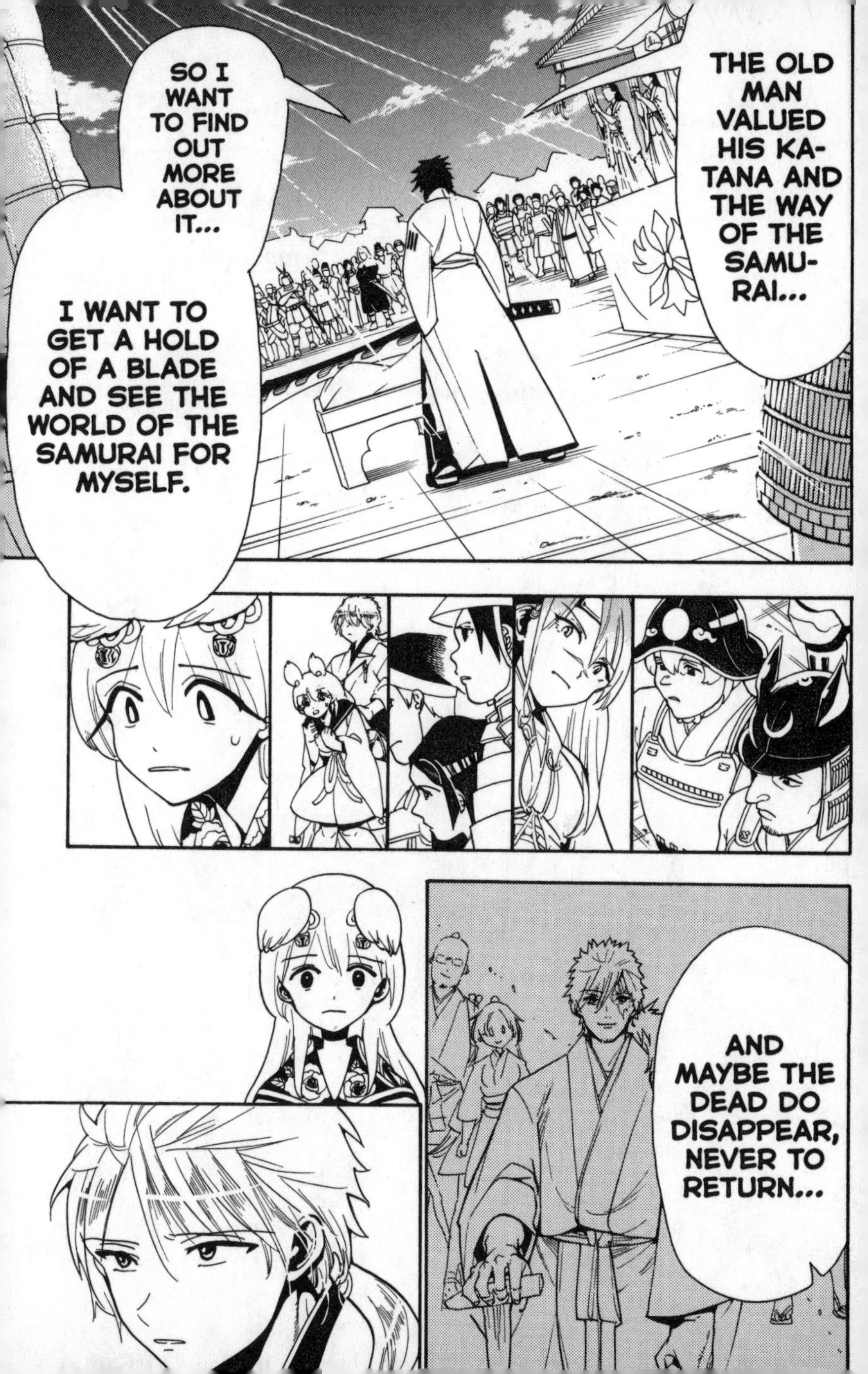
THE OLD MAN VALUED HIS KA-TANA AND THE WAY OF THE SAMU-RAI...
SO I WANT TO FIND OUT MORE ABOUT IT...
I WANT TO GET A HOLD OF A BLADE AND SEE THE WORLD OF THE SAMURAI FOR MYSELF.
AND MAYBE THE DEAD DO DISAPPEAR, NEVER TO RETURN...

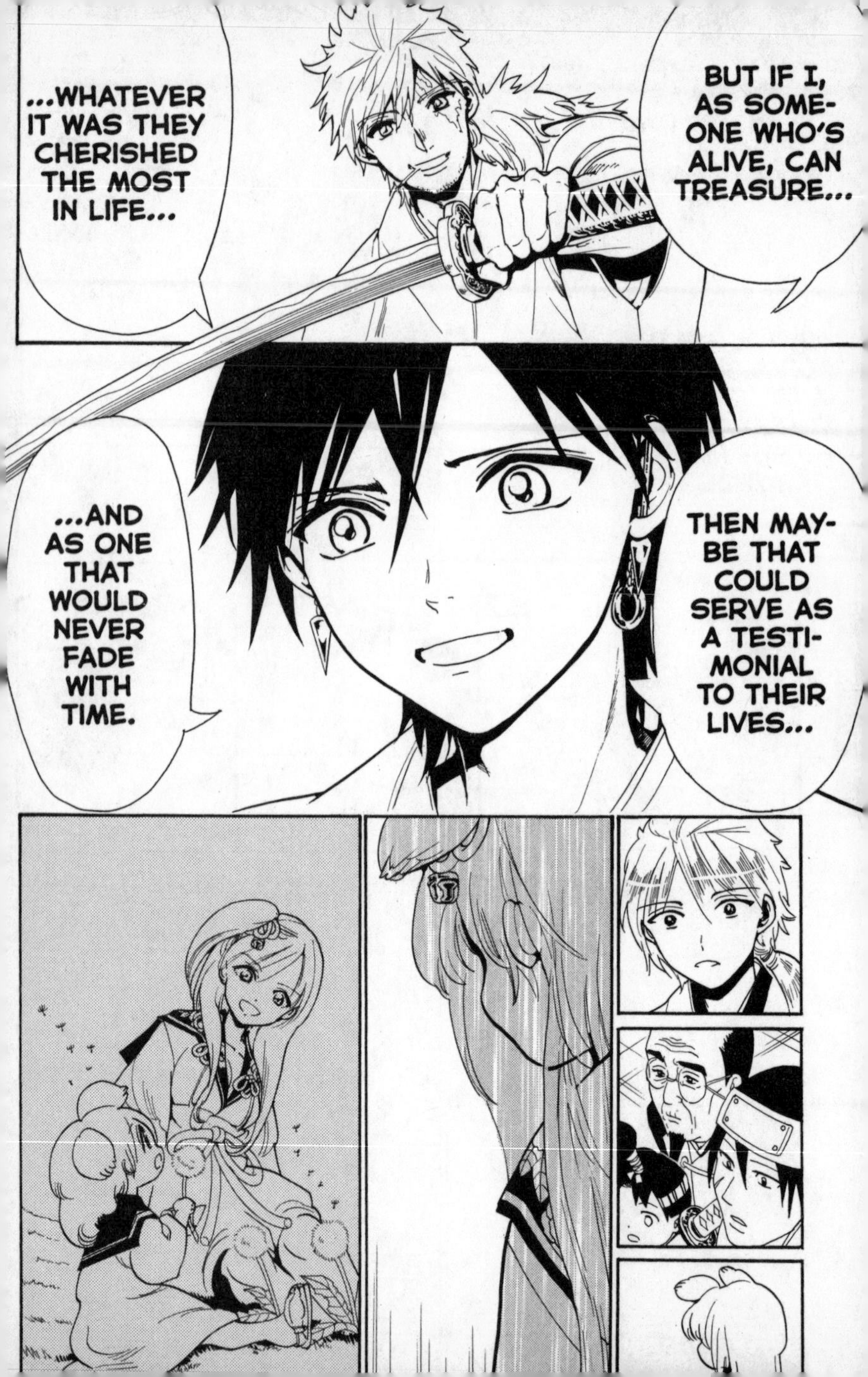
BUT IF I, AS SOMEONE WHO'S ALIVE, CAN TREASURE...
...WHATEVER IT WAS THEY CHERISHED THE MOST IN LIFE...
THEN MAYBE THAT COULD SERVE AS A TESTIMONIAL TO THEIR LIVES...
...AND AS ONE THAT WOULD NEVER FADE WITH TIME.

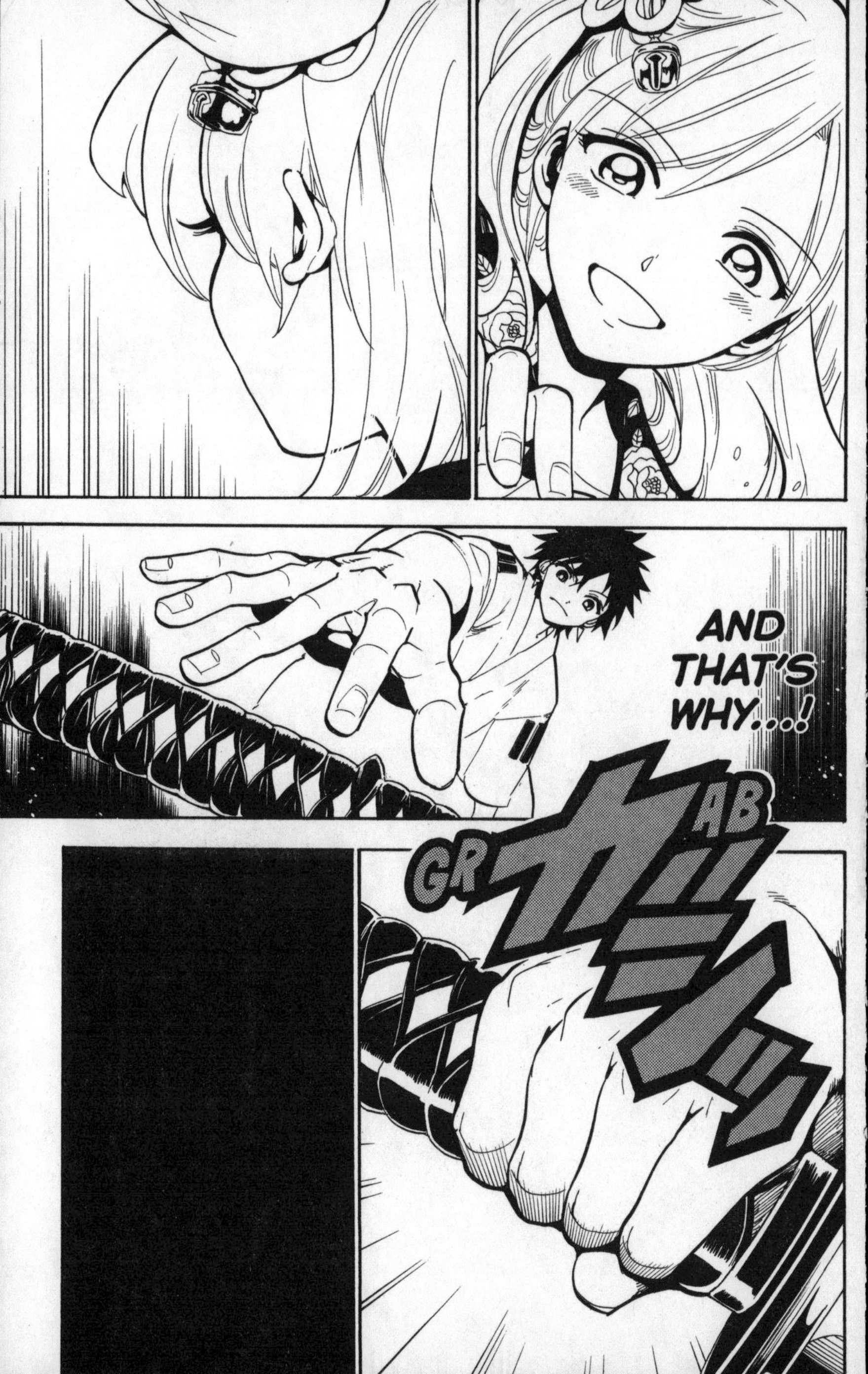
AND THAT'S WHY...!
GRAB

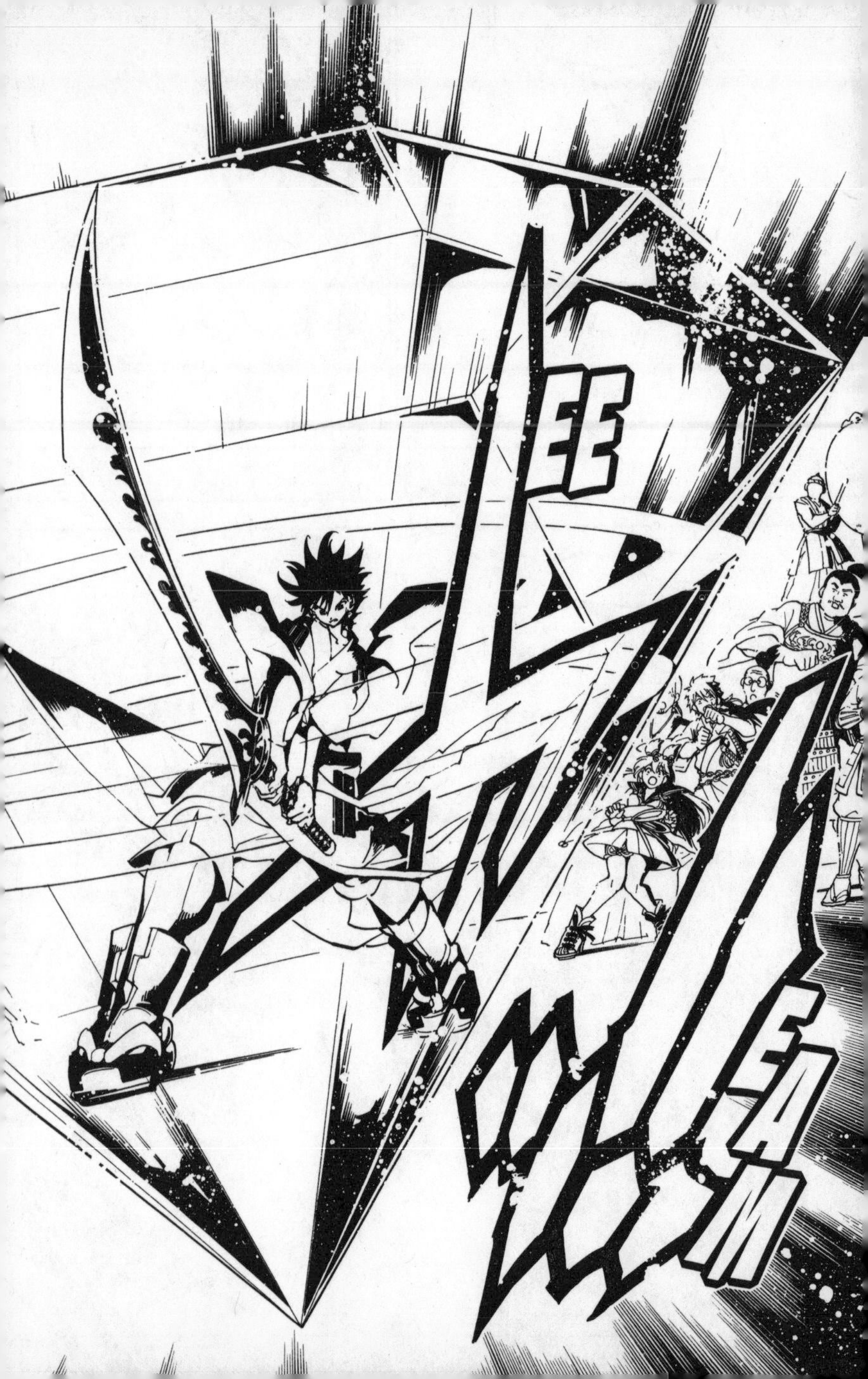
EE
EAM

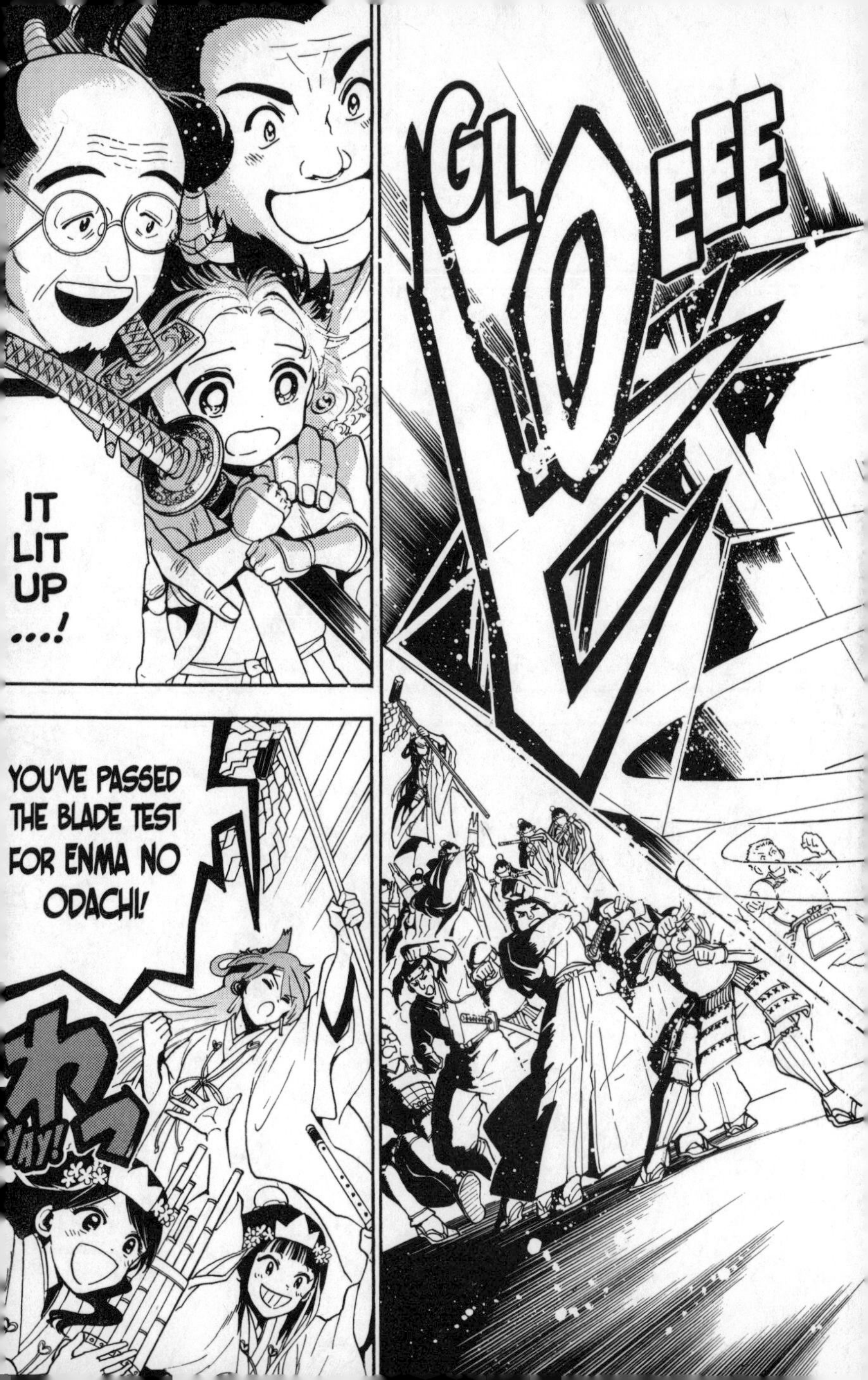
GLEEE
IT LIT UP...!
YOU'VE PASSED THE BLADE TEST FOR ENMA NO ODACHI!
YAY!

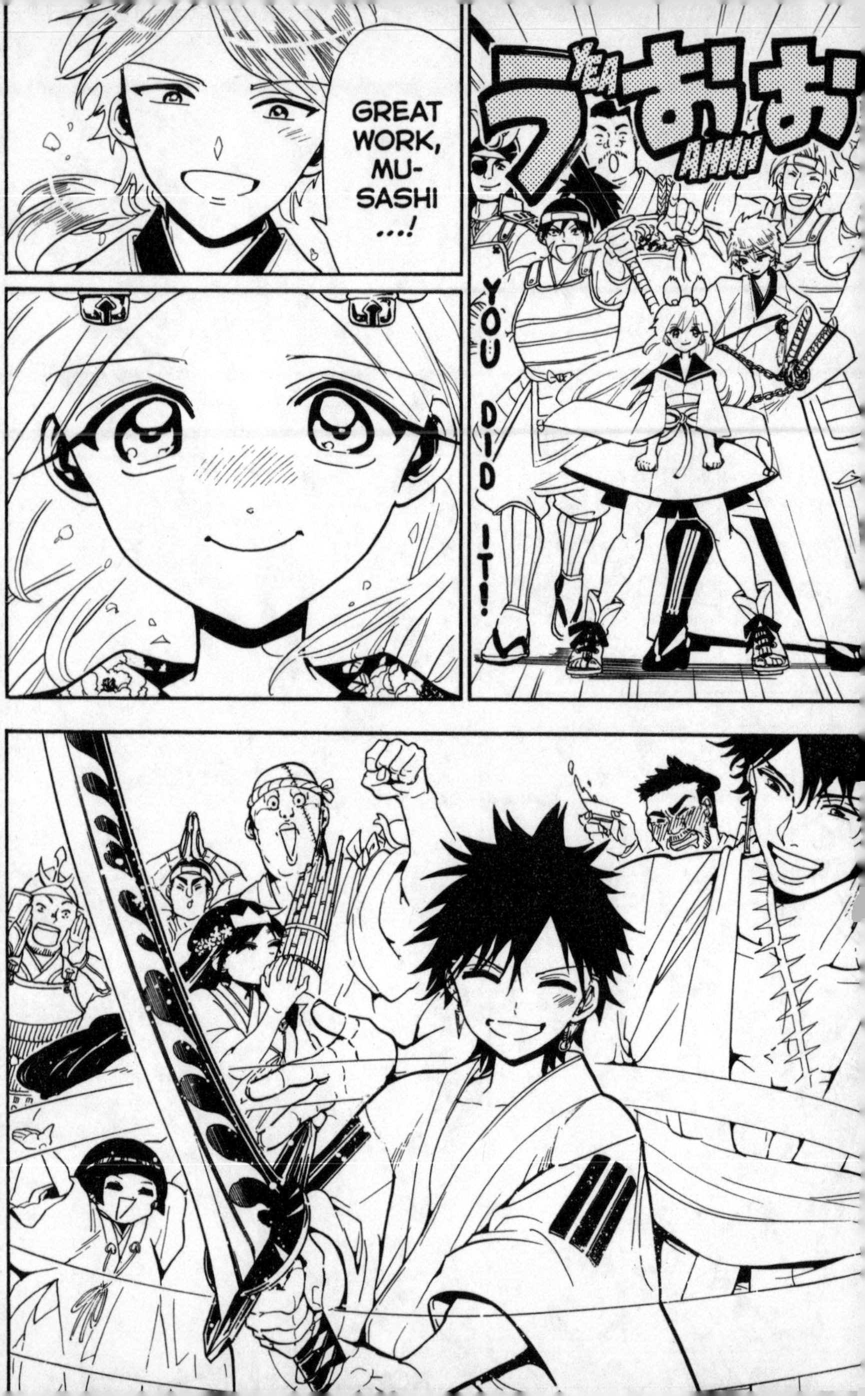

ゔおお
YEAH
AHHH
YOU DID IT!!
GREAT WORK, MU-SASHI ...!

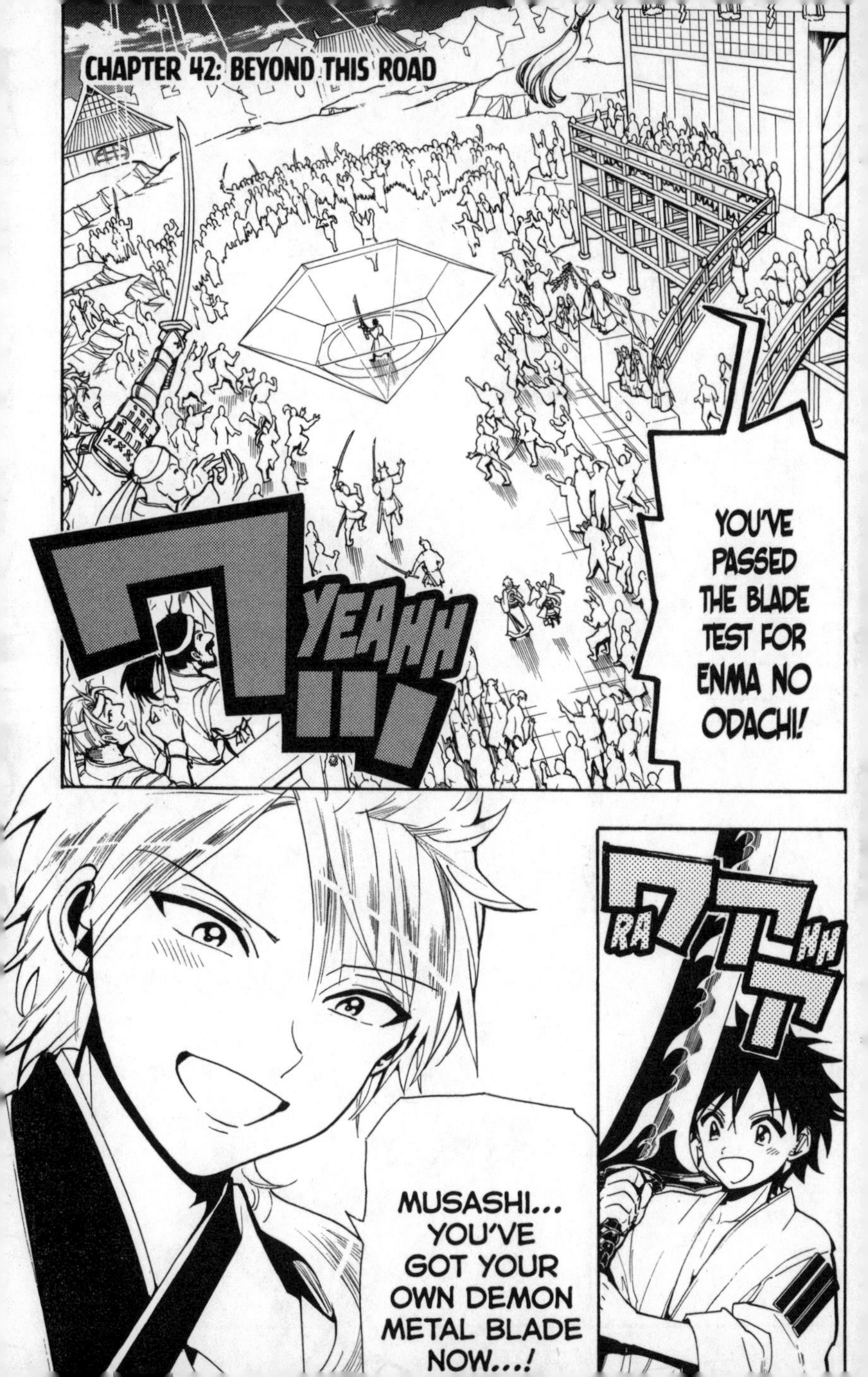
CHAPTER 42: BEYOND THIS ROAD
YOU'VE PASSED THE BLADE TEST FOR ENMA NO ODACHI!
YEAHH!!!
RAHH
MUSASHI... YOU'VE GOT YOUR OWN DEMON METAL BLADE NOW...!

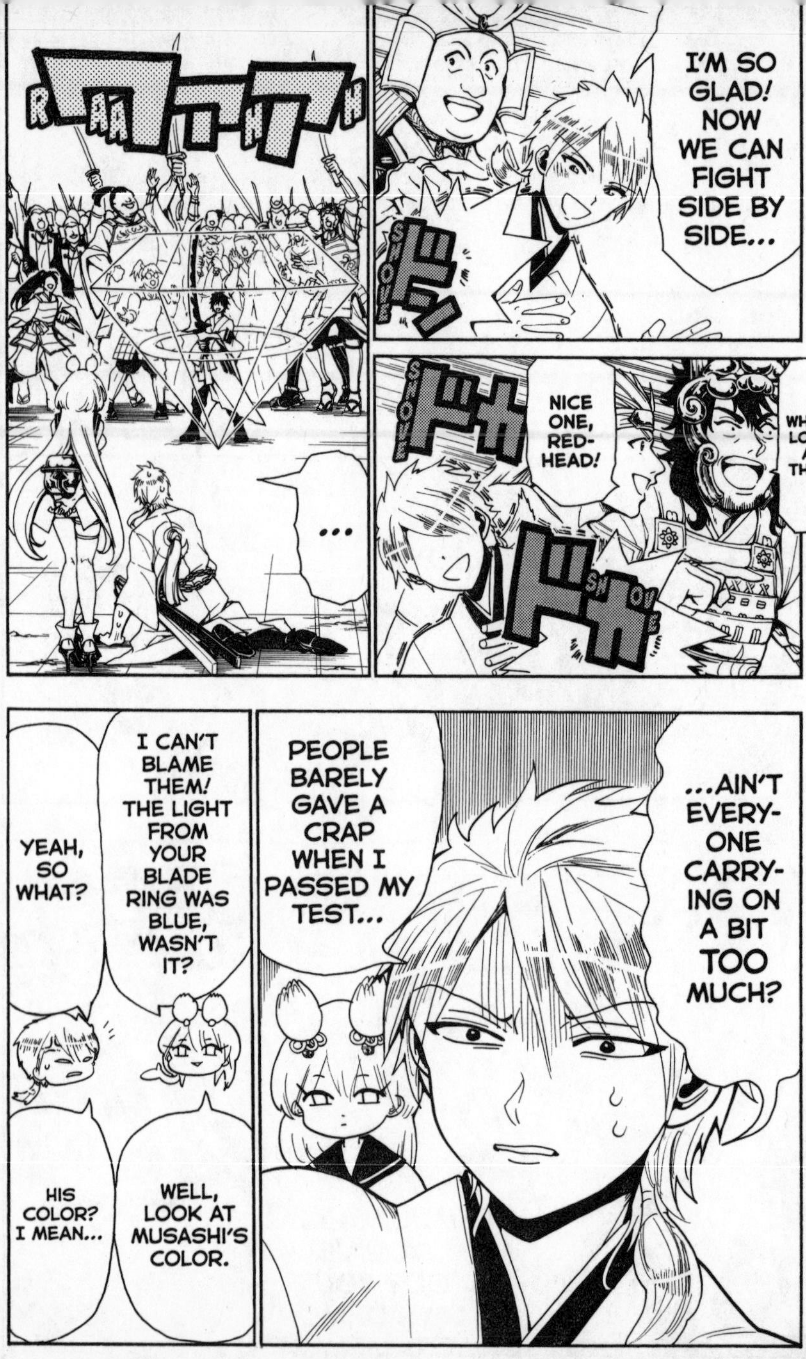
SHOVE
I'M SO GLAD! NOW WE CAN FIGHT SIDE BY SIDE...
SHOVE
WHOA, LOOK AT THAT!
NICE ONE, RED-HEAD!
SHOVE
RAAHH
...
...AIN'T EVERYONE CARRYING ON A BIT TOO MUCH?
PEOPLE BARELY GAVE A CRAP WHEN I PASSED MY TEST...
I CAN'T BLAME THEM! THE LIGHT FROM YOUR BLADE RING WAS BLUE, WASN'T IT?
YEAH, SO WHAT?
WELL, LOOK AT MUSASHI'S COLOR.
HIS COLOR? I MEAN...

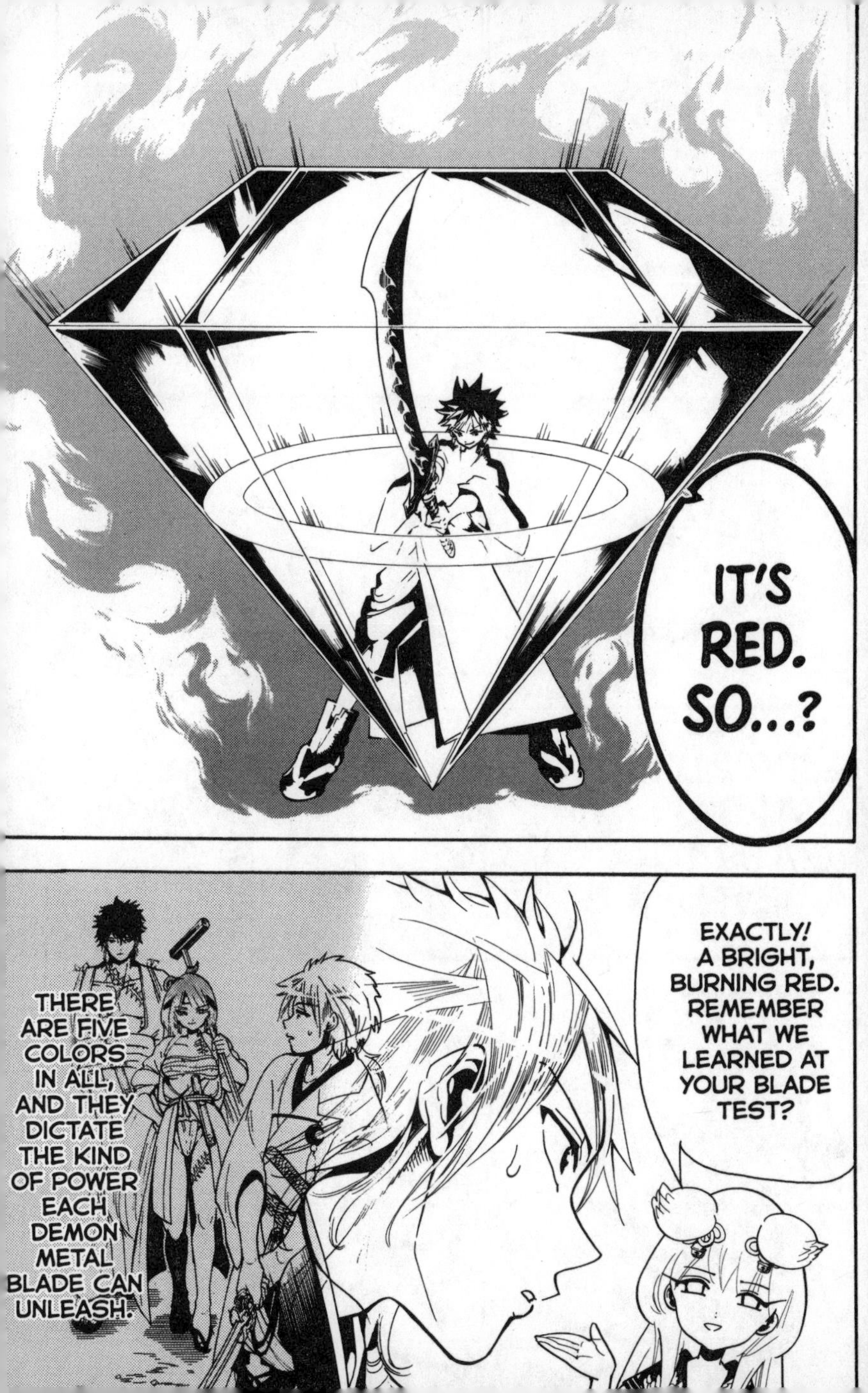
IT'S RED. SO...?
EXACTLY! A BRIGHT, BURNING RED. REMEMBER WHAT WE LEARNED AT YOUR BLADE TEST?
THERE ARE FIVE COLORS IN ALL, AND THEY DICTATE THE KIND OF POWER EACH DEMON METAL BLADE CAN UNLEASH.

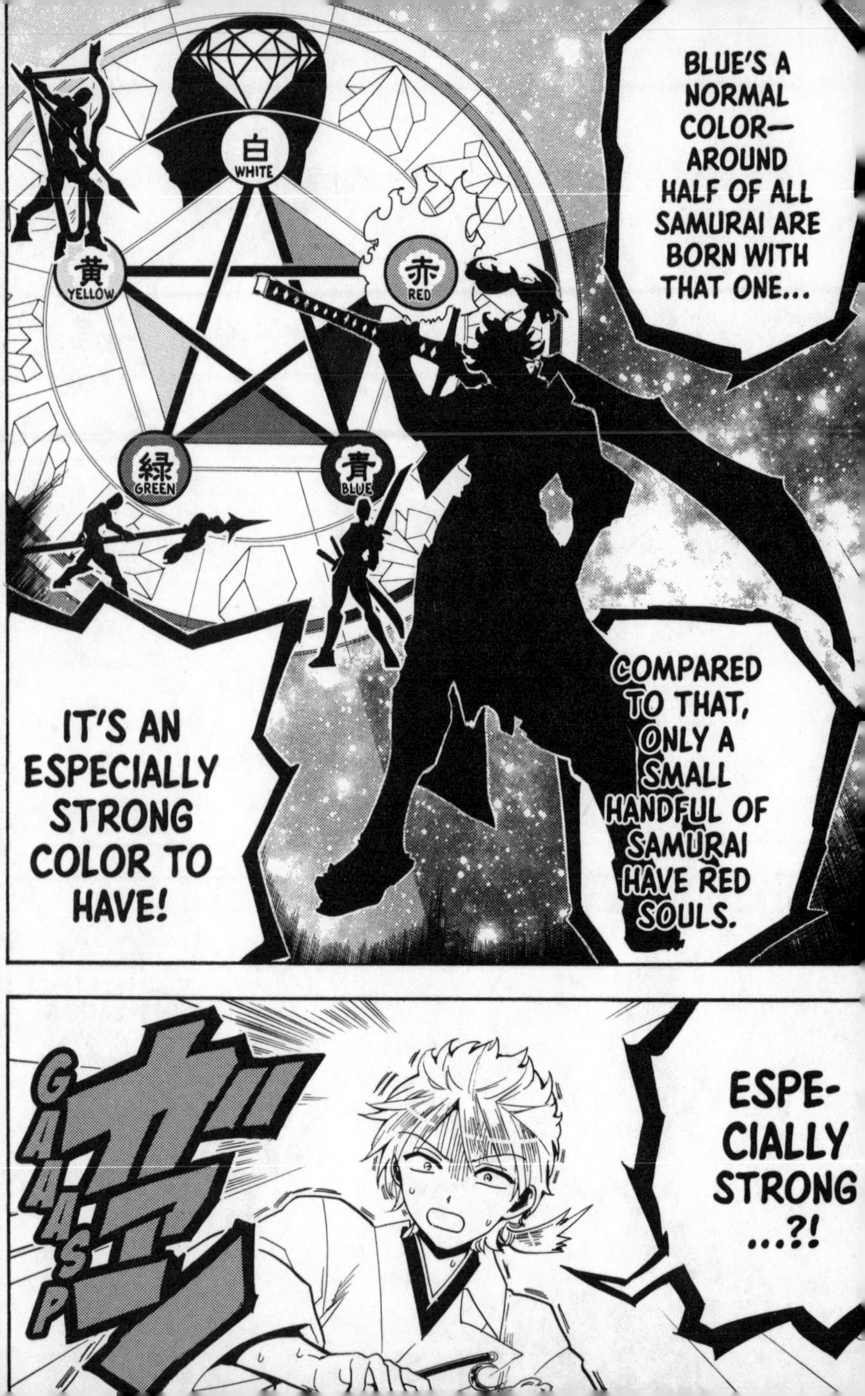
BLUE'S A NORMAL COLOR—AROUND HALF OF ALL SAMURAI ARE BORN WITH THAT ONE...
白 WHITE
赤 RED
黄 YELLOW
緑 GREEN
青 BLUE
COMPARED TO THAT, ONLY A SMALL HANDFUL OF SAMURAI HAVE RED SOULS.
IT'S AN ESPECIALLY STRONG COLOR TO HAVE!
ESPE-CIALLY STRONG ...?!
GAAASP

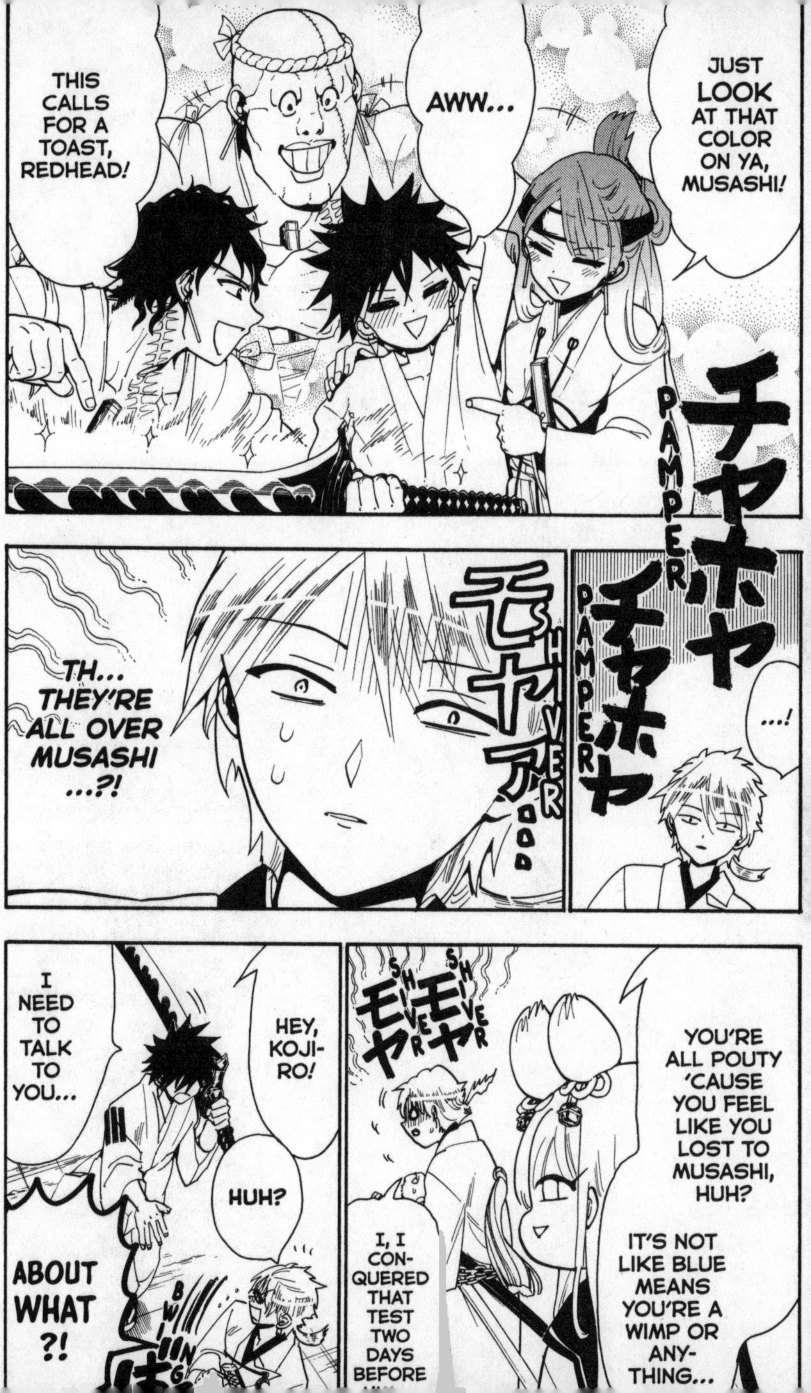
JUST LOOK AT THAT COLOR ON YA, MUSASHI!
AWW...
THIS CALLS FOR A TOAST, REDHEAD!
チヤホヤ PAMPER
チヤホヤ PAMPER
...!
モヤア SHIVER
TH... THEY'RE ALL OVER MUSASHI ...?!
YOU'RE ALL POUTY 'CAUSE YOU FEEL LIKE YOU LOST TO MUSASHI, HUH?
モヤ SHIVER
モヤ SHIVER
IT'S NOT LIKE BLUE MEANS YOU'RE A WIMP OR ANY-THING...
I, I CON-QUERED THAT TEST TWO DAYS BEFORE
HEY, KOJI-RO!
I NEED TO TALK TO YOU...
HUH?
ABOUT WHAT ?!
BWIIING

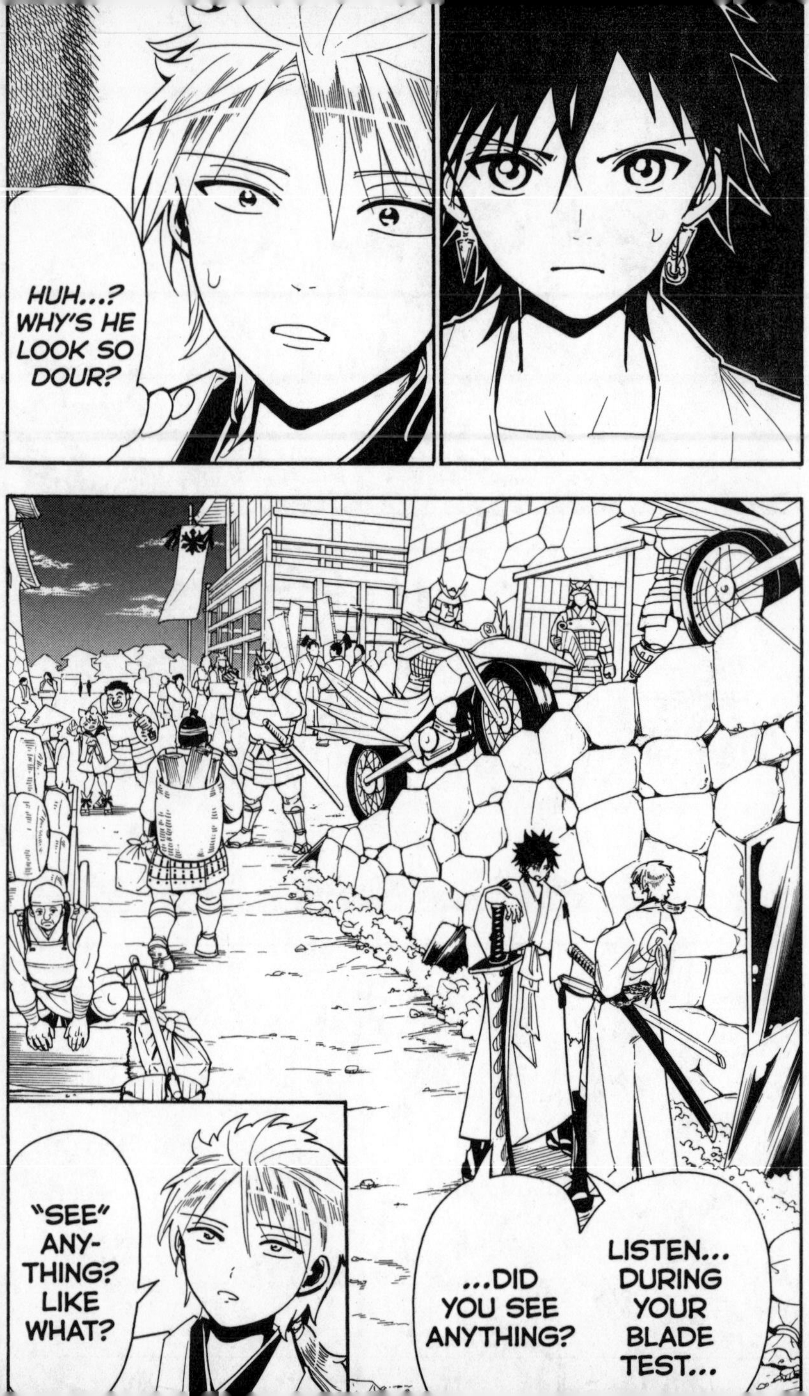
HUH...? WHY'S HE LOOK SO DOUR?
LISTEN... DURING YOUR BLADE TEST...
...DID YOU SEE ANYTHING?
"SEE" ANY-THING? LIKE WHAT?

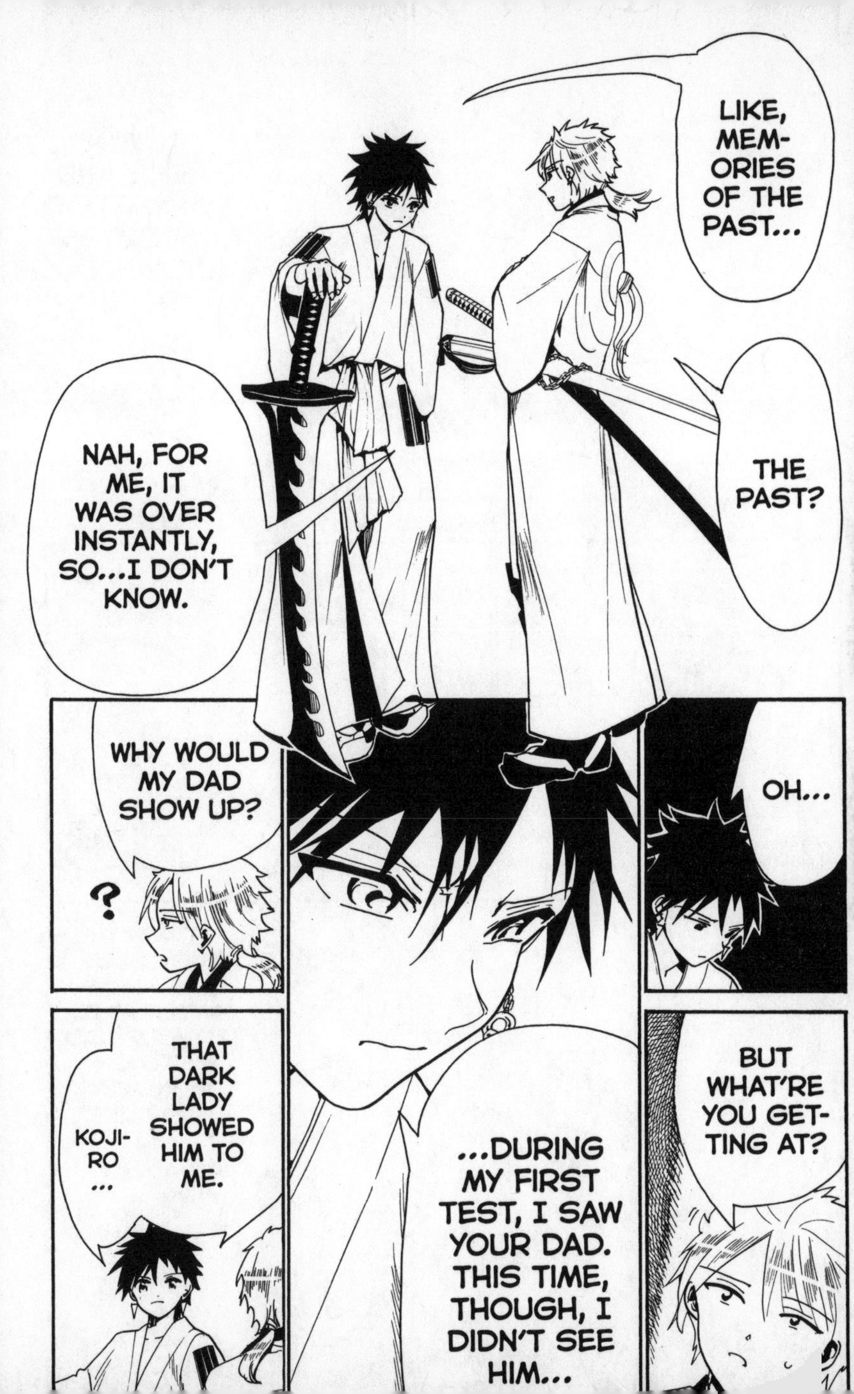
LIKE, MEMORIES OF THE PAST...
THE PAST?
NAH, FOR ME, IT WAS OVER INSTANTLY, SO...I DON'T KNOW.
OH...
BUT WHAT'RE YOU GETTING AT?
...DURING MY FIRST TEST, I SAW YOUR DAD. THIS TIME, THOUGH, I DIDN'T SEE HIM...
WHY WOULD MY DAD SHOW UP?
?
THAT DARK LADY SHOWED HIM TO ME.
KOJIRO...

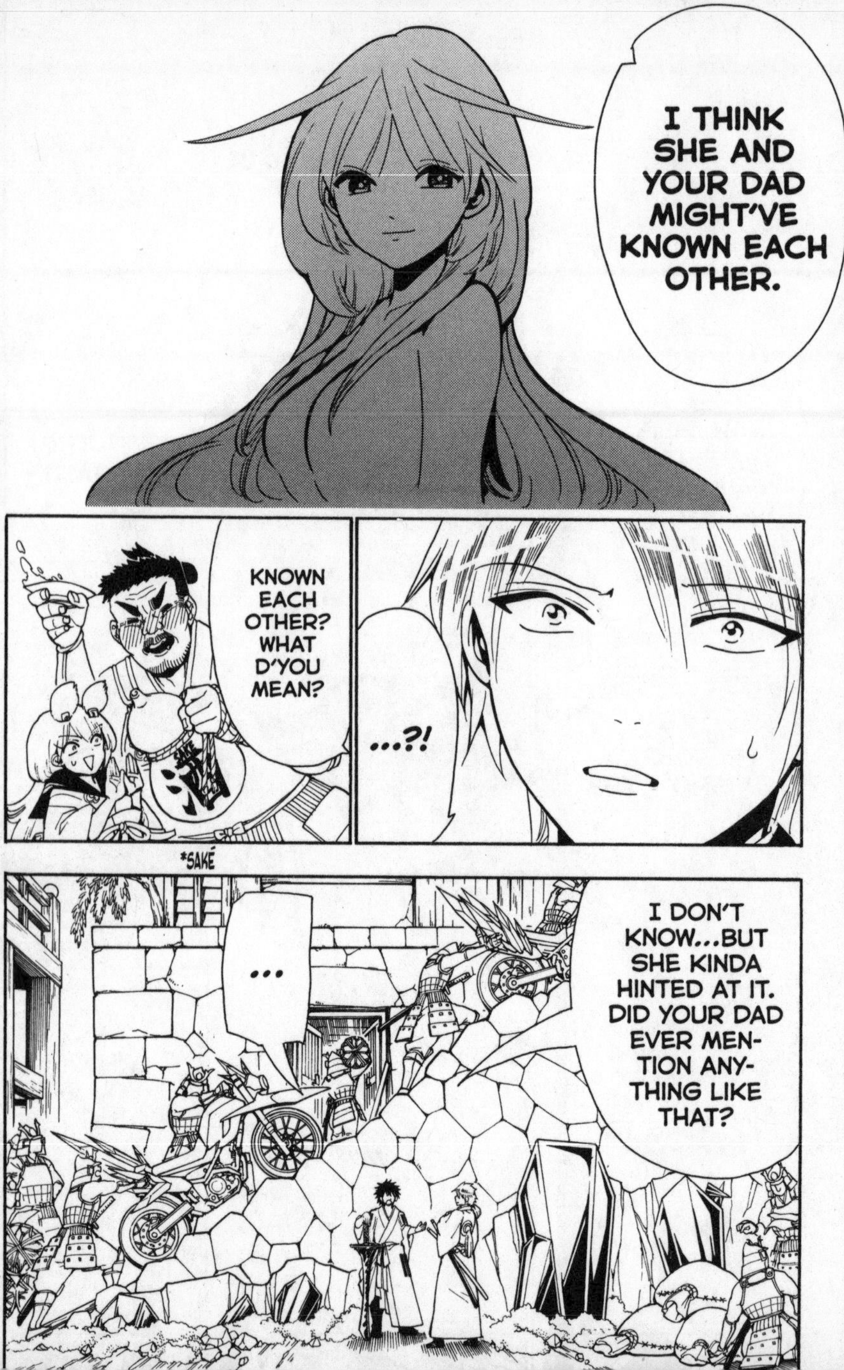
I THINK SHE AND YOUR DAD MIGHT'VE KNOWN EACH OTHER.
...?!
KNOWN EACH OTHER? WHAT D'YOU MEAN?
SAKE
*SAKÉ
I DON'T KNOW...BUT SHE KINDA HINTED AT IT. DID YOUR DAD EVER MEN-TION ANY-THING LIKE THAT?
...

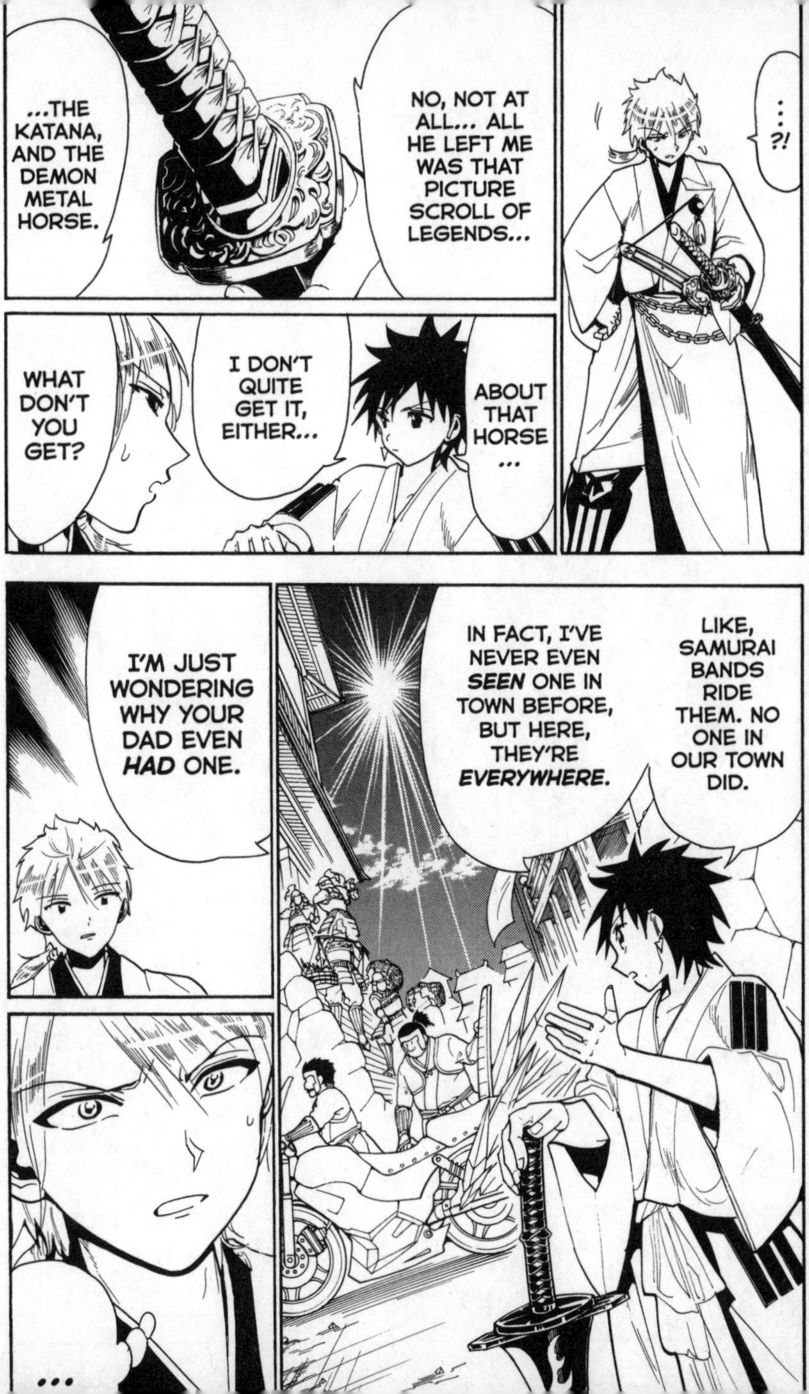
...?!
NO, NOT AT ALL... ALL HE LEFT ME WAS THAT PICTURE SCROLL OF LEGENDS...
...THE KATANA, AND THE DEMON METAL HORSE.
ABOUT THAT HORSE...
I DON'T QUITE GET IT, EITHER...
WHAT DON'T YOU GET?
LIKE, SAMURAI BANDS RIDE THEM. NO ONE IN OUR TOWN DID.
IN FACT, I'VE NEVER EVEN *SEEN* ONE IN TOWN BEFORE, BUT HERE, THEY'RE *EVERYWHERE*.
I'M JUST WONDERING WHY YOUR DAD EVEN *HAD* ONE.
...

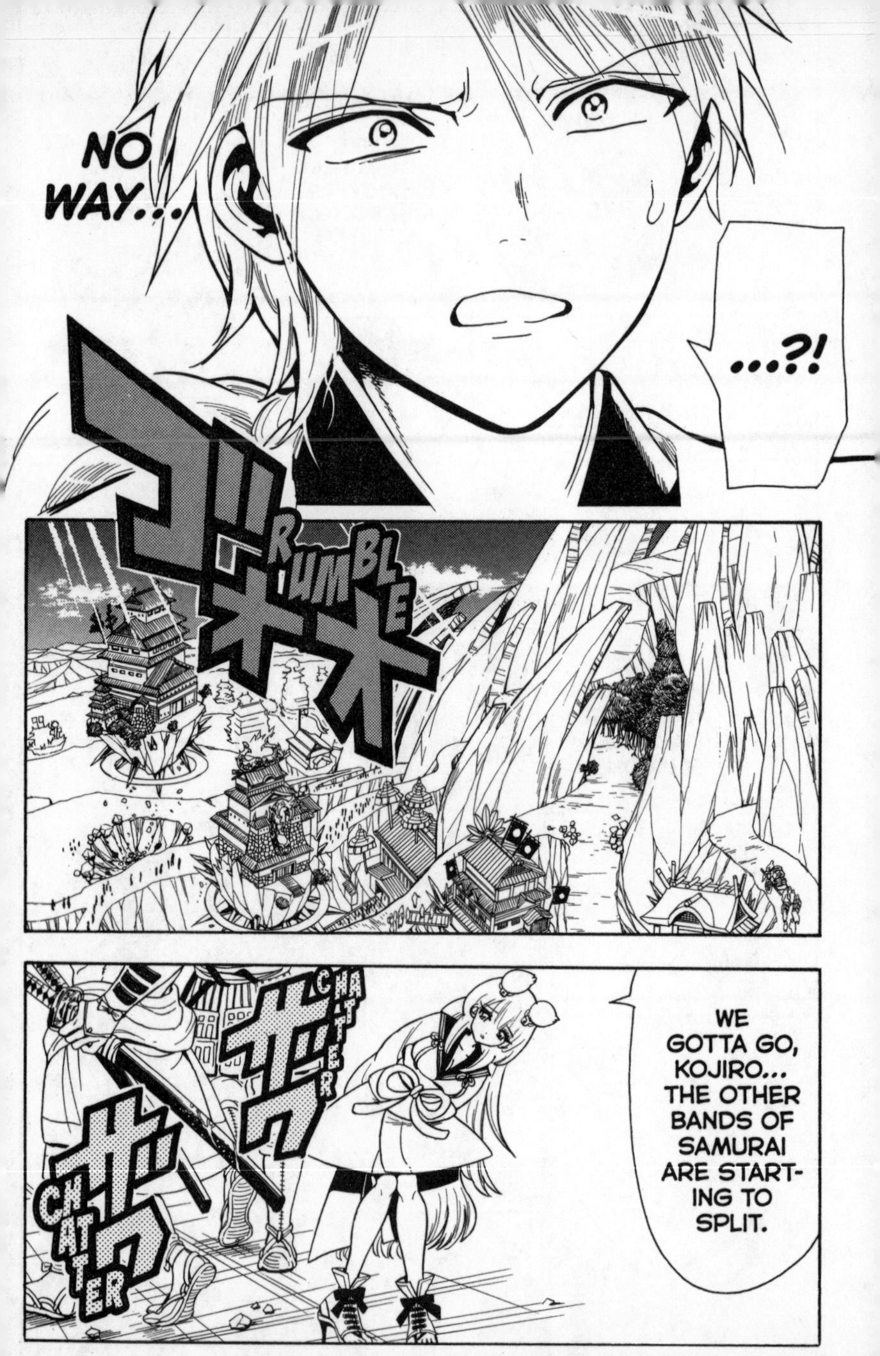
...?!
NO WAY...
RUMBLE
WE GOTTA GO, KOJIRO... THE OTHER BANDS OF SAMURAI ARE STARTING TO SPLIT.
CHATTER
CHATTER

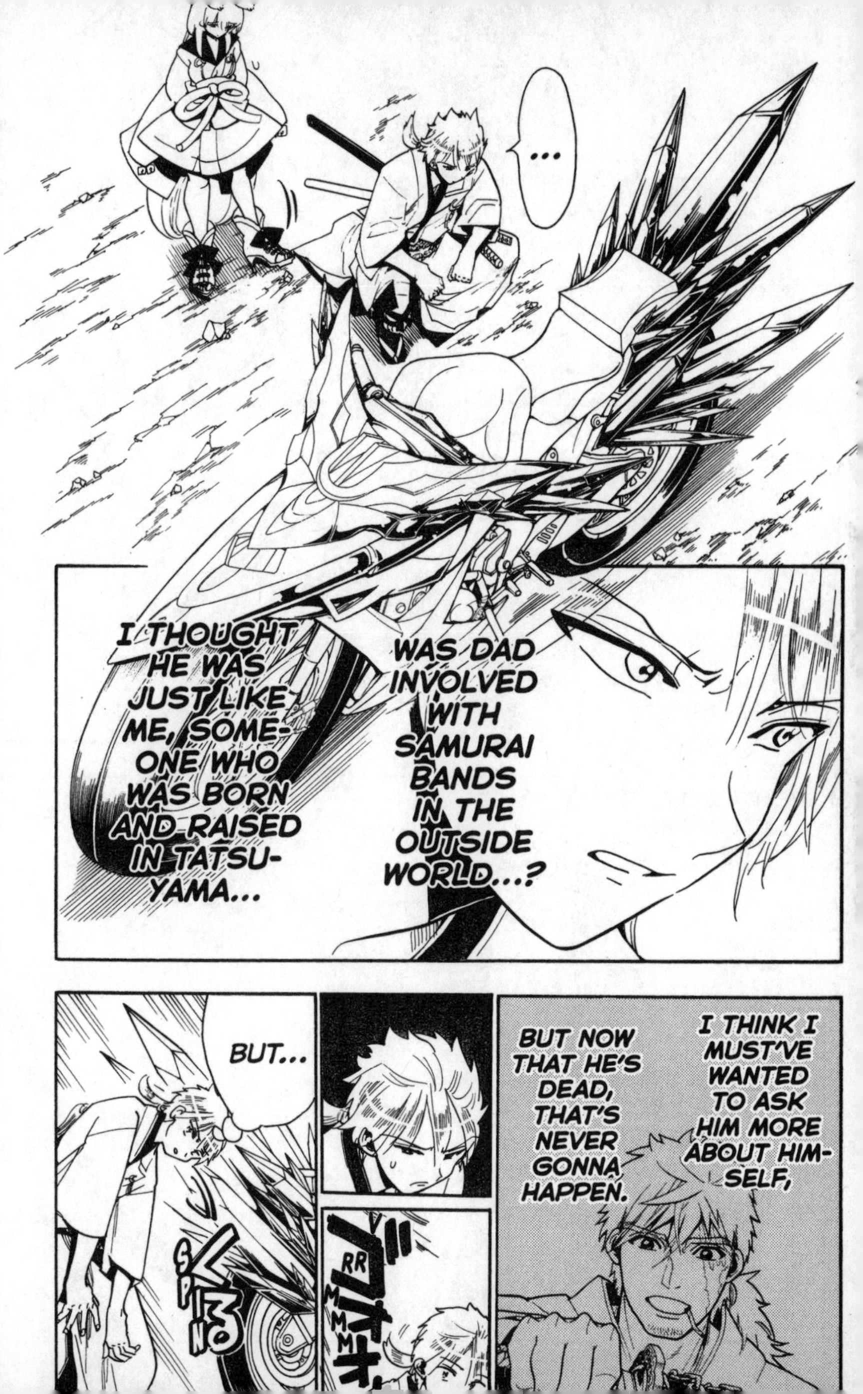
...
WAS DAD INVOLVED WITH SAMURAI BANDS IN THE OUTSIDE WORLD...?
I THOUGHT HE WAS JUST LIKE ME, SOME-ONE WHO WAS BORN AND RAISED IN TATSU-YAMA...
I THINK I MUST'VE WANTED TO ASK HIM MORE ABOUT HIM-SELF,
BUT NOW THAT HE'S DEAD, THAT'S NEVER GONNA HAPPEN.
VRRMMMM
BUT...
SPIN

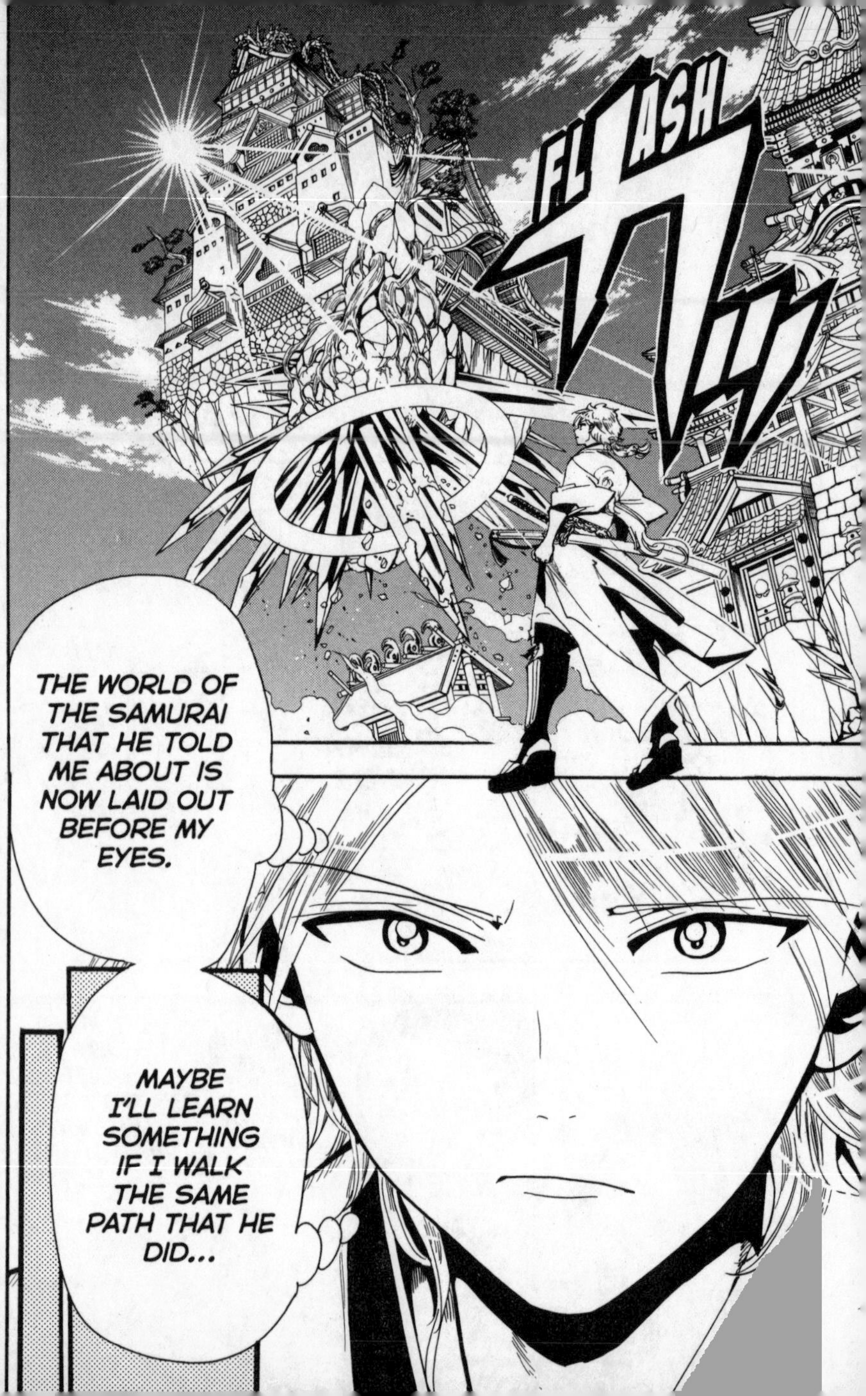
FLASH
THE WORLD OF THE SAMURAI THAT HE TOLD ME ABOUT IS NOW LAID OUT BEFORE MY EYES.
MAYBE I'LL LEARN SOMETHING IF I WALK THE SAME PATH THAT HE DID...

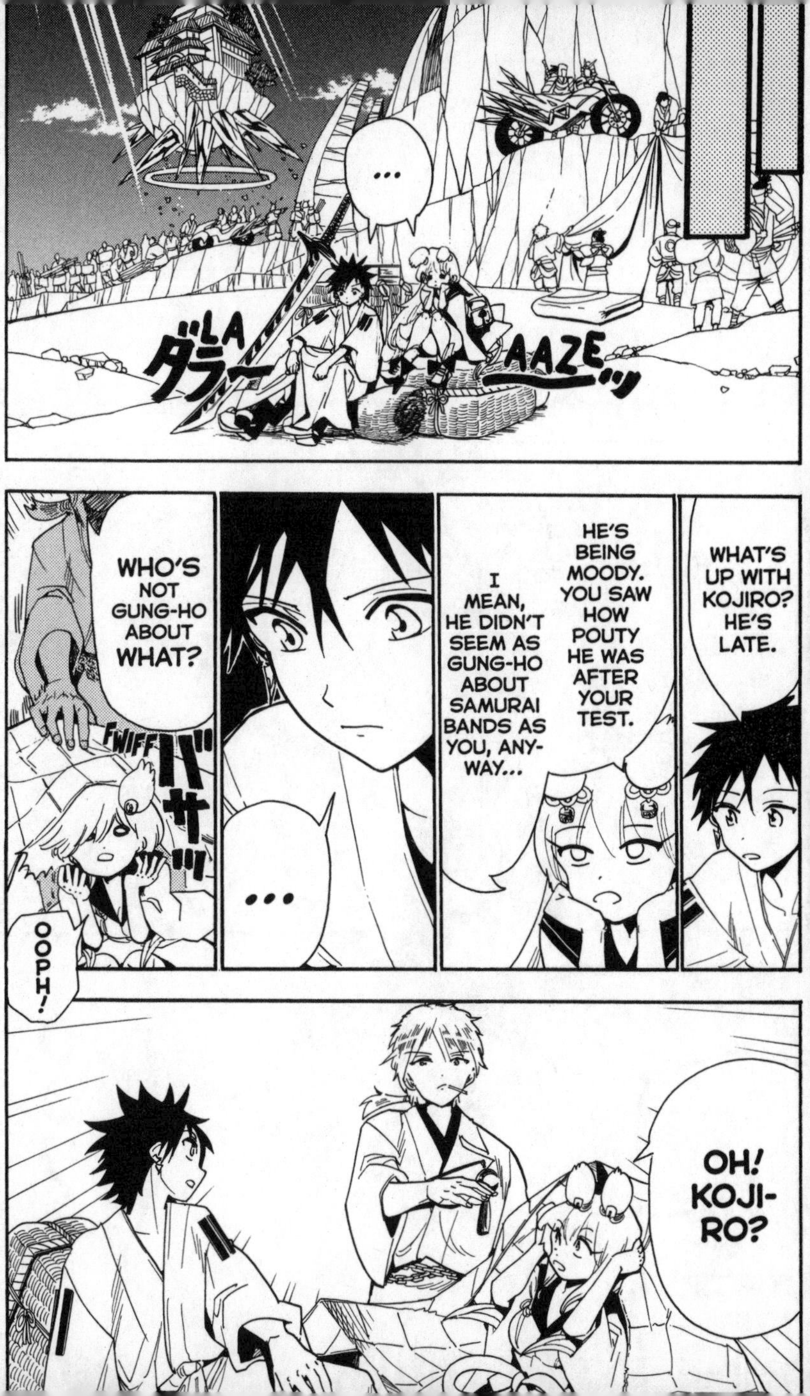
...
LA
ダラー
AAZE
WHAT'S UP WITH KOJIRO? HE'S LATE.
HE'S BEING MOODY. YOU SAW HOW POUTY HE WAS AFTER YOUR TEST.
I MEAN, HE DIDN'T SEEM AS GUNG-HO ABOUT SAMURAI BANDS AS YOU, ANY-WAY...
...
WHO'S NOT GUNG-HO ABOUT WHAT?
FWIFF
バサッ
OOPH!
OH! KOJI-RO?

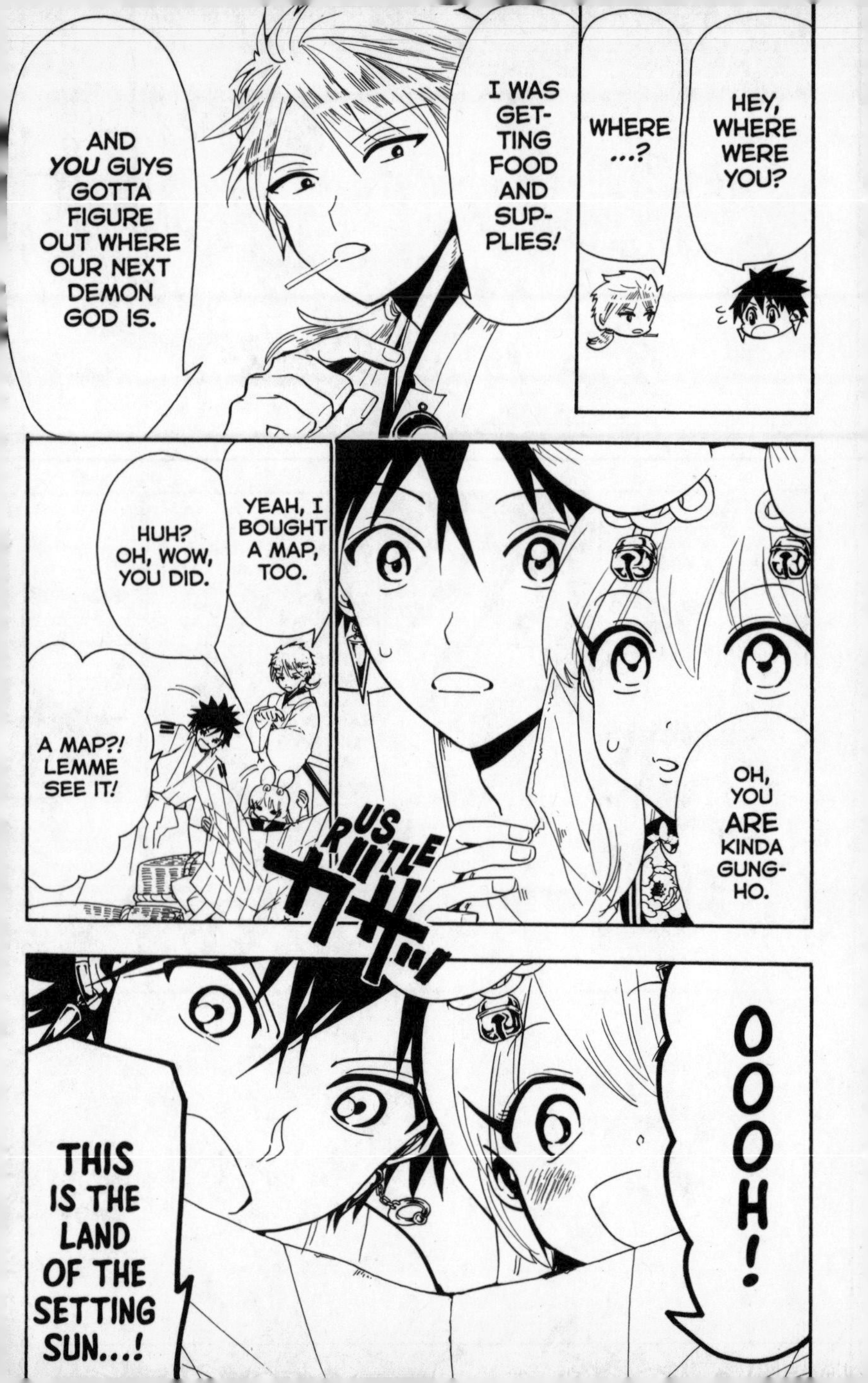
HEY, WHERE WERE YOU?
WHERE ...?
I WAS GET-TING FOOD AND SUP-PLIES!
AND *YOU* GUYS GOTTA FIGURE OUT WHERE OUR NEXT DEMON GOD IS.
OH, YOU ARE KINDA GUNG-HO.
RUSTLE
YEAH, I BOUGHT A MAP, TOO.
HUH? OH, WOW, YOU DID.
A MAP?! LEMME SEE IT!
OOOOH!
THIS IS THE LAND OF THE SETTING SUN...!

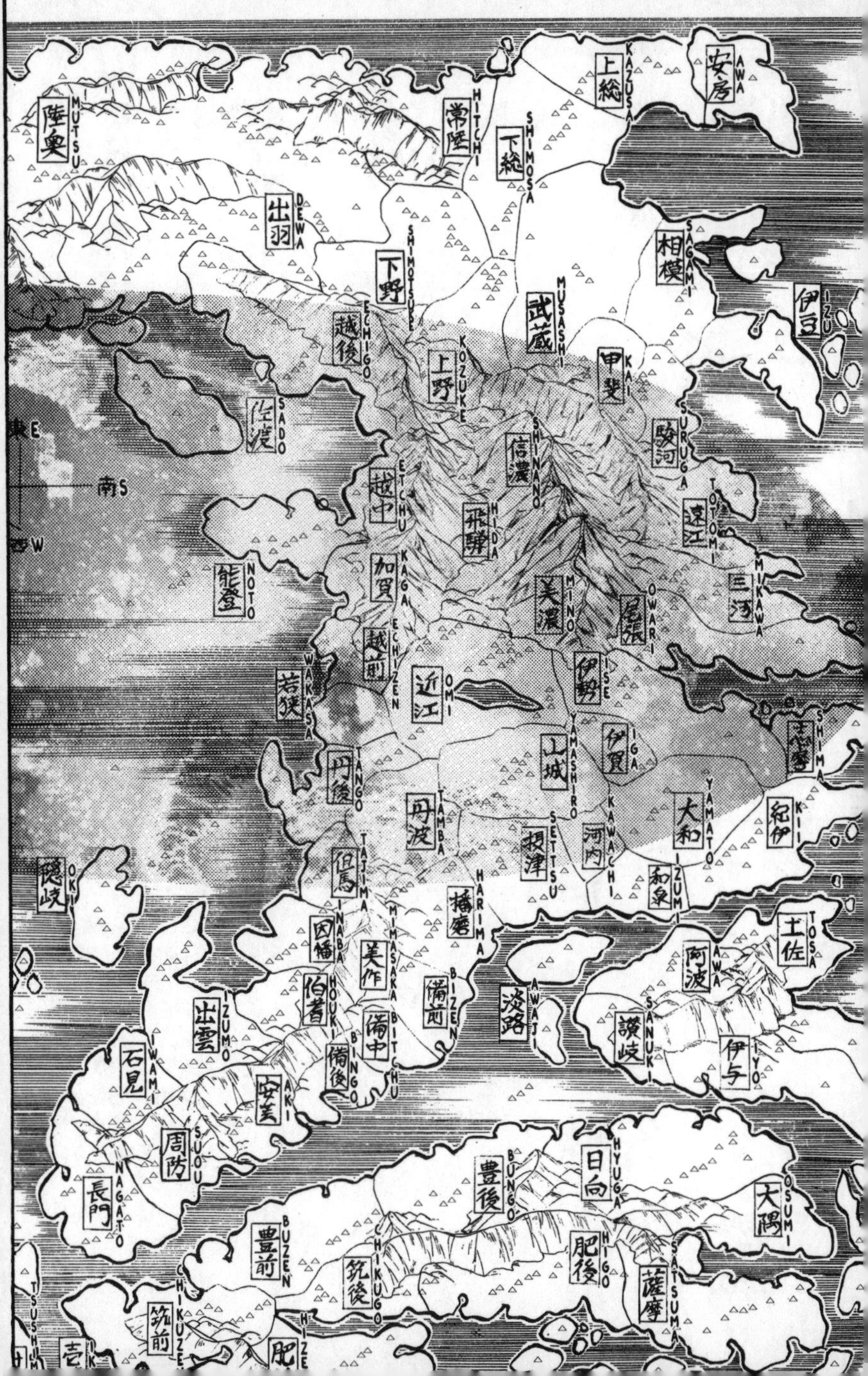

東 E
南 S
西 W
陸奥 MUTSU
常陸 HITCHI
上総 KAZUSA
安房 AWA
下総 SHIMOSA
出羽 DEWA
下野 SHIMOTSUKE
相模 SAGAMI
武蔵 MUSASHI
伊豆 IZU
越後 ECHIGO
上野 KOZUKE
甲斐 KAI
佐渡 SADO
駿河 SURUGA
信濃 SHINANO
越中 ETCHU
飛騨 HIDA
遠江 TOTOMI
能登 NOTO
加賀 KAGA
美濃 MINO
尾張 OWARI
三河 MIKAWA
越前 ECHIZEN
若狭 WAKASA
近江 OMI
伊勢 ISE
志摩 SHIMA
伊賀 IGA
山城 YAMASHIRO
丹後 TANGO
丹波 TAMBA
大和 YAMATO
紀伊 KII
河内 KAWACHI
摂津 SETTSU
和泉 IZUMI
隠岐 OKI
但馬 TAJIMA
播磨 HARIMA
因幡 INABA
美作 MIMASAKA
土佐 TOSA
阿波 AWA
伯耆 HOUKI
備前 BIZEN
淡路 AWAJI
出雲 IZUMO
備中 BITCHU
讃岐 SANUKI
伊与 IYO
石見 IWAMI
備後 BINGO
安芸 AKI
周防 SUOU
長門 NAGATO
豊後 BUNGO
日向 HYUGA
大隅 OSUMI
豊前 BUZEN
筑後 CHIKUGO
肥後 HIGO
薩摩 SATSUMA
筑前 CHIKUZEN

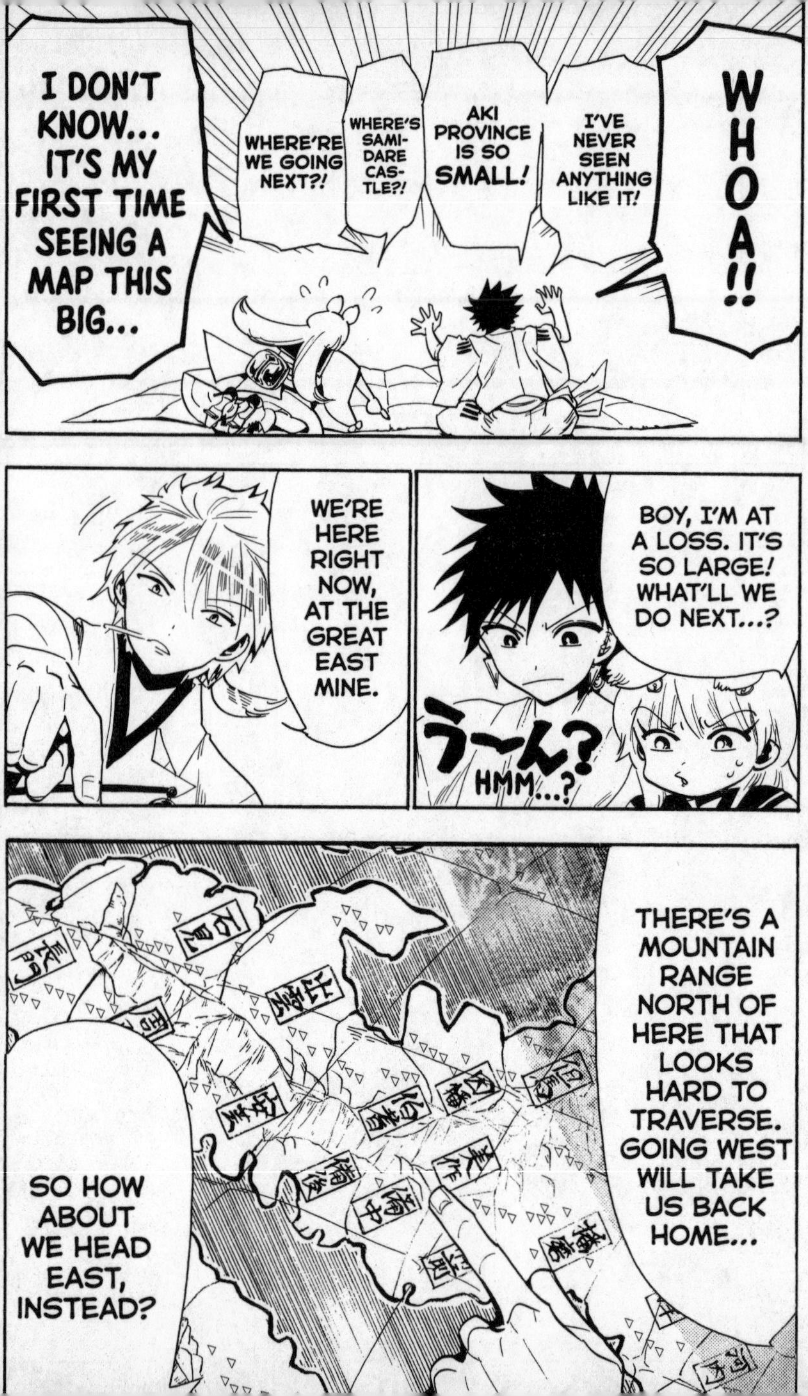
WHOA!!
I'VE NEVER SEEN ANYTHING LIKE IT!
AKI PROVINCE IS SO SMALL!
WHERE'S SAMI-DARE CAS-TLE?!
WHERE'RE WE GOING NEXT?!
I DON'T KNOW... IT'S MY FIRST TIME SEEING A MAP THIS BIG...
BOY, I'M AT A LOSS. IT'S SO LARGE! WHAT'LL WE DO NEXT...?
うーん？
HMM...?
WE'RE HERE RIGHT NOW, AT THE GREAT EAST MINE.
THERE'S A MOUNTAIN RANGE NORTH OF HERE THAT LOOKS HARD TO TRAVERSE. GOING WEST WILL TAKE US BACK HOME...
SO HOW ABOUT WE HEAD EAST, INSTEAD?

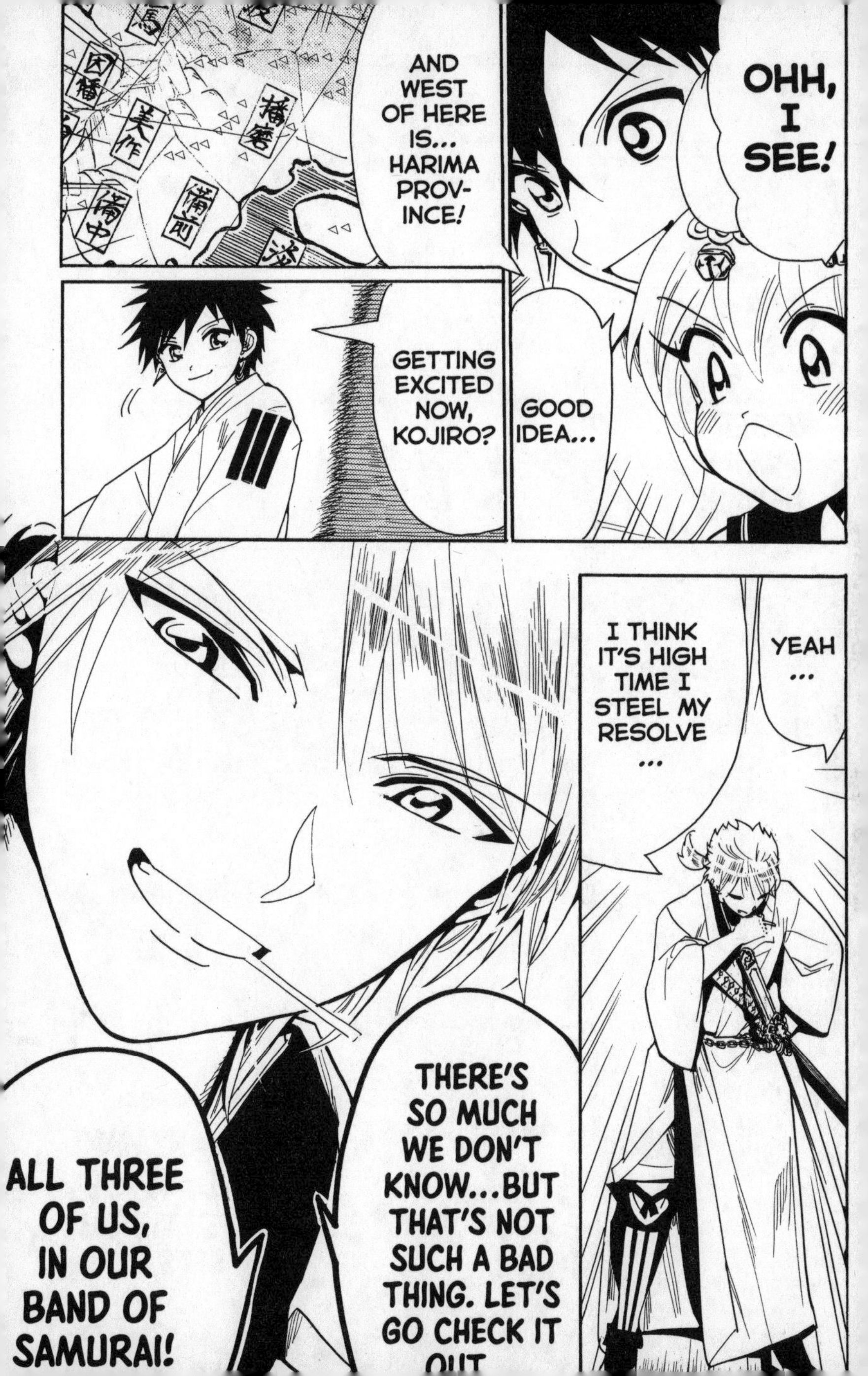
OHH, I SEE!
GOOD IDEA...
AND WEST OF HERE IS... HARIMA PROVINCE!
GETTING EXCITED NOW, KOJIRO?
YEAH ...
I THINK IT'S HIGH TIME I STEEL MY RESOLVE ...
THERE'S SO MUCH WE DON'T KNOW...BUT THAT'S NOT SUCH A BAD THING. LET'S GO CHECK IT OUT.
ALL THREE OF US, IN OUR BAND OF SAMURAI!

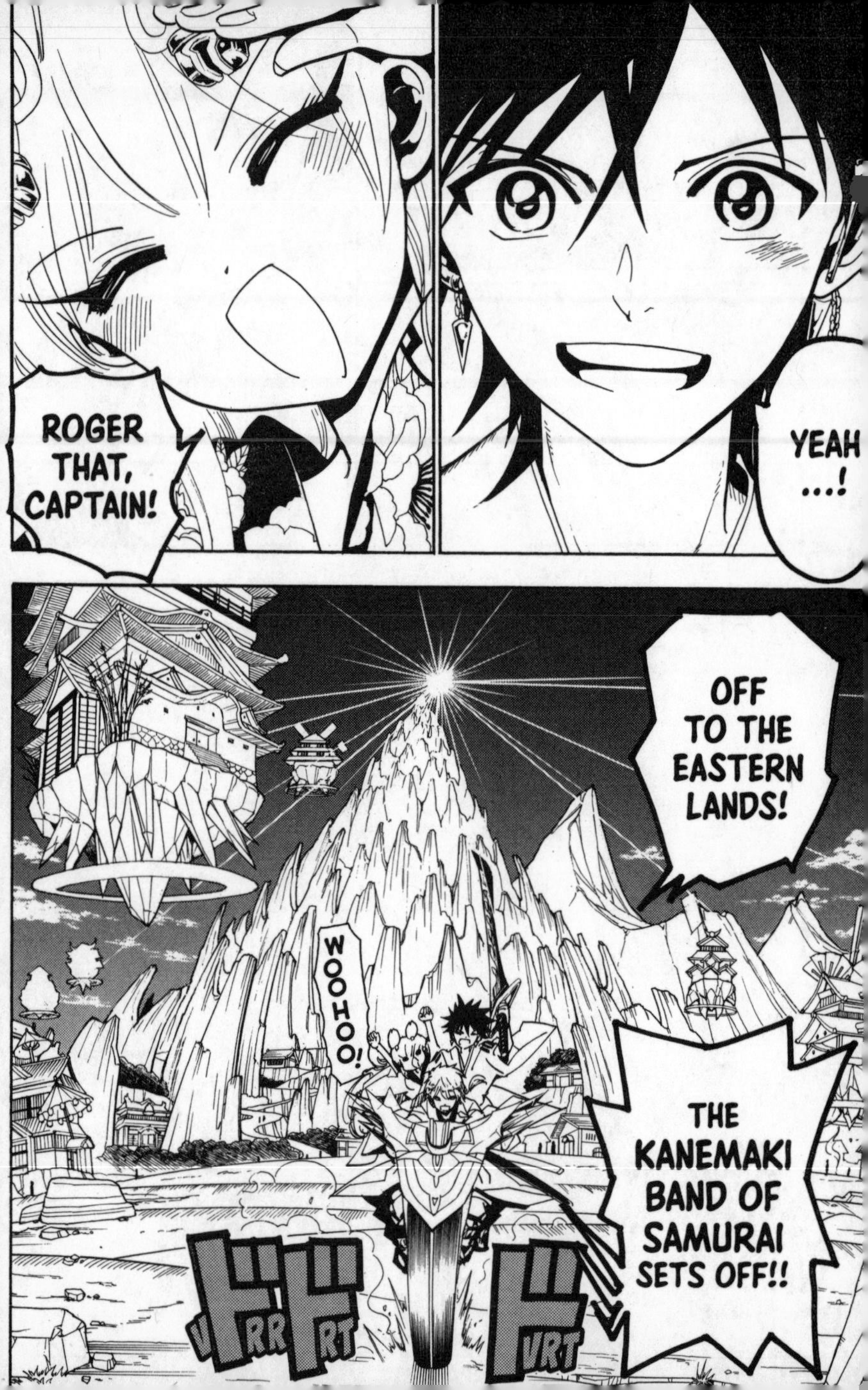

YEAH ...!
ROGER THAT, CAPTAIN!
OFF TO THE EASTERN LANDS!
WOOHOO!
THE KANEMAKI BAND OF SAMURAI SETS OFF!!

✦ STAFF ✦

REGULAR ASSISTANTS

舞嶋 大
Hiro Maizima

秋山 有緒子
Yuiko Akiyama

メギ
Megi

吉田 真美
Mami Yoshida

石後 千鳥
Chidori Ishigo

中村 犬彦
Inuhiko Nakamura

EDITORIAL TEAM

詫摩 尚樹
Naoki Takuma

菊地 優斗
Yuto Kikuchi

長塚 雅彦
Masahiko Nagatsuka

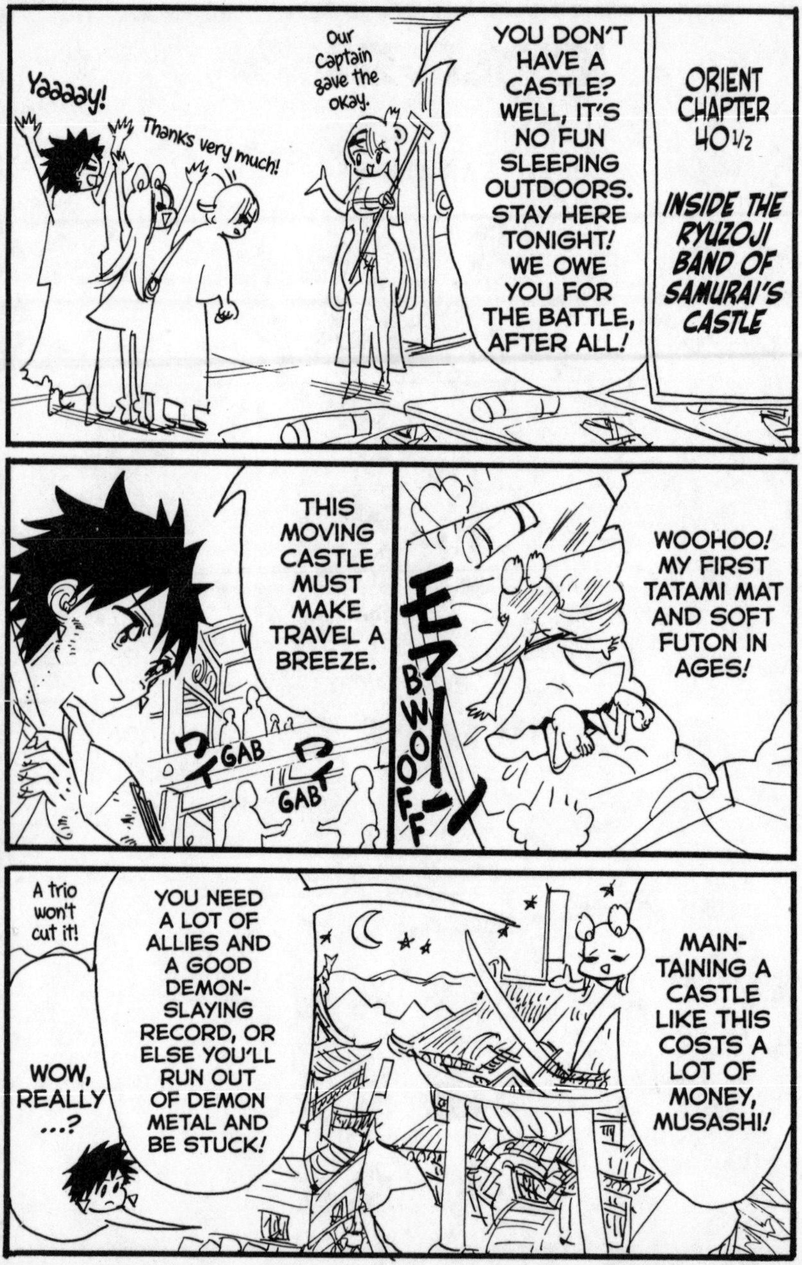
ORIENT CHAPTER 40 1/2
INSIDE THE RYUZOJI BAND OF SAMURAI'S CASTLE
YOU DON'T HAVE A CASTLE? WELL, IT'S NO FUN SLEEPING OUTDOORS. STAY HERE TONIGHT! WE OWE YOU FOR THE BATTLE, AFTER ALL!
Our Captain gave the okay.
Thanks very much!
Yaaaay!
WOOHOO! MY FIRST TATAMI MAT AND SOFT FUTON IN AGES!
BWOOFF
THIS MOVING CASTLE MUST MAKE TRAVEL A BREEZE.
GAB
GAB
MAIN-TAINING A CASTLE LIKE THIS COSTS A LOT OF MONEY, MUSASHI!
YOU NEED A LOT OF ALLIES AND A GOOD DEMON-SLAYING RECORD, OR ELSE YOU'LL RUN OUT OF DEMON METAL AND BE STUCK!
A trio won't cut it!
WOW, REALLY ...?

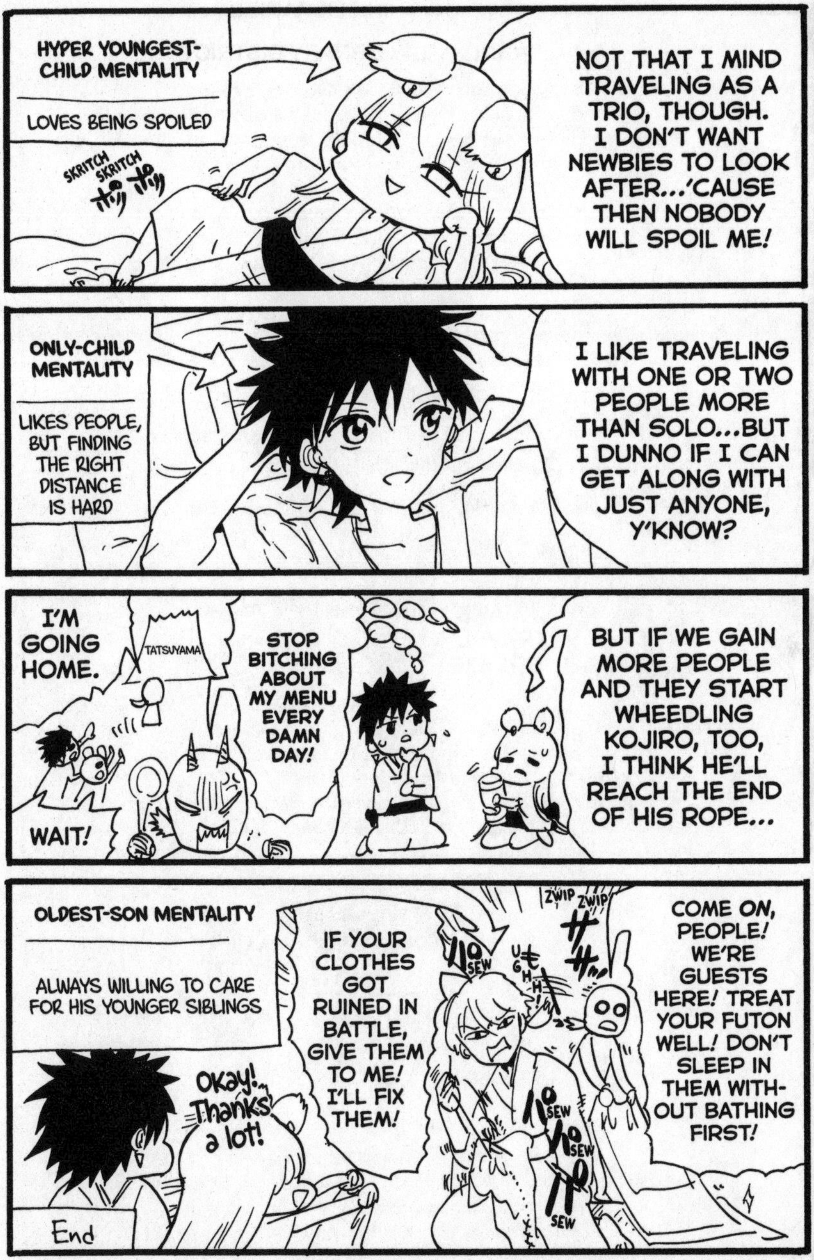

NOT THAT I MIND TRAVELING AS A TRIO, THOUGH. I DON'T WANT NEWBIES TO LOOK AFTER...'CAUSE THEN NOBODY WILL SPOIL ME!
HYPER YOUNGEST-CHILD MENTALITY
LOVES BEING SPOILED
SKRITCH SKRITCH
I LIKE TRAVELING WITH ONE OR TWO PEOPLE MORE THAN SOLO...BUT I DUNNO IF I CAN GET ALONG WITH JUST ANYONE, Y'KNOW?
ONLY-CHILD MENTALITY
LIKES PEOPLE, BUT FINDING THE RIGHT DISTANCE IS HARD
BUT IF WE GAIN MORE PEOPLE AND THEY START WHEEDLING KOJIRO, TOO, I THINK HE'LL REACH THE END OF HIS ROPE...
STOP BITCHING ABOUT MY MENU EVERY DAMN DAY!
TATSUYAMA
I'M GOING HOME.
WAIT!
COME ON, PEOPLE! WE'RE GUESTS HERE! TREAT YOUR FUTON WELL! DON'T SLEEP IN THEM WITH-OUT BATHING FIRST!
ZWIP ZWIP
UGHH!
SEW SEW SEW SEW
IF YOUR CLOTHES GOT RUINED IN BATTLE, GIVE THEM TO ME! I'LL FIX THEM!
OLDEST-SON MENTALITY
ALWAYS WILLING TO CARE FOR HIS YOUNGER SIBLINGS
Okay! Thanks a lot!
End

Orient 5 is a work of fiction. Names, characters, places, and incidents are the products of the author's imagination or are used fictitiously. Any resemblance to actual events, locales, or persons, living or dead, is entirely coincidental.

A Kodansha Comics Trade Paperback Original

Published in the United States by Kodansha Comics, an imprint of Kodansha USA Publishing, LLC, New York.

Publication rights for this English edition arranged through Kodansha Ltd., Tokyo.

First published in Japan in 2019 by Kodansha Ltd., Tokyo.

ISBN 978-1-64651-262-1

Printed in the United States of America.

www.kodansha.us

1st Printing

Translation: Nate Derr, Kevin Gifford
Lettering: Belynda Ungurath
Editing: Megan Ling
Kodansha Comics edition cover design by Phil Balsman
YKS Services LLC/SKY Japan, INC.

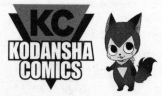

Publisher: Kiichiro Sugawara

Director of publishing services: Ben Applegate
Associate director of operations: Stephen Pakula
Publishing services managing editors: Madison Salters, Alanna Ruse
Production managers: Emi Lotto, Angela Zurlo